MEN AND POLICIES

MEN AND POLICIES

ADDRESSES

BY

ELIHU ROOT

COLLECTED AND EDITED BY

*ROBERT BACON

AND

JAMES BROWN SCOTT

Essay Index Reprint Series

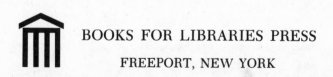 BOOKS FOR LIBRARIES PRESS

FREEPORT, NEW YORK

First published 1924
Reprinted 1968

LIBRARY OF CONGRESS CATALOG CARD NUMBER:

68-22942

PRINTED IN THE UNITED STATES OF AMERICA

CONTENTS

I. SOME AMERICANS

PAGE

THEODORE ROOSEVELT 3
Address presiding at a Meeting of the Century Association,
New York City, February 9, 1919.
Address at the Rocky Mountain Club Dinner on the Anniver-
sary of his Birth, New York City, October 27, 1919.

JOSEPH H. CHOATE 17
Memorial in the New York City Bar Association, December 20,
1917.
Address in presiding over the Century Association, New York
City, January 19, 1918.

ANDREW CARNEGIE 49
Address at a Memorial Meeting under the Direction of the
Authors' Club, New York City, April 25, 1920.

JAMES RUSSELL LOWELL. 58
Address as Chairman at a Dinner on the Centenary of Lowell's
Birth, given by the American Academy of Arts and Letters to
British and Canadian Authors, New York City, February 20,
1919.

ABRAHAM LINCOLN 63
Address at Parliament Square, London, presenting Saint Gaudens's Statue of Lincoln to the British People, July 28, 1920.

LINCOLN AS A LEADER OF MEN 69
Reprinted by permission from *Republicanism of 1920*.

ALEXANDER HAMILTON 76
Address as Chairman of the Board of Trustees of Hamilton
College, accepting a Statue of Hamilton presented by Thomas
R. Proctor, Clinton, New York, June 17, 1918.

GROVER CLEVELAND 88
An Introduction to Robert McElroy's *Grover Cleveland — the
Man and the Statesman. An Authorized Biography*.

ROBERT BACON 93
Introduction to *Robert Bacon — Life and Letters*, by James
Brown Scott.

ADDRESS AS PRESIDENT ON THE SEVENTY-FIFTH ANNIVER-
SARY OF THE CENTURY ASSOCIATION 99
New York City, April 22, 1922.

ADDRESS AS VICE-PRESIDENT ON THE FIFTIETH ANNIVER-
    SARY OF THE METROPOLITAN MUSEUM OF ART . . .   105
    New York City, May 18, 1920.

ADDRESS ON THE FIFTIETH ANNIVERSARY OF THE ASSOCIA-
    TION OF THE BAR OF THE CITY OF NEW YORK . .   111
    February 17, 1920.

II. LAW AND ITS ADMINISTRATION

THE CONSTITUTION OF THE UNITED STATES   121
    Address at Carnegie Hall on the Anniversary of the Signing,
    New York City, September 17, 1919.

ADDRESS AT A DINNER GIVEN BY THE ASSOCIATION OF THE
    BAR OF THE CITY OF NEW YORK TO LORD CHIEF
    JUSTICE READING, AS AMBASSADOR TO THE UNITED
    STATES   130
    April 5, 1919.

JUDGES AND LEGISLATURES   135
    Remarks to the Judicial Section of the American Bar Associa-
    tion, at Boston, September 4, 1919.

THE STANDARD OF LEGAL EDUCATION.   141
    Speeches in the Conference of the American Bar Association
    Delegates, Washington, February 23, 24, 1922.

THE RESTATEMENT OF THE SUBSTANTIVE LAW   158
    Opening Address as Chairman of the Bench and Bar Meeting
    to Organize the American Law Institute at Washington, Feb-
    ruary 23, 1923.

III. THE WAR AND READJUSTMENT

LETTER TO THE PRESIDENT OF THE NATIONAL SECURITY
    LEAGUE   169
    February 16, 1918.

SPEECH AT A MEETING IN HONOR OF THE ARCHBISHOP OF
    YORK   173
    New York City, March 7, 1918.

SPEECH BEFORE THE NATIONAL SECURITY LEAGUE IN PHILA-
    DELPHIA   178
    April 24, 1918.

ADDRESS AS CHAIRMAN OF THE ANNUAL MEETING OF THE
    NATIONAL SECURITY LEAGUE   185
    New York City, May 8, 1918.

PUBLIC STATEMENT FOR THE NATIONAL WAR SAVINGS COM-
MITTEE IN NEW YORK CITY   190
     July 2, 1918.

THE DUTY OF THE OPPOSITION PARTY IN THE WAR   192
     Address as Chairman of the New York Republican State Con-
     vention, Saratoga, New York, July 18, 1918.

THE RESUMPTION OF INDIVIDUAL LIBERTY   202
     Speech at Lincoln's Birthday Dinner in Utica, New York,
     February 12, 1919.

THE RESTORATION POLICIES OF THE UNITED STATES . . .   210
     Address as Chairman of the New York Republican State Con-
     vention, New York City, February 19, 1920.

WAR MEMORIALS   232
     Speech at the Convention of the National Federation of Arts,
     held in the Metropolitan Museum, New York City, May 15,
     1919.

NEW YORK REGIONAL PLAN   238
     Remarks in Behalf of a Project of the Russell Sage Founda-
     dation, in the Engineering Society's Building, New York City,
     May 10, 1922.

IV. INTERNATIONAL AFFAIRS

THE LEAGUE OF NATIONS   247

SPEECH AT A MEETING UNDER THE DIRECTION OF THE NA-
TIONAL REPUBLICAN CLUB, IN THE PRESIDENTIAL
ELECTION OF 1920   277
     New York City, October 19, 1920.

THE SECOND HAGUE PEACE CONFERENCE   295
     Instructions to the American Delegates to the Conference of
     1907.

LATIN-AMERICAN COÖPERATION.   315
     Letter of Instructions to Robert Bacon, July 20, 1913.

THE CARNEGIE ENDOWMENT FOR INTERNATIONAL PEACE . .   320
     Remarks before the Board of Trustees, Washington, April 21,
     1922.

THE PERMANENT COURT OF INTERNATIONAL JUSTICE . . .   324
     Remarks as Member of the Advisory Committee of Jurists at
     The Hague, prefaced by Letters of Invitation from Mr. Frank L.
     Polk, Secretary of State *ad interim*, and Sir Eric Drummond,
     Secretary General of the League of Nations, June 17 to July
     24, 1920.
     Address before the Association of the Bar of the City of New
     York, October 21, 1920.   391

Annual Address as President of the American Society of International Law, Washington, April 26, 1923. 405

THE CONDITIONS AND POSSIBILITIES REMAINING FOR INTERNATIONAL LAW AFTER THE WAR 427
Annual Address as President of the American Society of International Law, Washington, April 27, 1921.

THE PROHIBITION OF SUBMARINES AND POISONOUS GASES . 446
Speech at the Fifth Plenary Session of the Conference on the Limitation of Armament, Washington, February 1, 1922.

INTERNATIONAL LAW AT THE WASHINGTON CONFERENCE ON THE LIMITATION OF ARMAMENT 452
Annual Address as President of the American Society of International Law, Washington, Apri l27, 1922.

DEMOCRACY AND FOREIGN AFFAIRS 469
Speech at the Banquet concluding the Discussions of the Institute of Politics at Williamstown, Massachusetts, August 26, 1921.

A REQUISITE FOR THE SUCCESS OF POPULAR DIPLOMACY . 479
Article contributed to the First Number of *Foreign Affairs*, September 15, 1922.

THE EDUCATION OF DEMOCRACY IN FOREIGN AFFAIRS . . 489
Speech in the Committee on Foreign Relations and National Defense of the National Civic Federation, Washington, January 17, 1923.

HOW TO INTEREST DEMOCRACY IN FOREIGN AFFAIRS . . . 498
Remarks in the Executive Committee of the Committee of One Hundred on Foreign Relations, National Civic Federation, New York City, March 1, 1923.

INDEX 503

INTRODUCTORY NOTE

THE collected addresses and state papers of Elihu Root, of which this is one of several volumes, cover the period of his service as Secretary of War, as Secretary of State, and as Senator of the United States, during which time, to use his own expression, his only client was his country.

The many formal and occasional addresses and speeches, which will be found to be of a remarkably wide range, are followed by his state papers, such as the instructions to the American delegates to the Second Hague Peace Conference and other diplomatic notes and documents, prepared by him as Secretary of State in the performance of his duties as an executive officer of the United States. Although the official documents have been kept separate from the other papers, this plan has been slightly modified in the volume devoted to the military and colonial policy of the United States, which includes those portions of his official reports as Secretary of War throwing light upon his public addresses and his general military policy.

The addresses and speeches selected for publication are not arranged chronologically, but are classified in such a way that each volume contains addresses and speeches relating to a general subject and a common purpose. The addresses as president of the American Society of International Law show his treatment of international questions from the theoretical standpoint, and in the light of his experience as Secretary of War and as Secretary of State, unrestrained and uncontrolled by the limitations of official position, whereas his addresses on foreign affairs, delivered while Secretary of State or as United States Senator, discuss these questions under the reserve of official responsibility.

Mr. Root's addresses on government, citizenship, and legal procedure are a masterly exposition of the principles of the Constitution and of the government established by it; of the duty of the citizen to understand the Constitution and to conform his conduct to its requirements; and of the right of the people to reform or to amend the Constitution in order to make representative government more effective and responsive to their present and future needs. The addresses on law and its administration state how legal procedure should be modified and simplified in the interest of justice rather than in the supposed interest of the legal profession.

The addresses delivered during the trip to South America and Mexico in 1906, and in the United States after his return, with their message of good will, proclaim a new doctrine — the Root doctrine — of kindly consideration and of honorable obligation, and make clear the destiny common to the peoples of the Western World.

The addresses and the reports on military and colonial policy made by Mr. Root as Secretary of War explain the reorganization of the army after the Spanish-American War, the creation of the General Staff, and the establishment of the Army War College. They trace the origin of and give the reason for the policy of this country in Cuba, the Philippines, and Porto Rico, devised and inaugurated by him. It is not generally known that the so-called Platt Amendment, defining our relations to Cuba, was drafted by Mr. Root, and that the Organic Act of the Philippines was likewise the work of Mr. Root as Secretary of War.

The argument before The Hague Tribunal in the North Atlantic Fisheries Case is a rare if not the only instance of a statesman appearing as chief counsel in an international arbitration, which, as Secretary of State, he had prepared and submitted.

The miscellaneous addresses, including educational, historical, and commemorative addresses, the political speeches in days of peace, and the stirring and prophetic utterances in anticipation of and during our war with Germany, delivered at home and on special mission in Russia, should make known to future generations the literary, artistic, and emotional side of this broad-minded and far-seeing statesman of our time.

The publication of these collected addresses and state papers will, it is believed, enable the American people better to understand the generation in which Mr. Root has been a commanding figure, and better to appreciate during his lifetime the services which he has rendered to his country.

Robert Bacon died on May 29, 1919, after the distinguished civil and military career set forth so carefully, so lovingly, and in such masterly fashion by Mr. Root in the following pages. The present editor is unwilling to have the volume go to press without Mr. Bacon's name, for the plan was the plan of both, although the present volume is necessarily the work of the surviving editor. Mr. Root concurs in this view, and Mrs. Bacon has graciously permitted this use of her distinguished husband's name. It is, therefore, retained.

*ROBERT BACON.
JAMES BROWN SCOTT.

WASHINGTON, D.C.
AUGUST 3, 1924.

I

SOME AMERICANS

THEODORE ROOSEVELT

ADDRESS PRESIDING AT A MEETING OF THE CENTURY
ASSOCIATION, NEW YORK CITY, FEBRUARY 9, 1919

Theodore Roosevelt, twenty-sixth President of the United States, was born in New York City, October 27, 1858, graduated from Harvard University in the Class of 1880, served in the Assembly of New York Legislature, 1882–1884, organized and became Lieutenant Colonel and Colonel of the 1st U. S. Cavalry, known as the "Rough Riders" in the Spanish-American War, in action at Las Guasimas and San Juan Hill, Governor of New York, 1899–1900; was nominated on the ticket with Mr. McKinley for the Vice-Presidency in 1899, elected and served as Vice-President, March 4, 1901 until the death of President McKinley, September 14, 1901, succeeding him as President for the balance of the term. Nominated and elected President in 1904, he served in his own right from March 4, 1905 until March 4, 1909.

After the Presidency, he made a famous hunting trip in South Africa, returning to the United States June 18, 1910.

In 1912 he was nominated by the Progressive Republicans for the Presidency of the United States. Mr. Woodrow Wilson was elected, receiving 6,000,000 popular votes and 435 electoral votes; Mr. Roosevelt, 4,000,000 popular and 88 electoral, and Mr. Taft 3,500,000 popular and 8 electoral votes.

During the World War he was a strenuous advocate of preparedness, and his life was spared to see the success of the Allied and Associated Powers and the capitulation of Germany registered in the Armistice of November 11, 1918. He died at his home, Sagamore Hill, Oyster Bay, Long Island, January 6, 1919.

Both before and after his Presidency, Mr. Roosevelt was a writer of books and essays, and in spite of his busy life, he is perhaps the only President who may claim to be a man of letters. Among his many contributions to American history, the *Winning of the West* (4 volumes, 1889–96) stands out as a work of research and learning, and is, like his life, an inspiration especially to his young countrymen.

THEODORE ROOSEVELT can never be forgotten by the men of his time, and his memory can never be neglected by the historians who come in the future to estimate the forces effective in what now appears to be a period of vital change in the life of civilization.

In common with millions of men and women who have come directly under the influence of his personality, we have met upon this selected day to join in tribute to this very great man who has been so potent for so many years in the public life of our Country; and to do our part toward sending to generations to come, in the printed records of the day, our fragment of testimony to the effect produced by the living man upon the generation that knew him.

Here, in this Association, we respond of necessity to very personal and intimate factors of judgment and of feeling. Wherever in this world Theodore Roosevelt went, his tremendous personal power diffused an atmosphere within which all the men and women there grouped about his central figure, and that spot of earth seemed not foreign, but home for him. Yet, after all, this was his home. In this city he was born and bred. From this home he launched his first and ever-recurrent flights of adventure and achievement into the great world of universal human life that was forever calling to his eager and dauntless soul. In this club — dedicated to Arts and Letters — he was a member for thirty-four years, from the days of his youth, and it was his father's club from the time of the Civil War. He was in harmony with the spirit of the club. He loved and cultivated literature. A perpetual reader, with swift and alert grasp of the matter and the thought expressed in the print, sensitively responsive to poetry, and stirred to great joy by poems of sublimity and power. His first strivings for expression found vent in the ambition of authorship, and we know that he was no mean author. It is hard to estimate the value to the literary standards of the American people in having things that he has spoken and written go into the schoolbooks of the country, where they stand as examples of simple, sincere, direct, strong expressions of definite ideas, free from all attempts at rhetoric and adornment. He scorned style for style's sake, but with strong desire to implant his thought in the minds of others, and with intuitive understanding of human nature, he often sought and found terse phrases that crystallized general truths, and pierced through the barrier of indifference, and touched the springs of feeling and of action in the multitude — master words that will be potent long after all the fine writing of his generation has been forgotten.

He loved and practised the simplicity of life, in which literature and art live at their best. He scorned the meretricious and the decadent. He loved nature, its beauty, and its grandeur, from the great spaces of plains and mountains to the bird singing in the thicket, and he loved it with affectionate companionship, striving for definite knowledge and understanding.

He had a genius for friendship, and unfailing sympathy with his fellows, real interest in their lives and fortunes, tender consideration of their shortcomings, pride in their successes. He combined the highest degree of loyalty to his own convictions and confidence in his own powers with an entire absence of self-conceit. He had no petty pride of opinion. He gave freely of his own thought to others, and he eagerly sought and availed himself of all the wisdom of others' experience and knowledge. He was the most advisable man I ever knew, and the most independent and fearless in acting upon his own final conclusions. He was great-hearted, giving bounteously credit and praise to others. He had the saving grace of abundant and ever-present humor. He had purity of character, which kept his mind and heart open to all good influences. He had manifest sincerity of purpose that disarmed suspicion. He was incapable of deception, and thoughtless of it. He had the gift of social inspiration, and he had charm.

Many of us here have known him since his early youth, and have loved him for his noble and appealing qualities. And we have cared for him all the more because we have been near enough to see the trifling defects of his great virtues — the little foibles without which greatness remains coldly unapproachable and unloved. There is an intuitive sense of what a man really is — almost infallible in the community in which he lives from boyhood. All of us have absorbed that judgment upon the character of Theodore Roosevelt. We are qualified to say, and do say to the world that knew him in public, in high station, and in his great efforts and achievements, "All that he seemed to you he was — only a thousand times more admirable, more lovable, and more to be mourned."

Consider the qualities which were his beyond dispute.

Dauntless courage; fortitude; indomitable resolution.

Decision of character; an ingrained habit of mind, swiftly grasping all available data, and converging to immediate action. He was not at all an administrator, but he was an almost perfect executive.

A fixed philosophy of life which set a high standard of service to the point of sacrifice, and of scorn to spare one's self.

Public spirit; love of country; intense loyalty to ideals.

Sincerity; hatred of shams; love of justice; honor.

Family affection; capacity for friendship; purity of character; cheerfulness; hopefulness; humor; magnanimity.

Breadth of vision; intuitive sympathy with the feelings and interests of all men; an inevitable impulse to help the under-dog.

Essential constructiveness; never seeking to tear down except as part of a definite practical scheme of betterment.

He was not infallible; the swift decisions of a true executive make some mistakes inevitable. But we can affirm with confidence in the agreement of all who knew him best, that he never decided upon a course of conduct or a public action which he did not believe to be for the best interests of his country, and in which that consideration did not stand first in his mind.

Behind these qualities came the driving force of high ambition for achievement, of combativeness that rejoiced in conflict, and an amazing virile energy.

An unexpected and unsought election to the New York Legislature when he was but twenty-three years of age, just out of college, with all the initiative of youth unabated, turned him from the study and the writing of history to the practical business of government, and the study of men upon which the successful conduct of that business depends.

He was a natural reformer, saved from fanaticism and folly by humor and the sense of proportion which humor gives, by absence of self-conceit, by hospitality to advice, by fondness for the study of history, by intuitive judgment of the practicable, and by scorn for futile theory. His reading of history became a biological study of human nature, its development, and its reactions under past experiments. A recognized evil in government made instant demand upon him for a new experiment directed toward the abolition of the evil, and the substitution of something better. He wasted no time in weak protest or aimless discussion. He attacked instantly without the slightest apprehension of consequences to himself. On the 30th of April, 1884, writing to a friend who had approved his course in the New York Legislature, he said:

DEAR MR. NORTH,

I wish to write you a few words just to thank you for your kindness toward me, and to assure you that my head will not be turned by what I well know was a mainly accidental success.... I have very little expectation of being able to keep on in politics; my success so far has only been won by absolute indifference as to my future career; for I doubt if anyone can realize the bitter and venomous hatred with which I am regarded by the very politicians who, at Utica, supported me, under dictation from masters who were influenced by political considerations that were national, and not local in their scope.

I realize very thoroughly the absolutely ephemeral nature of the hold I have upon the people, and the very real and positive hostility I have excited among the politicians. I will not stay in public life unless I can do so on my own terms; and my ideal — whether lived up to or not — is rather a high one.

For the thirty-five years of strenuous life that followed he never varied from that attitude. It was always he, and not the politicians or even the constituencies, that set the conditions upon which he held public office, and the conditions were always formed upon the standard established by the ardent boy in his first adventure. No hardening of the heart ever brought to him indifference to the dreams of youth.

He continually attacked abuse. It used to seem as if every morning at daybreak the slumbers of the comfortable were disturbed by his vibrant voice summoning to instant action against wrong. His voice reached the minds and hearts of the people of the United States as no other voice ever had in their history. So just was his judgment of fundamentals, so manifest the sincerity of his purpose, so tremendous the power of his personality, that everywhere dim and vague feelings that something was wrong and uneasy dissatisfaction over unwilling acquiescence in what was wrong, hailed him as a leader, and rallied to his support; so he established a short circuit between himself and the voters, which cut out formal leadership, and created the greatest direct following upon the morals of government as distinguished from the followings determined by organization that has ever been known in the history of democratic self-government.

It is too early to estimate the value of his work. We were all too much affected individually in one way or another by what he did to leave it possible that we could have the detachment necessary to impartial judgment. The events which are now occurring in the world, however, cast a light backward upon what he did, and emphasize — if they do not measure — its value.

He came into the public life of this great self-governing democracy as a phase of development in civilization was drawing toward a close. The application of science and of organization to production had resulted in a vast and almost inconceivable increase in the wealth of the world, and in the power to multiply wealth. It was plain that this increase of wealth ought to make life more comfortable, more rich, more desirable for the inventors and discoverers whose brain-work made it possible, for the investors who risked their capital in the successful and the unsuccessful experiments, for the laborers who were producing so much more than ever before, and for the consumers whose supplies were costing less labor than ever before. The economic struggles of the last half-century had been steps in the process of adjustment toward this ideal distribution of the new wealth. But the process had lagged. The investor having the first opportunity had naturally and inevitably received the lion's share of the new wealth, and he had clung to it, and maintained it long after the risks of development had largely decreased. There had come to be a general feeling among the people that the investor was getting more than his fair share, and the other elements in producing the new wealth were getting less than their fair share. Our simple form of government, established long before these conditions arose, was not adjusted to the solution of this problem, and so the investor kept his initial advantage. A crust was forming over our national life. A class could be dimly recognized as rising with power and privilege and assumption of superiority on the basis of wealth. Underneath were vague but slowly growing dissatisfaction and resentment at that condition.

Biological study of human nature and his instinct taught Mr. Roosevelt that this crust must be dissipated and a fair equilibrium must be established, by the peaceful processes of government, or the crust would be broken by explosion, as it was once broken in France, as it has been broken in Russia. He addressed himself to that task — not as a matter of charity to the poor, not seeking popularity, but as a matter of governmental policy based upon political justice. He insisted upon the application of the underlying principles of our government, and the orderly process of its machinery, to set right what was plainly wrong. He appealed not to the baser but to the higher impulses that move men. He awakened a sense of responsibility and a renewed belief in the adequacy of our political institutions among the people who had begun to feel that our system of government was a failure. Each step in the unfinished process of readjustment under his leadership was a cheerful augury for the future, and an argument for confidence in representative government.

I think it safe to say that, when the test of American Democracy came with the Great War, the fact that the American people had preserved such memory of their ideals, such confidence that their liberty was united with justice, such affection for their country and respect for its institutions, as to be able to meet the test with the overwhelming power of unanimous action, is due more to the influence of Theodore Roosevelt than to all the other public men of his day. When the great test came, and the people of the greatest of all democracies had to determine whether they would turn from their peaceful lives, from their comfort, their ease, their prosperity, their wealth, and gird themselves again to fight for their liberty, ready for sacrifice and suffering and death that American liberty and justice might live, and that America might do her part for the liberty of the world, Theodore Roosevelt was out of office, out of political control, out of favor with official power. He was denied his dearest wish to fight upon the battle front with the four strong sons whom he had trained in all the traditions of heroism. He had no source of influence save his life, his character, his intense convictions; but it was then that he rose to the greatest height of his wonderful career. Day by day and month by month he appealed with passion and power to the people who had loved him; and that clear, insistent call to courage, and honor, and duty, and the noble ways of a nation's life, rousing to action the driving power of the American people, did more, I think, to bring America in arms to the battle-line before it was too late and to defeat the autocracy of Germany than any public officer — civil or military — for whom the flags are dipped as the victorious regiments pass in review.

ADDRESS AT THE ROCKY MOUNTAIN CLUB DINNER ON THE ANNIVERSARY OF HIS BIRTH, NEW YORK CITY, OCTOBER 27, 1919

WHEN Colonel Thompson asked me to come here and say a few words, a very few words, about Theodore Roosevelt, on his birthday, it seemed to me very appropriate, for the great mountains from which you draw your inspiration as a society were to him, next to his home, the dearest place in the world. Like Antæus of the Greek fable, there he renewed his matchless energy by the touch of Mother Earth. He loved every peak and plain and valley from the Bad Lands to the Flat Tops.

He loved the brave and simple people of the mountains; he knew them, he respected them, and he prized the influence of their lives upon his. So many of us loved him! The mystic chords of memory draw the hearts of so many of us back to that life so magnanimous, so kindly, so affectionate, so appealing to the best in all our natures, so full of genuine interest in our fortunes, so appreciative of what was good in us, so kindly and considerate of our failings! We love him! We could not celebrate his birthday as we do were it not for our deep affection.

But, that is not the cause of our gathering. He rendered great service, he did great deeds for us and for our country. With the swift intuitions in which he surpassed all men of his time, he pierced through the complications and uncertainties of political and economic life to the fundamental principles upon which rest our whole political and social system, the fundamental truths which underlie American institutions and which underlie all government of Justice and of Liberty. He saw that in the marvelous development of human wealth and human power to produce wealth we had gradually slipped away from the old, simple relations of equality among our people, that a crust was forming of power and privilege and superiority based upon wealth, and a steadily, certainly growing discontent was making its way among the people of our country. And he undertook, though there was no crisis, to make one, and to bring the people of America back to the supremacy of law for liberty. The millions who were beginning to feel that our free institutions were failing, he taught to understand that there was a remedy by law; and he forced a passage through the difficulties, doubts, and obstacles for law and for the application of the great principles of free government through law; and in order to prevent revolution, he went up and down the land, preaching the principles of justice and freedom — not merely solving particular questions of corporations and trusts and the use of capital, but laying down the rules by which all questions for all time must be solved in a free, democratic government. With unthinking and instant courage, he declared in clear tones heard throughout the land, "All must obey the law. Wealth must obey the law. Labor must obey the law." He flinched from no power, from no political power, from no social power, in the just and equal and uncompromising assertion of principles of American liberty and justice for rich and poor, for capital and labor, for the great and for the weak.

Where should we be now, called upon as we are to deal with the grave and terrible questions that are before us, if Theodore Roosevelt had not restored to the plain people of the United States, the men and women of small means, of simple lives, confidence in our institutions, an abiding faith in the capacity of our democracy to maintain the equality of independent manhood among rich and poor alike?

Where should we have been in those fateful days when the people of the United States were called upon to gird themselves anew and offer their fortunes, their lives, their dearest affections, in terrible war for the preservation of our liberty, if Theodore Roosevelt had not been able to appeal to the affection and the confidence and the trust of the American people for a system of free institutions in which he had taught them to believe? But as it is not for our affection, so it is not for his deeds that we are now met to honor him. He did more than solve the questions of his time. He presented to our country and to the world a great and inspiring example to enforce his teaching; it is not what he did, but what he became. The *man* was the spirit he worked in.

Sermons are forgotten; men are remembered. Truths are told in ten thousand volumes and pamphlets, from a thousand pulpits and rostrums. They are forgotten. For a moment they enter the mind, and in a moment they are displaced. But the perpetual lesson of a great example, inseparably united to a great truth, carries on the work of a lifetime through generations and ages to come.

And this example is one which appeals so readily to all. Every American boy can be Theodore Roosevelt's follower. He was not different, not some strange phenomenon unlike the rest of us. He was like us all, only more so. There was, as the French Ambassador has said, radium in the clay of which he was fashioned, that carried to the nth power every great purpose, every noble conception, every deep truth that possessed him.

Every Boy Scout may imitate him. He was strong, powerful, but he began weak and puny. He trained himself to strength and power. So can all American boys. He was born and bred under the disadvantages of wealth and fashion, with the paving stones of a city between him and the earth. He broke over the barriers and became the friend of every farmer, of every ranchman, of every huntsman, of every laborer, of every good and true man and woman in this great land. No pent-up city, no learned institution, no social convention restrained his universal and mighty sympathy. He trained himself to the habit of courage. So can every American boy. From the habit of courage came the natural reaction of truth. That is within the grasp of every American boy. He was sincere and simple, not ornate and florid. He spoke not the tongue of the poet or the philosopher. He had not what Macaulay credited to Gladstone, "a command of a kind of language, grave and majestic, but of vague and doubtful import." No one ever misunderstood what Theodore Roosevelt said. No one ever doubted what Theodore Roosevelt meant. No one ever doubted that what he said, he believed, he intended, and he would do. He was a man, not of sentiment or expression, but of feeling and of action.

His proposals were always tied to action. He uttered no fine sentence, satisfied that that was the end, the thing accomplished. His words were always the precursors of effective action. He cultivated promptness in action until it became his natural reaction and made him an almost perfect executive — not an administrator, but an executive gifted with the power of swift and unerring decision. Yet he was as free from self-conceit as any man I ever knew. His consciousness of strength was in the strength of his purpose, in the cause he advocated, and not at all in his own merits. He was as modest as a girl about himself. He was the most hospitable to advice of all the men I ever knew. He was eager for knowledge. He thirsted for knowledge, and in the performance of his public duties he sought everywhere, from all manner of men, to know their thought, their contribution of information. He talked little about common counsel, but he practised it universally and always, and he did come to know the very heart of the American people by actual contact. He was no unapproachable genius, unlike everyone else.

He did not originate great new truths, but he drove old fundamental truths into the minds and the hearts of his people so that they stuck and dominated. Old truths he insisted upon, enlarged upon, repeated over and over in many ways with quaint and interesting and attractive forms of expression, never straining for novelty or for originality, but always driving, driving home the deep fundamental truths of public life, of a great self-governing democracy, the eternal truths upon which justice and liberty must depend among men. Savonarola originated no truths, nor Luther, nor Wesley, nor any of those flaming swords that cut into the consciousness of mankind with the old truths that had been overlooked by indifference and error, wrong-heartedness and wrong-headedness. Review the roster of the few great men of history, our own history, the history of the world; and when you have finished the review, you will find that Theodore Roosevelt was the greatest teacher of the essentials of popular self-government the world has ever known.

What we are here for is to perpetuate that teaching, lift it up, striking the imagination, enlisting the interest of the country and the world, by signally perpetuating the memory of our friend, the great teacher.

The future of our country will depend upon having men, real men of sincerity and truth, of unshakable conviction, of power, of personality, with the spirit of Justice and the fighting spirit through all the generations; and the mightiest service that can be seen to-day to accomplish that for our country is to make it impossible that Theodore Roosevelt, his teaching and his personality, shall be forgotten. Oh, that we might have him with us now!

Be it our duty and our privilege, in our weak and humble way, to keep him with us, to keep him with our country in all the trials before it, and so pay to him the honor that he coveted most, the highest accomplishment of his noble and patriotic purpose.

JOSEPH H. CHOATE

MEMORIAL IN THE NEW YORK CITY BAR ASSOCIATION,
DECEMBER 20, 1917

Since Mr. Root's address was delivered, Mr. Choate's long and useful life has been told in a series of letters by Edward Sandford Martin, *The Life of Joseph Hodges Choate* (1920). His own impressions of the Second Hague Peace Conference, of which Mr. Root speaks, are found in a series of lectures (The Stafford Little Lectures) which he delivered at Princeton in 1912, under the title of *The Two Hague Conferences* (1913).

JOSEPH HODGES CHOATE was born in Salem, Massachusetts, January 24, 1832, and died at his home in the City of New York, May 14, 1917, in the fourth month of his eighty-sixth year. He was graduated from Harvard College in the class of 1852, and from the Harvard Law School in 1854. He was then for a year a student in the office of Leverett Saltonstall of Boston, and he was admitted to the Bar of Massachusetts in 1855. In September of the same year he removed to New York City; and after passing a few months in the office of Scudder & Carter, he entered the office of Messrs. Butler, Evarts & Southmayd, where he remained for nearly three years. In the meantime, in 1856, he was admitted to the Bar of New York. In August, 1858, he formed a law partnership with Mr. W. H. L. Barnes, subsequently a leader of the Bar of California; but early in the following year he returned to his former associates, and became a partner in the law firm of Evarts, Southmayd & Choate, a relation which continued throughout the entire professional lives of the partners.

He was married in October, 1861, to Miss Caroline Dutcher Sterling. There were five children of the marriage, three sons and two daughters, of whom three survive, one daughter and two sons, one of whom bears his father's name and is a member here.

Mr. Choate was one of the founders of this Association, a signer of the preliminary articles by which it was created in December, 1869. He was President of the Association in 1888 and 1889, President of the Bar Association of the State of New York from 1906 to 1908, President of the American Bar Association in 1898 and 1899, and President of the New York County Lawyers' Association. He was a member of the Commission of 1890 appointed by the Governor under legislative authority to report a revision of the judicial system of the State of New York. He was President of the Constitutional Convention that in 1894 framed the Constitution under which the people of the State still live.

In January, 1899, he was appointed Ambassador from the United States to Great Britain, and he served his country in that office for six years, until May, 1905. On the 10th of April, 1905, the Bar of England claimed him as a fellow of that great company by electing him to be a Bencher of the Middle Temple. Upon his return to his home he resumed his activity at the Bar; but in 1907 he was again made Ambassador, and the head of the Delegation from the United States to the Second Hague Conference, where he contributed an important part to the substantial advance in the establishment and definition of International Law and Procedure accomplished by that Conference. Upon his return from The Hague he again resumed practice, less actively, of course, than in earlier years.

In the meantime he had come to be a Doctor of Laws of Amherst, Harvard, Yale, Williams, Union, the University of Pennsylvania, of McGill and Toronto, of Cambridge, Edinburgh, St. Andrews, and Glasgow, and a Doctor of Civil Law of Oxford.

The forty-three years which elapsed between admission to the Bar in 1856 and the Embassy to Great Britain in 1899 were filled by the work of the pure lawyer. Neither business

Bar at its best of real devotion to justice and liberty, that the finest thought and feeling of the profession came to follow him, and to look to him as a leader, not merely because he tried causes more skillfully or argued them more powerfully than others; but also, because he put the power and prestige of his great reputation in the courtroom behind the thrust of advocacy of the honor and public service of the Bar as a whole. He has told us what his conception of advocacy was, and his whole life helped mightily to establish that high standard. He said:

I maintain that in no other occupation to which men can devote their lives is there a nobler intellectual pursuit or a higher moral standard than that which inspires and pervades the ranks of the legal profession. To establish justice, to maintain the rights of man, to defend the helpless and oppressed, to succor innocence, and to punish guilt, to aid in the solution of those great questions, legal and constitutional, which are constantly being evolved from the ever-varying affairs and business of men, are duties that may well challenge the best powers of man's intellect and the noblest qualities of the human heart.

Thus, the recognition of power and promise which he commanded from his seniors in the eighteen-sixties was gradually succeeded by universal admiration, deference, and pride in his leadership among the juniors of his later years. Wherever the class-consciousness of the Bar of New York sought expression in the comradeship of social intercourse, in protest against abuse, in repelling assaults upon the administration of justice or in demands for its improvement, in concerted action upon any great public question, his came to be the sympathetic leadership, his the clear voice, the commanding authority, the unimpeachable representation of the noblest impulses of the profession. The great leaders and colleagues of his early and middle life passing from the stage left him alone, without an equal or a rival, the most eminent, the most admired, and the most revered advocate and counsellor of the Bar, not only of New York but of our country.

In this country of popular self-government, however, it did not satisfy him to be successful in the trial of causes, or to win the respect and admiration of the Bar alone. To be a great American lawyer in the broadest sense, one must be a great Citizen, and Mr. Choate was that. He realized that our system of law, striking its roots far back in the customs and struggles in which the liberties of England were developed, shaped by the fathers of the Republic to suit the conditions of a freer life, adapted from generation to generation to meet the new requirements of national growth, rests always upon the foundation of general public conviction that it is fit and adequate to secure justice and to preserve individual liberty. He knew that public respect for law, public confidence in the judicial system through which the law is administered, public faith in the wisdom and rightfulness of those great rules of conduct which we have written into our Constitutions for the limitation of official power in its relation to the life, the liberty, and the property of the private citizen, are essential to the maintenance of the most vital rights which from day to day we assert in the courts. He welcomed the privilege of the American lawyer, not merely to insist upon the application to his client's case of the principles of American law, but to assert and defend the principles themselves before the great governing body of American citizens who make and can unmake the law. He understood that American lawyers cannot rightfully be a separate body cultivating a mystery; that they ought to be an active part of the citizenship of the country, sharing in the formation and expression of its opinion, in its social and political life, and by virtue of their special knowledge and training, leaders of opinion among their fellows in the community. He said to the Chicago Bar in February, 1898:

But at all times, and especially in this our day, great public duties await us. So long as the Supreme Court exists to be attacked and defended (that sheet anchor of our liberties and of our Government); so long as the public credit and good faith of this great Nation are in peril; so long as the right of property which lies at the root of all civil government is scouted, and the three unalienable rights to life, to liberty, and the pursuit of happiness — which the Declaration of Independence proclaimed and the Constitution has guaranteed alike against the action of Congress and of the States — are in jeopardy; so long will great public service be demanded of the Bar.

Let us magnify our calling. Let us be true to these great occasions, and respond with all our might to these great demands; so that, when our work is done, of us at least it may be said that we transmitted our profession to our successors as great, as useful, and as spotless as it came to our hands.

These functions of the American lawyer Mr. Choate performed with unwearying interest and devotion, and with signal distinction. He received from his Massachusetts ancestry and brought with him from his old Salem home a large measure of that amazing formative power, which, proceeding from the few scanty settlements on the Atlantic shore, has moulded this vast Continent with its hundred millions of people according to the course of the common law, and to conceptions of right inspired by the spirit of Magna Charta, and of the immortal Declaration of rights unalienable, to secure which governments are instituted.

The blood in his veins, the influences of early environment, of education and training, the foundations of his political belief, all made impossible for him the conception of a free community in whose public affairs it was not the duty of every private citizen to take an active part. He took such a part as a matter of course, and with an effectiveness natural to his exceptional powers. His intense and instinctive patriotism made him keenly alive to the welfare of the Nation, and of the State and City in which he lived. The strain of labor in the Courts never prevented him from doing his full share both in government, and in the public movements and private enterprises through which a democratic community develops the best side of its nature.

At the age of thirty-five he was President of the New England Society in New York, the organization which for more than a century has done honor to the history and spirit of his race. At forty-one he was President of the Union League Club, that institution created in the darkest days of the Civil War to promote, encourage, and sustain absolute and unqualified loyalty to the Government of the United States. He was President of the Harvard Club, of the Harvard Law School Association, of the Century Association. For forty years before his death he was a Governor of the New York Hospital. He was President of the New York Association for the Blind. He was President of the State Charities Aid Association. He was one of the incorporators of the Metropolitan Museum of Art, and one of its trustees for the forty-seven years which followed its organization in 1870; and for many years before his death he was Chairman of its Law Committee, and a member of its Executive Committee, and Vice-President. He was one of the incorporators, and during all its existence a trustee, of the American Museum of Natural History. He was an active trustee and the Vice-President of the Carnegie Endowment for International Peace. He was Vice-President of the Society for the Judicial Settlement of International Disputes. He was a member, and Chairman of the Sub-Committee on Elections, of the Committee of Seventy, which roused the honest citizenship of New York to the rescue of the city from the shame of the Tweed Ring control. He was Honorary President and an active coadjutor in the National Security League, which did so much to arouse the patriotic people of our country to realize the deadly peril to their liberty of possible German military domination, and to make them understand that the time had come when American institutions must be defended again by force of arms, or must perish.

He was not a dreamer, to reject the natural agency of political parties in popular self-government, and he did not hold himself aloof from the activities of the party which seemed to him the best agent of government. He never changed or wavered in his political allegiance. He made his first public political speech for Frémont in 1856, and his last for Hughes in 1916; but he conceived of a political party as an organization by which many citizens, agreed upon major questions of principle and policy, may give practical effect to their opinions in actual government. His interest was in the public effect of party control, not in office or emoluments. His activity was in the leadership of opinion, not in party management; he took little or no part in that. He sought no office, and he entered into no combinations. He held no party office. I remember that moving, some forty years ago, into a new neighborhood, and attending for the first time the Republican Association of the old 21st Assembly District, I found him there attending to his duties as a citizen; and he was there as one of the rank and file. He was always in the ranks. But, when the time of conflict came between opposing parties or against misleading leadership in his own party; when serious decisions were to be made by the instructed judgment and conscience of the people, then he was wont to come as a champion from the ranks with all the weapons in the armory of debate, with clarity of statement and destructive satire, and power of appeal, and charm of persuasion, against things sordid and corrupt, against the follies of ignorance and prejudice, against indifference and decadence and for the cause he deemed just, for the living spirit of American institutions.

He did not reserve himself for great occasions and great efforts; but gave without reserve to the everyday activities which taken together fill so great a part of the life of the community. In the multitude of gatherings half-public, half-social through which the members of a community are

welded together in sympathy of good fellowship and of opinion, he played a leading part for almost half a century. It is
hard to understand how any man engaged in the exhausting
labors of a crowded professional life could find the strength
and resiliency of body and mind to make speeches in vast
number at public dinners and luncheons and meetings for all
sorts of objects, where he delighted and instructed the crowd
year after year during his long active life; yet, he did so with
undiminished brilliancy until the end. It would have been
impossible but for a strong and active interest in the life of
the world, in everything that went on in the community, and
a genuine liking for the people among whom he lived, sympathy with their feelings, and understanding of their characters. He was never uninteresting. His wit and humor
never obscured or belittled his serious thought, and his serious
thoughts were never dull. He richly merited the great fame
he acquired as an after-dinner speaker. In viewing that
phase of his activity as a whole, it is plain that he made it the
means of great influence and useful service. He promoted
causes and institutions in which he was interested, and inspired in the tens of thousands who listened to him, not
merely admiration and grateful remembrance, but respect
for his authority, and acceptance of his ideas.

The reputation of many great lawyers is confined to their
own profession; but the wide range of his activities extended
a knowledge of his great abilities and commanding character
to the public at large, and brought appreciation from the
general body of good citizens. To achieve a commanding
position in the public life of this great country ordinarily requires the holding of high office. The office itself cannot give
the holder such a position, but it carries to the minds of the
great multitude, who have to form their judgments chiefly
upon hearsay, a presumption of a right to be heard in public

affairs. The presumption may not be justified and may fade out of existence, but it is the door of opportunity, and few men acquire great public consideration without it. Almost entirely without the aid of office, Mr. Choate acquired universal recognition as a great public character, a significant figure in the public life of his time, speaking with authority and entitled to leadership of opinion. This position was fully established before he was appointed Ambassador to Great Britain, and he was appointed to that office because of it. The basis of that great position was achievement at the Bar, and the devotion of powers trained at the Bar to the duties of a private citizen in the service of the community and the country.

Nature was very kind to him. She gave him a sound body, a constitution capable of enduring without injury the strain of long-continued and severe effort, and a temperament which saved him from the exhausting effect of worries and fears and passions and vain regrets; and she gave him a physical presence most impressive and attractive. He was tall, fully six feet in height, slender and erect in his early years, broad-shouldered, and carrying an impression of poise and balanced strength; the leonine head was set perfectly in its place, and his face was luminous even in repose with the beauty of intellect and nobility of character, sublimated and manifestly active and dominant. His voice was clear, pleasing to the ear, and far-carrying. I do not recall that he ever strained it, or seemed to be forcing it unduly. He was never oratorical even in passages of greatest force and feeling. His manner was dignified and courtly, but perfectly simple and unaffected, and it was the same everywhere and to everybody. Forty-odd years ago, when we were in the beginnings of a friendship which has been for me one of the chief satisfactions and joys of life, I used to think that he was the most beautiful and splendid specimen of manhood I had ever seen. I have revised my judgment upon this; for, after the Declaration of War with Germany, when he knew that the manhood and honor of his country had reasserted themselves, in the benign and radiant face with its lines of old experience and wisdom, made purer and gentler by trial and high endeavor, still alert with intelligence and feeling, shining with the joy of unselfish patriotism, and in the massive form bowed under the weight of a noble life, there was a beauty surpassing that of conquering youth; and the memory of it is a benediction.

His mind was strong, well balanced, and wonderfully alert and rapid in action. Its response to the emergencies which so continually arise in court was instantaneous, and apparently intuitive. Extraordinary power of discrimination and a sense of material and crucial questions relieved him of the burden of bothering over immaterial matters, and enabled him to work with great ease. This faculty, combined with his vast experience, led some younger men who were with him as juniors to think that he worked very little; but that was a mistaken idea. He worked very hard and with great intensity, but he was happy in escaping the great mass of unnecessary work which most of us have to do. When he came to New York in 1855 he brought a letter from his father's cousin, Rufus Choate, to Mr. Evarts. He prized this letter very highly, and I am sure that he would not have exchanged it for any patent of nobility. I will reproduce it here:

BOSTON, 24 September, 1855.

MY DEAR MR. EVARTS,

I beg to incur one other obligation to you by introducing the bearer, my friend and kinsman, to your kindness.

He is just admitted to our bar, was graduated at Cambridge with a very high reputation for scholarship and all worth, and comes to the practice of the law, I think, with extraordinary promise. He has decided to enroll himself among the brave and magnanimous of your bar, with a courage not unwarranted by his talents, character, ambition and power of labor. There is no young man whom I love better, or from whom I hope more or as much; and if you can do anything to smooth the way to his first steps the kindness will be most seasonable and will yield all sorts of good fruits.

Most truly,

Your servant and friend,

RUFUS CHOATE.

The particular expression of this letter which he valued most was the reference to his "power of labor," and he never regarded as a compliment the suggestion that he reached his results without the exercise of that power.

This letter points to one of the chief influences in the development of his character and the direction of his life. No one who has watched his career, and has read the address in which he paid his tribute to the majestic and lovable personality of Rufus Choate, can fail to be convinced that, widely as they differed in temperament and in their surroundings, admiration and reverence for his great kinsman was one of the controlling influences of the younger life. Much as they differed, there was a striking resemblance in the standards of life, the intensity of application, the tenacity of purpose, the ardor of conflict, combined with the broad and kindly view, the strong sense of humor, the love of literature and reliance upon its broadening and humanizing influence to correct the narrowing effect of exclusively professional interests, the impulse for public service and the intense love of country: all these were found in both the older and the younger Choate. One was the spiritual successor of the other. Rufus Choate came to the Bar in the year 1823, and he continued for four years after his young relative's admission. Thus, for almost a hundred years these two men, of the same name and family, products of the same influences, and inheritors of the same traditions and the same ideals, adorned and ennobled the American Bar, and each in his turn rose to great heights of honor and renown. The younger man was fortunate also in associating during the formative period of his career with really great leaders whose influence tended along the same lines of development. How could there be broader scope or loftier spirit than he found in Mr. Evarts, the advocate and statesman, eloquent, philosophical, delightful companion, the wittiest lawyer of his time, and Mr. Southmayd, the typical solicitor, learned, logical, cautious, independent in judgment, stubborn in opinion, caustic in expression. They were not merely partners, they were friends, and nothing could be more delightful than the intercourse between them.

Our friend was enabled to use his intellectual power to the highest advantage by two qualities of the first importance. One was his clear and instinctive courage. He was wholly free from any impediment of timidity. This quality did not impress one as being the kind of courage which overcomes fear, but, rather, as a courage which excluded fear. With him no such emotion as fear seemed to exist. The other closely allied quality was a universal and invincible cheerfulness. In all my varied opportunities for observation for many years, he was the same. I never knew him to be sullen, or sour, or bitter, or cross, or fretful. He strongly condemned some things and some men with force and picturesque expression, but never with the least tinge of malevolence. He had his griefs, which sank deep in his heart, but his buoyant spirits and high courage forbade them to control his conduct; and, through them all, he presented the same bright and cheerful face to the world. He brought to the breakfast table always the same genial and cheery lifting of spirit which made him such a welcome guest at the banquet tables of New York. He was as lively and interesting with a dozen friends, or with one friend, as with five hundred, because he was entirely free from false pretense; and he was the same man with the public audience that he was with his close and private friends. He had a most serene and imperturbable temper. He never lost his self-possession or entire control of his powers. Safe upon this ground of vantage, he took special delight in making his adversary angry, and in reaping the benefits.

He was a loyal and devoted friend, as he was loyal to every cause he espoused, and to every case he undertook; and he left no debt of friendship unpaid. No trouble was too great, no labor too arduous for him to help a friend. His power of satire and ridicule were terrible weapons, and he used them unsparingly, always most fatally when he was most gentle and childlike in manner. When engaged in battle he used all his weapons without respect of persons, and his thrusts often wounded his friends at the Bar more deeply than he probably knew. Yet I think he never lost a battle through friendship, or lost a friend through what he said or did in battle. It was impossible to cherish resentment against him. He fought as those gay and debonnaire youths of Dumas, who drew their swords with alacrity, and, rejoicing in their skill, fought joyously upon all suitable occasions without anger or malice, to death or victory or eternal brotherhood. Before a jury he was a master of the art of appearing surprised, and of appearing indifferent; but nothing was further from his habit than personal display. Anyone with his appearance and talents might be pardoned for thinking of so agreeable a subject as his own person; but he never appeared to do so. He was thinking always of his object, and carefully studying the minds and feelings of those to whom he spoke. He studied his juries, his judges, and his audiences with sympathetic insight, and his favorite method of capturing their judgment was by boldly invading the field of their personal experience and interest, making himself at home with them, and when he departed, leaving his own ideas with his audience as a part of their household goods. He very seldom told a story. His wit and humor did not percolate through him from the *gesta Romanorum*, or from the pages of American humorists. They were the natural reaction of his own mind from his perception of the persons and events that surrounded him at the time. He was a fountain, not a conduit, of humor. His speeches were interesting because his way of looking at men and life was fresh and original.

It is quite inadequate to say that he was always cheerful and interesting. He had in him something far beyond that, which I cannot describe to myself better than by calling it the eternal boy in him. He rejoiced in life. He spurned dull care. He bubbled over with fun. He dearly loved a little boyish mischief. That was rather a dangerous faculty, but the danger gave it zest. There is an old story (I think it belonged to Mr. Evarts) of an American assuring an Englishman that Washington could throw a dollar across the Potomac because he had thrown a sovereign across the Atlantic. Mr. Choate would never have deigned to tell that ancient joke here; but when he got to England and before an English audience, he could not resist the desire to see his English friends contemplating the aërial flight of their sovereign, and he told it, I think, several times. It befell me to sit near him at a famous St. Patrick's Day dinner, and he stopped at my chair and made a remark which indicated that he was having huge enjoyment with himself over something he was going to say. When he suggested that the Irish in America should redeem poor unhappy Ireland by going home, he was following the same kind of boyish impulse for mischief which leads schoolboys to carry their disconcerting pranks to the limit of audacity.

He had great force and nobility and purity of character. He made the world his debtor by great usefulness in many fields. He deserved and received great praise and admiration for his achievements; but, after all, I think it was the delightful "boy" in him that made us love him. It was that which, joined to his other qualities, made him so different from ordinary men. It was that blithe spirit which gave color and life and light to the whole character.

He had something that superior intellect and character do not always give — he had distinction; and above all, he had charm — that inexplicable quality whose origins are veiled among the mysteries of life.

Mr. Choate owed his selection as a delegate at large to the Constitutional Convention of 1894 largely to the fact that there seemed little probability of a Republican success in the election of 1893. He was so much of a free lance, his shafts of ridicule had wounded so many organization leaders, that in ordinary times there was little chance of his receiving a nomination really desired by any of the faithful. The Democrats were then, however, under the astute management of Senator Hill in control of the machinery of the State Government. They were in possession of the National Government also, and the influences which had driven the Republicans from power both in the Nation and the State seemed still to be dominant. The Republican ticket for 1893 was accordingly made up rather less than usual under the influence of a desire to distribute party rewards, and rather more than usual with a view to present a list of candidates who would secure all the chances of success possible, and whose defeat might be regarded with philosophy on the part of the Organization. In addition to this, the fact that the work of the Constitutional Convention of 1867 had been rejected by the people, and that the work of the Constitutional Commission of 1890 had not received sufficient popular support to prevent its being ignored by the Legislature, had created an impression that the work of the proposed Convention would have no practical results. There was accordingly little pressure for nominations to the Convention, and Mr. Choate's name readily found a place at the head of the delegates at large as a means of giving distinction to the whole ticket.

When it turned out that there had been a political revolution in the State, and that the Republicans had a majority of the Convention, including all the delegates at large, his selection as President of the Convention followed as a matter of course; and for a period of nearly five months during which the Convention was in session, he presided in the most delightful and effective way. He did not trouble himself very much about the technical details of parliamentary procedure. He preserved the substance of it, of course; but he was very fond of getting things done, and would sometimes make the most surprising shortcuts to reach results — always results, however, which would certainly have been reached by the more cumbrous process of slower minds, and never at the sacrifice of the substantial rights of the minority; and he always maintained his positions in such a way as to fill the souls of the majority with joy and command their enthusiastic support. Occasionally, when there was a heated debate, he would take the floor, and his speeches were always of great power and cogency. I always thought of the Olympians joining the fray under the walls of Troy.

Two speeches that rest especially in my memory are one in support of the new judiciary article, and one on the public schools. There had been an attempt to insert in an article reported by the Committee on Education a clause which would authorize State aid to schools under religious control. This was regarded by some of us as dangerous in the highest degree, tending to break down the separation between Church and State, and to destroy our whole unsectarian public school system. The attempt succeeded in the committee of the whole; but, when the article was reported to the Convention, there was a counter-attack, and Mr. Choate left the chair and came down to the floor, and made a fine and noble speech. The real nature of the thing that was being done was made plain, and the vote was reversed, and the obnoxious provision was defeated.

It was my good fortune to be by his appointment Chairman of the Judiciary Committee of the Convention, and that position carried by custom the leadership of the majority on the floor of the Convention, so that we were obliged to be in constant conference over the business of the session. Accordingly, we took a house together near the Capitol, and kept house jointly during the entire period, and I had exceptional opportunity to know about the influence which he exercised over the conduct of affairs. We kept open house for the members of the Convention, and almost every important Convention question was considered and discussed there. He was practically a member of every committee, and his clear vision and sound practical sense made themselves felt in every department of the Convention work through those personal conferences and discussions which properly play so great a part in shaping the judgment and directing the action of every deliberative body.

Mr. Choate's service in the foreign affairs of the country was of the highest value. When he was appointed Ambassador from the United States to Great Britain at the age of sixty-seven, there were several very serious and difficult questions between the two countries, which required to be treated with great skill and judgment if serious controversy was to be prevented. The very positive defiance of Great Britain in Mr. Cleveland's Venezuela message of December, 1895, and the general expression of American feeling in support of that defiance, had created an atmosphere not altogether favorable to mutual concessions. This had been modified, but not wholly dispelled, by Great Britain's discouragement of European intervention during our war with

Spain, and by the wisdom and good sense of Mr. Hay and President McKinley on the one side and Lord Salisbury on the other during the first two years of the McKinley Administration.

Only a few months before Mr. Choate's appointment a Joint High Commission established for the settlement of a formidable array of Canadian questions, sitting alternately in Canada and Washington, with Lord Chancellor Herschel at the head of the British section, and Vice-President Fairbanks at the head of the American section, had reached an *impasse*, and had dissolved without any settlement. The chief and apparently insuperable obstacle which barred the Commission from settlement upon any question was the deadlock over the Alaskan Boundary. That was a serious and critical matter, because at any time a new gold discovery in the disputed territory was liable to bring the miners on either side of the line into actual hostilities, and to set all Canada and Western America aflame. Under the diplomacy of Mr. Choate in London and Mr. Hay in Washington a *modus vivendi* was established; and a treaty was made providing for the submission of the boundary questions to a tribunal composed of an equal number from each country, charged to hear the evidence and decide according to law. The tribunal sat in London in the year 1903, and by its judgment the controversy was finally determined. With that stumbling-block removed, every other question which was before the Joint High Commission of 1898 has since been satisfactorily settled and disposed of.

When Mr. Choate was appointed, the United States had just reached a full realization of the necessity of a canal across the Central American Isthmus under American control. We were forced to that realization by the results of the war with Spain, the cession of Porto Rico, and the responsibility for the protection of Cuba; by the growth of population

and commerce on the Pacific Coast; by the acquisition of
Hawaii and the Philippines; by the appearance on the horizon
of grave questions of international policy toward the Far
East. It was necessary for our internal commerce and our
naval protection that our Atlantic and Pacific coasts should
be united by a ship canal under our control; but the way was
blocked by the Clayton-Bulwer Treaty of 1850, under which
the United States and Great Britain had agreed that any
such canal should be practically under a partnership of the
two nations. The object could not be attained while that
Treaty stood. Under the wise and highly competent diplomacy of Mr. Choate in London and Mr. Hay in Washington
the partnership was abandoned, and the obstacle of the
Clayton-Bulwer Treaty was removed upon the sole condition
of equal treatment to the commerce of the world in the canal
to be built and controlled by the United States.

When Mr. Choate went to London, China seemed to be on
the verge of partition by the great Powers, who had established naval and military stations and spheres of influence in
Chinese territory, and who, mutually suspicious, were reaching out, each for more control, in order to prevent other
powers from acquiring it. There was no escape from partition, except by stopping that process. With partition the
door for American trade with China would be closed, and the
opportunity of China for liberty and self-government would
disappear. America alone was free from suspicion, and from
that vantage-ground Mr. Hay undertook to stop the process
of partition by proposing a universal agreement on the principle of the open door. Without the agreement of Great
Britain effort would have been useless. It fell to Mr. Choate
to secure that agreement from the British Government, and
it was given cheerfully and ungrudgingly, and the principle
of the open door was established in China. So far it has saved
for China her territory and her opportunity to try out her

experiment of self-government under republican institutions. Incidentally, it was the relation of mutual confidence established by that agreement, which made it possible for the troops of America, England, Japan, France, and Russia, to coöperate in the march to Pekin, and the rescue of the legations in the Boxer uprising in 1900.

The diplomatic correspondence of that time shows the great part Mr. Choate played in these most important affairs, and how great was the skill and competency he exhibited in the negotiations which they involved. There were many other important things done — and well done — during his six years of service. Let no one suppose that results in the negotiation of such affairs come of themselves. They require long and patient labor, quick perception, judgment of character, tact, skill, and wisdom. Incompetency is fatal.

His service in direct relation to the people of Great Britain was perhaps even greater than his service in negotiation with the British Government. The most important thing in the relations between modern democracies is the feeling of two peoples toward each other. If they like each other and trust each other, any question can be settled. He carried to Great Britain the same readiness for service, the same social unselfishness, the same cheerful, brilliant, and interesting qualities as a public speaker, which had made him so admired and beloved at home. He accepted countless invitations to attend countless banquets and cornerstone layings, and openings of institutions, and unveilings, and celebrations, and meetings of all kinds, and to make countless speeches. Ambassadorial dignity did not injure him in the slightest degree. He must have been wearied often, but he was never bored, for he really interested himself in the affairs and the characters of the people. He talked to them in a sympathetic way about their affairs, and he told them simply and interestingly about the great men of our history and what Americans were doing, and thinking, and feeling. He was clever and stimulating, and enveloped his serious thought there as he did here with a mantle of humor and fun. He must have kept our British cousins guessing for a while at first, but they soon came to know him, and to understand him with undiluted enjoyment.

Upon formal and serious occasions he delivered carefully prepared addresses, admirable in literary form and in serious thought — on Benjamin Franklin, on Alexander Hamilton, on Lincoln, on Emerson, and on John Harvard, on the Supreme Court of the United States, Education in America, and, appealing to the common sympathies of both countries, on the English Bible. He represented the people of the United States to the people of Great Britain for so long a period on so many occasions in so many ways and so delightfully, as to create an enduring impression of the highest value. We did not see then as fully as we see now that a good understanding between Great Britain and the United States was no ordinary international affair, but that these two nations inspired by the same ideals of individual liberty and free self-government were destined to fight together, and stand or fall together, in defense of their common liberty against the hateful dominion of military autocracy; and that our friend's six years of unwearied labor to unite the two nations in strong ties of good understanding and kindly feeling was a special service to civilization.

The selection of Mr. Choate as an Ambassador Extraordinary at the head of the American Delegation to the Second Hague Conference in 1907 followed naturally upon his career at home and in Great Britain. No other man in the United States had shown himself possessed in so high a degree of so many of the qualities necessary for that service. He had learning without pedantry, power of expression which never sacrificed accuracy to rhetoric, or sense to sound, courage saved from rashness by quick perception and long experience, the lawyer's point of view and the statesman's point of view, the technique of forensic debate, and the technique of diplomatic intercourse. His brilliant success in the Embassy to Great Britain and the high position which he had acquired there had made his great reputation known to the public men of Europe, who at that time ordinarily knew little and cared less about American lawyers, so that he was able to speak at The Hague with great personal prestige and authority. His work at The Hague fully met the expectations of his Government, and fully justified his selection, for he became one of the great leaders of the Conference and held a commanding position in its deliberations, and under him the whole American delegation worked together with admirable team play. If any part of his work were selected for special praise, it should be his addresses upon the immunity of private property at sea, on International Arbitration, and on the establishment of an International Court of Justice, all of which show very strikingly how much this country lost when New York failed to send Mr. Choate to the United States Senate in 1897.

The events of the Great War have tended to obscure in most minds the value of the things done in the Hague Conferences; but that is only because the irresponsible brute force of Germany and her allies has thrown over the whole world the dark shadow of a revolt of barbarism against modern civilization. Notwithstanding the fact that all the rules of international law declared or agreed upon in the Hague Conferences have been flouted and broken and ground to powder during the past three years, and notwithstanding that the idea of a peaceable settlement for international disputes seems for the moment to have slipped back into the company of idle dreams, yet the declarations and agreements of those Conferences took many fundamental principles and rules of the law of nations out of the obscurity of inaccessible treaties and conflicting text writers, and made them a distinct and known basis on which the world has rendered its judgment of condemnation upon the conduct of Germany and her allies. And when modern civilization reasserts its control, — as it is sure to do, — the community of nations seeking to regulate its affairs so that peace rather than war may be normal will inevitably make its starting-point the platform established by Mr. Choate and his colleagues at the Second Hague Conference. A multitude of plans for the reorganization of the world after the war have been appearing continuously ever since the war began. Most of them settle everything except the difficulties; but they are all alike in one respect. Their postulates are identical with the conclusions reached by the Second Hague Conference on questions which had been doubtful and controverted.

But the greatest of all the services which Mr. Choate rendered to his country in his long and useful life was at the close, when he realized — as he did very soon after the beginning of the war — that the independence and liberty of the United States were threatened less immediately but not less certainly than those of England and France, by the German grasp for military dominion. With all the vigor and strong conviction of youth he abandoned the comfortable leisure to which the ninth decade of his life entitled him, and threw himself with enthusiasm into the task of making his countrymen see as he saw the certain dangers that lay before them, and the duty that confronted them to rouse themselves and act, for the preservation of their own liberties and the liberties of the world. With voice and pen he pressed his appeal with all the authority of his great reputation, with the wisdom of his experience, the power of an intellect undimmed, of a heart still warm, with the intensity of a great and living patriotism. When that appeal and the appeal of others who thought and felt with him were answered, and the great de-

cision was made that committed a slowly awakening people
to struggle and sacrifice for the preservation of the institutions which he had defended all his life, a great relief and joy
possessed him. He was made Chairman of the New York
Committee for the reception of the Commissions from England and France under Balfour and Viviani and Marshal
Joffre, who came to America after the declaration of war to
confirm and help to make immediately practical and effective
the new league of Democracy for the war against autocracy.
It was his part to lead the people of his own City in a reception of our new allies, so generous and warm-hearted as to
strike the imagination of the people of all three countries.

He met the French Commission and then the British Commission. He welcomed them in our behalf with gracious and
impressive hospitality. He rode with them through the
streets thronged with cheering crowds, and shared with them
the respect and homage accorded to the significant and representative figures of that great and unique occasion. He
attended all the receptions and banquets, and public and
private entertainments, by day and by night, which attended
their visits. Daily, and sometimes twice and sometimes
three times a day, he made public addresses, appropriate and
dignified, and full of interest and deep feeling. His adequate
representation filled his own people with pride, and aroused
their patriotism and their noblest qualities, and he impressed
our guests with confidence and satisfaction.

When the final service of the crowded week was finished,
at the Cathedral of St. John the Divine, on Sunday, the thir-
teenth of May, he bade Mr. Balfour good-bye with the words
"Remember, we meet again to celebrate the victory"; and
with stout and cheerful heart he bore the burden of his years
to his home, to meet the physical reaction that he had been
warned was inevitable; and in a few hours the great heart
filled with the impulses of noble service and with love of

country, and liberty, and justice, ceased to beat. He had given his life for his country.

ADDRESS IN PRESIDING OVER THE CENTURY ASSOCIATION, NEW YORK CITY, JANUARY 19, 1918

IT is peculiarly grateful to me that the first occasion of performing the duties to which your too partial judgment has called me should be in memory of the noble and dear friend who has been our President during these past years. Many organizations and institutions have done honor to his memory. He was a lawyer whose exceptional talent in some directions rose almost, if not quite, to genius, and the lawyers have with one acclaim paid honor to his memory. He was a diplomatist of the highest quality, and the public men of this country and of Europe have testified to their high appreciation of his work and his achievements. He was a great citizen, imbued with a sense of duty to his country, to the community in which he lived, to his fellowmen — during all his long life laboring without ceasing ungrudgingly for their benefit.

He was a patron of the arts, for more than forty years devoting his time first in the organization, then in guiding the feeble steps of the Metropolitan Museum of Art, and to the last devoting his time to its service, — as a member of its Board of Trust, a member of its Executive Committee, Chairman of its Law Committee, Vice-President, — never for a moment feeling that the time expended for the education of the people of his own city, his own country, to higher standards of art, education in the love of all that is beautiful, was time wasted.

He was full of human charity. He worked for the poor with deep comprehension of all their troubles, their sufferings, their sorrows. As President of the State Charities Aid Association, as Governor of the New York Hospital, as

President of the Society for the Blind — in all his busy life always ready to give his time and his effort in that cause.

And from all these associations of his long life have come expressions of sorrow over his loss, of admiration for his career, and of gratitude for the things that he accomplished. We meet, we, his old friends in The Century, meet for something far different. We meet to celebrate the man as we knew him, his personality. As I look back over his life, with more than forty years of which I was very familiar, it seems to me that, as I sum up what he did in all the directions to which he turned his high abilities, as I sum them all up, the man was greater than they, the man was greater than what he did.

But there is little that we can say or do to perpetuate the memory of that fine and gracious personality. Words may awaken the memories of those who knew him; words may call up from the hidden layers of consciousness recollections of this incident and that, of this act and that, of the influence of his presence, of the unexpressed and undefined impression which we received; but words can do little or nothing to carry to the minds of those who did not know him or to perpetuate in future generations any conception of what the man was. Garrick said, you will remember: "One common grave covers the actor and his art." That is the universal truth: one common grave covers the person and his personality. All the exquisite, the subtle, the delicate, the lambent, the bright, the shining light of his life must die with us, and lives now only with our memories, and with our memories it must cease to be.

Yet, this is the truest memorial, this memorial of the Choate we knew; and all that the lawyers and the diplomatists and the citizens can say and record and perpetuate in print is but the outside, the shadow of the man we knew. We can say that he had high courage, clear, lofty courage;

he feared the face of no man; no power, no dignity abashed him or caused the slightest tremor in that clear and instant courage. We remember the uniform, the constant, bright, and genial cheerfulness under all circumstances, dominant and diffusing itself among all the surroundings.

Grief was not unknown to him; bitter sorrows came into his life, but that beautiful and bright, cheerful courage rose above them all and presented always to the world the same steady and beaming countenance. Serene and imperturbable temper went with him everywhere, under all circumstances. He was never sour, or bitter, or fretful, or cross; never gave way to passion; never allowed himself to be swayed by personal animosity; of kindly judgment, but not mushy, not a negation of spirit, the kindly judgment that comes from a knowledge of man's infirmities and an even balance of the temptations and the obstacles to right conduct.

I do not know any man with a more genuine interest in human life than he had. The secret of the interest that others found in him, the reason why for so many years in countless banquets and meetings of all kinds he always found something that was interesting and inspiring for his audience, lay in the fact that he was genuinely interested in his audience, interested in everything in life about him, interested in everything that went on in the world.

All those things we remember, and when we put them all together we make some little approach to the reasons why we think of him and feel of him as we do. And there is the reason for his humor: his humor was the reaction of the people and the events about him, his individual reaction; it was not borrowed. He was always interesting because what he gave to his audiences was his own fresh and original way of looking at the events of the times and of studying the characters of the people about him. Every speech that he made was his own contribution to a study of life. He had, I think, in the highest degree what we have no word in our language for and what the French call *esprit*. He of all the men we know embodied to our understanding what they mean by *esprit*. He had what is so rare and what the highest ability and the longest experience and the greatest achievement do not give: he had distinction; his personality stands up among all those of this great city, of this great country as having distinction — and he had charm. I cannot define it; we do not know whence it comes; we do not know what it is; we do not know why it is, but he had it; and we cannot communicate to anyone else in the world the impression which comes from charm, the charm that he had. He was beyond imitation; he was himself, and there never will be another.

There was a little book — many of you have seen it — privately printed the other day by his family, a few copies printed but not published.[1] Two or three years ago when he was quite ill and was kept in bed by his physicians for wearisome weeks, he yielded to the urgent requests that his family had been making for a long time to leave some account of his early years. Influenced, I think, to some degree by the fact that in undertaking to write a memorial upon an old friend for the Bar Association he had found it so difficult to learn anything about his friend's early life — lying in his bed, he had his secretary come, and day by day he dictated some of his early recollections. It is one of the most delightful and charming pieces of literary work that I have ever seen. It is the man himself. And I think that there you find the key to a great deal of his character, and the reason why with all his intellectual force and power, with all the habits of a

---

[1] The little book to which Mr. Root refers was privately printed in 1917, under the title of *The Boyhood and Youth of Joseph Hodges Choate*. It gives Mr. Choate's account of his early days, to which he looked back in his old age with something akin to amusement, and which he has described with unfading charm, ending with his settlement in New York in 1861. The little volume now forms the introduction to Mr. Martin's *Life of Joseph Hodges Choate* (1920).

lawyer, with all the skill with which he used the weapons of sarcasm and of ridicule, nevertheless all who knew him loved him. For there you find that through all his long life he had treasured in his heart the memories of his early youth in the simple surroundings of his home; they never lapsed back into the past with him; they continued with him always.

He says, "In my bedroom there are the photographs of eighty-five of the members of my college class" — all but three of that college class from which he separated in 1852; and he says, "I frequently put myself to sleep in calling the roll of the class, which is as familiar to me now as it was when I graduated." He tells how William, his brother, whom we know, led him by the hand when first he was taken, two and one-half years of age, to the Dames' School. He tells about the school and its little incidents. He dwells with peculiar interest and humor upon the records in the family Bible; how the Choates — old seafaring family, born and bred upon the borders of Salem Harbor — recorded the births not only by date and hour but by the state of the tide. "George, born about nine in the morning, just at high tide"; "William, born three in the afternoon, four hours of ebb tide"; and so through the long list. There is something about it evidently that carries him back to old Salem. He dwells with most charming and pathetic love upon the sacrifices that his parents made to send him and his brothers to college. His father — he says he had known him to pay out what must have been nearly the last dollar in his pocket toward their education — four brothers in the Harvard Catalogue of 1848–49, at one time; and he says: "This done when the ordinary fees of the hard-working country physician were seventy-five cents for a visit and $7.50 for bringing a new child into the world." And with manifest joy he recounts the pleasure that must have been his parents' when he and his brother sandwiched the college class between them, William, who he says was superior to all other students, having no second, being the valedictorian and he, Joseph — how it happened he cannot tell — made salutatorian, so that they appeared upon the commencement stage at either end of the class.

Those reminiscences carry the very breath of Salem, of old Salem, and when I had read them I took down some volumes of Hawthorne and turned them over; it seemed to me that I was going to a next friend when I did that, and that I found the same charming spirit there. It was that side of his nature, living always, under the brilliant career, under the high endeavor, under the great achievements, that kept him the dear delightful youth that he was, with his blithe spirit and his tender sympathy and his loyalty to friends; it was this that made us love him, and it will keep his memory green in our hearts — the memory of the real man.

In all the long career of The Century, it has never done honor to anyone whose spirit it was more honorable to honor than when it made him our President and surrounded his old age with the glory of affection that accompanied him to his end.

ANDREW CARNEGIE

ADDRESS AT A MEMORIAL MEETING UNDER THE DIRECTION OF THE AUTHORS' CLUB, NEW YORK CITY, APRIL 25, 1920

Andrew Carnegie was born in Dunfermline, Scotland, November 25, 1835, and died at Lenox, Massachusetts, August 11, 1919. He was brought to the United States at an early age (1848) by his parents, who settled in Allegheny City, Pennsylvania. Later, in Pittsburgh, by introducing the Bessemer process in the manufacture of steel, he amassed a great fortune, and devoted it to the purposes mentioned by Mr. Root in the following address.

Since the delivery of Mr. Root's address, Mr. Carnegie's *Autobiography* has been published (1920), in which the full details of his remarkable life and achievements are stated entertainingly and in a literary style, by Mr. Carnegie himself.

THE possession and expenditure of great wealth obscures the personality of the possessor. The worship of wealth, whether it be that kind of worship which finds its expression in mere longing for possession or in sycophancy, or whether it be that kind of worship which finds its expression in envy and bitterness, will dazzle the eyes and prevent people from seeing through to the man. It is very much as with the people of a strange and ill-understood race: the racial similarity obscures the individual characteristics, and they will all look alike to us.

A great many of the people of the United States and of the world have learned to think of Mr. Carnegie as a man who had amassed a great fortune and had given away large sums of money. That is a very inadequate and a very inaccurate view. He did amass a great fortune and he did in one sense, a very limited sense, give away great sums of money, but he was predominantly of the constructive type. He was a great constructor, a builder, never passive. He disposed of his fortune exactly as he made it. He belonged to that great race of nation-builders who have made the progress and development of America the wonder of the world; who have exhibited the capacity of free, undominated individual genius for building up the highest example of the possibilities of freedom for nations.

Mr. Carnegie in amassing his fortune always gave more than he gained. His money was not taken from others. His money was the by-product of great constructive ability which served others; which contributed to the great business enterprises that he conceived and built up and carried to success, and through those enterprises gave to the world great advance in comfort and the possibilities of broader and happier life. The steps by which mankind proceeds from naked savagery to civilized society are the steps that are taken by just such constructive geniuses.

When Mr. Carnegie had amassed his fortune, the magnitude of which rested upon the introduction into America of the Bessemer method of making steel, with all the advance and the progress that that means; when Mr. Carnegie had amassed his fortune and had come to the point of retiring from money-making enterprise, it was impossible for him to retire. His nature made it impossible that he should become passive and he turned his constructive genius and the great constructive energy that urged him on, by the necessities of his nature, toward the use of the money which he had amassed. He never, in the ordinary sense, gave away his fortune. He used his fortune, and what may seem to some casual observer the giving away was the securing of agents for the use of his fortune to carry out his purposes.[1]

---

[1] "This, then, is held to be the duty of the man of wealth: To set an example of modest, unostentatious living, shunning display or extravagance; to provide moderately for the legitimate wants of those dependent upon him; and, after doing so, to consider all surplus revenues which come to him simply as trust funds, which he is called upon to administer, and strictly bound as a matter of duty to administer in the manner which, in his judgment, is best calculated to produce the most beneficial results for the community — the man of wealth thus becoming the mere trustee and agent for his poorer brethren." Andrew Carnegie, *The Gospel of Wealth* (1901), p. 15. See, also, the chapter on "The Gospel of Wealth" in Mr. Carnegie's *Autobiography*, pp. 255–267.

He brought to the work in the second period of his life, this greatest work of his life, some very marked characteristics. First was the urgency to do, to continue to do something. Another was the distinct understanding of the difference between using his money for the purpose that he had in his own mind and being a mark for others to make an instrument of him for their purposes. He had also a very distinct understanding of the difficulty of making a good use of money. He knew how easy it was to waste it. He knew what a danger there was of doing harm by the use of it, and he applied to the problem of its use the same sagacity that he applied to the problem of making steel and marketing it.

Long ago, before he retired from business, he had stated his idea in an article in the *North American Review* where he said:

"The main consideration should be to help others by helping them to help themselves, to provide a part of the means by which those who desire to improve may do so; to give those who desire to rise the aid by which they may rise; to assist — but rarely or never to do all. Neither the individual nor the race is improved by almsgiving." So he never held the grab-bag, and he brought to the consideration of the way in which he should use his money not only great sagacity but great pains and assiduity and continuous labor.

Another thing which played a great part in this second period of his life was that he had a very definite conception as to what would contribute to human happiness. In that conception, the mere possession of money played no part. It did not enter his mind that he could in general make men happy by giving them money; but he had brought from his boyhood memories of the longings of the little Scotch weaver's boy. From close, intimate contact with the poor, from the daily round of dreary toil, he had brought a knowledge of the human heart, such as Lincoln brought to the problems of our country during the stress of the Civil War from his experience as a boy.

Doubtless, as he watched the stationary engine which was his task in Pittsburgh, as he stood at the machine of the telegrapher, as he went to his daily duties as Division Superintendent of the Pennsylvania Railroad, he had had his dreams. He had built his palaces in the clouds, and from the heart of the boy, that never left him, he translated his longings into his theory of the possibilities of human happiness.

He said something in his letter to the trustees in establishing the Dunfermline Trust which told the story. He said to them that it gave him great pleasure "to bring into the monotonous lives of the toiling masses of Dunfermline more of sweetness and light."

Then there is the last characteristic that I shall mention. He was the kindliest man I ever knew. Wealth had brought to him no hardening of the heart, nor made him forget the dreams of youth. Kindly, affectionate, charitable in his judgments, unrestrained in his sympathy, noble in his impulses, I wish all the people who think of him as a rich man giving away money he did not need could know of the hundreds of kindly things that he did unknown to the world — the old friends remembered, the widows and children cared for, the tender memories of his youth, and all who were associated with him.

And so with this great constructive energy, with this discriminating Scotch sagacity, with this accurate conception of the possibilities of the use of money, with these definite views as to the sources of human happiness, and with this heart overflowing with kindness, he entered upon his second career, undertaking to use these hundreds of millions and not to waste them.

The first thing that he did was to turn to the associates of his early struggles and his early successes. He had done many charitable things, as men ordinarily do, while still engaged in business. But when he came to the dividing line between money-getting and the money-using epochs, he turned to Pittsburgh. And he first attempted there to apply his theories to the possibilities of giving happiness. He began with a library, the endowment of a great library, and he tells us what it was that led him to that.

It was the memory of a library of four hundred volumes which Colonel Anderson of Allegheny, over across the river from Pittsburgh, had opened for the use of the boys when Andrew Carnegie was too poor to buy a book. The first thing he did was to use his money to swing open for others the doors of knowledge which gave to him the bright light, the little learning, that could come from Colonel Anderson's four hundred volumes.

He endowed a great library. And then he established the Institute of Pittsburgh. That was the first great reaction of this hard-headed steel-maker — the establishment of the Institute of Pittsburgh in which he invested nearly $30,000,-000. Under it he established an art museum and a music hall and a museum of science. For he knew by the knowledge that came from the experience of his life that after men and women have all that is necessary to eat and to wear and for shelter, come great opportunities for increase of happiness in cultivation of taste, in the cultivation of appreciation for the beautiful in the world.

And so after the library came the art museum, and then the music hall and then the museum of science. And those he followed with the establishment of a technical school for the education of the working people of Pittsburgh.

And the next development was at the home of his childhood, his parents' home in Dunfermline. I have read to you the reason which he gave in his letter to the Trustees of Dunfermline, and he worked that out by presenting the

Trustees for the use of the people of Dunfermline, these toiling masses, a great park in which he set gardens, playgrounds and gymnasiums and swimming baths, and a sanitary school and a library, in order that recreation and joyful things might come to lighten up the days of toil.

Then he made his gift to the four universities of Scotland — St. Andrews, Glasgow, Aberdeen, and Edinburgh. Ten million dollars he gave to them — these universities, toward which he had never been able to bend his steps in youth — one half to be used for improving the university and developing the teaching of science, history, economics, and modern language, and one half to pay the fees of the young men of Scotland who were unable to pay for themselves, giving to all the Scotch boys the opportunity that had been denied to him.

And then having expressed his feelings in the home of his childhood and the home of his success, he broadened out and he established and endowed richly the Institution of Washington, the institution for research and the application of science for the good of mankind.

Then he established the Foundation, still broadening, for the Advancement of Teaching, with its pension fund, so that the teachers of America might not look forward to poverty in the old age that follows the laborious life of the teacher. And he added to that a separate fund for investigation and study in the methods of teaching under which teaching is gradually being standardized, and its defects, faults, shortcomings discovered, so that the institution is not only providing for the teachers but for systematic education by the teachers.

Still broadening in his view, he turned his attention to the maintenance of peace, and with an impulse so natural to establish a hero fund for encouraging and noting properly the heroism of those who lived in peace and in competition with the popular worship of heroism in war. That fund is being administered by trustees, and heroic acts in civil life are being signalized by medals, by money gifts, by providing homes, by pensions for widows — whatever seems the most appropriate to the occasion.

And he moved one step further and established the Endowment for International Peace. And that designed to go a little farther than the mere expression of feeling, the feeling that war is horrible, detestable; the feeling that peace should be made permanent and secure. That endowment was designed and adapted to securing the evidence upon which argument and persuasion in favor of peace and against war may be based; and it has been publishing and making available for all scholars, all students, all intelligent men, the true facts regarding international relations, the law of nations, the rights and wrongs and duties of nations, in the great books that have been written from which men may learn their international rights and duties; in another division it has been making careful scientific studies of the economics and history of war, and in another promoting international intercourse and education.

Incidentally, as he was developing these plans in all these different directions, he seized upon special occasions for doing particular things which would further his plans. He built the great Peace Palace at The Hague, to strike the imagination of the world with the idea of peace rather than war. He built the Pan-American building at Washington, to furnish a centre for good understanding and friendly intercourse between North and South America. He built a great building for the Central American Court of Justice in Costa Rica. He established another trust for the special use of the churches in their work in favor of peace.

All those things were but special occasions and incidents in the course of his development of his great plans. The plans, of course, grew as he went on; and then, having his five great trusts in this country, he added to his trust in Europe by creating the United Kingdom Trust, which was chiefly for the purpose of building libraries; and he developed his own work of library building in America, as a result of which nearly 3,000 libraries built by Andrew Carnegie now open their doors for the people of America as Colonel Anderson opened his door to Andrew Carnegie so many years ago.

And as he studied education, he turned his mind toward the colleges, and chiefly toward the poor colleges, chiefly toward the smaller colleges to which the poor boys go, and with most solicitous examination and discrimination he put his money where he thought it would be used to best advantage, here and there and there, until finally more than five hundred American colleges are using his money to-day — money amounting to over $20,000,000.

And before the end came he organized a single corporation. He incorporated his activities in the Carnegie Corporation, and he put into the Board of Trustees of that Corporation the heads of the five principal, special institutions which he had created in this country — the President of the Institute of Pittsburgh, the President of the Research Institution of Washington, the President of the Endowment for International Peace, the President of the Hero Fund, and the President of the Foundation for the Advancement of Teaching. They make up the majority of the Board of Trustees.

To that Corporation he gave the great bulk of the remainder of his fortune amassed during his lifetime, $125,000,000, to promote the advancement and diffusion of knowledge and understanding among the people of the United States; and he continued, as President of that Corporation, to direct its affairs and the use of its money during his life.

I said that he had not been giving away his money in the strict sense. Far from it. He secured as the agents for the use of his money, for the accomplishment of his noble and beneficent purposes, a great body of men whom no salaries could have attracted, whom no payment could have induced to serve; but who served because the inherent value of the purposes to which Mr. Carnegie summoned them commanded them to serve — Joseph H. Choate, John Hay, Dr. S. Weir Mitchell, President Eliot, Andrew D. White, Major Higginson, Alexander Agassiz, John S. Billings, John L. Cadwalader, and many others who have already passed from their active labor, as has Mr. Carnegie. Of that group President Eliot alone remains, as President Emeritus of Harvard, a wise observer of the development of the times. But that group of citizens, to whom Mr. Carnegie gave control of the institutions he created, have been endeavoring to seek, and find, as one by one they pass off the stage, new and competent agents to execute Mr. Carnegie's great policies.

The world has not been able yet to appreciate Mr. Carnegie. We who knew him and loved him and honored him can now express our judgment, but we are about to pass away. Yet the works that he inaugurated are upon so great a scale and are designed to accomplish such great purposes that as the years, the generations, and the centuries go on, they will the more clearly exhibit the true character of the founder. Centuries later men of science will be adding to human knowledge, teachers will be opening the book of learning to the young, friends of peace will be winning the children of civilization from brutality to kindliness; and Andrew Carnegie, the little Scotch weaver's son, will live in the evermore manifest greatness of the achievement that was the outcome of his great and noble heart.

JAMES RUSSELL LOWELL

ADDRESS AS CHAIRMAN AT A DINNER ON THE CENTENARY
OF LOWELL'S BIRTH, GIVEN BY THE AMERICAN ACADEMY
OF ARTS AND LETTERS TO BRITISH AND CANADIAN AUTHORS,
NEW YORK CITY, FEBRUARY 20, 1919

WHEN that stout English navigator, Henry Hudson, sailed the *Half Moon* into this harbor three hundred and odd years ago, the height of land to the north was inhabited by a league of nations — Indian nations, five great powers of the aboriginal world, bound together by mutual covenants. By force of their organization they held sway over all the savage tribes from the Penobscot to the Mississippi, from Carolina to the Great Lakes of the Northwest. Their union did not depend solely upon the binding force of agreements. Across the lines of national or tribal division ran the lines of clanship. In each of the five nations the members of the clan bearing the totems of the bear, the deer, the wolf, the beaver, were brethren of the members of the same clan bearing the same totem in each of the other nations. All the members of the clans were bound together by the traditions of brotherhood and sympathy in the most sacred ideals of Indian faith. The warp and woof of these double ties, of political loyalty to the nation and personal loyalty to brotherhood in the clan, created a fabric of so firm a texture, of such quality of resistance against all tendencies toward disunion and dissension, that the League of the Iroquois seemed destined to become the origin of a new civilization, until the whites came with superior numbers and applied science, and a religion not perfect in its restraint.

The American Academy of Arts and Letters welcomes the brethren of its clan from across the boundaries of Britain and

Canada, to the American Republic, with cheerful confidence that the ties of brotherhood in literature, of common traditions and sympathies and ideals, may bind more firmly together in harmony of purpose and of action the several nations whose sons we are.

We have come together to celebrate the one hundredth anniversary of the birth of James Russell Lowell, American author of English blood, born in Cambridge, Massachusetts, February 22, 1819; [1] a descendant of Percival Lowell, who came from Bristol, England, to Newburyport, Massachusetts, in the year 1639; raised by his pen to be Minister representing the United States in Great Britain, and, thereafter, by natural sequence, representing the best thought and feeling of Great Britain to the people of the United States; a graduate of Harvard, Doctor of Civil Law of Oxford, Doctor of Laws of Cambridge, some time Rector of the University of St. Andrews, some time Professor of Belles-Lettres and lecturer at Harvard; a gentleman of breeding and manners, a democrat of conviction and practice, a poet of noble thought and charm of expression, an essayist of insight and felicity, humorist, wit, satirist, a man of courage, of vision, worthy of trust, kindly, lovable, exhibiting the best qualities of his race. He illustrated in his own person, his character, his life, the essential unity of the race. He belongs to all of us. No one of us can say to another, "We celebrate your Lowell." We all of us are celebrating our Lowell, and when we honor him we are all honoring the great qualities of character and achievement wrought out in the long progress of the generations of the peoples from whom we spring. He was not of the greatest, with fame transcendent for all time, but he had his marked and conspicuous place in the long succession of men of genius from Piers Plowman and Chaucer down to the last great rendezvous with death in the battle-lines of France and

[1] Died at Cambridge, Massachusetts, August 12, 1891.

Flanders, the seers through whom the nobility of the race found voice.

He saw his country in one of those strange lethargies which come at times to all peoples under the septic poisoning of prosperity. The compromise between freedom and slavery which made the American Union possible had endured so long, and had been followed by such vast material success, that the general vision of his countrymen had become obscured; right and wrong had grown to seem to them strangely alike; and, when the vital question whether America should be slave or free demanded a decision, it found a people with consciences asleep, confused amid questions of expediency, halting upon timid counsels.

Then Lowell spoke for the better nature, for the deep underlying nature of his people. Now in stately and noble verse, and now in quaint and homely exaggeration of Yankee dialect, with the power of intense conviction, with pathos and wit and satire, and intuitive understanding of their natures, he reached the hearts and minds of his countrymen; he drove away the mists that obscured their sight, he awakened the memories of their past, their traditions, their ideals, their sense of justice, their love of liberty; and, under his influence more than that of any other save Lincoln alone, the soul of America rose above its timid materialism, and, by sacrifice and suffering, redeemed America for freedom.

When we come to honor James Russell Lowell, we do more than honor the man; we honor literature, the interpreter of the Divine spirit in man. Will anyone question that there is an essential unity of spirit served by that great company of poets and philosophers, historians and essayists and dramatists, the seers and prophets from all our lands, who by written word have destroyed the false by showing the truth, and driven out what was base by revealing what was noble, throughout the long struggle for ordered freedom wedded to justice, for truth, for liberty of thought, of religion, of expression and of action — the hard struggle through all the centuries from before Magna Charta until now Britain, her ancient kingdoms, her dominions and colonies, and her mighty offspring of the West, inspired by a single conception of public right and personal liberty, are together the chief hope and bulwark of the peace and liberty of the world. We honor that great company when we pay our tribute to Lowell, their brother.

If anyone does question, let him tell me how it is that, for thousands of miles from the place where we now meet, south to the Gulf and the Rio Grande, north to the Arctic, west to the Pacific, more than a hundred million people, drawn from all the races upon earth, order their lives according to the course of the common law of England, base their political faith on the principles of liberty and justice established against unwilling governments by the Commons of England, and embodied in the limitations of official power in the American Constitutions; rear their children upon the nursery rhymes whose origins are lost in the mists of the Saxon Heptarchy; form their religion from the texts of the English Bible; make their laws, transact their business, and carry on their social intercourse in the speech of our Spenser and Shakespeare and Milton. Here was power, the most tremendous formative power the world has seen since the prime of the Roman Empire. It was the power of the unity of the single spirit of the composite race, wrought out in the speech and life of humble folk, made manifest and guarded and handed down from generation to generation by the men of English letters, whose brotherhood of common service and common inspiration we celebrate this night.

All over the world the shock of universal war has broken the bonds of habit. Old postulates are denied, old customs abjured, old faiths forgotten. New dreams beckon. Nations tread unaccustomed paths that may lead to a millennium, or back into barbarism. From every part the peoples call to one another for sympathy and guidance and help. Deep calls unto deep. The fateful question: "What ideals shall rule the world?" hangs in the balance.

We join together for greater courage and hope and power, to the end that the ideals we have inherited and served may endure and prevail. We rest in faith that

> The single note
> From that deep chord which Hampden smote
> Will vibrate to the doom.

Ladies and gentlemen, I ask you to join me in a toast to the English-speaking peoples of the world — the Children of the Lion!

ABRAHAM LINCOLN

Born on "Rock Spring" farm, near Hodgenville, Kentucky, February 12, 1809. President of the United States, March 4, 1861 until the day of his death, in Washington, April 15, 1865.

ADDRESS AT PARLIAMENT SQUARE, LONDON, PRESENTING SAINT GAUDENS'S STATUE OF LINCOLN TO THE BRITISH PEOPLE, JULY 28, 1920

BY authority of His Majesty's Government a statue of an American has been set up in the Canning Enclosure, where on one side Westminster Abbey and on another the Houses of Parliament look down upon it; where it is surrounded by memorials of British statesmen whose lives are inseparable parts of the history of the Kingdom and of the Empire; and where the living tides of London will ebb and flow about it. The statue is the work of Augustus St. Gaudens, son of a French father, native of Ireland, and greatest of American sculptors. The American commemorated is Abraham Lincoln, sixteenth President of the United States. In behalf of the American donors, I now formally present the statue to the British People.

Abraham Lincoln was born on the 12th of February, one hundred and eleven years ago, in a log cabin among the mountains of the State of Kentucky. He came into a frontier life of comparative poverty, labor, hardship, and rude adventure. He had little instruction and few books. He had no friends among the great and powerful of his time. An equal among equals in the crude simplicity of scattered communities on the borders of the wilderness, he rose above the common level by force of his own qualities. He was sent by his neighbors to the State Legislature, where he learned the rudiments of government. He was sent to the Congress at Washington, where he broadened his conceptions to national scope. He was admitted to the bar, and won high place as a successful and distinguished advocate.

He became convinced of the wickedness of African slavery, that baleful institution which the defective humanity of our fathers permitted to be established in the American Colonies. He declared his conviction that slavery was eternally wrong, with a power and insistence that compelled public attention. He gave voice to the awakened conscience of the North. He led in the struggle for freedom against slavery. Upon that issue he was elected President. In that cause, as President, he conducted a great war of four years' duration in which millions of armed men were engaged. When in his wise judgment the time was ripe for it, then upon his own responsibility, in the exercise of his authority as Commander-in-Chief, invoking the support of his country, the considerate judgment of mankind, and the blessing of God upon his act, he set free the three million slaves by his official proclamation, and dedicated the soil of America forever as the home of a united liberty-loving commonwealth.

The act was accepted; it was effective; African slavery was ended; the war was won — for union and for freedom; and in the very hour of victory, the great emancipator fell at the hand of a crazed fanatic.

It was not chance or favorable circumstance that achieved Lincoln's success. The struggle was long and desperate, and often appeared hopeless. He won through the possession of the noblest qualities of manhood. He was simple, honest, sincere, and unselfish. He had high courage for action and fortitude in adversity. Never for an instant did the thought of personal advantage compete with the interests of the public cause. He never faltered in the positive and unequivocal declaration of the wrong of slavery, but his sympathy with all his fellowmen was so genuine, his knowledge of human nature was so just, that he was able to lead his countrymen without dogmatism or imputation of assumed superiority. He carried the Civil War to its successful conclusion with inflexible determination; but the many evidences of his kindness of heart toward the people of the South, and of his compassion for distress and suffering, were the despair of many of his subordinates; and the effect of his humanity and considerate spirit upon the conduct of the war became one of the chief reasons why, when the war was over, North and South were able during the same generation to join again in friendship as citizens of a restored Union.

It would be difficult to conceive of a sharper contrast in all the incidental and immaterial things of life than existed between Lincoln and the statesmen whose statues stand in Parliament Square. He never set foot on British soil. His life was lived and his work was wholly done in a far distant land. He differed in manners and in habits of thought and speech. He never seemed to touch the life of Britain.

Yet the contrast but emphasizes the significance of the statue standing where it does.

Put aside superficial differences, accidental and unimportant, and Abraham Lincoln appears in the simple greatness of his life, his character and his service to mankind, a representative of the deep and underlying qualities of his race — the qualities that great emergencies reveal, unchangingly the same in every continent; the qualities to which Britain owed her life in the terrible years of the last decade; the qualities that have made both Britain and America great.

He was of English blood; and he has brought enduring honor to the name. Every child of English sires should learn the story and think with pride, "Of such stuff as this are we English made."

He was of English speech. The English Bible and English Shakespeare, studied in the intervals of toil and by the flare of the log fire in the frontier cabin, were the basis of his education; and from them he gained, through greatness of heart and fine intelligence, the power of expression, to give his Gettysburg address and his second inaugural a place among the masterpieces of English prose.

He was imbued with the conceptions of justice and liberty that the people of Britain had been working out in struggle and sacrifice since before Magna Charta — the conceptions for which Chatham and Burke and Franklin and Washington stood together, a century and a half ago, when the battle for British liberty was fought and won for Britain, as well as for America on the other side of the Atlantic. These conceptions of justice and liberty have been the formative power that has brought all America, from the Atlantic to the Pacific, to order its life according to the course of the common law, to assert its popular sovereignty through representative government — Britain's great gift to the political science of the world — and to establish the relation of individual citizenship to the State, on the basis of inalienable rights which governments are established to secure.

It is the identity of these fundamental conceptions in both countries which makes it impossible that in any great world-emergency Britain and America can be on opposing sides. These conceptions of justice and liberty are the breath of life for both. While they prevail, both nations will endure; if they perish, both nations will die. These were Lincoln's inheritance; and when he declared that African slavery was eternally wrong and gave his life to end it, he was responding to impulses born in him from a long line of humble folk, as well in England as in America, who were themselves a product of the age-long struggles for the development of Anglo-Saxon freedom.

The true heart of Britain understood him while he lived. We remember the Lancashire workmen brought into poverty and suffering through lack of cotton. When the Emancipation Proclamation had dispelled all doubt as to the real nature of the struggle in America, six thousand of them met in a great hall in Manchester and sent to President Lincoln a message of sympathy and support. This was his answer:

Under these circumstances, I cannot but regard your decisive utterances upon the question as an instance of sublime Christian heroism, which has not been surpassed in any age or in any country. It is indeed an energetic and reinspiring assurance of the inherent power of truth, and the ultimate and universal triumph of justice, humanity, and freedom. I do not doubt that the sentiments you have expressed will be sustained by your great nation, and on the other hand I have no hesitation in assuring you that they will excite admiration, esteem, and the most reciprocal feelings of friendship among the American people. I hail this interchange of sentiment, therefore, as an augury, that, whatever else may happen, whatever misfortune may befall your country or my own, the peace and friendship which now exist between the two nations will be, as it shall be my desire to make them, perpetual.

We may disregard all the little prejudices and quarrels that result from casual friction and pinpricks and from outside misrepresentations and detraction, and rest upon Lincoln's unerring judgment of his countrymen and his race. We may be assured from him that whenever trials come, whenever there is need for assurance of the inherent power of truth and the triumph of justice, humanity and freedom, then peace and friendship between Britain and America will prove to be, as Lincoln desired to make them, perpetual.

This man, full of sorrows, spoke not merely for the occasions and incidents of his own day. He expressed the deepest and holiest/feelings of his race for all time. Listen to the words of his Second Inaugural:

Fondly do we hope, fervently do we pray, that this mighty scourge of war may soon pass away.

Yet, if God wills that it continue until all the wealth piled by the bondman's two hundred and fifty years of unrequited toil shall be sunk, and until every drop of blood drawn by the lash shall be paid by another drawn with the sword, as was said three thousand years ago, so still it must be said, "The judgments of the Lord are true and righteous altogether."

With malice toward none, with charity for all, with firmness in the right, as God gives us to see the right, let us strive on to finish the work we are in; to bind up the nation's wounds; to care for him who shall have borne the battle, and for his widow and for his orphan; to do all which may achieve and cherish a just and lasting peace among ourselves, and with all nations.

Consider this letter which he wrote to Mrs. Bixby of Boston:

I have been shown on the file of the War Department a statement of the adjutant general of Massachusetts, that you are the mother of five sons who have died gloriously on the field of battle. I feel how weak and fruitless must be any word of mine which should attempt to beguile you from the grief of a loss so overwhelming; but I cannot refrain from tendering to you the consolation that may be found in the thanks of the republic they died to save.

I pray that our Heavenly Father may assuage the anguish of your bereavement, and leave only the cherished memory of the loved and lost, and the solemn pride that must be yours to have laid so costly a sacrifice upon the altar of freedom.

More than half a century has passed, but is this the voice of a stranger to the men and women of Britain in these later years?

Because under the direct tests of national character, in the stress of supreme effort and sacrifice, in the Valley of the Shadow of Death, the souls of both Britain and America prove themselves of kin to the soul of Abraham Lincoln, friendship between us is safe; and the statue of Lincoln, the American, stands as of right before the old Abbey where sleep the great of Britain's history.

LINCOLN AS A LEADER OF MEN [1]

THE life of Abraham Lincoln is full of appeals to the imagination; its dramatic quality absorbs attention. The humble beginnings, the early poverty, the slender opportunity for even the simplest education, the swift rise from the ordinary lot to the heights of station and of power, the singular absence of those aids by which personal ambition commonly seeks its ends, the transcendent moral quality of the cause which he came to lead, the desperate struggle, the triumphant success, the tragic ending, the startling contrast between the abuse and ridicule to which he was so long subjected, and the honor and glory for all time which he achieved—all these tend completely to fill the minds of those who read or listen to the story of Lincoln.

There is another view of Lincoln's life, however, which we ought not to overlook, and from which a useful lesson may be learned. He was intensely practical. While he never for a moment lost sight of the great ends toward which he struggled, or wavered in his devotion to the eternal principles which justified those ends, he never assumed that his conclusions would be accepted merely because he knew they were right, however clearly he might state them. He did not expect other people to have their minds work as his mind worked or to reach his conclusions because he thought they ought to reach them, or to feel as he felt because he thought they ought to feel so. He never relied upon authority or dictation or compulsion upon the minds of others. Never concealing or obscuring his ideals, avowing them, declaring them, constant to them, setting them high for guidance as if among the stars, he kept his feet on the earth, he minded his steps, he studied the country to be traversed, its obstacles, its possible aids to prog-

[1] Reprinted by permission from *Republicanism of 1920;* copyright, The Journal Company, The Evening Journal, Albany, William Barnes, President.

ress. He studied the material with which he had to work —
the infinite varieties of human nature, the good, the bad, and,
predominantly, the indifferent; the widely differing material
interests of sections and of occupations; the inherited traditions and prejudices, the passions and weaknesses, sympathies and dislikes, the ignorance and misunderstanding, the
successive stages of slowly developing opinion, the selfishness
and the altruism. He understood that to lead a nation in
emergency he had to bring all these forces into such relations
to his design and to each other that the resultant of forces
would be in the direction of his purpose. This was the field of
Lincoln's great struggle, and here he won by infinite patience
and sagacity. During those terrible years of the Rebellion he
was not disturbing himself about what principles he ought to
maintain or what end he ought to seek. He was struggling
with the weaknesses and perversities of human nature at
home. He was smoothing away obstacles and converting
enemies and strengthening friends, and bending all possible
motives and desires and prejudices into the direction of his
steady purpose. Many people thought, while he was doing
this, that he was trifling, that he was yielding where he ought
to have been splendidly courageous and peremptory. He
understood as they did not how to bend his material without
breaking it; he understood as they did not how many a jest
bridged over a difficult situation, and made it possible to
avoid a quarrel injurious to the Union cause.

Lincoln's whole life had been a training for just this kind of
struggle. He had begun at the bottom, in a community of
simple, poor, and for the most part uneducated people, and
he had learned in his contests for the State Legislature to
win the support of those people by actual personal contact
and influence, standing absolutely on a level with them, and
without any possible assumption of superiority or right of
dictation. He had moved along up the scale of association

with people of broader minds and greater education and more trained intelligence, developing himself as he moved on, but never changing his method of winning agreement. This was always by a frank and honest declaration of principle and purpose, accompanied by the most skillful and sympathetic appeal to the human nature of the man with whom he dealt, based upon a careful study of the capacities and prejudices and motives of that man.

He had three qualities of the highest value. The first was sympathy — genuine appreciative sympathy for all his fellow men. Contemplation of human nature furnishes nothing more encouraging than the general response of mankind to such a quality; it cannot be simulated; it must be real; and then it begets its like in others. Secretary Stanton used to get out of patience with Lincoln because he was all the time pardoning men who ought to be shot; but no one can tell how much the knowledge of that quality in him drew the people of the country toward him and won their confidence and support. Above all, that quality enabled him to understand men, to appreciate how they felt, and why they acted as they did, and how they could be set right when they were wrong.

The second quality was a sense of proportion, with which is always associated humor, or a sense of humor. He knew intuitively what was big and important and must be insisted upon, and what might seem big, but was really small and unimportant, and might be sacrificed without harm. Such a statement may seem a matter of course and of little consequence; but, if we look back in history, we can see that a large part of the most bitter controversies in politics and religion and statecraft and opinion in all fields have been about matters which really were not in themselves of the slightest consequence; and we may realize how important it is in great crises to have leaders who can form the same kind of judgment about the relative importance of questions at issue that future generations may readily form in the reading of history.

The third quality of Lincoln's was his subordination of himself to his cause. He liked to get on in the world, of course, as any normal man does; but the way he got on was by thinking about his job, not by thinking about himself. During all these years he was not thinking about making Abraham Lincoln famous; he was thinking about putting an end to slavery and preserving the Union. It is interesting to observe that the two who have attained the highest pinnacles are not to be found among the millions of Americans who have dreamed of power and fame for themselves. Washington and Lincoln reached their preëminence by thinking about their work and forgetting themselves.

Lincoln never made the mistake of using words — either oral or written — merely for his own satisfaction. Many fine sentiments are uttered about public affairs, which are not really designed to have an effect upon anybody except the speaker or writer whose feelings are gratified by expression. They are like the use of expletives — profane and otherwise — which simply relieve the feelings of the speaker. Lincoln never made this mistake. When he spoke or wrote, his objective was always the mind of somebody else. His method with individuals is well illustrated by the incident when a committee of gentlemen called upon him to object to the use of negro troops. They said they were all patriotic citizens, that their sons were serving in the Union Army, and were cultivated gentlemen, and they objected to having negroes put upon the same level. Mr. Lincoln said: "Well, gentlemen, if you would rather have your sons die for a black man than have a black man die for your sons, I suppose there is nothing more to be said." This was a wholly new view of the subject. The objectors were prepared to stand for all time against arguments designed to force them to abandon their prejudice. Lincoln, however, had instantly found the line of least resistance, which left the prejudice undisturbed and at the same time left them nothing to say; so the objection ended.

Another illustration on a broader field is to be found in the great debates with Douglas. From first to last, in these debates, he insisted upon the fundamental proposition that slavery was morally wrong and ought not to continue. He knew, however, that the conservatism and the material interests and the unawakened conscience of the North could not then be arrayed in favor of destroying slavery in the Slave States at the expense of destroying the Constitution. Accordingly, he carefully and consistently disclaimed any such proposal, and limited himself to demanding that slavery should be restricted to the states where it already existed under the protection of the Constitution, and that its extension should be prevented just as it had been prevented by the ordinance for the Government of the Northwest Territory in 1787, in confidence that, if restricted, it would die a natural death, just as the framers of the Constitution believed it would die when they agreed to the compromises of the Constitution. Upon that proposition, to prevent the extension of slavery because slavery was wrong, he enlisted the public opinion of the North and made possible the election of a Republican President in 1860. In the struggle of the South against that proposition a new situation was created, and in 1863 the whole North accepted the complete emancipation upon which they would have divided fatally five years before.

The Emancipation Proclamation itself illustrates the same wise solicitude to keep the people upon whose support he relied close behind his leadership. After declaring that the slaves shall be free, he concludes with the following paragraph: "And upon this act, sincerely believed to be an act of

justice warranted by the Constitution upon military necessity, I invoke the considerate judgment of mankind and the
gracious favor of Almighty God."

It would be difficult to conceive of a broader appeal to
more varied kinds of men and phases of opinion than is contained in this single sentence of thirty-three words. It commands the interest and conciliates the support of all who love
justice, of all who revere the Constitution, of all who are
determined that the sacrifices of the country in the war shall
not have been in vain, of all who regard the judgment of mankind, of all whose sympathy is enlisted by action reverent in
spirit and seeking for Divine guidance. It claims no credit for
Abraham Lincoln but it places the great act, with a fitting
sense of proportion, on a basis to command universal approval and support.

One of the most valuable results of Lincoln's training was
that he understood the necessity of political organization for
the accomplishment of political ends. He knew that to attain a great public purpose multitudes of men must be induced to lay aside or postpone or in some way subordinate
their minor differences of opinion, and to move together on
the lines of major policy. He used all the resources of party
organization to hold the people of the North to the support of
the Northern armies in the field. Lincoln was a politician,
the best practical politician of his time. If he had not been
that, the Northern armies would have been abandoned; the
Union would have been broken, to the infinite injury of both
sections; and slavery would have continued, no one knows
how long — probably until another war had been fought. It
will be useful to remember that Abraham Lincoln was a
politician. The word is often used as a term of reproach.
Such a use indicates the most superficial thinking, or, rather,
failure to think. To be a corrupt and self-seeking politician
ought of course to be a reproach, just as it is a discredit to be

a corrupt or unfair business man. Politics is the practical exercise of the art of self-government, and somebody must attend to it if we are to have self-government; somebody must study it, and learn the art, and exercise patience and sympathy and skill to bring the multitude of opinions and wishes of self-governing people into such order that some prevailing opinion may be expressed and peaceably accepted. Otherwise, confusion will result either in dictatorship or anarchy. The principal ground of reproach against any American citizen should be that he is not a politician. Everyone ought to be, as Lincoln was.

ALEXANDER HAMILTON

Born on the Isle of Nevis in the West Indies, January 11, 1757; died in New York City, July 12, 1804.

ADDRESS AS CHAIRMAN OF THE BOARD OF TRUSTEES OF HAMILTON COLLEGE, ACCEPTING A STATUE OF HAMILTON PRESENTED BY THOMAS R. PROCTOR, CLINTON, NEW YORK, JUNE 17, 1918

IN behalf of the Board of Trustees of Hamilton College, I have the honor to accept this statue of the great man who 126 years ago gave his name to the Institution, and who stood first in the list of the Incorporators and of the Trustees appointed by the charter for the Hamilton Oneida Academy which twenty years later was invested with the collegiate powers and privileges we now exercise.

The generous loyalty that moved you to this gift is consistent with the long career of unselfish citizenship that marks you as an inheritor of the great tradition of public service which is the most precious possession of our Country, and which found its highest inspiration in the life of Washington, and second only to him, in the life of Alexander Hamilton.

The title of the College to a special share in the memory of the statesman whose name it bears, and the title of this memorial to its place on the College campus, may be read in the early records of the Regents of the University of the State.

On the 12th of November, 1792, a petition was signed for the establishment of an academy here on the edge of the Oneida woods, for the education of Indians and whites, and this petition was considered by the Board of Regents on the 29th of January, 1793. The journal record of the meeting reads:

The respective applications of Samuel Kirkland and seven other persons, praying that Alexander Hamilton and fifteen other persons for that purpose nominated may be incorporated by the name and style of the Trustees of Hamilton Oneida Academy at Whitestown in the County of Herkimer, and of Joseph Yates and twenty-three other persons, praying that Abraham Yates Jr. and twenty-three other persons nominated in the said application may be incorporated by the style of the Trustees of the Academy of the town of Schenectady in the County of Albany, . . . were severally read and committed to the Vice Chancellor General Clarkson and Mr. Verplanck.

[After a favorable report by the sub-Committee]

The Board resolved itself into a Committee of the Whole to take the above report into consideration; and after some time spent thereon the Chancellor resumed the chair and General Schuyler from the said Committee reported that they had agreed to the report of the sub-Committee, whereupon

RESOLVED That the Board agree to the said report.

ORDERED That the Secretary prepare instruments in the usual form for incorporating the said Alexander Hamilton and the other fifteen persons for that purpose named, and the said Abraham Yates and the said twenty-three other persons named in the said application, and that the Chancellor affix the seal of the University to the said instruments.

The General Schuyler named in the journal as reporting the agreement of the Committee was Philip Schuyler, the always loyal and affectionate father-in-law of Hamilton, the true hero of Saratoga, the noble gentleman whose name was borne by that Fort Schuyler then standing in the valley upon which we look from this hillside, in the place where since that day the noble city of Utica has come into being.

The other Academy named in the resolution has grown into Union College and Union University.

So the Charter was prepared as the resolution directed, and was signed by George Clinton as Chancellor of the University, and incorporated Alexander Hamilton and his associates into the institution which now does him honor, and which is itself a monument to his name.

I will read the list of the Trustees appointed by the Charter. They were:

Alexander Hamilton, John Lansing, Egbert Benson, Dan Bradley, Eli Bristol, Erastus Clark, James Dean, Moses Foot, Thomas R. Gold, Sewal Hopkins, Michael Myers, Jonas Platt, Jedediah Sanger, John Sergeant, Timothy Tuttle, Samuel Wells.

The first three of these were men of nation-wide reputation. John Lansing, later Chief Justice and Chancellor of the State, had been General Schuyler's military secretary, and was one of Hamilton's colleagues in the Convention of 1787. Egbert Benson, the first Attorney General of the State, was Hamilton's companion in the Annapolis meeting of 1786 which called the Convention of 1787, and was his close ally in urging the adoption of the Constitution.

Of the others there is hardly one but played a conspicuous and honorable part in the history of this region, and their descendants may well look with satisfaction upon the record which links their fathers' names in association for a beneficent undertaking with this great figure of the world's history.

Hamilton's interest in the new enterprise was not merely casual or personal. He was then Secretary of the Treasury and the dominant spirit in the cabinet of Washington's first Administration. The troublesome race question at that day was not black, or yellow, or brown; it was red. For thousands of miles westward from the comparatively feeble settlements on the Atlantic seaboard extended a vast and unknown wilderness peopled by savage and warlike Indians. Hatred for the whites and a fierce determination to prevent further encroachment prevailed from the St. Lawrence to the Gulf. Every frontier community lived in dread of their sudden and remorseless forays. The Indian menace hung always like a black cloud on the Western horizon, threatening the infant Republic.

Samuel Kirkland, the brilliantly successful agent of Washington during the Revolutionary War for the management of the Iroquois, was a most trusted adviser of the Administration upon Indian affairs. He proposed to remedy the evil by educating, civilizing, and Christianizing the Indian. He prepared a plan of education which he urged upon the Administration. It appears to have been referred to Timothy Pickering, then Postmaster General, and the paper containing his approving discussion of the plan has been preserved. This institution was a part of the plan. It was to try out the plan by educating Indians and whites together; so the new enterprise enlisted the interest of the members and friends of Washington's Government. Pickering approved it; Hamilton became a part of it; Schuyler reported favorably upon the Charter; Baron Steuben laid the cornerstone of the new Academy. Alas, the plan of education was a dream. The Indians in general proved incapable of receiving education, and the whites alone have profited by what was done.

There was another reason for Hamilton's participation. He was deeply interested in education in his own state. It was Hamilton's Committee in the New York Legislature which reported the Act of 1787 creating the University of the state. It was Hamilton who drafted the report; it was his constructive genius which gave form to the educational system of the state that endures to this day; and the first act of the Regents of the University in exercise of the power to create institutions of learning vested in them upon Hamilton's initiative was to incorporate the institution for which he stood sponsor, and to write his name at the head of the long and honored list of citizens who have given their free service to the cause of public instruction under the Constitution and laws of this state.

But all this was a secondary incident in a great career. It explains why the statue should be here, but it does not explain why there should be a statue.

We raise statues to Alexander Hamilton because the lessons of a century and a quarter have shown that the people of the United States owe to him a greater debt for the creation of the American Republic than to any other man save Washington.

He was not greater than Washington, but the high quality and power and intense devotion and splendid achievement of his service for the cause of ordered liberty through self-government set him next to Washington. The two supplemented each other and worked together in perfect confidence and affection, with a single purpose and the same just conception of the essence of a government that should reconcile liberty and obedience to law, independence, and peace, sovereignty, and honor. Together they endured detraction and public abuse, and strove against ignorance and folly, and selfishness and prejudice and malice, against intriguers and demagogues and traitors, through the critical period which followed the recognition of independence, when the principles of the new Nation had to be determined, and the institutions to give them effect had to be established. At the end of that first formative period the great-hearted character of Washington, and the marvelous insight of Hamilton's genius into the principles that control human conduct, had given to the future of mankind the institutions of government which, after a century's test of human weakness, of domestic and foreign war, of vast growth and prosperity, now bind together one hundred million people in the effective exercise of power to preserve Christian civilization, and to defend their liberty and the world's liberty.

Hamilton was not greater than Lincoln, but if there had been no Hamilton, probably there would have been no Lincoln, because there would have been no Union for Lincoln to save.

The treaty which closed the Revolutionary War removed the external force that alone secured any semblance of united

action among the thirteen colonies, and there speedily en-
sued a state of confusion and absence of general direction
and control almost comparable to the condition of Russia
to-day. The Continental Congress under the old articles of
Confederation had no power whatever. It could not levy
taxes or command money to pay its own expenses; it could
not raise troops or maintain them. It could pass resolutions, but could not enforce them. It could make treaties,
but could not keep the promises they contained. There was
no national lawmaker or executive, or judiciary. There
could be no action, except by the unanimous agreement of
all the thirteen states; and when the war was over they ceased
to agree. Each state was jealous of its own independent
power, and absorbed in the pursuit of its own selfish advantage; burdensome and vexatious interstate tariffs and commercial restrictions prevailed. Bitter controversies had come
to the verge of war. No national consciousness had been
awakened; and a people individually honest appeared to
have no sense of collective or national honor. The obligations
of the treaty of peace were grossly violated. The treaty
promised security for the property of Loyalists. The separate states confiscated their property. The treaty promised
justice in the Courts. The states nullified the promise.
Foreign countries would not make commercial treaties with
an alleged nation whose word was worthless. No one would
loan money to a government that was unable to raise money
to pay. Issues of inconvertible paper money speedily de-
preciating to nominal values completed the destruction of
public credit. The specie in the country disappeared. Business returned to the method of barter. There was no security
for the fruits of enterprise. There was general stagnation
and distress. The farmers of Western Massachusetts —
ignorant of the true nature of the evils which oppressed
them — rose in rebellion against the state government. The

Southwest discussed the formation of a separate confederacy. The failure of the American Colonies to maintain any effective government seemed to have been demonstrated.

With the instinctive comprehension of political problems in which he was superior to all other men of his time, Hamilton perceived the essential causes of demoralization which were urging the infant Confederacy toward its ruin, and the nature of the remedies which were necessary. He saw that the Divine Right of Kings finds its support among men in the necessity of government, that justice and peace are impossible without government possessed of power to compel obedience to its laws. He saw that, if the members of a political community would be free, they could not rest with the repudiation of superior authority, but must supplement that repudiation by subjecting themselves as individuals to the control of an effective government, resting upon their own collective authority; that the organized power of self-government must take the place of the organized power of royal government, or liberty would perish in anarchy. He was not alone in this understanding; but he surpassed all others in the clearness of his vision, in capacity to apply theory to the practical affairs of life, so that untrained minds of narrow scope could understand what it meant for them, in power of clear and compelling exposition, in determination to make the people of his country see what he saw so clearly, and in the high courage and intensity of the warrior spirit striking for the victory of a great cause.

In the Annapolis meeting, where but five states were represented, he drafted the address which called the Convention of 1787. His presence in the New York Legislature of 1787 was for the specific purpose of securing the appointment of delegates from New York to that Convention. He did his part in the Convention hampered by colleagues who reflected the hostility of George Clinton to the movement. It is probable that he himself could not have brought about the compromises of the Constitution which were necessary to its acceptance. It is certain that he believed a far stronger government to be desirable; but he alone signed the Constitution as a representative of New York, and he had the largeness to hold all minor questions of difference of no account compared with the overwhelming importance of creating a real national government.

When the Constitution was signed, he became the first of its champions. A majority of the people of the country were against him. Local prejudices and personal interests opposed him. A great multitude in all the states were jealous of their individual liberty, and unwilling to surrender any portion of it upon the demands of a public policy which they had never learned to understand. The contest which followed, and its result, stand forth as the supreme example of the capacity of an unlettered democracy to yield its prejudices to the force of reason made plain by high intelligence and driven home by the fervor of sincere patriotism. The letters of "The Federalist," the major part of which Hamilton wrote, were read and studied in town and village and farmhouse. They furnished the material for discussion in the state conventions called to act on the new Constitution. They were not mere theoretical discussions. They dealt with the workings of human nature under government, and with the effect of the proposed provisions upon the daily life and affairs of the plain people. They overcame all opposition of argument, and instructed and convinced the candid minds of the multitude to whom they were addressed. The book which now contains them is universally recognized as one of the greatest, if not the greatest, of all works upon government.

The most stubborn obstacle to the adoption of the new system was the political power of George Clinton in the State of NewYork. When the Convention of that state met, two thirds of the people of the state, and four sevenths of the members of the Convention, were opposed to the Constitution. On the 17th of June, 130 years ago this day, Hamilton entered the Convention for a parliamentary battle, which in merit and in fame has no equal in American history, except in the great debate when Webster replied to Hayne. He faced a solid adverse majority bound together by political allegiance to Clinton, with their minds determined, and apparently not open to argument. For more than a month, with undivided leadership on the floor of the Convention, with splendid courage and persistency, and with unrivalled power of persuasive and compelling argument, he incessantly assaulted this solid and sullen phalanx. He broke the phalanx by convincing the judgment of the most logical and able of his antagonists, and by sheer force of personal power he destroyed the political organization which opposed him, and won the majority of the Convention to the adoption of the Constitution.

When the new Government was formed, it still remained to make it a real and not a paper government. Adequate and effective organization must be created for the exercise of its powers. Sound principles must be followed in laws under which enterprise would revive; foreign relations must be established upon a basis to command respect and ensure the dignity of independence and the benefits of commercial intercourse; obedience to national authority must be compelled. Without these things, the experiment would still fail.

Here again Hamilton was the man of the hour. As the first Secretary of the Treasury, he made the organization of the Treasury Department which has endured to this day, and which, after more than a century, is in this present month of June, with perfect order and accountability, receiving four billions of taxes after marketing within the year at par over ten billions of bonds at low rates of interest. He raised the public credit from the dust, and industry and enterprise revived. He established a conception of national honor which has become a national tradition, proof against all assaults. As the dominant spirit in Washington's cabinet and the acknowledged leader of the Federal Administration, always in unison with Washington himself, his clear vision led the way against the opposition of the Department of State to the policy of neutrality and abstention from European quarrels, and to the ratification of the Jay Treaty, that landmark of liberal diplomacy, against a tempest of public protest. Without military office he directed and controlled the first exercise of armed power by the Government of the United States, before which the Whiskey Rebellion of 1794 faded away, and the power of government under the Constitution to compel obedience was established.

He did all these things under storms of abuse and vilification which now seem incredible. He had no weapons of defence but integrity, the broad wisdom of his action, and power of exposition and argument. He had no faculty for political combination or securing political favor. He had the ardent ambition of youth, but it urged him always to achieve great ends rather than selfish advantage. No consideration of personal popularity ever for an instant hindered or modified the expression of his convictions. He appealed to the nobler against the baser motives of his countrymen. He overcame prejudice and selfish impulse by impressing the common intelligence with the fundamental and eternal truths upon which in all ages and places the order of human society depends. So great came to be the respect of his associates for his extraordinary powers and their confidence in the sincerity of his purposes, that John Adams speaking of his own administration said: "Hamilton was all the time the

Commander-in-Chief of the House of Representatives, of the
Senate, of the Heads of Departments, of General Washing-
ton, and last and least, if you will, of the President of the
United States."

Hamilton's work was not for his own day alone. He translated thought into action, and gave to his political conceptions the demonstration of permanent institutions founded
upon them; and the descendants of the people for whom he
wrought have given to his ideals the immortality of a noble
tradition.

Self-government is an art which does not come to man by
nature. It must be learned. Terrible experience proved that,
when the French overthrew the Bourbons, when the Mexi-
cans overthrew Diaz, when the Russians overthrew the
Romanoffs. Alexander Hamilton was the greatest teacher
of the art of self-government in the history of the world. To
him more than to any other save Washington is due that intelligent conception of the relation between liberty and law
which enables this great, free people, more than a century
after Hamilton's death, voluntarily, with alacrity, without
the slightest fear of endangering their liberties, to vest in the
President at Washington, as Commander-in-Chief of their
Army and Navy, the mightiest power ever exercised by a
single man, with millions of soldiers and sailors in arms,
millions of workmen making warlike supplies, billions of
money, — quantities beyond realization, — universal restrictions upon food and fuel and the conduct of business and
of life, hard to bear, but cheerfully borne. It is due to Hamilton more than to any other save Washington that this
people have a conception, a tradition, an ideal, of a Nation
whose power is a bulwark of liberty, so that they are willing
to make sacrifice for it, feeling that when they give up for it
their means and their peaceful careers, and their lives, and

the lives of those dear to them, they are laying their offerings on the altar of liberty, enlarging power for the moment, that liberty may live.

This granite may crumble, this bronze may corrode, this College may be dissolved; but the monument of his work will remain.

GROVER CLEVELAND[1]

(Stephen) Grover Cleveland was born at Caldwell, New Jersey, March 18, 1837; died at Princeton, New Jersey, June 24, 1908. He was the twenty-second President of the United States, holding office from 1885 to 1889, and from 1893 to 1897. He was the first Democrat to hold that exalted office since the Civil War. In the Presidential election of 1888 he was nominated by his party but defeated by Benjamin Harrison. He was the first, and so far, the only President of the United States elected with an interval between his two terms of service.

WE have been told recently that there are too many biographies. The complaint indicates a sense of compulsion to read them. This can come only from a belief that they probably contain something which ought not to be overlooked. The real ground of the condemnation, therefore, is not that biographies are not worth reading, but that they ought to be read and that they therefore impose additional obligations upon men who may perhaps feel overburdened. The condemnation thus becomes a justification.

The most obvious appeal of a biography to the generations which have direct or close knowledge of the man written about — which have knowledge of the things he has done, of the affairs in which he has played part, of the men with or against whom he has worked — is really a very narrow and minor function of biography. The more important function is as an effective mode of presenting history for the benefit of the future, which has to get its knowledge entirely from books or traditions. Biography makes a period interesting by throwing a high light on a central figure and establishing a relation between all the conditions and incidents of the time and that figure. If only one of the significant figures of a period were made the subject of biography, there would be an

[1] An introduction to Robert McElroy's *Grover Cleveland — the Man and the Statesman. An Authorized Biography.* — Harper & Brothers, 2 vols., 1923. Reprinted by permission of the publishers.

effect of disproportion due to overemphasis. But that is seldom if ever the case. Men worth writing about are naturally grouped in periods. Their biographies reproduce the same background with different emphasis. On looking at the period from all these different points of view taken together, we see life in the round standing out from the canvas, with a quality of human interest which it seems quite impossible for any impartial historian to create. Of course there must be balance. If you read Morley's Gladstone, you must read Monypenny's Disraeli and the rest of the great Victorian biographies. If you read the life of Jefferson, you must also read the lives of Hamilton and of Marshall and of Adams. If you read Cavour, you must also read Garibaldi and Mazzini. The important question is not whether there are too many or too few biographies, but whether the biography of an important period in the world's life is well balanced, whether all the personal points of view, from which enlightenment and correction may come are adequately represented, so that the aggregate biographies of a period, as a whole, will convey a correct as well as an interesting conception.

The biography of Grover Cleveland, which Professor McElroy has now completed with great labor and sympathy, is of special importance to the understanding of a very critical period in American history — the period of readjustment to the new conditions created by the Civil War. The readjustment involved, not merely a recovery from the enormous losses of the war, which included the entire abolition of property in slaves, but also the great reconciliation between the peoples of the two sections, who, after four years of fighting, of killing and wounding each other, were to try the experiment of living together again as parts of the same people, sharing in the conduct of the same government. It was a reconciliation which had to be effected by the same generation which fought the war; because, if that generation died unreconciled, bequeathing its resentments and hatreds to a younger generation, the undertaking would have been almost hopeless. Inherited hatreds are almost ineradicable. That the reconciliation was effected within the life of that generation, and that survivors of the Union and Confederate armies came to work together with harmony and mutual confidence in the government at Washington, is one of the greatest of American achievements.

It was not an easy process, but it was aided by two reactions in the sober sense of the North. One, the reaction against the grave error of reconstruction legislation, which went upon the theory that by merely giving a vote to the negro he would be made competent to govern. The North became rather ashamed of the exercise of power which inflicted real injustice upon the people of the South by the application of this false theory. The other reaction, also in the dominant North, was against the undue use made by political managers, for personal and organization purposes, of the old spirit and memories and shibboleths of the war. For the first twenty years after the war these feelings served to control in the selection of the members of government at Washington. But as the dominant political organization, during this long lease of power, became more compact and autocratic, great numbers of people in the North who sympathized with the war feeling became quite unwilling that it should be utilized for the benefit of a political organization in which they had no practical voice. Under these circumstances the Democratic party, which could not hope to secure control in the nation except by Southern votes, was fortunate enough to find in Mr. Cleveland a man of such a strong personality and such clearly demonstrated capacity upon lines quite outside of the old Civil War contest, that his nomination for the Presidency would divide the Northern vote.

As we look back forty years, we can see that it was time

for new motives to assert themselves in American politics. There could not be a real reunion of States in patriotic sympathy without moral as well as legal amnesty, without really letting bygones be bygones. So long as the control of government turned upon the sympathies and resentments of the Civil War, it was inevitable that there should be a sense of proscription by the defeated party which revived bitter feelings upon both sides in every election. The only way in which a change could come was by making the control of government turn upon the new issues which the developing life of the country was bringing on, and which did not depend at all upon the old Civil War divisions.

There is a certain satisfaction in considering how perfectly Mr. Cleveland was adapted to the requirements of that situation. He was a Northerner and a Democrat, and so available. He was a party man without answering to the ordinary conception of a politician. He belonged to a party as a natural incident to the business of citizenship. He inherited traditions from the earlier days, not so very far remote, when it was considered every man's business to do his part toward maintaining the peace and order of the community. He accepted that as a part of a normal American life; but he never was a political leader in a personal sense, and he never tried to be. He never tried to collect about himself any group of followers who would promote his fortunes in the expectation that he would promote theirs. As an incident in the career of a young lawyer, he came to be appointed Assistant District Attorney in Buffalo, and in that subordinate office he exhibited qualities which led after a time to his being made sheriff, and then mayor of Buffalo, and then governor of the State of New York. He had strong common sense, simplicity and directness without subtlety, instinctive and immovable integrity, perfect courage, a kindly nature with great capacity for friendship, and with great capacity also for wrath, which made him a dangerous man to trifle with. There was nothing visionary or fanatical about him, but he had a natural hatred for fraud and false pretense, and a strong instinct for detecting the essential quality of conduct by the application of old and simple tests of morality. There was no self-seeking about him. In all his public employments he thought about his job and not about himself. His official judgment was never disturbed by any question as to the effect upon his personal fortunes. He had an exceptionally good mind; a still more exceptionally rugged strength of character; altogether a powerful and attractive personality. When the Presidential nominations of 1884 came to be made, Grover Cleveland in his various offices had done more of the honest and courageous things which good government requires and which decent people like to have done, than any other Democrat. That made him the available candidate to change the current of American politics. His election upon that record practically closed the old era of politics dominated by the past and began the new era of politics looking to the future. The strength and courage of his administrations as President confirmed the new departure. No thoughtful and patriotic American, to whatever party he may belong, and however much his opinions may differ from those of Mr. Cleveland, can read the story of those administrations without admiration and sympathy, or without a sense of satisfaction that his country can on occasion produce and honor such a man as Grover Cleveland.

ROBERT BACON [1]

I T is difficult for anyone who knew Robert Bacon well to
write about him with such reserve as will commend itself
to strangers. To his friends only superlatives seem adequate.
To them, what he was seems infinitely more than the record
of any career could possibly be. It was a distinguished and
useful career, yet his usefulness consisted not merely in what
he did, but still more in the impression produced by his persuasive and compelling personality and his intense convictions upon the great events in which he played a part.

His life began in the year before the American Civil War
and it ended in the year after the great World War. It covered a period of extraordinary development and change
throughout the world — a period in which, consciously or
unconsciously, the whole world was in motion, and when
directing influences for good or evil were potent beyond experience. He was born on the shore of Massachusetts Bay,
and he received from an unbroken line of Puritan ancestors,
by direct succession, the essential underlying qualities of
character which have made the spirit and developing force of
Puritan New England such an amazing formative power in
the life of this continent. He was educated at Harvard, and
in later life was long an elected Overseer of the University,
and finally he became a Fellow, one of the little group of five
who, with the President and Treasurer, constitute the College Corporation and direct its affairs. He became a banker
in Boston, and then a banker in New York. He was made
Assistant Secretary of State, and then Secretary of State,
and then Ambassador to France, and finally an officer of the

[1] Introduction to *Robert Bacon — Life and Letters*, by James Brown Scott (1923).
Reprinted with permission of Doubleday, Page & Company.

American Army in France. These things came to him without any intriguing or wire-pulling or pushing or use of influence. They followed his qualities naturally; they were the by-products of strenuous labor for others, unselfishly directed with little or no thought of self, inspired by sympathy, friendship, loyalty, love of country, humanity, idealism.

He was a man of curious and delightful combinations and contrasts. He was a superb creature physically. It was a pleasure to behold him, as it is to look upon any natural object which approaches the perfection of beauty. But he was altogether modest and free from conceit. He never gave the impression that he was thinking about his own perfections, because he really was always thinking about something else; and the high light of his manly beauty was in the face always luminous with kindly thoughts and sympathies for other persons and other things. He was a renowned athlete in college, and he was an athlete and a sportsman all his life long — an all-around devoted enthusiastic sportsman. But underlying the joyfulness in sport there was still a Puritan conscience which regulated the control of life. The incident of the boat race illustrates this very well. He was Assistant Secretary of State at Washington. The Harvard–Yale boat race was about to occur at New London. It was most interesting for him. He had rowed in the Harvard crew himself when in college. On this particular occasion his three sons were to row, one in each of the three Harvard boats. He was most anxious to see it, and to join the multitude of college friends who would be there. He had been overworking and overdriving himself in Washington. Everybody in the State Department wanted him to get the recreation, and he started by the evening train. The next morning he appeared at the State Department and explained that he had left some things undone in his office, and that by the time he had got to Jersey City, he found that he simply could not go on; and so he took the midnight train back to Washington to attend to his duties, and let the boat race go. A conscience born in Puritan England some centuries before had made the admired and joyous sportsman incapable of neglecting a duty for a pleasure.

The material which the devoted friendship of Doctor Scott has selected and arranged in this book indicates that Robert Bacon was a full member of what before the war used to be called "Society," on both sides of the Atlantic. His love of sport, education and training, and wealth and personal attractions naturally put him into that relation. He had two very rare and admirable qualities — he had charm and he had distinction, qualities that cannot be defined or even described, but which can be felt; and he had highly developed the social instincts and sympathies. He was everywhere admired and welcome, and he was a part in a great number of affectionate friendships, which with intimate acquaintance and good manners form the true basis of social life. He was in and of society; yet he was the most domestic of men — faithful, loyal, devoted, with a heart always full to overflowing with love for his home and his wife and his children. He was responsive to a multitude of friends; always ready with universal sympathy; intensely interested in difficult and engrossing tasks, yet he was always a wonderful lover for one woman only throughout his life. What the war and all its overturnings may have done to that old pre-war social life no one can yet fully measure. It was a product of aristocracy, but the war has demonstrated that it possessed some qualities which the world, democratic or otherwise, cannot afford to do without.

Bacon fell naturally into the first rank; as an undergraduate, as an alumnus, as a banker finding his place in the greatest of American banking houses, and as a diplomatist. He brought to American diplomacy qualities and attainments of the highest value; a strong sense of right and courage to maintain it, entire freedom from subserviency or timidity, sympathetic consideration and kindly feeling for other peoples, and a most effective sincerity and frankness. He helped mightily toward substituting the new method of frank and open intercourse for the old type of subtlety and deception in diplomacy. He had the social training that is so useful; and he always understood his subject; no pains were too great for that. He was fair and honest in diplomacy as he was in sport and in business.

The greatest public services of Robert Bacon's life, however, were rendered on the basis of comparatively little official authority. His genuine affection for the French people, added to the strong predilections of his English descent, his knowledge of European politics, his intimate acquaintance with the men and women who were significant in the public life of England and of the continent, his special interest in European affairs incident to his service as ambassador, all gave to him a sense of the true meaning and possibilities of the Austrian assault upon Servia and the German assault upon Belgium at the end of July, 1914. He saw in this concerted movement, immediately, the purpose and the danger of world-domination; and he saw America resting in a condition of complacent incredulity similar to that which confronted Lord Roberts in Great Britain when he strove to make the British people understand that Germany was preparing to attack. His whole soul rose in protest against the fatuous indifference which remains blind to danger until it is too late; and he became an active and ardent apostle of immediate military preparation and speedy entry into the war. He repudiated indignantly the idea of neutrality between right and wrong. With voice and pen, in private and in public, he urged immediate action. He went up and down the country, arguing and exhorting, demonstrating the danger and pointing out the need of American liberty for defense on the battle-line where the liberties of western civilization were at stake. He and his devoted wife threw themselves with enthusiasm into the work of that American aid for the care of the wounded in France, before our entrance into the war, which did so much to express and to foster American sympathy with the Allied cause. While he superintended construction and drove ambulances and arranged with officials, Mrs. Bacon raised vast sums of money and secured material and organized personnel in America, and they became the foremost single agency in that beneficent work which did so much for the wounded and so much more for America. When the training camps, to which Plattsburg has given its name, were organized, the former Ambassador, distinguished, wealthy, far up beyond the military age, but an athlete still, set the example of service in the ranks to do the uttermost that it was possible for an American to do toward meeting the inevitable emergency. He should be counted as one of the greatest of the personal forces which gradually moved the American people to the point of entering the great conflict just before it was too late.

Robert Bacon rendered one further public service of the first importance. The great danger of composite forces carrying on war together is in misunderstandings, unsettled differences of opinion, personal discords and resentments, and the feebleness and irresolution which flow from divided councils. We all remember the repeated efforts made by Germany through all sorts of agencies during the war to bring about informal conferences upon the aims of the war. Many very good people thought such overtures should be accepted as a matter of course in the interest of peace; but many, better informed or more mindful of the working of human nature, perceived that the true object and necessary effect of such conferences during hostilities would be to put the Allies into controversy and destroy their unity of action. That is, that if discussions were opened then upon the aims of the war, just what has happened in Europe since the Armistice would have happened with the German army still in the field, and Germany would have won against a divided foe.

In a war carried on by allies, however friendly, one of the first and most difficult requisites is to keep the allies together, pursuing a single purpose by concerted action. When America entered the war, she introduced not only a needed element of strength, but another element of possible misunderstanding and divided purpose. Robert Bacon was not *persona grata* with the Administration — the rôle he had played in urging preparation and action made that impossible; but the experience and sound judgment of General Pershing led him to see that here was an agent of the first force for the accomplishment of the vital military purpose of maintaining real harmony among the Allied forces. Accordingly, after a sufficient experience as commandant of the headquarters at Chaumont, to become thoroughly familiar with American organization and military opinion, Colonel Bacon assumed the head of the American Military Mission to the British Headquarters of Sir Douglas Haig. From that coign of vantage until the close of the war every quality Robert Bacon possessed was actively devoted to the purpose of maintaining good understanding and harmony among the leaders of the Allied forces. All his experience in business and in diplomacy, his Anglo-American traits, his Franco-American affections, his tremendous and untiring energy, his knowledge of languages and of manners, his liberal education, his familiarity and facility in sports of every kind, his social training, his personal charm and distinction, his kindliness and consideration, his intense devotion to the common purpose — all of these fitted him above all other men whom America could produce to prevent the fatal misfortune of dissension and discord.

ADDRESS AS PRESIDENT ON THE
SEVENTY–FIFTH ANNIVERSARY OF
THE CENTURY ASSOCIATION

NEW YORK CITY, APRIL 22, 1922

IT is seventy-five years since Gulian Verplanck, William Cullen Bryant, Henry W. Bellows, Daniel Huntington, Jonathan Sturges, Asher B. Durand, and a little group of their sympathetic friends, forty-two in all, joined in founding The Century for the purpose of promoting the advancement of art and literature.

They called their organization simply "The Century." Ten years later the Legislature granted them a corporate charter under the name "The Century Association." As the years passed, the demands of intimate fellowship developed the accessories and methods of a club, and the associations of friendship were preserved by the familiar scenes of a club home. For corporate purposes and by legal definition we are "The Century Association." We can probably be described best to the world at large as "The Century Club." But here, among its members, the institution is as it was in the beginning, simply "The Century"; and the meaning of the name is to be learned, not from the dictionary, but only from the traditions and memories and living purpose evoked in the life of the institution by the never-ceasing stream of influence from a spiritual impulse sent forth by the great-hearted founders.

I do not think it was ever anybody's intention that The Century should perform its function of promoting the advancement of art and literature by becoming an institution for the education of others outside of its membership. It was an association to learn rather than to teach, to help each other in acquiring knowledge, appreciation, discriminating judgment, and true feeling in art and literature, through the interaction one upon the other of sympathetic and friendly natures. So the purpose of The Century has prevented it from becoming didactic or reforming toward the rest of the world, and has enabled the "authors, artists, and amateurs of letters and the fine arts," composing its constitutional membership, to live together in the unruffled harmony of modest friendship.

We are living in a different world from that in which The Century was founded. That was a quiet and leisurely world. The good Queen Victoria was in the early years of her long and serene reign. Gladstone and Disraeli were young members, who had not yet found themselves, in the House of Commons. No one had yet heard of the British Empire. Louis Philippe sat on the throne of France. Germany was a multitude of petty independent states, apparently absorbed in the ponderous and trivial etiquette of opera bouffe courts. Bismarck was in that year, at the age of thirty-two, making his first appearance in the Prussian Landtag.

Italy was a geographical expression for the region in which Austrian possessions and states of the Church and decadent principalities faintly continued ancient intrigue. The star of Cavour had not risen. Garibaldi was an unnoted exile in South America. In Austria, Francis Joseph had not yet begun the long reign which was to end in such tragic disaster. In Russia, a nation of serfs was chained to the soil under the iron hand of Nicholas I. The Turk ruled the Balkans. The first few treaty ports of China had just been opened for trade with the foreign devils. Japan was hermetically sealed, and the Shoguns ruled within. Throughout the continent of Europe the fires of the coming revolution slumbered unnoted. Throughout South America the process of internal fermentation, which seems as necessary to the making of republics as it is to the making of beer, was pursuing its conventional and externally negligible course.

In the United States there was quiet, hardly disturbed by the sideshow of the Mexican War. Webster and Ashburton had just settled the northeastern boundary. The Oregon Treaty had just been signed. California and the vast mountain regions to the east of it were Mexican territory. Individual enterprise was winning the west in family formation. Polk was leading the procession of mediocrity in Executive office. Procrastination, by a succession of futile compromises, was feebly endeavoring to avert the inevitable conflict over slavery. Whittier and Lowell were voices crying in the wilderness. The period of Irving and Cooper and Bryant was passing. The period of Emerson and Hawthorne and Longfellow and Holmes and Parkman was just beginning. In that very year the Brook Farm phalanx was dissolved.

Morse and Eliot and Huntington were tending the cradle of art in America. The Bessemer steel process had not yet been invented. There were but few short local railroads, not amounting to one fiftieth part of our present railroad system, scattered throughout the country. Steam navigation was still in its feeble and experimental stage. It was less than three years since Morse had demonstrated the success of the first telegraph line, in messages between Baltimore and Washington. Men were still practically in the age of the stage coach and the sailing vessel. Great corporations as we see them were unknown. Great labor organizations as we see them were unknown.

No one had realized the tremendous power of organization for peaceful enterprise. No one had realized the tremendous power of mechanical transportation and swift communication, which are breaking down the physical barriers between

peoples and making all the nations of the earth interdependent, and changing the community of nations from a convenient working theory of international relation to a necessity vital to national independence because vital to national
life. There were no radio stations, no telephones, no tele-
graphs, no aeroplanes, no automobiles, no elevators, no sky-
scrapers, no stenographers, no typewriters. Life was lived
at long hand. Farming was an occupation but not yet a business. The vast multiplication of human power to produce
wealth was still in the future. The comparative poverty of
mankind favored simplicity. The physical obstacles to speed
of action assured opportunity and time for reflection and
mature judgment. The tardy steps of news discouraged the
spectacular and sensational.

The highly accelerated speed of life in these later days
cannot fail to affect character. The multiplication of ob-
jectives in life, the multitude of material prizes for enterprise,
the imperative need for alert perception, swift decision and
sudden action, cannot fail to create new habits of thought
and feeling.

How comes it that, after all, The Century is the same and
the spirit of the founders of three quarters of a century ago
still remains among the associates who know them only by
tradition? Good fellowship and friendship, a sane and
gentle philosophy of life, sympathy in love of beauty in art
and literature and character, have not been frightened away
by the rude alarums and excursions of a turbulent world.
I think it is because those benign spirits were seeking something of more worth than all the wealth and power of this
wonderful age of material progress. They formed an association not for the purpose of doing something, but for the
purpose of being something.

Many members of The Century have done fine things.
Paintings and sculptures and noble buildings, and books that

will live, and unselfish service to the community, have come from them. But the test in The Century is not what it has done, but what it has become. Thousands of associations for profit and power and glory of their members, to instruct and educate others, to prevent civil society from pursuing conduct which they disapprove and to insist upon its following conduct which they approve, to reform and regenerate the world, fill the air with a great noise. The Century has no such mission. Its objective is in the influence of its members on each other to care for sincerity in art and literature and in character, to achieve the liberal spirit, the habit of kindly judgment, to be unimpressed by the external displays of life, to care for our fellows because of what they are, not because of what they may achieve.

These things which make for the building of character and the growth of the spirit are what the founders of The Century sought; and from their day, influence upon character has formed character, extending the influence to new generations, standards of judgment accepted have become habits of thought and feeling, memories have ripened into traditions and, as the generations have passed, through the miracle of spiritual succession, the founders live and will continue to live though their names be forgotten. In that spirit The Century has kept itself simple. In an age of marble palaces and eastern magnificence it has kept itself inexpensive so that wealth should not by any means become a requisite for membership.

There is a motto — I don't know whence it came. I saw it years ago over a doorway in the office of an old-fashioned banking house in Holland. It runs like this: "L'âge d'or est l'âge où l'or ne régnait pas." The Century has lived in the spirit of that motto. Joseph de Maistre said: "One's country is an association upon the same soil, of the living and the dead, with all who are yet to be born." Such an

alliance in The Century, in a peculiarly personal sense, between ourselves, the living, and all the Centurians of the
past, and all who are yet to come, we celebrate upon this
anniversary. As our memories drift back over the periods of
our own membership in this Association, how full of feeling
they must become!

We may be dimly conscious that back in the past were the
founders whom we have never seen, but after Verplanck and
Bryant and Bancroft we begin to remember faces and forms
and we begin to fill the familiar spaces of the club with the
memories of Huntington and Bigelow and Potter and Choate
and Evarts and Carter and Beaman and Henry E. Howland
and Loyall Farragut and Gilder and Richard Hunt and Lau-
rence Hutton and John LaFarge and McKim and Stanford
White and St. Gaudens and Frank Millet and Tom North
and Stoddard and Weir and Weston. Each one of us can go
on with the list according to his own special affections. What
fine and noble fellows they were! How interesting and admirable! What wit, what humor, what spirit, what genius
for friendship! What dear and lovable fellows they were!
A blessed thing, is it not, to have the memory of them as a
part of our lives? All the mines of Nevada could not buy
such a thing. We are better and more human because of
them. We are grateful in recognition. We are affectionate
in memory. We have a feeling for the places where we knew
them, and we cry "Long live The Century!"

ADDRESS AS VICE–PRESIDENT ON THE FIFTIETH ANNIVERSARY OF THE METROPOLITAN MUSEUM OF ART

NEW YORK CITY, MAY 18, 1920

IT has seemed to the trustees of the Museum fitting that, upon this celebration of the close of the first half-century of the Museum's existence, the names of the founders and the benefactors during that critical period should be inscribed in permanent form and in conspicuous place amid the works that have lived after them.

On the 23d of November, 1869, there was a meeting of a little group of men in the hall of the Union League Club in this city, for the purpose of considering a proposal to establish a museum of art in the City of New York. They appointed committees. They agreed upon a constitution. They applied to the Legislature and received a charter granted in April, 1870 — fifty years ago last month. The conditions under which they met and acted it is very difficult for us to realize now. It is difficult even for those of us who can remember them. We were just approaching the close of that dreadful period of taste which extended from the presidency of Jackson to the presidency of Grant — that dreadful period which found its consummate flower among the French in the meretricious adornment of the Second Empire, and which has associated the idea of goodness with the idea of ugliness in the term "Victorian Period." The newly awakening desire of the American people for art was finding expression in sawed-scroll work ana basswood-towers. The women of America, with all the innate and natural tastes of womanhood, were pressing autumn leaves and doing crude worsted work as an expression of art. The reign of Mullet was just before us — the reign of that incredible architecture which has given to us the New York Post Office, and in Washington the State, War, and Navy building, with its job-lot of granite columns opposite the beautiful relic of colonial days in the White House.

Long rows of brownstone, high-stooped houses expressed the idea of New Yorkers in regard to living. In the homes of the American people who had about them all the beauties of nature Prang chromos expressed their ideas of art. More than twenty years were yet to come before that wonderful white city on the shore of Lake Michigan was to strike the imagination of the American people with a new idea that the beautiful was better than the squalid.

The giving habit had not been cultivated — hardly created in New York. Fortunes were small. There were many faint hearts in the group that gathered in the Union League Club. There was so little art for the public that it was not understood, and there was so little public for art that it was hardly manifest. There were no considerable museums. There were some praiseworthy private attempts on a small scale, but not here. There were no sources from which to draw. Our conception of art was of something far away in the Old World. The men who gathered in that meeting and resolved to establish an art museum played the rôle of Columbus. And what they did has the same relation to what we are doing that the courage and faith of Columbus bore to the ordinary matter-of-course voyage of the master of an ocean steamer on the Atlantic to-day.

But the development of this free, intelligent, individually independent people had been passing through the stage I have attempted to describe, and had come to the beginning of a new era; and like the faint breath of the breeze before the dawn, something touched the spirit of the men who gathered at the call of enthusiasts, to consider the project of establishing a museum in New York. It was felt, not here alone, but in Boston, and faintly stirring in favored places throughout the land. The men who gathered included artists and authors and lawyers and clergymen and men of affairs. There were Hunt, Ward, Johnston, and Kensett, and Olmsted, whose art is living now. There were Bryant and Curtis. There were Bellows and Thompson, Choate and Barlow. And there were John Taylor Johnston and Dix, Aspinwall, Blodgett, Putnam and Marquand, and other names of the great business men of New York, to whom at that time, as a youth, I looked up as to the gods upon Olympus. They belonged to that great class of nation-builders — men whose strength of character and ability and power, through the process of natural selection, made them the leaders in the march of the American people toward the amazing development of our country in the last half-century.

And, like all men of distinguished success in business as well as in literature and in art, they had the quality of imagination. Inspired by the artists and authors who joined with them, they overbore the doubting and vacillating — the men of little faith — and determined to accomplish the apparently almost hopeless task. There was one man whose inspiration was the most valuable of all, and whose name should not be omitted here — George F. Comfort of Princeton University, who was not only an enthusiast in art, but a reformer with the instincts of reform, with the enthusiasm of propaganda, and devoted to sharing his love of art and his joy in it among all the people of this country. His knowledge and direction and inspiration played a great part in making the effort a success.

Under that kind of influence, and with that character, the men who undertook to begin the establishment of the museum formed a sound conception of what it was they were undertaking. They knew that their task was something more than the establishment of a depository for works of art. They understood that the cultivation of taste is one of the mightiest agencies in the eternal conflict, the struggle for happiness against the discontent and the tedium of life. They knew that when, for rich and poor alike, food and drink and clothing and shelter have been supplied, still comes the question of happiness. They knew that then Satan enters into the empty chambers of the soul that has no spiritual interest in life. They knew what we see to-day, that the great problem for the laboring people of America, with their higher wages and their shorter hours, is what to do with their higher wages and their leisure hours. They knew that no wealth and no material things can fill the void in human nature. And with that deep knowledge they proceeded with a breadth of view worthy of all honor. They determined to establish an institution which should exist not to gratify curiosity, but to educate taste, which should be not for amusement but an essential means of high cultivation. And they declared that they were determined to establish an institution which should gather for the education of all the people the human documents of art in all its phases and in all its possibilities, — painting and sculpture, the graphic arts, handiwork, textiles, and metals, music, the arts of East and West, of the present and the past, — all were to be made to contribute toward the cultivation of that taste which makes for human happiness.

And the institution which they founded upon that broad basis has stood the test of common judgment. It has been accepted as not a foible of the rich, but a benefit for the whole community. It has justified and brought about the support of government in the City and State, and it has commended itself to a long line of spiritual successors of the men who founded it — of successors inspired by the same high purpose, capable of the same faith and instinct, with the same spirit of service. John Taylor Johnston, founder and benefactor; William T. Blodgett, who without authority made the purchase of 174 paintings in Europe and borrowed the money to pay for them, so that the Museum had to go on; Marquand and Rhinelander, and that greatest of art collectors, Pierpont Morgan, and many another whose names you will presently see graven in marble, have carried on the purpose, have kept the faith, and have brought fruition to the hopes of the little group of men who founded the institution fifty years ago in the meeting-room of the Union League Club.

It is impossible for me here upon this occasion, which permits but brief remarks, to do justice to the devotion and lofty spirit and enthusiasm of such men as Mr. Johnston and Mr. Marquand and Mr. Rhinelander and Mr. Morgan and Mr. De Forest. The nobility of the work has found in them fitting association, and I doubt not that they have received in full measure from that work a reward for the noble service they have rendered. It is especially grateful to me, and I know it must be to all of you, that while the first name on the list of the founders and the first name on the list of the benefactors is that great citizen of New York, John Taylor Johnston, the last names on the list of benefactors are his daughter Emily Johnston De Forest and his son-in-law Robert de Forest. In the character of the founders, in the universal public approval of their work, in the knowledge that they have swung open the doors of vision to the school and the factory, the children and the teachers, the artisans, the laborers, the millions who are wearied by the dull and squalid sights of a great city, in the succession of noble men who have kept alive the work they began, we find an augury inevitable for the future of the institution. The spirit of great and noble citizenship lives still in America. The instinct of service, the habit of benevolence, the urge of patriotism, the love of beauty, and devotion to humanity live still in America. And so long as our free republic retains its freedom, this institution and all the ranks of other institutions which have come along in the same cause and are inspired by the same spirit will live and increase and be a blessing to mankind.

ADDRESS ON THE FIFTIETH ANNIVERSARY OF THE ASSOCIATION OF THE BAR OF THE CITY OF NEW YORK

FEBRUARY 17, 1920

I HAVE often thought that the best corrective for the despondency of the men who think that everything is going to the devil is to be found in reading history, and comparing the conditions of one's own time with what one finds in the past. I think we can especially indulge in that process as we consider the most interesting paper Mr. Davies has read to us about the conditions that existed fifty years ago and those at present. With all that we find to cause apprehension and distrust to-day, the candid observer must realize that the standard of public and official purity and integrity is far better now than it was then; the interest of the public in political and public affairs of all kinds is far greater and more effective now than it was then. There has been a great advance in the art of self-government, always, it is true, followed by an increase in the complexity and difficulty of such government, but still an advance that presents a most cheerful augury for the future of our institutions.

I think that the organization of this body is a very excellent illustration of the way in which people living under self-governing institutions make their appeals to answer to the needs of the community. The conditions in 1869–1870 were very different from those that we have to-day. This was a rather small provincial town at that time. I don't remember the precise figures for 1870, but four years before, when I came down from the country to go into the law school here, there were less than 750,000 people in New York. Fewer than there are in Cleveland and Detroit and several other

111

American cities now. This was just beginning to be a considerable city. It was small in area, crowded down in the lower part of the island. The highest uptown of all the theatres was Wallack's at 13th Street and Broadway. The principal hotels were down in the neighborhood of Bleecker and Houston streets, the St. Nicholas, the Metropolitan, the Southern. The Fifth Avenue Hotel had just made a great new departure and had gone up to 23d Street. Everything was very simple.

I looked over the list the other day to see how many there were of the men who were about me when we signed the Constitution in 1870, and I could find but twelve in all of the more than two thousand members of the Association, so that I feel at liberty to talk to the members of the Association a little about what things there were then.

There were not any elevators then, and the principal law offices were on the second story, and the young fellows went up to the top floor. I came out of Man & Parsons' office just a year before this call was signed, and went up to the fourth floor, 43 Pine Street, in the effort to begin practice. There were no typewriters, no telephones, practically no stenographers. Everything was done in longhand. Mr. Parsons, when I first went into his office, handed me a paper that he had drafted in his own handwriting and told me to make a fair copy of it. I did. The request was never repeated.

Fourteen years afterwards, on going into the United States Attorney's office to help John Clarke enforce the laws of the United States, I found there was no stenographer allowed, and I had a great row with the government about my saving a sum of money out of my appropriation to hire a stenographer to take down in shorthand the proceedings of trials.

At that time if a woman was seen below Canal Street everybody turned and looked at her, and drew inferences

either very highly favorable to her fortune or unfavorable
to her character. Now, you can't go through the streets for
them, walking two by two or four by four; and when you are
in a hurry and trying to get up to court to answer the call of
the calendar, you know how very difficult it is to make time.

Well, we had just begun then the business of having a big
city, and we had not learned how. That is one of the reasons
why these things Julien Davies has told about occurred.
Our election laws were very crude, inefficient, and ineffective.
They were adapted for rural use where everybody knew
everybody else; and it was exceedingly easy to circumvent
them in the city districts. Whoever happened to have control of the machinery could do just about what he pleased;
and while I was not familiar with the affairs of the city at
that time, it is quite evident looking back after acquiring a
good deal of familiarity with election laws and machinery,
that the Tweed Ring could have kept itself in complete
power by merely controlling the election machinery and cast-
ing the ballots, or counting the ballots whoever cast them, if
it had not been for some external force coming in to break
them up. The fact that we hadn't learned how to have a big
city, how to handle people in mass, together with the era of
speculation which followed the war, and one other thing, that
is, that the country had just begun the era of great corporate
undertakings — the combination of all these things was the
fundamental cause for the conditions as described by Mr.
Davies in his interesting paper. The community was quite
untrained in dealings both with corporations and with a
great city, and it required leadership. In response to that
necessity, the formation of this Association furnished the
leadership of men who knew how to lead. They were men
who knew the law, and knew the procedure, and knew what
government was and how it ought to be conducted, and the
city got leadership both of opinion and of action through

this Association, to the great good of this community which was sound and honest then as it is now. The formation of the Association was not a sporadic event. It was the result of a natural development of our institutions. It was the application to the new conditions here of the principles which the Bar of England had applied for centuries in its gradual growth. We never had a real Bar before. It never had been necessary to have a real Bar before, in which lawyers regarded the administration of the law as a whole instead of regarding the administration of the law separately in their particular cases. The need for that was answered by the natural growth of American institutions following along the same line by which England's liberty has been wrought out ever since Magna Charta.

There are thousands of organizations formed every day which run for a while, have their worthy objects, and then wither and die. There are thousands of abuses which go unchallenged. There are thousands of offenders against good morals and common honesty who go unwhipped. It is only when the need and the institution come together that you have progress as a result, and fifty years ago the need and the institution came together. It was a natural growth, a natural response to a need; and the ability of the institution to respond is shown by what has followed throughout the country ever since. There are more than a thousand state and local associations in the United States now, following the example of this Association. There is an association in practically every state, and then there is the great American Bar Association, with its ten or fifteen thousand members, all at work steadily, many of them hardly conscious of the full scope of what they are doing, but all at work gradually creating an American Bar to administer American justice, to spread throughout the whole of this land, where we grow every year more and more interdependent, the standards of American justice, the conception of sound morals, of sound procedure, and of true devotion to the administration of law. And I look upon this Association as being a great event in a progressive development of institutions for the maintenance of justice throughout this land.

We no longer have to meet the crass corruption, frauds, thievery which prompted the Bar of 1870 to its original organization. But there are still duties. One of the things about the Bar fifty years ago and the community fifty years ago is very striking when we look back from our present conditions; and that is the fact that at the close of the Civil War there was a sense of security for the principles for which the Bar has stood. Some things were determined. A man could plant his feet upon the ground of the Constitution, and if he could hold himself there he was safe. Certain principles were established and stood out strongly after the decisions of Marbury and Madison, Gibbons and Ogden, McCullough and Maryland, Cohens and Virginia, Sturges and Crowningshield, Vicksburg, Gettysburg, Lookout Mountain and Appomattox — all conflicts for the establishment of the same great safeguard for the justice and the liberty of our country, the sacredness of the American Union, founded upon the principles of the Constitution of the United States. Those great battles were gone through so that we might be safe, and we were safe. But to-day all the old and tried institutions and traditions are questioned — some of them denied. New theories of government assert themselves with varying opinions as to the method by which they may drive out the old theories. It is not only missionaries from Russia, it is not only the parlor Bolshevists; but all through the community we find people who are in doubt as to whether somebody has not, after all, got hold of something better, of some better scheme of things which will make us all vastly happier. You will find a great number of people who think or feel that, after all, the best way is for men to do what seems to be right at the time, and that it is all wrong that we should be limited by so many constitutional provisions. They feel that we have too much law. The background of all this thought is the assumption that, if the inconveniences of so many rules and limitations, so much red tape of the law, could be done away with, then the best possible thing under all conceivable circumstances would be done by the best possible men, never for an instant reading history to see that the rule of law is all that stands between civil society and the destructive hordes of barbarism.

Now, how are people who spend their time in manufacturing, or farming, or buying and selling, — or teaching, for that matter, — to be made to understand what will happen to them if they succeed in overthrowing the rule of law, if they succeed in demolishing the limitations and the rules of right conduct which were wrought out in the struggles for civil liberty in England and were embodied in our Constitution when we established our government? How are they to reach a sound conclusion? It is only by the leadership of opinion that the Bar can furnish. A great duty is before the Bar. It is not to urge the consideration of their particular cases upon the judge, but to defend the law on which the rights of all their clients depend, before the community whose support only can preserve the law. The growth and development of our civil society has produced this Association and the thousand other associations of lawyers all over America, so that they are here ready for the performance of that duty. It is the highest duty that can come to a citizen of a self-governing community, far beyond the vision of the men who formed this Association a half-century ago. Here are the means for the preservation of all they held sacred, for our civil liberty cannot be preserved without every effort, in season and out of season, to bring to the minds of clients, friends, associates, and the public, the eternal truth of the great underlying principles of our system of government and our system of rendering justice.

This great library has been extended far beyond the needs of the ordinary practitioner in order that, in the good time for which it was being unconsciously prepared, scholars might come from all the four quarters of the land to study the jurisprudence that underlies the law. This body of lawyers has been trained to association and combined action through the efforts of its Judiciary Committee and its Grievance Committee and all its various agencies, in order that in God's good providence it may be able with the power of organization to meet the great and pressing need of our country for the maintenance of its institutions. It is a fair prophecy that in another half-century men will look back and make speeches telling of the service of this Association, far greater in the next fifty years than in the past fifty years; that in the next half-century of usefulness the accomplishments of the Association within the past fifty years will be dwarfed in comparison. The possibilities of an association like this, the spirit of an association like this, the competency of its members, the power of its associated action are a material possession for our future.

II

LAW AND ITS ADMINISTRATION

THE CONSTITUTION OF THE
UNITED STATES

ADDRESS AT CARNEGIE HALL ON THE ANNIVERSARY OF THE
SIGNING, NEW YORK CITY, SEPTEMBER 17, 1919

Youthful as is the Republic of the United States, its Constitution, signed September 17, 1787, and the Government thereunder organized March 4, 1789, is the oldest written Constitution of any nation still in effect. By its Nineteenth Amendment, ratified in 1920, it is one of the youngest of written instruments of government.

WE have met to celebrate the signing of the Constitution of the United States by the members of the Convention, who framed it 132 years ago.

What is it? We are apt to forget. We have been free so long that freedom is unnoted and hardly prized. Peace and order have preserved the opportunity for useful and happy lives, have preserved safe and contented homes, freedom of religion, freedom of thought, freedom of speech, independent manhood and womanhood and the right to rule the conduct of one's own life, so long that we forget whence these blessings come. They come through a system of government maintained by the resolute loyalty of a great people. When that system of government fails, something else will come. We cannot tell what it will be, but this we may know: that the system of government which has preserved our peace and order and security and opportunity and growth in prosperity and in grace, will no longer protect us.

You all recall the immortal words of the Declaration of Independence which declare that all men have unalienable rights, to secure which governments are organized. That was a declaration which joined issue with all the theories of government in the past. The theories of all the monarchies and all the ancient republics were that the state was the main thing, and that the rights of the individual were derived from the State. The Declaration said the unalienable rights are those of the individual. The State is organized to secure them. But a thousand noble declarations of principles have been made in this world and have passed into the mist of oblivion without effect. No mere declaration of principles is effective for the control of human affairs except it be supported and applied by practical rules of conduct, which impose upon the powers, upon the men, the individuals who exercise the powers of government, specific and definite duties to give effect to the principles.

And that is the office of the Constitution of the United States. For the first time in the history of the world definite and certain rules, clear and unmistakable, were put upon paper, so that all could read, were printed, distributed, recorded, to make effective the unalienable right of the individual, which includes life, liberty, and the pursuit of happiness, and to make government the servant of the individual right.

There are several things to be said about a written Constitution — several characteristics. One is, that it settles things. There are many rules of conduct which are not in themselves so important one way or the other, but as to which it is of vital importance that there be rules. In some countries, vehicles upon the highway turn to the left, as in England. In some countries, vehicles upon the highway turn to the right, as they do here. It is of little consequence which way they turn, but it is of vital importance that there be a general rule so that they will turn the same way. Otherwise, if the millions of automobiles in the United States all set forth in the morning, each driver having his own rule and no one knowing what the rule of the others may be, you will have at least five hundred thousand collisions before the day is over.

All the world is now in a state of nervous reaction. The declarations of noble sentiments, which were to receive effect upon the close of the Great War, have set half the people of the world agog with the idea that all their dissatisfactions in this weary life are to be wiped out, and that they are all to have what they think they ought to have. A very singular febrile condition exists. Everybody wants to do something else. The people who are crying the loudest for labor do not want to work. The people who make the most noise about the high cost of living are crowding the jewelers' shops. They raise so much trouble about paying the baker, but there was never such good business in cheap jewelry and in furs and in laces and in feathers and in silks. Articles of luxury are going like hot cakes.

Everyone wants to be self-determining. Wherever the shoe of the law pinches, there is a loud outcry against the system of government. Now, the Constitution settles things; it settles certain rules, and so long as they are settled, good people can attend to their own business, earn their own living, go to their own church, bring up their own children and go on with their lives, accomplishing the object for which all government is intended; but if you wipe out the rules, so that nothing is settled and everybody is disputing about every question as to how everything shall be done, then there is no peace or security for anybody in living his life.

Another thing to be said about a written Constitution is that it lays down the fundamental rules of right conduct for the enforcement of the great general principle declared by the Declaration of Independence, or whatever declaration in any country may have set forth the principles in which the people believe. A Constitution lays down the rules of right conduct for the enforcement of those principles; and those rules are established impersonally, abstractly. They are established, as in the case of the Constitution of the United States, by a

convention sitting apart, concerning themselves with no concrete or temporary question. So in our states, constitutions
are prepared by conventions which do nothing else, and are
submitted to the people. Ordinary laws answer to the impulse of the moment. Ordinary laws deal with the concrete
difficulties that arise from year to year. But a constitution,
made calmly, impersonally, for all the future, without reference to specific needs or specific impulses, declares the general
rules of right conduct; and that is in accordance with the
teaching of all religion and all human experience.

We have all of us learned from childhood up that we cannot trust the impulses of the human heart under temptation.
The passions sway us; temptation draws us; the worst elements of our natures are brought to the fore by strong desire,
by hatred, by the heat of conflict; and if we leave ourselves
in the affairs of our government to do what we want to do at
the moment, we forget the teachings of that religion which
says to us that life must be guided not by impulse but by
principle — eternal principle. The Constitution of the United
States for more than a century has held up before the eyes of
the people of the United States and the whole world the im-
perishable rules of justice in the exercise of government, in
the exercise of that mighty power by which the whole people
constrains the action of each individual.

Another thing to be said is that a written Constitution
such as ours limits the powers of the men who govern. Never
forget the importance of that. That is the vital thing for the
preservation of liberty. No king by any name among a free
people! Give to any man in this free land a great office, call
him Mayor, or Governor, or General, or President, and so
long as by virtue of that office he is administering the law, so
long as he speaks the voice of the law, he is your superior and
mine as the representative of law, of our law; but the moment
he passes the border of that lawful power which is limited by

the Constitution, that moment he is our equal and not our superior.

I have seen a hundred times submissive, good, peaceable citizens on the continent of Europe tremble before some petty minister of the law, bow before him as before a superior, because they did not know the limits of his authority; and having power not limited to their knowledge he was universally their superior and they were his inferiors. Let me tell you this. In that great army which crowded across the Atlantic and went to the battle-line in France, — as General Mangin said of the soldiers at Château-Thierry, "They ran to the fight as one going to a feast," — in that great army, composed of the best military material in the world, since the dreadful slaughter of those early years had destroyed the noblest and the best of England and Belgium and France, — in that great army, the vital and conspicuous element of strength was the independence of individual manhood, which came from a self-respecting life in free America. Nothing can defend liberty but the character of a people who deserve to be free; and nothing can preserve the character of independent manhood except the kind of limitation upon the power of all officers of all governments which is imposed by the Constitution we meet here to-night to celebrate.

The Constitution was framed by a group of men such as never had met before in this world; not that there were not as good, as patriotic, as able men in other countries; but these men had become familiar with the practical working of free self-government during one hundred and fifty years of colonial life. They were not theorists like the men who initiated the French Revolution.

They applied to questions of government a knowledge of the character of the material with which government has to deal, that is to say, human nature with its multitude of feelings and impulses and passions and weaknesses. They were not as a man who, seeking to build, builds of iron as if it were stone, or of brick as if it were wood, or of wood as if it were concrete. They knew their people, and they knew how their people would act under the provisions which they discussed, so that it was the most practical instrument ever written for government.

But that is not all. These men represented colonies which were the inheritors of a great tradition, and they embodied in the instrument which they made for their country all the results of that age-long struggle during which for more than six hundred years, since before Magna Charta, the Commons of England with labor and agony and sacrifice had been working out the practical principles of Anglo-Saxon liberty. They embodied in that instrument the spirit of Magna Charta and the Petition of Right and the Bill of Rights and the Habeas Corpus Act, of all that made the people of England great, and an adaptation of those great principles to American life through the practical working of one hundred and fifty years of American government. So that the Constitution we meet to celebrate is the embodiment of the principle, the spirit, the ideals of American institutions at their best; and when we celebrate this Constitution, we declare our loyalty to the American type of liberty and order; for the signing of it is the one act which illustrates, presents sharply and distinctly, the whole spirit of American institutions. If we mean to preserve the rules of conduct and the system of government which have made us free and great, prosperous and powerful, we shall defend the Constitution of the United States against all assaults and against all detraction.

The Constitution is worthless unless it is applied. It is of no use to have a Constitution if you pay no attention to it.

There are some countries that have followed the American Constitution, practically copied it for themselves, but have allowed the exigencies of the moment, the passions of the time, the strong desire of this leader or that, this faction or that, to cause them to forget, to pass over and fail to apply the rules of the instrument they had adopted. Those countries have struggled through marshes and mountains of difficulty. They have been poor and war-torn and oppressed by warrior bands and harsh dictators, because they forgot the gospel of their liberty, and failed to make a living thing of the constitution that would have preserved it.

There is now universal unrest, there is a universal questioning of old postulates and raising of new questions, and discussion of all sorts of issues; but I am mistaken if we are not here to say that the Constitution of the United States is not in question. We are not going to begin over again at the beginning and discuss with the gentlemen whose names were read to you by Colonel Lydecker, so anxious for American Liberty, so anxious for it that they came here. We are not going to begin over again and discuss with them the principles upon which our government was founded. We may instruct them upon what those principles are. But the principles are settled, and they are written down. They are our Constitution. They represent American institutions, and the men who are not willing to live in accordance with those institutions may, and ultimately shall, go to other lands. We cannot maintain this Constitution without insisting upon its being followed. We cannot maintain it by laughing at those who try to make a joke of it. We cannot maintain it by being tolerant and liberal and indifferent toward those who attack it. We must stand for it when it is challenged. And it is being challenged to-day, here and there in a hundred directions. Most noticeably it is challenged by the police strike in Boston now. That raises distinctly the question whether our system of government represented in this Constitution is to be abandoned or not. Somebody says no.

Think a minute. This Constitution provides for free, popular
.government. Under it we have a democracy in which all the
people have their part in government. Every officer, legislative, executive, judicial, military, is the servant of all the
people — not of any class, not of any group, not of any calling, not of any race, not of any religion; but all. And that is
fundamental to our democracy. Now, what does the police
strike in Boston mean? It means that the men who have
been employed and taken their oaths to maintain order and
suppress crime, as the servants of all the people, are refusing
to perform that solemn duty unless they are permitted to
ally themselves, affiliate themselves, become members of a
great organization which contains perhaps three per cent of
the people. Now, if that is done, that is the end, except for a
revolution. Government cannot be maintained unless it has
the power to use force.

The provisional government of Russia, composed of good
and patriotic men who were doing their best to give the
people of Russia an opportunity to set up their own government by universal suffrage, had not the force, had not the
power to use force, and Lenin and Trotsky and their associates came along, and with German money and helped by
German agents, they got together a force that was willing to
kill to accomplish their purpose, and they set themselves up
in the place of the Tsar, and are ruling now. The people of
Russia are deprived of the opportunity to rule now as much
as they were when the Tsar was there, because these men got
control of the force of arms, and if the power to use force
passes from the 97 per cent of the whole people of the United
States, or from the 100 per cent of the whole people of the
United States to this organization of three per cent, the 97
per cent are no longer a self-governing people. The effects
may not come to-day or to-morrow, but the effect of the
passing of power to enforce laws, the power to punish crime,

the power to maintain order, from the whole people of the United States to one section of the people of the United States is as certain to come in destroying the liberties of the whole and subjecting them to the part, as sunrise is sure to come to-morrow.

Thank Heaven, those millions of young men who went abroad to fight for their country have come back better patriots, more fitted for the duty of citizenship, more determined to preserve our liberty and peace than ever before. Thank Heaven, the spirit of the people of the United States, awakened by the trials and sacrifices of these recent years, is more ready than ever since the earliest days to do whatever their country needs for the preservation of its institutions. We must be vigilant and we must be earnest — but we shall be, and we shall preserve for generations to come and for the peace and blessing of our children and children's children, that liberty and order which this Constitution has given to us.

ADDRESS AT A DINNER GIVEN BY THE ASSO-CIATION OF THE BAR OF THE CITY OF NEW YORK TO LORD CHIEF JUSTICE READING, AS AMBASSADOR TO THE UNITED STATES

APRIL 5, 1919

Lord Reading's special mission to the United States — which he performed to the satisfaction of the country which sent him and the country which received him — lasted from January 1, 1918 to May 10, 1919.

He began life in very humble circumstances as Rufus Isaacs, and after shipping as a cabin boy, took to the study of law. He was admitted to the Bar in 1887, and rapidly distinguished himself in his profession, becoming Solicitor-General in 1910, on which occasion he was knighted. He was Attorney-General in Mr. Asquith's Liberal Ministry, resigning to become Lord Chief Justice in 1913. Eight years later, in 1921, the Earl of Reading resigned the Chief Justiceship in order to accept the Viceroyalty of India, to which important post he was appointed in the course of that year.

IT is quite impossible for any one voice to express the peculiar attitude of the American Bar toward a Lord Chief Justice of England. To the elder among us — I do not know how it is with the youngsters to-day — Barnwell and Cresswell, and Adolphus and Ellis, were as familiar friends as Wheaton and Hill and Denio. What your predecessors said, my Lord, upon the bench, their words of pithy wisdom, their illustration of the justice which we wrought to maintain, made us feel, each one of us, as the humble friend to them. It has been the honor and pleasure of our Bar to meet for a day or so at a time, upon brief visits to this country, I think, all your predecessors, my Lord, for the last fifty years, with one exception, the exception of that noble gentleman who became endeared to your bar under the name of Sir Richard Webster, and better known to the world upon the bench which you adorn as Lord Alverstone. This is the first time that we have had a Lord Chief Justice come to live among us, to meet us as a human being without wig or gown, the first time that we have been able to see in one person a Lord Chief Justice and an ambassador. We respect ambassadors, but no ambassador can rank in our minds and hearts with a Lord Chief Justice. I will take leave to observe however, that, in view of the vast multitude of statutes which are making it criminal for any of us to indulge his natural inclinations, it is a wise thing that a Lord Chief Justice upon visiting America should be made an ambassador, in order to have immunity from arrest.

You have represented your country here in many delicate and important relations between your government and ours, resting upon negotiations and mutual assurance and the faith of treaties. I wonder if your people at home and ours appreciate that it is really as Lord Chief Justice that you represent the true bond between Great Britain and the United States. Treaties may be signed, sealed, and ratified, faith may be pledged in words. All the history of the world concentrated and accentuated by recent experience shows that treaties, agreements, promises, are of little worth if there be not underneath them the substantial agreement and purpose of the people whom they purport to bind. Really as Lord Chief Justice you represent to the American people the common history of those struggles through which the free men of England through centuries wrought out the liberties that we enjoy to-day. Wherever English law goes, the American breathes freely. Wherever American law goes, the Englishman finds himself at home. We know how each other's mind works. We understand each other against the background of long centuries of development of English and American law, of British and American freedom.

Common understanding among the millions of people, allegiance to the same ideals, unconscious possession of the same purposes in life, the same conception of right conduct,

the same deep sense of what constitutes justice, the same
method of doing business and dealing with our fellows — all
those make it possible that the people of Great Britain and
America shall forever have a common interest in the development of civilization the world over. And that you represent
as Lord Chief Justice, while as Ambassador you represent
treaties that are worthless but for the substratum of law and
liberty and common understanding and common purpose
and common ideals.

We are told by the newspaper that a convention is now
being discussed in Paris. We have little other information
about it, but it has been repeated so often by the press that
we begin to be impressed by a belief in its truth. A convention which proposes the formation of a league of nations, to
do two things: first, to continue, for the garnering of the
fruits of the Great War and the reconstruction of Europe and
the Near East necessary to the establishment of peace, that
virtual alliance, without treaty but based upon a common
purpose, that has been in existence for the two years that are
passed; and next to seek to continue far into the future an
organization of the civilized nations who love peace and
abhor war, for the purpose of preserving the peace of the
world. There has been much discussion about it here which
you have doubtless observed, but I beg to say to you, my
Lord, that it is the earnest hope of the American people that
in due form and by wise and suitable provision the country
which you represent and our own may unite for effective and
perpetual organization to preserve the peace of the world for
all the centuries to come. Toward that alliance for the en-
thronement of public right to control the world, I believe the
American Bar upon all its traditions of justice and liberty
stands with you and stands with all the Allies by whose side
we have fought. We would not have it that American boys,
who died upon the fields of Flanders by the side of the young

men of Great Britain fighting against a common foe, have wasted their lives. And the same sense of loyalty that kept them side by side charging against death must keep our countries side by side to make certain the fruits of their victories.

We are in alliance, my Lord Chief Justice, alliance for the preservation of that Anglo-Saxon liberty that was wrought out during all the seven hundred years from Magna Charta, through the Petition of Right and the Bill of Rights, through the Declaration of American Independence, when our fathers fought for the liberty of the Anglo-Saxon race against the soldiers of the German king who then ruled Great Britain. We are in alliance for the preservation in the world of the common principles of English and American law. We are in alliance for the preservation of all the charms and joys and pathetic loyalty of France, of Notre Dame, of the French Academy and the Sorbonne, of the literature and the art and the science, that the great civilizing influence of France shall never fall before the onslaught of barbarism. We are in alliance that the art and literature and patriotism of Italy may never be driven back into the sad old days of despotism and strife from which she was rescued but so brief a time ago. And we are in alliance to make the great sacrifice for honor and faith of little Belgium earn its true reward.

No matter how much we discuss about particular measures and particular provisions, my Lord Chief Justice, when you go back to your place on the bench, to administer the laws of England, never doubt that we, on this side of the Atlantic, will sustain the fundamental principles which you apply, against all new Bolshevist ideas; against all internationalism and destruction of law, against all tearing down of true democracy, to substitute the despotism of the proletariat; and that the great free people of America, led in opinion to no slight degree by the members of her bar, would stand as a bulwark against the destruction of all that you devote your life to making real in the affairs of your countrymen. You may go back to your home and your duties feeling sure that you have done your part by this knight-errantry which took you from your quiet seat upon the bench into strange duties in a strange land; that you have done your part, not merely in administering justice between man and man in the particular case, but toward making strong and living and perpetual the fundamental principles of the law which you represent in your high office.

JUDGES AND LEGISLATURES

REMARKS TO THE JUDICIAL SECTION OF THE AMERICAN BAR
ASSOCIATION, AT BOSTON, SEPTEMBER 4, 1919

WHILE more than fifty years have passed since I became a member of the Bar, I still take an interest in the judiciary. There are some very interesting things that I observe in the development of our law, and the administration of it, and public opinion in regard to it.

In the first place, you have a double function under our system. You are to apply in concrete cases, for concrete needs, the laws which are enacted by the national and state legislatures. In that way, you are an arm of the legislative branch. You are necessary for its effectiveness. The laws which the legislative body passes will be ineffective unless you apply them.

But, on the other hand, you are the natural enemies of the legislature. The whole course of constitutional development in this country has been to pile up, one after another, a continually increasing set of limitations upon the actions of legislative bodies, prohibiting them from doing this and doing that and doing the other, and requiring them to do this and that and the other thing, under certain restrictions and safeguards against unconsidered action, or action under what Mr. Conkling used to call forbidden and abhorrent forces.

Now, those limitations which the people of the different states have imposed upon their legislatures, because they do not trust the legislatures, because they find so much human weakness on the part of the legislators, amount to nothing unless you enforce them against the legislatures.

That has been ground into us since John Marshall's time; and, with the exception of here and there a crank, some fellow who simply knows it all, we assent to it.

At the same time, the legislatures are continually tying you up in threads, cords, ropes, and chains of legislation about procedure. I have been for a good many years now sputtering about it, coming as near swearing about it as one well could in a parliamentary way, and declaring, as I now again declare, that one great trouble about the administration of law in the United States is that our legislative bodies will not permit the judges to do justice.

There is this peculiarity about all these practice and procedure statutes: when a man has a lawsuit, and he thinks, either as plaintiff or as defendant, that it is necessary to have certain interlocutory relief, if he thinks it is right there should be an injunction, or an attachment, or a receiver, or the examination of a party, or a commission or an order, to take testimony of some other witness, if he is at liberty to go to the judge and appeal to the judge's sense of what is fair to do, in order to get at the merits of that case, he will get it; and if the judges have established rules regarding the way in which he should act, nevertheless those rules do not give any right against what the judges consider to be fair and just. But if the legislature has made a series of provisions, each provision constitutes a legal right, and you cannot discriminate. The law is that a man shall have such and such a thing done in a particular way, according to the relief he wants. The law is that a man shall not have the interlocutory relief that he wants unless he goes in that particular way, and there is a legal requirement there that you have got to observe. So you have thrust into the litigations that come before you a long series of separate, independent, preliminary legal rights, and you have litigations about this legal right and that legal right and the other legal right, before the court ever gets to a

point where the legal right on which the parties came into
court can be tried.

Now, those things come up, not because legislatures are
malicious, but because, as a rule, a large part of the members
of the Bar who go into the legislature go in when quite young,
or are men with not very much practice. They have had experience in a few cases, and when something has worked
wrong in a particular case with them, when they think that a
particular case has not been treated as it should have been,
they go in and get a statute passed which applies to all cases,
for the purpose of remedying what that particular legislator
conceives to be a wrong. And another man does the same
thing, and another the same thing, and the next year some
other fellow will come in with his vision and will get the law
amended, and so it goes. The result is that, instead of having
the breadth of view which a general experience with the trials
and decisions of courts gives to the just judge, to determine
how causes should be brought into the condition of hearing
and determination, you get an infinite variety of special
views, based on the limited experience of the young men who
go into the state legislatures.

And I think a very large part of the trouble that Mr. Ran-
dall has been talking about in the reports comes from the fact
that you have got a swarm of separate legal rights to deal
with instead of being allowed to do justice in the case as it
comes before you, to enable the parties to get at the merits
of the case, and get it settled.

I do not believe in half-way measures about this. I would
wipe out the whole business. I think you can put the rules
of practice, which it is really necessary to impose upon the
judges to prevent their going wrong, on two sheets of paper,
and then wipe the whole burdensome mass of code provisions
out, and with that little series of fundamental rules leave it
to the judges to do justice.

The Bench has been hammered so, there has been so much abuse of the courts, there have been such loud outcries against the courts, that I think a good many judges are getting rather sensitive, and I do not think there is quite that sturdy independence in applying the Constitution that there was thirty or forty years ago.

Now, let me say this about it. Of course, every defeated litigant goes down to the tavern or, since prohibition, elsewhere, to swear at the courts. Of late years, the defeated litigants have got a hearing from the public that they did not have formerly. Sometimes they are great organizations; sometimes they have political power behind them; sometimes they are complaining at a decision which frustrates public feeling; and the defeated litigant has made more noise and got more hearing within the last fifteen years, ten times over, than he could get thirty years ago.

The real secret of it, the real reason for it, is not that the people of our country have lost their faith in the courts, not that they have lost their confidence in the judges, but that they are becoming less and less willing to be bound by law. We are going through a phase, — temporary, God grant, and I believe He will grant it, — a phase of public feeling, in which men are more restive under the restraint of law than they used to be. They resent having the impulse of the moment, or the desire of the moment, frustrated by prescribed rules of conduct. And they flout the judges and the courts, and complain in the press, because they are unwilling to submit to the restraint of law.

You are in a position where you have got to meet that, because you have got to enforce the law, and this feeling will pass away. The change of the law, the development of institutions, always has to move along a little ahead of the courts. Courts do not hang back. It is the development that hangs back. The courts have to apply the law as it is. God forbid that we should ever have a judiciary which abandons the law as it is, and undertakes to apply the law as it thinks it ought to be; for when you get that, you have a government not of law but of men, and you will no longer be courts; there will no longer be courts if you do that. Legislatures can do that, and executive officers can do that. As long as you are courts, you have got to apply the law as it is; and the people who think the law ought to be changed will, for a time, find fault with the courts because they do not change it. After a time, people, through the due and orderly methods of constitutional governments, make the change, and then the courts enforce the law as it has become. And then, presently, will come another public desire, and the same thing will go on again; and that condition of restiveness with the courts, because the people have not made the necessary changes of law to meet the changes of the conditions of life and business, will be always most aggravated in times of change.

We are just now at a time when everything is changing. For the last fifteen or twenty years changes have been in the air and in the desires of people; the change of conditions in business, occasioned by the great new wealth of the world, and the enormous enlargement of the productive powers of mankind, and the change of relations between capital and labor and employers and employees, and producers and consumers, caused by these great new opportunities and new facilities, all these changes of conditions fill the minds of people, properly and rightly, with a desire for development. We have got to develop; and after a time that phase will be passed, and people will recognize that the only thing that kept the whole establishment from blowing up, going to pieces instead of developing, was the judicial branch of our government, which always, step by step, enforced the law as it was at the time. Believe me, as an observer of the trend of the public mind of the people of the United States, underneath all the noise and newspaper talk and heroics in public meetings, underneath all this there is, among the American people, loyalty to their institutions, and confidence in the just and honorable men who are maintaining those institutions upon the bench.

THE STANDARD OF LEGAL EDUCATION

SPEECHES IN THE CONFERENCE OF THE AMERICAN BAR
ASSOCIATION DELEGATES, WASHINGTON,
FEBRUARY 23, 24, 1922

At the request, and under the auspices of the American Bar Association, a meeting was held on February 23, 24, 1922, in the City of Washington, to discuss the
steps to be taken in order to improve the practice of the law by requiring a higher
standard of admission to the American Bar. The recommendation of the American
Bar Association to be considered at the meeting was "that hereafter two years in
college and the equivalent to three years in a full-time law school, shall be required
as a condition of admission to the Bar."

The Section of Legal Education and Admissions to the Bar, of which Mr. Root
was Chairman, invited all the State and local bar associations to send delegates
to a Conference at Washington, and at this Conference Mr. Root delivered the
following address.

OLD Dr. Lieber, the great teacher of jurisprudence of the
last generation, had posted on the wall of his lecture
room the motto, "No right without a duty." It is my pleasant task to present to you certain action of the American
Bar Association upon which that Association appeals to you
for sympathy and assistance. It consists in certain resolutions designed to improve the standard of the incoming Bar,
and it is the result of many years of discussion, many committees, many reports, many drafts of resolutions. For
twenty-five years the American Bar Association has acted
under a continually growing feeling that the Bar was not
functioning quite right; and during all that time local associations and state associations have been appointing committees, receiving reports, and passing resolutions based upon
the same feeling.

Some nine years ago the American Bar Association formally asked the Carnegie Foundation for the Advancement
of Teaching, which had just accomplished a noteworthy

study of the teaching of medicine, the results of which had been very salutary to the medical profession, to make a similar study of legal education. That was undertaken by the machinery of the Foundation, and last summer the report of the gentleman who had been engaged in the study was produced. In the meantime the American Bar Association reorganized its branch devoted to legal education into a section on legal education and admissions to the Bar, with an executive council. The Section also appointed a special committee composed of half a dozen gentlemen from different parts of the country, to take up the question, what should be done to create conditions which would improve the efficiency and strengthen the character of those coming to the practice of law. That committee met in the City of New York, and it sent out questionnaires all over the country to the people who were supposed to be best fitted to make suggestions — to the heads of all the bar associations, state and local, to all the law schools, and to a great number of leaders of the Bar in different parts of the country. They got great numbers of answers, and these they collated and digested.

Then the committee met again, and they invited representatives of all sorts of experiences and opinions on the subject to come before them and instruct them. There was a long session in which the heads of the law schools and bar examiners and members of the Bar in active practice came in and talked to the committee and answered questions. As a result, the committee reported to the Section of Legal Education and Admissions to the Bar of the Bar Association a series of resolutions which they recommended, designed to take one step at least in the direction of having a more effective Bar, not only now but in the future. Those resolutions which were recommended by the committee went before the Section, at a largely attended meeting in Cincinnati last summer, and were fully debated. Representatives of certain law schools who were opposed came in and argued very fully in opposition. But the resolutions were adopted by an overwhelming majority by the Section and recommended to the Association; and in a very fully attended meeting of the Association there was another vote, and they were adopted then by an immense majority. I am now bringing them before you by the direction of the Association with a request for your kind consideration and all the help that you can give us.

I. The American Bar Association is of the opinion that every candidate for admission to the Bar should give evidence of graduation from a law school complying with the following standards:

(a) It shall require as a condition of admission at least two years of study in a college.

(b) It shall require its students to pursue a course of three years' duration if they devote substantially all of their working time to their studies, and a longer course, equivalent in the number of working hours, if they devote only part of their working time to their studies.

(c) It shall provide an adequate library available for the use of the students.

(d) It shall have among its teachers a sufficient number giving their entire time to the school to insure actual personal acquaintance and influence with the whole student body.

II. The American Bar Association is of the opinion that graduation from a law school should not confer the right of admission to the Bar, and that every candidate should be subjected to an examination by public authority, to determine his fitness.

III. The Council on Legal Education and Admissions to the Bar is directed to publish from time to time the names of those law schools which comply with the above standards and of those which do not, and to make such publications available so far as possible to intending law students.

IV. The President of the Association and the Council on Legal Education and Admissions to the Bar are directed to coöperate with the state and local bar associations, to urge upon the duly constituted authorities of the several states the adoption of the above requirements for admission to the Bar.

V. The Council on Legal Education and Admissions to the Bar is directed to call a Conference on Legal Education in the name of the American Bar Association, to which the state and local bar associations shall be

invited to send delegates, for the purpose of uniting the bodies represented
in an effort to create conditions favorable to the adoption of the principles
above set forth.

> ELIHU ROOT, *Chairman*, New York, N. Y.
> HUGH H. BROWN, Tonopah, Nev.
> JAMES BYRNE, New York, N. Y.
> WILLIAM DRAPER LEWIS, Philadelphia, Pa.
> GEORGE WHARTON PEPPER, Philadelphia, Pa.
> GEORGE E. PRICE, Charleston, W. Va.
> FRANK H. SCOTT, Chicago, Ill.

You will perceive that the first part of these resolutions —
all of the first two — is an expression of opinion by the American Bar Association. Of course that opinion cannot be
changed here, in another meeting, differently constituted.
What you can do, and what I hope you will do, is to range
yourselves by the side of the American Bar Association to
give effect to that opinion.

You will perceive that the second part of the resolutions
directs action. It directs two kinds of action. First, action
which will be effective in itself: that is, the Council of the
Section of Legal Education is directed to publish from time
to time the names of those law schools which comply with the
above standards and of those which do not, and to make such
publications available so far as possible to intending law students. Now, that is going on and will continue to go on, and
Mr. Sanborn, the Secretary of the Section, who is here, can
give you information about the very gratifying results of the
publication of these resolutions, in the way of responses from
law schools, a large part of which have already announced
their intention to make their qualifications conform to the
qualifications that should be established in the opinion of the
American Bar Association. So, no matter what we do here,
there will be put before the people of the country and the
thousands of young men who are seeking admission to the
Bar during this coming year, a list of the law schools which

conform to the opinion of the American Bar Association as to what a law school ought to be, and a list of the schools which do not conform to the opinion of the American Bar Association as to what a law school ought to be, with the natural result that all the young men and young women who are able to do so will go to the first-class law schools, and none who can get to the first-class will go to the others; and if they are true Americans, imbued with the traditional American impulse always to have the best, you will find the law schools that are what they ought to be, filling up and the law schools that are not what they ought to be, dwindling.

The second line of action directed in these resolutions is what has brought us here. It is a direction of the Association to coöperate with the state and local bar associations, to urge upon the duly constituted authorities of the several states the adoption of the above requirements, and a direction for the calling of this Conference, for the purpose of uniting the state and local bodies in an effort to create conditions in the several states favorable to the adoption of these principles.

You see those are two quite separate and distinct lines of action to give effect to these standards. First, the direct communication to the people of the United States upon the authority of the members of the Bar Association of an opinion as to the kind of law school their young men shall go to; and, second, an appeal to you members of the state and local bar associations to use your influence and power in the several states to get the state authorities to take over and put into force that same opinion.

Now, this appeal to you and to your associations is not without a basis in past history. The local bar associations have long been appointing committees, passing resolutions in some way to improve the standing and efficiency of the Bar, and particularly of the incoming Bar. And this is an appeal for that union which will make it possible for all the resolutions and all the good intentions of the state and local associations for twenty years past to become efficient and active.

There will be opposition to some of these provisions; and in order to determine how far the opinion of the American Bar Association is praiseworthy and sound and should be supported, it is important to look a little at the trouble which it seeks to cure. That there is trouble I think every one of us feels. It may not be trouble in this particular county, in this particular Bar, in this or that state; but it is trouble in so large a part of the Bar that it affects the whole Bar. You cannot have too many rotten spots in an apple and have the rest of it good. We have for years been hearing just such things as Judge Goodwin tells us out of his experience on the Bench, about the sacrifice of clients' interests, increased expense, the continual delays, the sending back of cases for new trial, notwithstanding their merits, owing to the inefficiency and incompetency of members of the Bar. Those reports have been coming from all over, and they have blackened the name of the Bar. They have led the public to observe the manifold defects of our administration of justice — its delays, its technicalities, its repeated and oft-repeated appeals and reviews, its long delays, which prevent the honest man of modest means from getting his rights, while the rich man, with abundant income, and the sharper, with subtle and adroit ingenuities, can put off indefinitely the granting of justice. That is the charge against us, against you and me; and what is worse still, it is a charge against our free institutions that is sapping the faith, the confidence, the loyalty of the millions of people in this land, in those institutions.

Apart from those evidences, there is enough in the general conditions to satisfy any one that either the Bar or somebody else is not quite doing its full duty. Vastly complicated our practice has become. The enormous masses of statutes and decisions have made it so. Twelve thousand to fifteen thousand public decisions of courts of last resort in a year! Twelve thousand to fifteen thousand more statutes from our Congress and legislatures! A wilderness of laws and a wilderness of adjudications that no man can follow, requiring not less, but more ability; not less, but more learning; not less, but more intellectual training in order to advise an honest man as to what his rights are and in order to get his rights for him. Are we doing it? No. The Bar stays still. It has been talking twenty-five years. The American Bar Association has been talking about it for twenty-five years, appointing committees, listening to reports and filing them. This is the first attempt, in any authoritative and conclusive way, to do something. I am here to ask you to help in it.

Not only has the practice of law become complicated, but the development of the law has become difficult. New conditions of life surround us: capital and labor, machinery and transportation, social and economic questions of the greatest, most vital interest and importance, the effects of taxation, the social structure, justice to the poor and injustice to the rich — a vast array of difficult and complicated questions that somebody has got to solve, or we here in this country shall suffer as the poor creatures in Russia are suffering because of a violation of economic law, whose decrees are inexorable and cruel. Somebody has got to solve these questions. How are they to be solved? I am sure we all hope they will be solved by the application to the new conditions of the old principles of justice out of which grew our institutions. But to do that you must have somebody who understands those principles, their history, their reason, their spirit, their capacity for extension, and their right application. Who is to furnish that? Who but the Bar? Is the Bar giving it? Is the Bar getting it? The public's judgment is that it is not.

Conditions have so changed from Abraham Lincoln's day
that the problem is different and the opportunity is different.
Not only that, but the material is becoming different.

I was for many years a member of the Character Committee in the City of New York, appointed by the Appellate
Division of the Supreme Court in that Department; and year
after year we used to sit, and all the applicants for admission
to the Bar came before us and presented their papers and
submitted themselves to such examination as we saw fit to
make regarding their characters. And every year, when it
was all through, we were compelled to confess to each other
that we really did not know anything about the character of
nine tenths of the young men who came before us. They
would get somebody to sign the necessary papers, and they
would furnish certain formal statements about their careers.
A young fellow just applying for admission to the Bar has not
much of a career. It is very difficult to tell much about his
character. We could not keep a young man out because we
did not know much about him. It would not be fair to de-
prive him of his chances. Nevertheless, I had, we all had, an
uncomfortable and unhappy feeling that we were admitting
to the Bar each year some scores and hundreds of young men
without any warrant for believing that they had the character that is the most essential thing in the administration
of justice.

The old practice of Lincoln's time, under which a young
man studied in a law office, got a little coaching, a little steer-
ing from the members of the firm, read a few fundamental
books and became educated as a lawyer in that way, has
passed. Here and there in the country districts it may remain, but by and large it has gone. That pathway is no
longer open to the young man who is seeking admittance to
the Bar. In its place has come the law school; and in place of
that assurance which the old lawyer in whose office a boy had

studied could give to the court upon his personal knowledge, has come the Bar examination.

Two things, I think, lie at the bottom of our difficulty here. One is that the old system which has passed away was a system that gave moral qualities to the boy. He took in, through the pores of his skin, the way of thinking and of feeling, the standards of morality, of honor, of equity, of justice, that prevailed in that law office; and the moral qualities are the qualities for the want of which our Bar is going down.

Lincoln did not need any such resolutions as we have here. Lincoln inherited and breathed in and grew into the moral quality that makes a lawyer useful, that makes a judge great.

The other difficulty is that examination is wholly incapable of testing that moral quality of a man. The young men whom I have been talking about, whom we had to see going through the examination and into the Bar were acute, subtle, adroit, skillful. They had crammed for their examinations. They could trot around any simple-minded American boy from the country three times a day. But the thing that we were troubled about in that Character Committee was: Have they got the moral qualities? And we had no evidence that they had. And the evidences are coming in all the time of a great influx into the Bar of men with intellectual acumen and no moral qualities. How are you going to test them? Not by an examination; not by going back to the law office. That is impossible.

There is another thing to be considered. A very large part of these new accessions, and particularly in the large cities, are young men who have come in recent years from the Continent of Europe. They have come from countries where there is a highly developed jurisprudence. They have necessarily, by inheritance, all those predilections and fundamental ideas which differentiate the continental systems of jurispru-

dence from the Anglo-American system. Do not underesti-
mate the importance of that. I am not saying that the systems of the countries from which they come are not just as
good as ours. I am drawing no comparison. But they are
different from ours. Do not mistake that. I had many years
ago to argue a case in the Supreme Court of the United
States, the case of Hilton *vs.* Guyot — you will find it along
about thirty years ago in the reports (159 U. S. 113) — involving the effect of a French judgment. After very careful
and long-continued study I came to this conclusion: That an
American stood little chance in a French court and a Frenchman stood little chance in an American court. I have thought
of that a thousand times since, when engaged in international
affairs, and I have seen it illustrated over and over and over
again. The great trouble in international affairs is that the
people of two different countries have two different sets of
pre-natal ideas in the backs of their heads. Every word that
is said and printed and written receives one meaning against
the background of one set of ideas, and another meaning
against the background of the other set of ideas. If you have
a week's conference, you can spend six days in trying to understand each other's back-of-the-head ideas. And if you
can get a little glimmer of an idea of what the other fellow is
really thinking about, then you can settle your difficulty in
five minutes.

These young men to whom I have referred come here, and
they are coming to our Bar by the hundreds, with continental
ideas born in them. No cramming for an examination will get
them out. They are not to be learned or dis-learned out of a
book. Those ideas can be modified or adapted to our ideas
only by contact with life, — contact with American life, —
taking in, during the processes of life, some conception of
what the American thought and feeling and underlying basis
of honesty and justice is.

Now, how can you get that kind of contact? The idea of this resolution, that the law school should require as one of its conditions for entrance two years in an American college, is an effort, and the only one that has been suggested, to require that these young men shall spend an appreciable time under such conditions that they will take in the morale of our country before they are admitted to the Bar.

I believe in the fundamental conceptions of justice and honor and good faith, out of which our American institutions grew. They were the conceptions that were wrought out by struggle and sacrifice during the long centuries of the Anglo-Saxon fight for freedom. They received a new birth, a new commission upon the American continent — an enlarged conception of individual liberty and manhood, of individual right, of justice, of duty to the state, of the common good, entertained by men who had no superiors, who looked up to no government above them, but *were* the government, through their own organization. That was the complex of conceptions that gave the formative power that has made this continent, that has carried the common law of England from ocean to ocean; that has made the individual enterprise of America, carried on by sovereign citizens, dealing with justice and rendering justice, a mightier force than the dictates of any empire or any sovereign.

I said a few moments ago that I do not criticize any continental view of jurisprudence. But I do take leave to say that we want *our* view here in this country to continue.

I do not want anybody to come to the Bar which I honor and revere, chartered by our government to aid in the administration of justice, who has not any conception of the moral qualities that underlie our free American institutions — and they are coming, to-day, by the hundreds.

I know of no way that has been suggested to assure to any considerable degree the achievement of such a view on the part of aspirants to the Bar, except this suggestion that they should be required to go to an American college for two years and mingle with the young American boys and girls in those colleges, be a part of their life, and learn something of the community spirit of our land, at its best; learn something of the spirit of young America in its aspiration and its ambition, seeking to fit itself for greater things. That is what they will get in an American college.

Somebody sent me the other day a card that had been circulated from some night school suggesting that this was a snobbish proposal. He who sent it knew little of the American college. We are told that this will keep poor young men out. Keep them out! Do you suppose such a thing would have kept Lincoln out? I have been, within the last year, to three American universities, each one of which had over 11,000 students. I never saw a more inspiring spectacle than I did in going into the great reading-room in the University of California and seeing there from a thousand to two thousand young men and women all at work, reading. My heart grew lighter in its view of the future in the faith of that spectacle!

I know American colleges, and I have seen for sixty years the plain boys trudging over the hills to get an education, in order that they might climb the heights of fame and fortune, in order that they might slake the thirst for learning, in order that they might make themselves something bigger and better; and I say to you there is no better democracy in this world than the democracy of the American college. And that is the great thing that is learned there; for in it the youth pass the most formative years of their lives before the spectacle of men who are happy in the pursuit of learning and of literature and of science — happy in their growth and achievements — without money, without display, without ostentation. There are to-day over 600,000 young Americans in these institutions. And can you tell me that a boy who is worth his salt, who is fit ever to have a client, who has the character that will enable him to assert and maintain rights, cannot find his way to one of those institutions and spend two years there? If he cannot, he does not belong in the Bar.

One other thing: Whence come these 600,000? Observe, that means every year that more young Americans are going into these institutions than there are in the whole Bar of the United States. They could duplicate the Bar of the United States every year, if all the youngsters that came out went into the Bar. Whence come they? They come from the people of every calling, all over our land, of every condition, from parents who are working hard to educate their children, and from conditions of life where the child has to serve itself. They are coming in response to the universal feeling of the American people that they must make progress. That is where these 600,000 come from. They come from a people who mean to do better, to be better, to be stronger, to do great and greater things.

Is the Bar alone to be free from that noble feeling? The Bar, which deems itself the guardian of the most sacred rights of humanity? Is the Bar to sit silent, passing futile resolutions, expressing pious hopes, and unwilling that its ranks shall be elevated by marching side by side with all the rest of the great and aspiring American people?

There is no trouble about a young man getting a college education in this country to-day — not the least. There is money enough wasted by incompetent, slovenly, ignorant practice, keeping honest men out of their rights, filling up the time of the courts, frustrating efforts at more prompt disposal of cases, and the granting of justice — there is more money wasted each year than would be necessary to pay for the education in college of all the men who will apply for admission to the American Bar for the next twenty-five years.

What is all this for? What is the vital consideration underlying all the efforts of the American Bar? We are commissioned by the state to render a service. What we have been talking about is the way of ascertaining or of producing competency to render that service. Upon what standard of judgment shall we consider and attempt to do that? Of our rights? Of the rights of the young men who come here crowding to the gates of our Bar? Is it a privilege to be passed around, a benefit to be conferred? Is there any doubt that that standard is inadmissible? Do we not all reject it?

The standard of public service is the standard of the Bar, if the Bar is to live; the maintenance of justice, the rendering of justice to rich and poor alike; prompt, inexpensive, efficient justice.

Shall we turn our backs on an effort to secure better public service, and go away and congratulate ourselves on the preservation of the privilege of charging fees for services, without regard to the great duty, the great obligation, the great responsibility, that our privilege carries with it?

The Bar of America has been fumbling for years, through the American Bar Association and state associations and local associations and in private conference and in public address, to find some way to render the public service that we all know we are bound to render, and that we all feel we are not rendering satisfactorily; and this is the one concrete and practical step proposed for the accomplishment of that purpose.

I hope that we shall have the enthusiastic and effective support of all the Bar associations of the country in the maintenance of that standard.

[February 24, after extended debate.]

Mr. Chairman, I have to leave in ten minutes to take a train; may I ask the indulgence of this body to use five minutes of that time? There have been two kinds of suggestions made in opposition to the approval of the action taken by the American Bar Association. One is in recognition of the serious evil with which our Bar ought to deal. The evidence that has been produced from many lips here during the past two days shows that this nation, more than one half of which has come to live in cities where men know little of each other, can no longer maintain a Bar of the quality and character that has built up this republic in accordance with the customs and usages of earlier and simpler times when men lived in rural communities and knew all about each other. But the recognition of that fact distinctly made, for example, by the gentleman from Florida, who proposed the substitute a few minutes ago, is accompanied by a pious hope, a resolution wholly ineffective to cure anything, just such as we have been having for a quarter of a century before the American Bar Association finally came to a concrete conclusion, which, if adopted, will accomplish something. I think that the proposal of my friend from Delaware, Mr. Marvel, is of the same general character. It is to approve the standard but remove the standard at the same time. Now, for heaven's sake, do not let us stultify ourselves. If there is something wrong, as there certainly is, let us deal with it, and not use weasel words about it.

Another class of objection was illustrated this forenoon by my friend, the former Senator from Colorado, Mr. Thomas, for whom I have had for forty years or more, since we first met in the Supreme Court of the United States, not only great admiration, but warm friendship. Now my good friend was responding not to a study of this subject, but to the natural reaction of a man who rather dislikes to have the old traditions of his life interfered with by somebody else.

I am willing to admit that if you concentrate your attention, as he did, upon Thomas and me, you do not need any cure. We are too old to be anything else. Whenever trouble comes, it comes in the fact that this Bar of ours is being filled up to the brim at every term of court by thousands of young men whom nobody knows anything about. And the question is how to get a line on them so that you can keep the fellows out that are merely trying to get an opportunity to blackmail and grind the face of the poor, merely seeking an opportunity for more successful fraud and chicanery by having a law shingle. How can you let in the good fellows, the earnest, sincere fellows, and keep out the black scoundrels of the future? I have not heard any suggestion that takes the place of saying that you shall have a period, in the nature of a period of probation, where two things shall happen to you: where you shall be under the observation of men whose testimony regarding your daily walk and conversation will be accepted as proving whether you are the right stuff or not; and the other, that you shall be under such conditions that you will be taking in through the pores of your skin American life and American thought and feeling.

My friend Thomas did not do himself justice in the story about the banker who said, "Damn your religion, show us your collateral." That is not his character. That did not come from Thomas. That did not come from his heart. It came from the nature of the proposition that he was arguing; and I am against it. God forbid that that shall be the principle applied to building up the American Bar of the future! Above all the stocks and bonds that can be made into collateral, stands as a guaranty of the future of our great and prosperous country the character of the men who come to be called to the Bar. I hope sincerely that this Conference of men who hold dear the good name and the prosperity and the moral qualities of the communities and states from which they come will not here vote to stop the only effort the Bar has ever made to answer the prayers of the good people who want our country better, and to answer the terrible responsibility that rests upon it to maintain the free institutions which are to perpetuate liberty and order in our dear country.

All that the opposition here comes to is simply to stop, to stop! to do nothing! stop the American Bar Association, disapprove them, tell them they should do nothing! How much better, instead of beating over the prejudices and memories of a past that is gone, it is to take dear old Edward Everett Hale's maxim, "Look forward, not back; look upward, not down, and lend a hand." [1]

[1] Thereupon the resolutions were approved.

THE RESTATEMENT OF THE
SUBSTANTIVE LAW

OPENING ADDRESS AS CHAIRMAN OF THE BENCH AND BAR MEETING TO ORGANIZE THE AMERICAN LAW INSTITUTE AT WASHINGTON, FEBRUARY 23, 1923

For many years, American lawyers and judges have been much impressed by the volume of judicial decisions of both the Federal and State Courts. Matters have come to the point where it is impossible for any one person to read the mass of reported decisions published during the year, even if he should devote his entire time to this ungrateful task.

Lawyers and judges have apparently approached the codification of the common law with reluctance, whereas the lawyers and judges of the Continent of Europe have welcomed and coöperated in the codification of the law of their various countries. As it is, the comparatively few principles of the law are in danger of being lost in the reams of judicial decisions. "We cannot see the forest for the trees." Law is suffering, and the administration of justice, with a lack of confidence in both on the part of the public.

Thanks to the initiative of the Association of American Law Schools, a Committee was appointed, May 10, 1922, on the Establishment of a Permanent Organization for the Improvement of the Law, the object of the Committee being "to make a report on the establishment of such an organization, its constitution, and the specific work which should be first undertaken," and the submission of the report to a representative gathering of the American Bar.

This representative meeting of the American Bar was held in the City of Washington on the 23rd of February, 1923, at which time and place, Mr. Root, Chairman of the Committee, delivered the following address.

For an account of the American Law Institute, its purpose and organization, see *The American Law Institute, Proceedings*, Volume I (1923).

GENTLEMEN of the Bench and Bar of the United States: It is an inspiring and cheerful spectacle upon which I now gaze, the spectacle of men eminent in the great profession of the law, who have come from high station and leadership in practice in the various courts of our country and from all parts of the Union, to participate in a conference upon the improvement of the law.

I have been requested by the Committee to make a brief statement in explanation of the proceedings which bring us

to the point where we are now. Most of you know that for
many years we have been talking, in the American Bar Association and in many State Bar Associations, about the increasing complexity and confusion of the substantive law
which is applied in all our states and in the Federal courts.
We have been talking about it. We have had committees
appointed; but nothing has been done; and about a year ago a
number of gentlemen interested in the subject began to consult as to whether something could not be done, and how it
could be done. It was apparent that the confusion, the uncertainty, was growing worse from year to year. It was apparent that the vast multitude of decisions which our prac-
titioners are obliged to consult was reaching a magnitude
which made it impossible in ordinary practice to consult
them. It was apparent that, whatever authority might be
found for one view of the law upon any topic, other authorities could be found for a different view upon the same topic.
The great number of books, the enormous amount of litigation, the struggles of the courts to avoid too strict an application of the rule of *stare decisis*, the fact that the law had become so vast and complicated that the conditions of ordinary
practice and ordinary judicial duty made it impossible to
make adequate examinations — all these had tended to
create a situation where the law was becoming guesswork.

You will find in the paper which has been distributed the
statement that a count made in 1917 showed 175,000 pages
of reported decisions in the United States, as against 7,000 in
Great Britain. Three years before that I had a count made in
the Library of Congress, the result of which I have often
stated. It showed that during the five years preceding 1914
over 62,000 statutes had been passed and included in the
printed volumes of laws in the United States, and that during
the same five years over 65,000 decisions of courts of last
resort had been delivered and included in the printed volumes of reports. And still it goes on.

It was evident that the time would presently come, unless something were done, when courts would be forced practically to decide cases, not upon authority but upon the impression of the moment, and that we should ultimately come to the law of the Turkish Kadi, where a good man decides under good impulses and a bad man decides under bad impulses, as the case may be; and that our law, as a system, would have sunk below the horizon. and the basis of our institutions would have disappeared.

The result of the conference was, first, to consider an attempt to secure a great meeting of representatives of the bar from all over the country; and then the suggestion was made that the meeting would have nothing to do of practical effect, because they would have nothing to work on, and that they would be driven to appoint a committee to study the subject and to report upon it at a further meeting. It was also suggested that for such a purpose, merely to come together and appoint a committee, it would be impossible to secure attendance from all parts of the country of the men who ought to be in such a meeting; and accordingly it was determined to constitute such a committee as everybody knew such a meeting would constitute, and to let them make a thorough, exhaustive study of this problem — How can the work of restating the substantive law, in clear and simple terms and in authentic form, be performed?

Accordingly, such a committee was got together. They secured funds, they employed competent and experienced assistants, and for nearly a year the work has been conducted; and the result of the work is this report which we make to this meeting as if we had been appointed by you to make this study and report, asking you to receive it and to consider it and act upon it.

Copies of the report have been circulated, sent, I think, to each one of you in sufficient time for you to have an opportunity to read it, and I assume it will not be necessary to spend the day in re-reading it here. The idea of the report is that, if we can get a statement of the law so well done as to be generally acceptable and made the basis for judicial consideration, we shall have accomplished at the outset a very great advance.

We recall the part played in judicial decisions by what Judge Story said, not only in his decisions, but in his textbooks and in his writings; the part played in judicial decision by what Chancellor Kent said in his great work. To take recent instances, take the work on equity written by John Norton Pomeroy. I have not followed the reports closely enough to know whether it still continues, but for a good many years after the publication of that work the courts quoted what he said with practically the effect with which they would have quoted a great judicial decision.

There is a work now which is playing the same part, Mr. Williston's work on contracts, which is being quoted in the same way.

Now, if you can have the law systematically, scientifically stated, the principles stated by competent men, giving their discussions of the theories upon which their statements are based, giving a presentation and discussion of all the judicial decisions upon which their statements are based, and if such a statement can be revised and criticized and tested by a competent group of lawyers of eminence, and when their work is done, if their conclusions can be submitted to the bar that we have here, if that can be done when the work is completed, we shall have a statement of the common law of America which will be the *prima facie* basis on which judicial action will rest; and any lawyer, whose interest in litigation requires him to say that a different view of the law shall be taken, will have upon his shoulders the burden to overturn the statement.

Instead of going back through ten thousand cases, it will have been done for him; there will be, not a conclusive presumption, but a practical *prima facie* statement, upon which, unless it is overturned, judgment may rest.

If such a thing is done, it will tend to assert itself and to confirm itself and to gather authority as time goes on. Of course it cannot be final, for times are continually changing and new conditions arise, and there will have to be revision after revision; but we shall have dealt with the past and shall have got this old man of the sea off our shoulders in a great measure.

It is a great work. It is a work before which anyone might well become discouraged. Unless the work can be done greatly, it is worthless. It is of no use to produce another digest, another cyclopedia. That kind of work is being done admirably. It is of no use to duplicate the work of the West Publishing Company, which has done so well. It must be so done as to carry authority, as to carry conviction of impartial judgment upon the most thorough scientific investigation and tested accuracy of statement.

Can it be done? If it cannot, why we must go on through this swamp of decisions with consequences which we cannot but dread. The great work of the Roman law had imperial power behind it; Theodosius and Justinian could command, and all the resources of a great empire responded. In the simpler and narrower work of the Code Napoleon, again, imperial will put motive power behind the enterprise. What have we? No legislature, no Congress can command; no individual can do the work. Men who come and go, who spend a little time from their ordinary occupations, and go, cannot accomplish it.

Means must be raised for an adequate force, for continuous application. Participation in the enterprise must be deemed highly honorable. Selection for participation must be deemed to confer distinction, it must be recognized as a great and imperative public service. How can it be done? It can be done only if the public opinion of the American democracy recognizes the need of the service, and that public opinion you here to-day represent and can awaken and direct.

That is why the Committee solicited your attendance here, to ask you whether you will put all that you represent behind the undertaking, so that the American democracy may be behind it.

You will perceive that it is a simple task in statement, that it stands by itself, and that the organization required is an organization specifically adapted to this particular work.

I have received a number of letters from friends in various parts of the country suggesting that certain other things ought to be done, especially that there should be a reform of the administration of the law, that there should be a reform of the criminal law. To that I agree, we all must agree. But that is another story. The American Judicature Society, a most excellent institution, is addressing itself to the subject of administration. There is a most excellent society in connection with the criminal law, which is dealing with criminal law. The trouble with the criminal law is chiefly a trouble of administration. In both branches of the law, civil and criminal, there are these existing organizations, which it is not desirable to duplicate or to substitute ourselves for; but further than that, to deal with defects of administration, great defects, requires an organization especially adapted to that purpose, and quite a different organization from one which would be available and effective for this purpose of the scientific study and restatement of the substantive law.

Defects in administration have been receiving the attention of the American Bar Association and of most of our State Bar Associations for many years. The trouble with reforming them comes when you run against the legislative bodies that have the power to pass the laws necessary to reform them. In my own state most thorough and excellent work has been done on the subject; and when it runs up against the legislature, there is always some little thing that the reform hitches on and fails to make progress, and the legislature adjourns without action; and that goes on year after year.

I busied myself for years in the Senate of the United States in trying to get through reforms in procedure that had been discussed and recommended over and over again by the American Bar Association. Quite often I would get a favorable report from the Judiciary Committee; but always there was some little difficulty which prevented their being enacted into law; and the trouble is plain, that the motive power behind the demand for reform is not strong enough. You get the real motive power of a people that demand reform behind the demand and no little hitch will occur in the legislature, either of the state or of the nation.

But while we are all for reform, we are mildly for reform; we do not put any beef behind it, we do not put any power behind it. Nobody is in danger of being run over by it if he gets in the way. That is the trouble with the demands for reform of judicial procedure, civil and criminal, because almost anyone in the State Legislature or the National Congress can stand in the way and stop it without danger of consequences to himself.

Perhaps we can help. The gathering of the distinguished leaders of opinion of America here in this hall to-day will help; the making of a permanent organization to accomplish this restatement of the law, with the earnest and real interest in the subject on the part of real men, will help; and as time goes on, the organization which you have made may accomplish such relations with other organizations and take on such additional duties, and avail itself of such opportunities, as to aid all along the line in the reform of law and the reform of procedure. But at present it seems plain that the thing to do is to form an organization adapted to this specific thing. Institutions which try to do everything do nothing. This great, difficult task will be load enough for us to carry if we can carry it.

Gentlemen, many competent observers, many thoughtful students of history, are beginning to fear that the competency of mankind to govern is not keeping pace in its development with the ever-increasing complexity of life in this new era of universal interdependence.

I have faith that our people will prove themselves equal to the ever-growing, ever-increasing demands upon them, of life, in these strange new years. I have faith; but they cannot do it by lying down. No free people, no democracy — and I include in this the American democracy — can maintain its institutions, its freedom, its justice, its opportunity for the future, unless there be general, practically universal effort, willingness to serve, desire for knowledge, determination to grapple with and deal with the difficult problems that confront humanity.

We may not succeed; but we can try. Here is one thing we can try It is something the need of which is universally recognized. It is something the responsibility for which rests especially upon us. It points the pathway where we shall be acknowledged the natural leaders of the democracy in its struggles toward better life, toward permanency of institutions. If we fail, who shall succeed? And if none succeed what becomes of the law which we are, each one of us, from day to day, appealing to, and demanding the application of, in the interests of our clients? What becomes of the great system of American law to which we have undertaken to devote our lives?

III

THE WAR AND READJUSTMENT

LETTER TO THE PRESIDENT OF THE NATIONAL SECURITY LEAGUE

The National Security League was organized in December, 1914, "to promote patriotic education and national sentiment and service among the people of the United States." From the date of its organization until the entry of the United States into the World War it advocated preparedness in the sense of universal military training. At the same time, it advocated patriotism through education. In the Report of the Security League for 1920, it is stated that "during the period that we were at war, the character of the League's work was symbolized by the slogans ' Win-the-War ' and ' Peace by Victory.' . . . After the Armistice, the subject of ' Americanization,' with all that the word implies, was the obvious mission of the League."

It was organized by S. Stanwood Menken, Esquire, of New York City. Robert Bacon was its first permanent President. Joseph H. Choate, its first Honorary President, was succeeded after his death by Mr. Root.

February 16, 1918

My dear Mr. Menken, —

As you know, I am unavoidably detained from the National Security Meeting on the 21st. I regret it very much, and I send you my best wishes for an inspiring and strengthening conference.

There are several things I had intended to say. One is about the relation between peace talk and fighting. There has been much recent discussion of terms of peace, not between the belligerents, but by the heads of governments making addresses to their own people. There have been two recent addresses to Congress by our own President, stating in the most admirable and statesmanlike way what the people of the United States are fighting for and will insist upon. Of course, the newspapers are filled with discussions of these addresses, with headlines from which one might infer that negotiations for peace are going on. Such an infer-

ence would be a great mistake. Such addresses are primarily
designed to make the peoples of the respective belligerents
understand clearly the position occupied by their own governments. In the meantime, the position which Germany
assumes does not come within a thousand miles of that assumed by the Government of the United States and agreed to
by our Allies. The things which we are fighting for and shall
insist upon Germany will not consider or discuss at all. The
things which Germany will insist upon we shall not consider
or discuss at all. There are not only no negotiations, but
there is no basis for negotiation. It is moreover perfectly
clear that Germany will not abandon her present position and
recede to a position which will make peace negotiation possible until she has had a thorough whipping, which we and
our Allies must give her, and shall give her; but that can be
done only by tremendous fighting and great loss of life and
suffering and sacrifice, and to do this fighting we must strain
every nerve and exert all our powers. We must not forget
that the statements of our peace terms mean not peace but
war until Germany is beaten into accepting them. We must
be careful that newspaper headlines about peace terms do not
distract our attention from the intense concentration of
effort upon war necessary to carry our country through the
supreme test of her power to maintain her liberty. Let us be
warned by poor Russia's present position. The Bolsheviki
were very eloquent about peace "without annexation or indemnities," and they filled the minds of Russian soldiers and
workmen with that idea to such an extent that they stopped
fighting and making munitions but when they got to Brest-
Litovsk, they found what the leaders probably knew all
along — that Germany had no intention of making any such
peace.[1] She wanted the Baltic provinces of Russia, and she

[1] On December 15, 1917, the then Imperial German Government, flushed with
victory, concluded an armistice with Russia, to go into effect December 17, 1917.

seized them and proposes to keep them; and Russia having stopped fighting in favor of the kind of peace she admired, finds herself in a position where, for the present, she has nothing whatever to say about the kind of peace there shall be. We must beware of anything in the remotest degree approaching that.

Another thing I wanted to say was about the effect of criticism on the conduct of the war. Of course, there have been mistakes and shortcomings. It would be a miracle if there were not. Everybody agrees to that. Nor is there any doubt that, when there are mistakes and shortcomings it is a good thing to have them pointed out. Sincere and constructive criticism of executive conduct is a very useful thing. But we must all be careful that neither shortcoming nor criticism tends in the slightest degree to divert or decrease the heartiness with which we al support and reinforce the President and his civil and military officers in carrying on this war.

Abraham Lincoln said something on this subject during the Civil War which is worth recalling now. He was speaking to the 164th Ohio Infantry in September 1864. He said: —

There may be mistakes made. Sometimes things may be done wrong, while the officers of the Government do all they can to prevent mistakes; but I beg of you as citizens of this great Republic not to let your minds be carried off from the great work we have before us.

The struggle is too large for you to be diverted from it by any small matter. When you return to your homes, rise up to the dignity of a generation of men worthy of a free government, and we will carry out the work we have commenced.

A series of treaties was concluded at Brest-Litovsk, March 3, 1918, between Russia and Germany and its allies. It was a peace imposed by the conqueror, and its terms were extraordinarily harsh.

The "Peace of Bucharest" of May 7, 1918, was imposed upon Rumania, which had, on August 27, 1916, entered the war on the side of the Allied and Associated Powers. It was likewise the peace of the conqueror.

These various treaties were declared null, void, and of no effect by Articles 290, 292, of the Treaty of Versailles, imposed upon Germany and signed on June 28, 1919.

That is the great thing — not to allow small irritations and petty prejudices and personal predilections to weaken our main purpose and prevent us from rising to this great occasion. This war must be fought and won by the power and momentum of this People moving, solid and wholehearted, behind the President at Washington, and not otherwise. This is to be the big hour of American life. God grant we may all be fit for it. May the spirit of the Second Inaugural rest upon your meeting.

Fondly do we hope, fervently do we pray that this mighty scourge of war may soon pass away.

Yet, if God wills that it continue until all the wealth piled by the bondsman's two hundred and fifty years of unrequited toil shall be sunk, and until every drop of blood drawn by the lash shall be paid by another drawn with the sword, as was said three thousand years ago, so still it must be said, "The Judgments of the Lord are true and righteous altogether."

With malice towards none, with charity for all, with firmness in the right, as God gives us to see the right, let us strive on to finish the work we are in; to bind up the nation's wounds; to care for him who shall have borne the battle, and for his widow and for his orphan; to do all which may achieve and cherish a just and lasting peace among ourselves, and with all nations.

    With kind regards and good wishes,

I am,

Always faithfully yours,

ELIHU ROOT

S. STANWOOD MENKEN, ESQ.,
    President.

SPEECH AT A MEETING IN HONOR OF THE ARCHBISHOP OF YORK, NEW YORK CITY

MARCH 7, 1918

The Most Reverend Cosmo Gordon Lang, Archbishop of York since 1908, visited the United States in the early part of 1918. A large and representative body of American citizens met in Carnegie Hall on the evening of March 7, 1918, to do him honor — among them the Governor of the State of New York. On this occasion and under these circumstances, Mr. Root delivered the following address.

ONCE before a message of the brotherhood of free self-governing peoples has come from Britain to the United States. The people of northern England, those who lived upon their labor in the manufacture of cotton fabrics from the staple produced in the Southern States, deprived of their raw material during our civil war, were thrown out of employment and the men and women and little children were thrown into poverty and hunger and suffering in the province of my Lord, the Archbishop.

Long the people of Europe doubted where was the right in our civil struggle; but when Lincoln had declared that the slaves should be free, the men of Manchester doubted no longer, and in a great meeting upon the last day of that dark year 1862, six thousand of them sent a message to Lincoln, saying that now they were sure that the victory of the Union forces meant striking the shackles from the slave, they were with the North with all their hearts. Let me read to you Lincoln's reply, or an extract from it. He said:

I know and deeply deplore the sufferings which the working men of Manchester and in all Europe are called to endure in this crisis. It has been often and studiously represented that the attempt to overthrow this government, which was built upon the foundation of human rights, and to substitute for it one which should rest exclusively on the basis of human slavery, was likely to obtain the favor of Europe. Through the action of our disloyal citizens, the working men of Europe have been subjected to severe trials for the purpose of forcing their sanction to that attempt. Under these circumstances I cannot but regard your decisive utterances upon the question as an instance of sublime Christian heroism, which has not been surpassed in any age or in any country. It is indeed an energetic and reinspiring assurance of the inherent power of truth and the ultimate and universal triumph of justice, humanity and freedom. I do not doubt that the sentiments you have expressed will be sustained by your great nation, and on the other hand I have no hesitation in assuring you that they will excite admiration, esteem and the most reciprocal feelings of friendship among the American people. I hail this interchange of sentiment, therefore, as an augury that whatever else may happen, whatever misfortune may befall your country or my own, the peace and friendship which now exists between the two nations will be, as it shall be my desire to make them, perpetual.

My Lord Archbishop, we now, in common with the people of Lincoln's land, renew to you, and through you to the men of Manchester and their countrymen, the pledge that Lincoln gave. They were speaking of striking the shackles from the slaves, a freedom for others, but we speak now of freedom for the men of Manchester themselves and the men of Lincoln's America themselves, for their children and our children in all time to come. We are with you in heart and soul, in judgment and conviction, in purpose and determination, proud to be with the men who have shown the manhood, the high courage, the self-devotion, the willingness to die for liberty, that the men of Great Britain have shown in these times. We are proud that our laws, our system of justice, our conception of liberty, our customs came from those fathers out of whose loins sprang the men in the trenches upon the British line.

Joseph de Maistre said many years ago: "One's country is an association upon the same soil of the living and the dead with all who are yet to be born." The association with the dead; loyalty to their memories by a free people scorning to be false to the ideals for which their fathers gone before have suffered and sacrificed. An association with those yet to be born, that nobility of character which forbids the self-respecting free man to fail to hand down to his children and his children's children the liberty and justice which he has inherited. It is these which bind together the people of a country, and not geographical expression or political lines; and if that be true, as it is true, then, my Lord, you are our countryman. For we cherish and owe from our hearts loyalty to the same dead. Your liberty and ours were one. It is one liberty; it was won by the long struggles of the centuries in which Anglo-Saxon freedom was beaten out. You and I and all of us owe our fealty to the example of those barons at Runnimede who extorted the great charter from the hands of John. You and I and all of us owe the same loyalty to Pym and Hampden and Eliot, the men who stood for the great gift to mankind of representative government. Washington and Franklin, equally with Chatham and Burke, were the inheritors of that great tradition of individual manhood and personal independence. And when in that great Civil War for the freedom of the race in Britain and America, which we call the Revolution, we wrote into our Declaration of Independence the fundamental principle that men are entitled to unalienable rights, among which are life, liberty and the pursuit of happiness, and that governments are created to secure those rights, we stated principles which have made Britain great, as well as the principles which have made America great. And now the inheritors of the same great traditions, in the peaceful enjoyment of the same conception of liberty and justice, we are called upon alike to win them again. In loyalty to the same dead, we, the living, undertake the same task; the same duty rests upon us. And for the future your children and ours depend upon the same struggle; for if the German conception of government is to control in this world, your children and ours will not be free.

We understand what it means. I am ashamed to talk about it, because we have talked so much; but we are acting about it; gradually, step by step, Britain came to understand what it meant, and gradually, step by step, the people of the United States have come to understand what it means — that the principles of Anglo-Saxon and American liberty and justice are denied by the greatest military power the world has ever known. They will be cast out and no longer have a place in the world, unless that power is stricken down. And it can be stricken down only by force of arms, not by negotiations, not by argument, not by settlement or adjustment, only by the strong arm of military force. It will mean vast sacrifice, and still more sacrifice; suffering and still more suffering; death lamentable to contemplate. "We shall drain our dearest veins, but they shall be free."

Is it strange that a clergyman should come upon this mission of war? Ah, no! The struggle is more than political. It is a struggle for the overthrow or the maintenance of all the progress that the civilization of a century has made toward Christianity. All, every step, by which kindly and enlightened men during this past hundred years have sought to bring the practice of nations nearer to the principles of the Christian religion, every step is to be retraced if Germany wins. It means the renewed ascendancy of the cruel and brutal and conscienceless power of a dark and horrid past, a wicked and heathen past, taking the place of that Christianity which we fondly hoped we were, little by little, approaching in these years.

No one has so much reason to protest, to cry the alarm, to rally his people, to urge resistance, as the man who gives his life that God's kingdom may come upon earth.

This war is not a war about boundaries or provinces or the distribution of territory; it is not a war in which we are entering because ships were sunk or because plots have been laid

and carried on within our boundaries or because attempts
have been made to foment attacks and partition our territory; it is not a war for Serbia or Alsace-Lorraine or Poland
or even for Belgium — it is a war between Odin and Christ.
It is a war to determine whether this world shall go back
under the Dominion of the Prince of Darkness, out of the
light back again to days of despair and ignorance and slavery,
or whether the good God who is just and compassionate may
still smile upon a world where He is worshipped in spirit and
in truth. There can be no half-way measures. There is no
other issue but this: Shall the German principle of evil, dark,
cruel, pagan, control this world and oppress our children?

[A Voice: It shall not.]

No, it shall not.

My Lord, please tell your people when you return that the
one hundred millions of America are not weaklings. They
are awake at last. They were slow to part with their peace,
but they are awake at last, and they are preparing to fight,
going to fight, beginning to fight, and will continue to fight,
with all the dogged persistency, the bull-dog courage, the incapacity to realize defeat, the unwillingness to realize defeat,
and therefore the capacity for victory which we rightly inherit from the men who made the liberty of the Anglo-Saxon
race.

SPEECH BEFORE THE NATIONAL SECURITY LEAGUE IN PHILADELPHIA

APRIL 24, 1918

I HAVE become honorary president of the National Security League partly because it was the thing at hand to do, and to satisfy an urgent longing to play some part in the great struggle of the ages in which we are engaged; partly to pay a debt of loyalty and affection to that dear and noble friend who was the first honorary president of the League, its adviser and its mainstay in all the time of its early struggles and efforts, Joseph H. Choate. I never respond to a call from that man of tremendous organizing capacity, who is the active President of the League, Mr. Menken, without feeling that Choate has called me and I am answering him.

I am bound to confess to you that I am so tired of talking and of hearing talk that it is difficult for me to reconcile myself to it. I have the feeling that we in America have talked so much that it is time to shut up and make good; that we should point to things done, not talk about what we are going to do; and the only justification for talking that I can see now is as a means of doing something more effectively. I felt, as many of us did when war was at last declared and the die was cast, as if a great thing was accomplished. I know that probably all of us here felt, when the bill for universal training and then for the selective draft was passed, that the great thing had been accomplished and now we would move on. I felt, when the first Liberty Loan was oversubscribed, that the die was cast again and a great thing had been done; and when the second Loan was accomplished, that the future was secure. Nevertheless, when we come to count up our advance, we see the hills rising before us, still, ever. It is a long and weary road upon which we have entered, and we shall not come to the end of it except by continued struggle and effort and sacrifice.

I have been much impressed by the effect produced upon the people of this country by what Germany has done in Russia. Germany did in Russia nothing but what I assumed she would do as a matter of course. It did not impress me much. She did what I knew she was going to do, and what I supposed everybody else knew she was going to do, but it evidently has struck great masses of people all over the world with a new sense of German professions regarding annexations and indemnities and the self-determination of peoples; and I realized in thinking about it that, while I had been convinced long ago of what Germany meant and what her domination would make certain, while I had been talking about it day after day and month after month and year after year, to people who seemed to agree with me, they did not really appreciate, understand, and feel it. I think that the effect of what Germany has done upon the minds of our people shows that, up to the time of that action of Germany, a great part of our people did not really feel in their hearts what Germany actually wants, did not really understand that the domination of Germany meant the death of liberty for the world. That should be a lesson to us. The people of this country have been gradually, very gradually, very slowly, moving toward that complete understanding. We are too apt to impute to all the rest of the world the same views that we have ourselves, the same estimate of affairs that we have ourselves; but the fact is that it is only very recently that a majority of the people of the United States have come to a true understanding upon this matter so vital to our future, and there still remain great masses of people in the United States, masses gathered together, and enormous numbers scattered throughout the country, who have not come to that understanding. It is vital to us that they should.

There are two things which we should understand about this war. One is that it has become a war to be won or lost by the exercise of moral qualities. In this great struggle between the principles of Christian civilization and the principles of pagan cruelty and brutal force, that party is to win which has to the last the higher courage, the stronger determination, the more inflexible will, and the greater capacity for sacrifice and self-devotion. These moral forces are not to be the mere forces of sentimentalism, not forces which spend their strength in words, in sympathies, but they must be forces which move the concrete, which are directed effectively toward the creation and the application of physical force. Civilization, which has been for so many generations elevating the conception of morals, the conception of humanity, of kindliness, of justice, of compassion, is brought face to face with the physical force which will make the exercise of those qualities impossible, because the liberty in which only they can exist, will be destroyed unless that force is met by force; and the moral qualities which are to win this war must be qualities which are effectively exercised in the creation and the maintenance of force. To win this war upon the battlefield, we have to win it by victory in arms against an enemy in arms, and the moral quality will win because it creates and maintains and energizes and makes effective the physical force that it stands behind.

There are two ways in which the moral forces of this country are to be exercised. One is in the furnishing of money, in the furnishing of men, in the building of ships, in the building of aeroplanes, the furnishing of all the material supplies of war. There is another. Money can be wasted. Money is wasted. It is inevitable that it should be. Men may remain idle. Ships may not be completed, may not be launched.

Aeroplanes may go wrong, machinery may go wrong. Nothing can be done by all the tremendous forces that have been liberated in this country by the slowly growing sense of national peril and national duty, except through that great machine that exists in Washington, which is calling out the men, carrying out the manufacture, laying the plans, putting troops upon the battle-line. And that machine is a representative machine. It does not work, as the German military autocracy does, of its own force for its own aggrandizement, for the extension of its own power. It is the representative of the people of the United States, and its vast, complicated operations cannot go on effectively without having behind them the driving power of the people of the United States.

No machinery works without somebody to work it. No great number of men engaged in complicated operations work together unless there is a driving power behind them; and we, you and I, the people outside these walls, in this great city, and outside of the city in this great State, in this vast country, have got to be this driving power in this, *our* war for *our* liberty. For that there must be no divided people. For that there must be through the length and breadth of the land a deep sense of the duty and a willingness for the sacrifice. We feel it. We have the sentiment, we have the feeling, we have the desire; but the work is not yet completed of carrying that sentiment, that feeling, and that desire throughout all the American people. No public feeling can become effectual without institutions to give it effect. It becomes but words that vanish in the air, or it becomes a mob that howls through the streets, without some definite, regular, coördinated machinery to give it effect. And if we are going on, if we are not going to allow our sentiment to vanish in the air, if we are not going to be satisfied with giving money, and sitting back congratulating ourselves, we have got to create, or assist in creating, the effective machinery to make every man and woman in the United States feel as we feel about the duty and the peril of this hour.

The National Security League was organized for the purpose of proffering to the people who were disturbed about the defenceless condition of the United States an organization, machinery, to give effect to their feeling, and it began two or three years ago to carry on a campaign for universal preparation for national defence. As it has progressed, it has found a keener appreciation of the necessity of its work. The requirement of further accomplishment has grown more rapidly than its accomplishment has grown, notwithstanding the passing of the act for universal service and for the selective draft, and it is now addressing itself to a systematic campaign of instruction, of edification, of exhortation here, and there, and there, and there, in the hundreds, in the thousands, in the tens of thousands of places in this country which have been found to be asleep or to be wrong upon these great and vital questions. It is working in a practical way. It has secured the coöperation of a great part of the educational institutions of the country, signally represented by Professor McElroy, the head of the department of political science of Princeton University, who has been loaned by the University to give his entire time to the organization and carrying on of the work of education. Great numbers of men from our universities and colleges are coming in, falling into the organization and engaging in this work. During this past month the League has had an exchange of instruction between Chicago and New York City. For a week, one week, two hours a day each day, in the city of New York thirty-one thousand teachers of the public schools were gathered by order, gathered to receive instruction in practical patriotism and the duties that lie before them. In the city of Chicago all the teachers of its public schools were gathered in the same way to listen to instruction coming from New York.

What has happened in Russia has caused a revulsion of feeling in a place where a few months ago there was, I suppose, a stronger opposition to the part of this country in the war against Germany than anywhere else between the Atlantic and Pacific, and that is the East Side of New York, which was peopled largely by Russians, largely by Russian Jews. The Russian Jews, bitter against the government of Russia, could not sympathize with Russia in the struggle, and being against Russia, their sympathies were practically and in effect with Germany. But what Germany has done in Russia, what they have never believed Germany would do because they did not believe what Germany was, opened their minds and their hearts and turned all that vast conclave of opposition to our country into enthusiastic support. There has been going on now for two weeks, a training school in the rooms of the Bar Association of New York, in which three hundred speakers, young men who had experience in recent political campaigns and had a knack for speaking, have been trained by men of experience and knowledge of the character of the East Side of New York, to go out on to the avenues of the East Side, on to the soap-box, and preach American patriotism against German militarism, to those men whose minds for the first time are opened.

That is what I mean by organization. That is what I mean by creating an institution through which sentiment and feeling can become effective. That is what this League is engaged in; and our hosts have called you here and have asked some of us who are familiar with the operations of the League to come here and talk to you, in the hope that you will have renewed determination to cash in your patriotic feelings, to turn them into concrete action, in order that there shall be no corner in this America of ours so dark that the light of patriotic purpose and courage and determination shall not enter in and give a new birth to its people.

Now it is only by making a united people, it is only by having the feeling universal, by having so strong a feeling, so earnest a desire, so stern a purpose to win this war upon the battlefield, that no politician will dare stand against it, that no casuist will dare argue against it, no coward will dare recoil from it, that this war can be won. It is not enough to speak, it is not enough to give money that may be wasted. Here is one more thing that you can do. You can get behind that organization which brings into force the power of the spirit to energize America to the winning of the war.

Now I have said what I came to say. I want to say one thing more. Do not be pessimistic. I hate to go to Washington, because so many people come and weep on my bosom and tell me about the things that are not done, the things that are delayed and postponed and that are wrongly done. That is true. It was doubtless inevitable. It is true, but many great things have been done. And many great things are being done. Please God, by the power of a great people, whose individual characters have been made strong by generations of liberty, the one great thing of winning the world for freedom will be done. You remember seeing a steam fire-engine go through a crowded street, a street through which it seems impossible that anybody or anything could go; and when the mighty power of the steam fire-engine comes, away go the crowds and through goes the engine. All the idlers and triflers, all the men who think they are getting along pretty well if they draw their pay and do a little something every day within office hours, all who are without a strong desire to move up further, will start for the wall when the mighty power of an aroused people, united universally in their determination that their work shall be done, makes itself manifest, pressing on the legions in Washington, whose action will give victory to the legions in Flanders.

ADDRESS AS CHAIRMAN OF THE ANNUAL MEETING OF THE NATIONAL SECURITY LEAGUE

NEW YORK CITY, MAY 8, 1918

THE length of the programme and the more important part of the performance to come, make it quite inappropriate that I should take the time to express all the grateful appreciation I have, of the honor which has been conferred upon me, on Mr. Menken's motion. There is a certain sadness about it; for I cannot help remembering that just a year ago there sat in the place of honorary president of this League that dear and noble friend, that democratic gentleman, that pure leader of opinion, of righteousness, of idealism in America, Joseph H. Choate. He has gone to his rest, leaving not only a blessed memory, but a lesson; for he gave the last remaining strength of his old age to the service of his country, as truly as the youth who falls in the trenches. I love to think that his spirit pervades this League which is met here tonight; that the sincerity of his purpose runs through all its efforts.

It is a League for National Security. There are others, there are many other organizations most admirable and efficient, under various similar names, each doing noble service to the country in its own way, and leading toward the same result. For national unity, for Americanism, for public defence, for national security, whatever the names may be, they are all the working out of the patriotism of our American citizens, accustomed to individual enterprise and individual independence, seeking to bring the power of general universal organization to our dear country in the trial which has come upon it.

Abraham Lincoln said that it had long been a grave question whether any government not too strong for the liberties of its people could be strong enough to maintain itself in the presence of a great emergency. That is the test which is being applied to us now. Is the government of the American democracy strong enough although not too strong for the liberties of its people? The government handed down to us by our fathers, the government under which we have enjoyed liberty of conscience, of political faith, personal independence; under which we have had security for the fruits of enterprise and industry, opportunity for the education of our people; under which we have known no superior; under which every man and every woman has been a sovereign in the independence of individual liberty — is that government, because it has been free, because it has left its people free, free men, free women — is it for that reason too weak to maintain itself in the presence of this great emergency?

That is the question we are to answer, you and I, not the men in the trenches alone, but you and I. And answer we must, with stout hearts, to back them up as they risk and sacrifice their lives, or with faint hearts to leave them unsupported. We must answer it with faith, faith in our fathers and our fathers' God; with courage, the courage that braved the seas and fought the savage and tamed the wilderness and built this mighty nation; the high courage that fears the face of no man — or with craven hearts surrendering our birthrights. We must answer it with determination that will outlast all discouragement, all doubt and pessimism, determined to win, and to win by force of arms; to win by the power and manhood of this great virile nation. And we must answer it with honor. Lincoln's test is before us, for good reasons, because we saw, and because those in whom the power had been placed to look out and to see into the future, for the safety and preservation of the American people, saw that the time had come when America must fight again for her freedom; and so we have entered upon this terrible war.

There are but two ways out of it. One is humiliation, retreat and slavery — for it will be slavery. The people of Russia have found what it meant to yield to Germany. The people of the Ukraine are finding out to-day what it means to yield to Germany. If we retreat, if we surrender, we shall learn what it means to become a people subject to the arrogant and brutal power of that military caste, which seeks to dominate the world by force of arms. And the other way! The other way is by the power of the manhood of this one hundred million people; by the unstinted use of the wealth that we have been piling up, in our security, for this century and a half; by the exercise of that individual strength and *morale* which have been nurtured and brought to maturity by generations of life in freedom — freedom from the domination of men; freedom from servility; the freedom of individual American manhood; by the virile power of this rich and strong and prosperous and free nation, to go on with men and money and arms and munitions, with courage and determination, doggedness, and irresistible onward power, till we win the victory, on the battlefield, over Germany.

We must be one. To do it, the impulses of all our hearts must move in the same direction. To do it, we must each one be willing to surrender all minor motives and desires, and have but one overwhelming purpose in life till this war is won; and that purpose is to help our country to win the war. He that has any other, the woman or man who has any other purpose or motive or desire that overtops that great patriotic desire, is a trifler and a dastard.

We are going to elect a Congress this coming fall. There

is one great predominant qualification for an election to that Congress, and that is a loyal heart. I do not care whether a man is a Democrat or a Republican or a Progressive or a Socialist or a Prohibitionist, or what not; he must have a loyal heart, or it is treason to send him to Congress. There are probably from twenty to thirty Congressional districts in this country where there is a loyal majority, but where there is so large a disloyal minority, that a division of the loyal majority may let a pro-German in. In every one of those districts, Democrats and Republicans and all loyal men should get together, and agree upon the loyal man of one party or the other, who is the surest to carry the district, and all unite on him without regard to party.

Any man who would not accept that idea and follow it, I would want to live a hundred years to vote and work against him. Human nature has not changed. There are going to be parties, going to be politics hereafter; but now they are subordinate, they are unimportant. The one thing only is to win the war, and put men in Congress who will represent the driving power of the American people; the driving power that is behind Congress, that is behind the Administration, and that, God grant, may make itself felt behind the men who are puttering over contracts and lingering on the road to victory. The great thing is to make Germany feel that the hundred millions of America are going, as one man, to beat them; to make every American feel that all the rest of the hundred millions are with him in his mightiest efforts to beat the German.

I have been a Republican all my life, but I count it as naught compared with this great issue. And I am proud of my life-long associates in that old party, of the splendid loyalty with which they rallied behind a Democratic administration to give all the best that was in them to support that administration, and I challenge all Democrats, all Democrats whatsoever, to support their own administration with the same loyalty of purpose, and if they can accomplish it, with more.

Well, that is what this League is working for, and it was not organized to make an opportunity for me to speak; and accordingly we will proceed with the programme of the evening.

PUBLIC STATEMENT FOR THE NATIONAL WAR SAVINGS COMMITTEE IN NEW YORK CITY

JULY 2, 1918

It is observed by Mr. Root in the course of the following address that the American people with small incomes were to be given an opportunity of contributing to the conduct of the war in which the United States was engaged from 1917 to 1918, with the Imperial German Empire and the Austro-Hungarian Monarchy.

It appears from an official statement of the Treasury Department that the people availed themselves largely of this opportunity. Thrift stamps, of the denomination of twenty-five cents, and Treasury Savings Stamps of one dollar, were non-interest bearing. The War Savings Stamps, of five-dollar denomination, bore interest. During the last two weeks of 1917 and in the final and culminating year of 1918, the amount totalled no less than $972,913,872.91.

THE fact that more than seventeen million separate subscriptions were received for the bonds of the third Liberty Loan is cheerful evidence that the people of the United States are united in loyal and earnest determination to make their liberty and future peace secure by vigorous and unrelenting prosecution of the war to a victory which shall destroy the power of the Imperial German Government to dominate and oppress the democracies of the world. Doubtless, millions more in America — if their means had sufficed — would have offered the evidence of their loyal support to their Government in the war. We hope these millions of loyal Americans will realize that it is especially to give them an opportunity to do their bit in the war that War-Savings Stamps and Thrift Stamps have been issued by the Government and can be purchased everywhere in the country in very small amounts. It is not the amount that counts the most; it is the spirit in which the service is rendered. It is not merely that you furnish money to the Country when you buy one of these stamps (useful as the money will be), but it is the weight of a great multitude joining in the defence of their liberty; it is the inspiration to our soldiers and sailors who are braving wounds and death; and it is the knowledge of all the world that not merely a government but a great and united people are carrying on this war. If the money invested in these stamps shall have been saved by cutting off some unnecessary expense, by going without some object of desire, then all the savings together will be a great conservation of the material and labor of the country, to be used in the war instead of being wasted unnecessarily; and those who save in order that they may give will also have their part in the nobler service of self-denial and sacrifice for their country's sake.

Deep will be the regret in after years of any who reject the opportunity to render service in this great struggle. Who is so poor in spirit as to receive Liberty as a gift from others, unwilling to do his own part toward preserving it?

THE DUTY OF THE OPPOSITION PARTY IN THE WAR

ADDRESS BEFORE THE NEW YORK REPUBLICAN STATE CONVENTION, SARATOGA, NEW YORK, JULY 18, 1918

THERE is only one thing I have come here to talk about, and that is the War. The immediate pressing question is, "How can we use our whole strength to the best advantage to secure a conclusive victory for the Armies of our country and her Allies?"

The object toward which we are all agreed to strive is distinct and certain. The general direction and lines of the course which we are all determined to follow are clear and free from doubt. Every man and every woman in this Convention is inspired by a single purpose. For many months each one of us has been anxiously seeking and seizing upon opportunity in many forms to do something according to our individual capacity to speed the War. As the people of this land have served their country, the blessings of unselfish service have descended upon them. For every heavy tax ungrudgingly paid; for every gift to war auxiliaries like the Red Cross, the Young Men's Christian Association, the Knights of Columbus; for all relief of suffering and distress; for the neglect of business and loss of income to render unpaid service in boards and commissions and committees; for all the bonds purchased; for all the economies to buy Thrift Stamps; for every cheerful compliance with restrictions upon food that our Allies may be fed; for the willing alacrity with which liberty of conduct has been submitted for the moment to unusual control of authority, in order that liberty may endure hereafter; for every garment knitted by the dear women whose hearts have urged them to minister as best they could to the health and comfort of their defenders; for the millions of eager youth counting life as nothing that they might do a man's part in the great battle for liberty and law; for all that vast multitude who have given their loved ones to danger of wounds and death, and bravely bear the heavy burden of waiting in fear and hope; and for those to whom the bitterness of loss has come, God has already returned a reward in the riches of the spirit which is the true life of men and of nations. The old indifference and selfishness are gone; the thick layer of materialism with which prosperity had concealed the better nature of a people born and reared in freedom has been stripped away; the old standards, the old ideals of earlier and simpler days have resumed their sway; and toward them the renewed and purified hearts of this people are turning in the spirit of sacrifice and service. The whole world regards America with new sympathy and respect, and, best of all, America is conscious of a new self-respect and a new strength of brotherhood.

Yet wars cannot be won by feeling and enthusiasm alone. Persistent and ceaseless effort, enduring faith, stubborn determination, must bind the American people together into a single unrelaxing force to win this War.

What can the organized power of the Republican Party contribute to that end? How can this great party, which for two generations has included approximately one half the people of the United States, use its power of organization, the relations of fellowship and leadership and influence, and all those ties that bind together men who have been fighting political battles side by side, to the end that our country may be strong and victorious in this War?

It is not enough for us to act individually. There rests in our hands collectively a tremendous force which should contribute to the national momentum. There are millions of

Americans on the farms, in the shops, in the factories, all over this vast country, who were born into the Republican Party and bred in it, whose loyalty to it comes by inheritance and training, and the habits of a lifetime. The strongest impulses move them to support and maintain the general judgment of that party in public affairs. It is the duty of Republicans to see to it that this tremendous force of party spirit and party loyalty is effectively applied in carrying on the War.

Here, too, the course is plain. We must clear our vision of those obscuring objects of desire for which parties ordinarily contend. The War has come while we are out of power at Washington. Of course, we would like to see the Republican Party return to power; but the War is here. It must be fought now; it must be fought under the direction and control of a Democratic President, Commander-in-Chief of the Army and Navy, and a Democratic Cabinet, acting under the influence of all those relations of personal intimacy and confidence within their own party which are inevitable whatever party is in power. That lawfully elected President and lawfully appointed Cabinet must continue in their place of leadership for nearly three years to come. It is only by supporting them that the War can be won. It is only by giving power to them and putting behind them the solid force and momentum of a united people terribly in earnest that the War can be won. That comes first. That is the present duty, and the supreme duty. Compared with the full performance of that duty, the question who shall hold the offices or what party shall hold the power at any future time is of no importance. To realize that truth as a party, and to make our words and acts conform to that, is the first duty of the Republican Party.

If the question be what can we do who are out of power, the answer is that the hardest and therefore the noblest duty rests upon us because we are out of power.

These one hundred million people of the United States, united and determined, with the strength of independent character formed under our conditions of free individual life, with our resources, and the preliminary training that we have already acquired for carrying on war, are capable of throwing into the field of conflict a military and naval reserve that will decide the war, and make the overthrow of the German military power as certain as sunrise to-morrow. There is but one danger — the danger of division, that faint hearts shall grow weary, that high enthusiasm shall cool, that selfish purposes shall divert effort, that personal pique shall hinder progress, that insidious propaganda shall confuse and mislead until we have come to that condition of internal jealousies and dissensions, which is the chief weakness of undisciplined democracy and the fatal disease that makes victory impossible. It is that condition which Germany has without ceasing sought to bring about in every country with which she is at war, including our own, and it is through fostering that condition far more than by her armies that she has acquired the mastery of Eastern Europe. Where in any people does the danger of division make its way? Not among the party in power, not among those who hold the offices and distribute the revenues and enjoy the honors, but among those who are out of office, who are naturally critical of the conduct of their political opponents, who see the defects without realizing the difficulties of policy, who are not consulted about the measures they are called upon to support, and who not without bitterness have seen themselves and their chosen leaders shoved aside with little honor from positions of consequence and authority. It is here, at this point of danger, that the deadliest foe will seek entrance silently as if by night; and it is here that the Republican Party, out of office, has the high privilege to stand on guard, vigilant and hostile to every act and thought and suggestion that may tend to divide or hinder or weaken the united power of this Nation in its forward sweep to the winning of the War.

It may be that this War could be won in no other way than by having in office the party that has cherished the traditions of local power, and having in opposition the party inspired by the great traditions of national power. The advocates of the two historic schools of American political opinion are curiously placed. The disciples of Jefferson, who have stubbornly contended for the narrowest limitations upon national authority and have thought in terms of the state rather than in terms of the nation, have confided to them the most extreme exercise of national power. They are compelled by the necessities of the War; they are bound by loyalty to the President of their own choosing; they cannot withhold approval of their own conduct of affairs; they cannot refuse to vest authority in their own administration. The retention of office, the exercise of authority, the disposal of vast revenues, the incense of popular applause, the instincts of self-preservation, all their political hopes for the future urge them on to the successful conduct of the War. For them to falter would be fatal.

On the other hand, the disciples of Washington and Hamilton and Lincoln, whose inheritance and conviction are for a vigorous and powerful national government, who are instinct with the spirit of American nationality, look on from outside the Government to see their country pressing forward upon the lines of their own political opinions under the guidance of the opposing party. We are denied the privilege of following the President whom we would have chosen; we are incited by no rewards of office or emolument or power or applause; as we contribute to success in the War we contribute to the success of our political opponents; but we have the traditions and the faith; we are born and bred to a conception of a nation great, powerful, honored, a nation independent and free, a nation with vision, with ideals, with a mission for self-government, consecrated to liberty and to equal justice, and to peace among men. We love the land for which Lincoln died, for which our fathers fought and suffered, in which lies the hope of our children's happiness. We need no persuasion of office, or emolument, or applause, to lead us to serve this nation in this time of its supreme trial with all our strength and the utmost devotion. We accept the service of self-abnegation and sacrifice — sacrifice of feeling and prejudice and selfishness, and of all desire except for the overwhelming and conclusive victory of our country. Never when the bells have rung for great majorities and elections gained has the Republican Party stood so high in the dignity of merit as it has in the splendid patriotism with which it has supported a Democratic President in waging this War for our country's sake. In this spirit we will continue, and we challenge our Democratic opponents to do more if they can; we challenge them to do less if they dare.

The first great function of Republican organization is now to encourage among ourselves this spirit of unselfish service by formal and public declaration, and by private expression and practice, and to make clear the understanding that this is a fundamental and essential qualification for the right to call one's self Republican. If anyone who claims to be Republican fails to answer to this test, he should be cast out and repudiated, denied the political fellowship, suffrage, and support of true Republicans. We may lose votes here and there, we may lose an office here and there; we can live without such votes and without office; but we cannot live without principles and without self-respect. This is no time for easy-going indifference. He is no true Republican who does not hate disloyalty and hold the disloyal man to be his enemy.

Second. The Republican Party will stand not only for a vigorous and aggressive prosecution of the War, but for its prosecution until a final and decisive victory has been won, and it will stand against every attempt to bring about an inconclusive peace. It will of course approve no conclusion which does not set Belgium free, and return Alsace-Lorraine, and give Italy her own again, and redress ancient wrongs of Poland, and bring the Serbians home, and take the foot of Germany from the necks of Russia and Rumania. But it will demand a broader conclusion still: it will consent to no peace until the power of the military aristocracy which has enslaved and demoralized the humble people of Germany, and has committed the foulest crimes of modern history to gain for itself the overlordship of the world, shall be put in a position where it cannot repeat the attempt. Overtures will be made for a peace attractive to a war-weary world but leaving the power of the German great General Staff practically intact. We must be alert for this, and see to it that such attempts are understood and rejected. Such a peace would be but a truce in the interest of our enemy. We are not fools or weaklings to stay our hand upon the red-handed criminal's request and leave half done the work on which depends the peace and liberty of the world.

Third. The Republican Party should insist upon thorough work for the War, through the prompt extension of the selective draft system to all men of military age, their selection for the duties for which they are best suited, and the training of those of them who are to fight, without waiting until they are needed, so that they will be ready when needed. Nothing can be more certain than the requirement of millions more of American soldiers to keep our faith and do our work in Europe. Now is the time to get them ready.

Fourth. The Republican Party should insist on a permanent policy of universal military training, based upon the principle that the rights and privileges of citizenship are inseparable from the duty of every citizen to take part according to his ability in the defence of his country. The time may come when it is safe to rely (as we once vainly relied) on the peaceable intentions of the rest of the world, but no eye can now foresee the coming of that happy day, and in the meantime our very national life may depend upon having our powers for defence ready for instant use.

Fifth. Republican organizations everywhere should make absolute loyalty, and sincere purpose to aid with might and main in the vigorous prosecution of the War until victory, a primary and essential qualification for all nominations to office; and in every Congressional district where there is the slightest danger that a division of the loyal vote on political lines will make it possible for pro-German voters to put into Congress a man of weak and shifty loyalty, there the Republican organization should join with the loyal men of all parties in agreement upon a single loyal candidate for all loyal votes.

Wherever danger from disloyal votes does not threaten, we should strive vigorously to elect Republicans to the Senate and the House of Representatives. The proper conduct of the War requires loyal Republicans in Congress. No government can afford to go on without the tests and criticisms of policy and performance which can hardly be furnished during the continuance of this War except by putting Republicans in Congress. With the tremendous power which the exigencies of war have vested in the executive branch of government, it is very difficult for legislative members of the party in power to express, or indeed to form, independent judgment, and to subject measures proposed for legislation to the process of correction and improvement by discussion and amendment — yet, without this, terrible mistakes are certain to be made. A study of recent legislation will show that the independent support of the Republicans in the Senate and in the House given to every forward step of the

President in the conduct of the War, not because a party leader told them to give it, but because their loyalty and judgment constrained them to give it, has been of the highest value. No nation can dispense with the kind of independent and fearless service which was rendered by Augustus Gardner of Massachusetts when he led the fight for preparedness, and by Julius Kahn of California when he led the House of Representatives in the passage of the Selective Draft Act. It is a moderate statement that a large part of the Democrats who exercise power in Washington are not very familiar with the vast and complicated industry and commerce and finance which underlie the taxpaying power of the United States. Nor are they very sympathetic with the men who are engaged in that industry and commerce and finance. There are some men among them who seem to feel that an element of punishment may properly be included in taxation. That is dangerous in the highest degree. Taxation should be absolutely controlled by the purpose to raise the necessary revenue and preserve the sources of revenue by fair distribution of the burden, and unless there is independence and courage to insist upon this principle we are liable to be hampered in the War by a sharp decline in our power to raise money.

There is another reason for sending Republicans to Washington, arising from the effect upon American political and social institutions which must result from the measures necessary to carry on the War.

We have been building up by a great mass of statutes an executive authority unprecedented in scope and absolutism. We have done it with alacrity, because it was necessary for the conduct of the War. We shall continue it so long as the War lasts. But when the War ends, all this system of executive government will have to be unscrambled, and we shall have to get back to a government of limited powers and individual freedom. We shall not go back where we were. That never can be done. And it ought not to be done, because we are learning valuable lessons and we must utilize them in the rearrangement which follows the War. But that rearrangement must be based upon the same fundamental principles which have made America great and free. Never in American history have brains and character been needed more in the Congress of the United States than they will be at the time, probably within the life of the next Congress, when Germany breaks and peace comes.

Beyond that day of victory, a new world will arise from the ashes of sacrifice. The new relations in a community of nations subject to the rule of law and morals, and the extension and development of the principle of self-governed freedom, will demand the highest capacity for political organization and public service. In that day the party that has been faithful to the right, without fee, the party that rises to the greatness of these spacious times with vision and unselfish devotion, will have its reward in the confidence and trust of the American people.

THE RESUMPTION OF INDIVIDUAL
LIBERTY

SPEECH AT LINCOLN'S BIRTHDAY DINNER IN UTICA,
NEW YORK, FEBRUARY 12, 1919

PUNCH, the English journal, said not long ago, "There
are eleven lunatics in Europe, each of whom thinks he
is the crown prince of Prussia, and one of them is right." If
I were to take to myself all that might be implied from the
generous warmth of your welcome to me, I wonder where I
would find the other ten. But it is a good thing for me to
come back home. I get a background from the valley of the
Mohawk and from the hillsides that slope down to the stream
which has never grown dim in my memory through all the
long years since I was a boy in Oneida County, and which
revives with tenfold force as I come into this old familiar
place.

The background takes in a farm in the town of Vernon,
County of Oneida, a simple little farmhouse in fields from
which my grandfather, whose name I bear, cleared the trees
with his axe before Utica was born. A quarter of a mile
down the road stands the white house in which lived Willett
Sherman, the grandfather of James Schoolcraft Sherman,
Vice-President of the United States.

Memories of plain men holding the plough-handle, driving
the lumber wagon, swinging the scythe, milking the cow.
Simple folk resting in unknown graves, taking into the scope
of their lives neither power, fame, nor wealth, but altogether
forming that conception of my country, my people, my home,
that I bear through life.

I was bred to reverence for the great names of our history, Washington, Hamilton, Jefferson, Lincoln, Grant, Sherman; but, after all, these plain farmers are to me the men who have handed down the traditions of noble purpose and established by their lives the destinies of the country. How did that life differ from the life of the peasant whom many a time I have seen plodding through his daily toil in the monarchies of Europe?

How could it differ from the countless millions of men who lived and died in the centuries that have gone? In this, that these farmers lived lives of individual independence; they loved freedom and they practised it. They knew no superior. All the millions of our country lived and practised liberty. They were obedient to law. They made their own laws and they obeyed them. The common opinion of the community demanded obedience to law. How did they reconcile liberty and law? How did they make that liberty ordered liberty? By establishing limitations upon official power. They knew by their sterling common sense, bred of many generations which had practised liberty, that if men were to be free from superior power, free of control by others, they must govern themselves. If their government was to be free, they must limit the powers of those who administered government. And these plain, humble men of the type from which I came, whose traditions were breathed into me through my home in Oneida County, are the exemplar of what must be, if it is to be at all, the liberty of the world.

And when, with the change of the world on which I look with eyes grown old, I come back here and think again of them, I am minded to preach a little sermon, and for that I am going to take a text from Abraham Lincoln. More than eighty years ago in a speech in Springfield, Ill., Lincoln said: "At what point is danger to our country to be expected? If it ever reaches us, it must spring up among us. It cannot

come from abroad. If destruction be our lot, we must ourselves be its author and finisher. As a nation of free men we
must live through all time or die by suicide."

Is there danger now? Is there danger that the ordered
liberty for which Lincoln lived and died, plain man of the
people, which these men I have been talking to you about
received from their fathers and passed on to us, shall go to a
suicide's grave? Is there not danger? Always there is! There
are no statics in the life of nations. There is no rest in all the
seething caldron of the world's life except the rest of death.
Always those who would be free are traveling a narrow, rocky
ledge on the one side of which there is despotism and on the
other anarchism; on one side the safety of being governed by
a superior power and on the other the danger of lawlessness;
on the one side the Tsar in his time and on the other the Bolshevik in his time. Always the balance must be held, and
there never is opportunity for rest.

We are now at a point in the development of our nation
which calls not for mere Hosannahs, but for devotion and
determination and service by all who would have this country
continue free. Whence does the danger come? Not from any
incidental invasion. There are many things in which if we go
wrong we can correct ourselves: the tariff, the currency,
merchant marine, big or little navy, or army. If we make
mistakes in these things we can cure them.

But there is such a thing as the heart of a nation and the
essential of unity. If that point be reached, take care that
consequences do not fall that you cannot repair. What is the
source of American power? I undertake to say it is not American wealth or American laws. It is the individual character
of each unit of the hundred millions of the American people.
Why is it that my friend Hicks is able to laud, as he has justly
done, the heroism of the American soldiers on the battle-line
in France?

I have received many letters from Europe during the War and the universal testimony of them all is that the American private was the best military material then in Europe. Our part of this War was won by the American private in arms and by the American private, man and woman, creating the material supplies and furnishing the moral power behind the American private in arms. It was not the President who won the War, not the Secretary of War, the general commanding, or any officer. It was the individual soldier, because the practice of liberty and the individual character created by independent manhood, that knew no superior, made the strongest manhood in the world for the winning of this War.

The voice that beyond all others brought courage to the swaying and fainting hosts of the Allies was the voice of Theodore Roosevelt calling to the consciences, the idealism, the love of country and liberty, the courage, determination and enthusiasm of the individual American. That was the greatest engine of the War.

There were thousands of boys in our army of German lineage or birth, and the experiment proved that these boys who had been living in America, who had grown to manhood in the practice of liberty, bowing to no superior, were better men in battle than the best disciplined soldier of the Kaiser could be. The power of liberty to make men is a miracle of life.

Now what have we got? With the purpose of winning the War we came to the administration through which the War has been waged. We brought our most precious possession and laid it down; not our money. The last time I was in this room I presided at a great war-loan drive, and the chairman reported that Utica from having raised half had gone way over the top in one day. But it was not money and it was not service, although the best men of the country crowded in and offered their service. It was not even the sacrifices of father and mother, of the dear women who saw the boys they loved best go forth to an unknown fate. It was what we all brought to the altar of our country and laid down before the administration to win the War with, and that was our liberty.

We made the President of the United States and his Cabinet the most powerful monarchs on earth. We threw aside all limitations of power which had been the safeguard of the manhood of America. We said, "Take all we possess, don't stand upon our rights, we are all for the service of the country. Take all possible power and win the War." They took it. No other constitutional monarch has ever before had the unlimited power given the President of the United States; but if we are Americans and the country is to continue an honorable, useful course, we must have that power back.

How is it to be got back? Alas, alas, the recipients of the power have given us fair evidence that they mean to hold it. Some, drunk with power, mean to continue it. Some, well intentioned, but weak, assent. Some, desiring to protest, are too cowardly to raise their voices. But the voice of the American people will be raised. Do I speak too strongly?

Look for a moment at the seizure of the cable, the telegraph and telephone systems after the Armistice had been signed, when Germany had given into the possession of the Allies the physical means of carrying on the War, after the President had made his address to Congress in which he gave an account of the Armistice and then said in this formal, official way, as President of the United States: "And so the War ends." After that, the power which we put into the hands of the administration for the purpose of winning the War was still exercised to get possession of the cable, the telegraph and telephone systems. Technically the War has not ended until the President has issued a proclamation.

The difference between the American citizen who proceeds along his independent life and the peasant in the German fields is that the American is governed by an officer whose power he has limited; he is governed by the law, and that is his own. Within the limitations of his official authority the governor, mayor, or police officer is respected because he represents the law; and when he goes beyond that he is no better than you or I. But in Germany the power is not so limited. The man who has the power is all superior to the private citizen, and the private citizen bows with submission. The men to whom we have given the power to carry on this War, without regard to our liberties, are using it by false pretense to carry out other purposes than the War, and are not regarding the limitations of constitution.

They seized the railroads as a war measure. I am not saying that it was not necessary or important. But now the administration is insisting in Congress that their holding of the railroads shall be continued, not until the technical closing of the War, but for five years more. Everybody who knows anything about the railroads knows that it means government possession and control.

These are but illustrations of what is going on. The men to whom we have given the power without limitation purpose to keep it, and we have got to get it back. They mean plainly enough government ownership of the railroads. What does that mean to us, to our liberty, and the subordination of our official class to the law and the respect of our official class for the limitations upon power? Think of it for a moment.

There are in the railroad and telegraph and telephone companies about two million employees. We have had a good deal of trouble in past years owing to the fact that men in control of political machinery could not be dislodged; that the citizen could not get his will because the power of organization made it impossible under the process of law. The body of officeholders stood behind the officials, and it has been exceedingly difficult to dislodge them. Once in a while the people would get up and overturn things and we would be glad we had got rid of the politicians; but the next morning we would find that the politicians were still in power.

What is going to happen if you have two million more men who are interested in controlling the political machinery? It is rare that presidents are elected by as many as two million votes. That addition to the man in office will carry every presidential election. That is not all: the same process may be continued as to industry. What industry can live in a quarrel with all transportation? You, manufacturer of Utica, what can you do if the railroads refuse to carry your product and you have no recourse except to go to the political head of a great official organization kept in power by the men who run the railroad.

Along with this is the control of the banks. The bankers of the country are afraid of their lives now, and do not dare to say their souls are their own for fear they will be ruined by government. The administration can ruin any dealer in food products. The trade commission can ruin any merchant, make or break him, destroy his credit in one day, by all this concentrated power. How are you going to overcome a party that gets possession of that power, except by revolution? That is n't the worst: this essence of our liberty, our prosperity, our development, must live upon individual initiative. It has received its life and grown to its splendid stature, which has made the upbuilding of America the wonder of the world, through individual initiative.

If you make it necessary that all the men who are carrying on these industries shall crook the pregnant hinges of the knee to official power, if you make them subject to official power, rather than to law, you destroy their individual initiative. More than that, independence of character lives only by self-independence. If you teach the people that for their prosperity and success in life they are to lie down on the government, if the railroad and banking facilities are to be enjoyed, they are to lie down on the government, then you have lost possession of the distinguishing characteristic that has made America what it is.

This great War with all its sacrifices and suffering has quickened into life the noblest impulses of humanity among the people of America. We are ten times as good a people as we were five years ago. Our country has taken new meaning from liberty and justice. American ideals have sunk into the minds of the people and will not be forgotten. Service, sacrifice and the noblest qualities of humanity have become commonplace in American patriotism.

Can it be that a people thus ennobled, thus renewed in their love of liberty and justice, thus devoted in their veneration for the great men who have sacrificed themselves that America might be free, can it be that this people will remain silent and inert while by false pretense and false title the officials of the American government proceed to destroy the individual initiative of American character? But how can it be prevented? Not by revolution, but by the exercise of the precious right of the ballot at the polls.

THE RESTORATION POLICIES OF THE UNITED STATES

ADDRESS AS CHAIRMAN OF THE NEW YORK REPUBLICAN STATE CONVENTION, NEW YORK CITY, FEBRUARY 19, 1920

Hostilities ceased on November 11, 1918, upon the signing of the Armistice by Germany. The Treaty of Versailles, imposing peace upon Germany, was signed by the representatives of the Allied and Associated Powers, among them, President Wilson, on June 28, 1919. The treaty went into effect on January 10, 1920, for the Powers which had ratified and deposited their ratifications.

The United States did not then, or later, ratify the treaty, but concluded separate treaties, with Germany at Berlin, August 25, 1921 (ratifications exchanged, November 11, 1921), Austria, at Vienna, August 24th (ratifications exchanged November 8, 1921), and Hungary, at Budapest, August 29th (ratifications exchanged December 17, 1921), incorporating in these treaties the portions acceptable to the United States contained in the treaties with Germany, signed at Versailles, June 28, 1919, with Austria, signed at Saint-Germain-en-Laye, September 10, 1919, and with Hungary, signed at the Trianon, June 4, 1920.

Congress took, as it were, several bites of the cherry. On July 11, 1919, it repealed the Joint Resolution approved July 16, 1918, authorizing the President to supervise or take possession and assume control of any telegraph, telephone, marine cable, or radio system or systems with power to operate them during the war.

February 28, 1920 an act was passed providing for the termination of Federal control of railroads and systems of transportation, to go into effect at 12.01 A.M., March 1, 1920.

March 3, 1921, the day before his successor took office, President Wilson signed a Joint Resolution declaring that an imposing list of Acts of Congress, Joint Resolutions and Proclamations, were to be considered as if war had ended, and the present emergency had expired.

On June 2, 1921, President Harding approved the Joint Resolution of Congress terminating the state of war between the United States and the Imperial German Government, and the United States and the Imperial and Royal Austro-Hungarian Monarchy. With this act, the war powers of the President, temporary and permanent, went out of existence for the time being.

ONE of the duties of a good citizen and of a good political party is to be alert when there is general indifference, and to be steady when there is general excitement.

The war has left the whole world in a condition of disturbed nerves; old habits are broken up; the machinery of production, transportation, trade and finance through which industry produces prosperity has been dislocated. After years of sustained excitement, with nerves keyed to the highest pitch of effort, old occupations seem tame and distasteful; there is a widespread desire for something different to be attained, no one knows how. Multitudes of people are neglecting their own affairs and distressing themselves over the shortcomings of others. It is a prevailing state of mind. It is an epidemic. It will run its course like other epidemics, and some day the world will realize that the cure is for each man to go to work himself, attend chiefly to his own business, perform his own duties, pull his own weight in the boat. Then the high cost of living will go down.

Our business as a party is to address ourselves with cheerful courage and confidence to the public problems demanding solution, and to bring our country back to normal. It is not to put the country back where it was, without profiting by the lessons of these wonderful years; but it is to reëstablish the effective control of the fundamental principles on which America's liberty, prosperity, and power for good in the world rest; and we must do this not by generalities, but by specific acts.

Thrift stands first on the list. An improvident and thriftless people who talk more than they work can never succeed. To prosper, a people — like a private individual — must earn more than it spends, must really earn by contributing to the wealth of mankind more than it consumes. It cannot live long by borrowing, nor can it live long by a system of taxation which absorbs the accumulations of the past, and gradually dries up the source of supply. It is true that a political party cannot make individuals thrifty; but a political party can produce the shining and potent example of thrifty and economical government. The useful thing is, not to have a government that preaches thrift, but a government which practises thrift, a government which makes people understand that their money is being saved, so that it will be worth while for them to earn and save.

All the world has been confused by the amazing financial figures of the war. Incredible amounts were raised by taxation and by loans, and were spent like water. There has been profligate expenditure. To some extent that was inevitable. I am not now criticizing that. There would have been less if our Government had begun to prepare for war years before it did, and when the plainest common sense demanded that it should begin; but I am not going to talk about that. There would have been less if when we entered the war the men whom the process of natural selection in American business had pointed out as competent to deal with great business affairs had been promptly called to Washington, and given power to act in that greatest of all business undertakings, instead of leaving authority in the hands of a group of men quite untrained in business affairs and distrustful of all who had achieved business success; but that is past.

The important fact now is that the officials and agents of the present Administration have acquired the habit of spending public money with both hands and they do not know how to stop. The Government departments are still running for the most part under the war-time appropriations made by the 65th Congress, which was elected in November, 1916, and they are going strong.

The American people may perhaps recall the fact that Republicans had no opportunity to acquire the bad habit of spending too much money under war-time appropriations; and they may well feel that the way to change the practice is to put out the men who have the habit, and put in those who have it not.

With a party in power free from responsibility for defending the mistakes and bad methods which are to be reformed, three great things can be done.

First, the vast mass of figures through which the finances of the Government are presented in such a way that hardly anybody can understand to what conclusions they lead, can be reduced to practical and instructive form by the establishment of an effective budget system, under which government will be obliged to start with its resources in order to determine its expenditures; under which the cloth will be measured before the coat is cut; under which, when a new or enlarged expenditure is proposed, the question will have to be asked: "Where is the money to come from?" and under which responsibility for extravagance can be fixed. It was quite right during the war to say, "Such and such things must be done immediately; we will find the money somehow"; but no nation can afford to conduct its peace expenditures in that way.

A second thing to be done is to secure executive departments that will stop urging and a Congress that will stop appropriating money for things which need not be done now, or need not be done so expensively, or need not be done at all. We should have both in the Executive and the Legislative branches men who will not be content with the assurance that a proposed expenditure is for a good purpose; but who will also enquire, "Are we justified at this time in adding to the already oppressive weight of taxation upon the American people in order to secure the money for this expenditure?"

The present Congress has done well. It has made enormous reductions in the estimates submitted by the Executive Departments for their expenditures in the next fiscal year, which will begin on the 1st of next July. After that time many reductions will be forced by the limits of appropriations. It is, however, very difficult for Congressional Committees to cut down the expenses of a vast and complicated business like that of the United States Government without assistance from the heads of departments and of bureaus. It is easy for a bureau chief to make expenditures appear absolutely necessary when they are really absolutely useless, and when his error can be discovered by nothing short of an investigating committee and cross-examining counsel. Effective economy requires coöperation between the Executive and Legislative branches. It requires courage and a sense of public duty to resist appeals, and it requires open public insistent declaration of the policy in aid of that resistance.

A third thing that can be done is to revise the system of taxation, and to make some serious changes in it indicated by experience of its effects.

It is a very difficult thing to make a good tax law, even with the most sincere purpose to distribute the burden fairly; but, if the men who make the law have other purposes, and are inspired by a desire to punish somebody by the imposition of taxes, they are sure to get into their law provisions which work badly. The men who framed the Revenue Laws of the Sixty-fourth and Sixty-fifth Congresses did not conceal the fact that they looked with suspicion and dislike upon the great body of successful business concerns of the United States, and upon the men who were conducting and had conducted them, and that they meant to take away as much of these men's money as they possibly could. Now, tax laws are curious boomerang-like things, and it requires some intelligence and knowledge of affairs to know where they are going to strike. No statute can determine who is really going to pay a tax. The most dangerous post is that of the innocent bystander who goes home grumbling about the high cost of living. It is time for the Republican bystander to ascertain how far these war revenue taxes are really paid through the cost of living by everybody who eats and wears clothes. Let him discover how far the excess-profit taxes for example are being added to cost, like other business expenses, so that we all pay them together with a profit on them; and then let him act.

The review of taxation will involve the tariff. In this, new conditions are to be considered. Before the war we were a debtor nation, paying annually interest and dividends upon from four to seven billions of American securities held in Europe, paying hundreds of millions upon letters of credit to American travellers and in the remittances of recent immigrants to their friends at home, and in freight and passenger rates on commerce both ways across the ocean; and we were much pleased to have a favorable trade balance, which reduced the amount of gold drained away from us in these ways.

All this has been changed. The United States has become a great creditor nation. Our debts to Europe have been paid. Europe does not merely owe the billions loaned by our Government to European governments, or the hundreds of millions of foreign securities sold in the American market; but the exhaustion of European supplies of the necessaries of life and the raw material for manufacture have led to enormous purchases and exports of American products during the past three years.

All these things have to be paid for. There is not gold enough in the world to pay, and we already have a very large proportion of what gold there is. That is one reason why exchange has gone down, so that a pound, ordinarily worth $4.86, in American money, was a few days ago worth only $3.37. The only way in which Europe can pay America and continue to buy from America is by producing goods and selling them. Thus, we have acquired an interest in the prosperity of Europe. It is our interest to facilitate her production and trade, just as a merchant is interested in the prosperity of the customers to whom he sells on credit.

Our new tariff law must be framed to meet the new and difficult problems presented by this change of conditions. It must be framed so that American industry will not be ruined, especially so that the manufacture of things which the war has shown to be necessary for the independence of the country shall not be stopped, and it must be framed so as not to destroy the export trade of Europe, which directly or indirectly will enable Europe to pay her debts and remain solvent.

All these things, if done well, must be done by a party which really sympathizes with American business and wishes it to prosper.

More important than all is the necessity that we shall restore our Republican form of Government, with the liberty of the individual citizen preserved by limitations upon official power, and put an end to the dictatorship which we created, in order to carry on the war. By a series of statutes unprecedented in scope and liberality, with singleness of purpose and patriotic devotion worthy of all praise, the American people conferred upon the President powers broader and more autocratic than were possessed by any sovereign in the civilized world. Our capacity for effort, our fortunes, our liberty of conduct, our lives, were freely placed at the disposal of an Executive whose authority was so vast that its limits were imperceptible. The authority was exercised by the President, by his heads of departments, his bureau chiefs, his government agents, and his personal agents, to the full, without question, because the people of America were ready for any sacrifice to win the war.

Peace has come, in fact, if not technically; but the war powers of the Executive still continue. They should be brought to an end. It is not a simple thing, for new conditions have been created, which should be dealt with at the same time by new statutes adapted to the conditions of peace, and subject to the limitations upon power of our Constitutional system.

There is a double immediate purpose to be served. One, to restore the habit of freedom. It is dangerous for a people to acquire the habit of bowing to power without limits. They soon become subservient, and then character essential to freedom degenerates. The other is to stop a multitude of interferences, ill-judged although well-meant, with the natural course of business, through which alone natural laws can operate to restore normal conditions.

It is not in human nature to relinquish readily power once possessed. Excuses for continuance readily suggest themselves to the possessor.

The appeal of President Wilson in October, 1918, for the election of a Democratic Congress, which the people refused by so great a majority, was not merely an injustice to the Republican Senators and Representatives who with splendid loyalty had supported every forward step of the Administration, and had responded to every suggestion for the grant of increased powers. It was a demand for the continuance of supreme power by the election of a Congress which would submit itself to the orders of an Executive acting at once as a party leader in politics and a dictator in government. It was the instinct of the American Democracy that repelled the demand. Such has long been the government of Mexico. Such must not be the government of the United States. A government with a Louis Napoleon at one end and a plebiscite at the other, and with naught but subservience between, is not a free republic. It is autocracy by consent.

The President's defiance of the authority of the Senate to advise upon the Covenant for the League of Nations, and to give or withhold its consent to the ratification of the treaty containing it, was an assertion of a right to continue the same autocratic power. It was not a question of senatorial dignity or consequence. We need care little for that. It was a challenge to the right of any officer of the Government of the United States to exercise his powers in any way which had not the approval of the Chief Executive. The President had the constitutional authority and duty to negotiate a treaty. The Senate had the constitutional authority and duty to advise, and to consent or refuse to consent in accordance with their judgment. The right to perform that duty was challenged. By all the tremendous power of a president commanding millions of civil and military subordinates and controlling the expenditures of billions of money, Senators were threatened if they did not submit their judgment to the presidential will. Many questions were difficult and doubtful. I personally differ from many gentlemen in the Senate upon some of those questions; but, whether their conclusions are right or wrong, I should have despised them if they had yielded their honest opinions to Executive threats, and I honor them for the courage and fortitude with which they have maintained the authority of the Constitution they were sworn to support, and discharged the duty of independent judgment imposed upon them by the people who elected them to office.

Nor have the long and painstaking discussions of the Senate been without most useful results. The treaty which it was their duty to consider was fatally defective in several respects, not only from the standpoint of the vital interests of the United States, but considered as an instrument designed to secure the future peace of the world. In private life we are at liberty to discuss the treaty without reading it, and to form and express conclusions based upon what someone else has told us. Not so with the Senators. They were bound to test the true meaning of every paragraph, to consider the conditions which the provisions were to meet, to estimate the human forces of self-interest and prejudice and

passion under the influence of which the treaty was to be
applied, and to form their own judgment upon the results
which would be produced for America and for civilization.
No man ever lived who could be trusted to negotiate a complicated and important treaty without having his work tested
by the independent judgment of men who were not direct
parties to the negotiation. Because in this particular case
the President himself was the negotiator of the treaty, the
Senate alone had the authority and the duty to perform this
necessary function of independent review.

The reservations adopted by the Senate remedy so far as
the United States is concerned the chief objections to the
treaty. They prevent our entrance into the League of Nations from being an abandonment of the Monroe Doctrine,
with irreparable injury to the United States, and no benefit
to the rest of the world. Especially important is it that they
prevent the incredible mistake of Article X. That article
contains an express agreement "to preserve as against external aggression the territorial integrity and existing political independence of all members of the League." If that
stipulation means anything, and is not mere sham and false
pretence, it will, if ratified, bind the United States when
occasion arises to defend every member of the League by
armed force against external aggression. It will bind the
United States to do that, no matter what our people at the
time think about the right and wrong of the controversy, or
about the wisdom or folly of entering upon it. It will require
the United States to fight on occasion for all the dispositions
of territory made by the Supreme Council in Paris, under the
influence of secret treaties and bitter animosities and political
expediencies — dispositions of territory many of which are
doubtful, and some of which are clearly wrong.

Two things seem plain. First: the sense of justice and the
independent and uncontrolled power of the United States to

throw its weight whenever occasion arises in favor of what it deems to be right in the affairs of the world is the greatest single influence toward that justice among nations which is the essential requisite of peace; and such an agreement as this (if observed) would rob the world of that influence, because the United States would be bound by this formula to act irrespective of its judgment at the time. Second: there is a practical certainty that if the United States entered into such an agreement it would not observe it. No human power can bring the people of the United States into a war unless, at the time when they are called upon to fight, they believe the cause to be just and worthy of sacrifice. If the occasion for acting under Article X when it came did not appeal to the judgment and sympathies of the people of the United States, it would be impossible to comply with the agreement, and the worst possible thing for the peace of the world would happen — that the United States should have made a solemn treaty and should break it.

It seems clear to me that in the interests of the world's peace, which all America desires to promote, this treaty ought to be ratified with the reservations of the Senate; and that without those reservations in their fair and honest substance it ought not to be ratified. I hope the treaty will be ratified with the reservations long before the presidential election. That will be done if the President permits it. If that is not done, then that is what I think the Republican Party ought to stand for.

Immediately after the fourth of March, 1921, a Republican President should urge upon the society of nations the reform of the League Covenant, so as to make it establish the rule of public right rather than the rule of mere expediency; so as to make the peace of the world rest primarily upon law, and upon the effectiveness and enforcement of law. A Congress of all nations should be called, to consider and declare what of international law still remains of binding force, and to provide for the further development and extension of that law, and for the application of the law to all justiciable cases of controversy between nations by impartial judicial tribunals, and to make the decisions of such tribunals upon questions of fact and upon questions of law binding and effective. That is the Old American doctrine, and that is the necessary method of democracies, for democracies can live only under governments of laws, and not of men.

The extreme effects of the possession of arbitrary power are seen in the extraordinary letters of the President to Secretary Lansing [1] published on the 14th of February, 1920, by which it appears that honest and independent advice from officers of the President's own selection is an offense, and that the exercise of the most ordinary powers of the heads of departments without consulting the President when his illness prevented consultation is cause for resentment.

It is interesting to observe that many citizens — official and unofficial — who are willing that the country should assume the startling obligations of Article X are opposing the system of universal military training, without which our obligation would be worthless, and which intensively applied enabled the United States to turn the scale of war against Germany. They say we have millions of young men already trained; but how long is the service which these splendid and patriotic youths have already rendered to their country to be made the ground for imposing upon them exclusively the burden of further service, and leaving the millions of young men who come to military age year after year untrained and unfitted to do their part for the defense of our country?

One result of the War and of the universal unrest which has followed it has been to force upon the American Democ-

[1] See Robert Lansing's *Peace Negotiations — A Personal Narrative* (1921).

racy a series of questions which involve the very life of the Nation. These questions arise from widely different causes, and each presents its own special problems: — Bolshevism, Americanization of Immigrants, the deportation or discipline of seditious aliens, the relations of capital and labor under the new conditions, the relations of organized labor to the public, the coal supply, the railroads, the preservation of public health, security for the life of the community, and opportunity for the pursuit of happiness by its members. Here is a great variety of subjects, but the method of treating all of them must depend upon a clear conception of what our system of government is, and what we mean it to be. Our Government rests upon certain very simple ideas.

First, that all men are equally endowed by their Creator with certain unalienable rights, including life, liberty, and the pursuit of happiness, and that governments are instituted to secure these rights.

Second, that the government which secures these unalienable rights is to be constituted and conducted pursuant to the will of those whose rights it is intended to secure, expressed through a majority vote of all of them.

There are three things essential to the maintenance of such a system of government. One is that there shall be universal opportunity for education, so that the governing body may vote intelligently. A second is that the governing body shall recognize its responsibility for justice in the broadest sense in maintaining the unalienable rights of the minority and every individual composing it. The third is that there shall be real opportunity for the individual citizen to better his condition and that of his family by industry, thrift, self-denial, enterprise, courage, skill, talent, genius. There must be security for the fruits of enterprise. No crust must form to hold down the aspiring. No human power must make the rewards of industry and idleness, ambition and indifference, intelligence and stupidity, the same.

The whole course of development of free self-government from monarchical and aristocratic forms has been in the direction of more and more universal suffrage, and more complete power of the majority of all who live under the government. We have reached a point where neither religion, nor occupation, nor color, nor race, nor property, nor poverty, nor degree of education, excludes any man from the opportunity to take part in his own government by his vote. In the greater part of the country, this is extended to both sexes. Our Government is a government directed by the majority of all who are governed.

Bolshevism is a government of all the people of a country by a part of the people constituting a single class called "The Proletariat," or the mass of industrial workmen who have no capital and depend for support on daily or casual employment. All others are grouped with the "Bourgeois," and are to have no part in government. This system has been tried for the past two years in Russia. Its purpose was set forth in an authentic statement from Petrograd in January, 1919, as follows:

The aim of the proletariat must now be immediately to conquer power. To conquer power means to destroy the governmental apparatus of the bourgeoisie, and to organize a new proletarian government apparatus. This new apparatus must express the dictatorship of the proletariat.

The dictatorship of the proletariat must be the occasion for the immediate expropriation of capital and the elimination of the private right of owning the means of production through making them common property.

The governmental apparatus of the proletariat employed in Russia is the Soviet system, under which the workmen in each industry, in each locality, select delegates to a kind of central Soviet or committee, which in turn selects a few men to exercise the powers of government. With the assent of the

Soviets, Lenin and Trotzky are now exercising absolutely despotic power in a large part of Russia in the name of the proletariat, through a reign of terror and violence which makes the French Revolution seem mild and conservative. Tens of thousands of people have been put to death without any form of trial, or any charge except the assertion by somebody or anybody that they were opposed to the dictatorship of the proletariat, or were friendly to those who were opposed. The despotic control extends to the workmen themselves. No strikes are permitted. No elections by Soviets have been permitted to stand, unless the persons elected were friendly to Lenin and Trotzky. It would seem as if the methods employed were designed to exterminate all who did not belong to the proletariat; but Trotzky in a signed article on January 10, 1919, explained that this is not so. He said:

While dispersing, arresting, and shooting saboteurs and conspirators, the proletariat says: "I shall break your will, because my will is stronger than yours, and I shall force you to serve me." . . . Terror as the demonstration of the will and strength of the working class is historically justified, precisely because the proletariat was able thereby to break the political will of the Intelligentsia, pacify the professional men of various categories and work, and gradually subordinate them to its own aims within the fields of their specialties.

In the meantime the economic condition of Russia has gone from bad to worse. The collapse of industry, the breakdown of transportation, the starvation and misery of millions of people, without any practical constructive measures of relief, are appalling beyond expression.

I am not going to discuss the merit of these two systems. There is no shadow of doubt as to which kind of government the people of the United States stand for. By an overwhelming majority the people of the United States and of every state mean to maintain Lincoln's government of the people, by the people, and for the people. They will no more be governed by a class of laborers than they will be governed by a class of aristocrats, or a class of plutocrats, or a class of soldiers. They will trust the justice and maintain the power and enforce the will of the American Democracy as a whole. That, of course, is where the Republican Party will stand.

This is so plain that there would be no justification for talking about it, except for two things.

The first is that Russian Bolshevism has set out upon a definite undertaking to destroy all existing democratic governments, and it is carrying on an extensive and vigorous propaganda to accomplish that end. It has a vast multitude of missionaries at work, not only in Europe, but in the United States, who by misrepresenting the actual and promising the impossible are trying to win labor over to their plan for establishing a dictatorship of the proletariat. They have made some headway in the United States, chiefly among the foreign-born laborers, and against the intelligent opposition of the great leaders of organized labor in America. The assault is too substantial to be wisely ignored. America is full of Intelligentsia, and we cannot afford to have them all turned by terror into parlor Bolsheviki.

We are already meeting the assault in two ways. When we find one of these Bolshevist missionaries or his converts inciting criminal overthrow of government by violence, we punish him or deport him. That is lawful and sensible. The right of free speech does not include the right to incite to crime. Yet, we must be careful not to overlook the distinction. Let there be fair hearing, and let no expression of mere differing opinion — however radical or distasteful — be punished.

One of the things the Republican Party has to do apparently is to clear a lot of Bolsheviki or sympathizers with the Bolsheviki out of the public offices of our Government. The administration of the law regarding these missionaries of sedition has been apparently very bad — illustrating that weak kind of government which tries to make up for being too lax at one time by being too severe at another. Let us hope for an administration that will put the control of this business in the hands of men sufficiently strong and impartial to be just at all times.

The chief means of meeting the Bolshevist assault, however, is by what we call "Americanization," an organized active popular movement to instruct the foreign-born in the principles, the history, and the character of American free institutions. That is to use the true weapon of free democracy. We must not confine it to the foreign-born. It must extend to all the children in the schools, and to that end it must be extended to all the teachers in the schools, not by any means excluding the professors in our colleges. There is not one of us — no, not one in this great country — who will not profit by learning more or hearing over again about the simple truths so often forgotten, upon which our liberty, the security of our homes, the opportunities of our children, rest; and about the duty of service by us if these truths are to be maintained.

Let the Republican Party give to the movement for Americanization the strength of its publicly declared and active support.

It is not enough, however, to teach Americanization. If the principles of our Government are to be maintained, they must be applied. It is hopeless to teach them unless we practise them. The relations between organized labor in the United States and the public call for the definite and conscious application of those principles in two distinct directions. The first is to assert the control of the whole people of the United States within its field, and of the whole people of each state within its field, over matters essential to the life of the community, to the exclusion of any class control over such matters. The second is to exercise that popular control by making and applying such laws, and establishing such institutions of government, as to secure justice within the law to the members of every class and calling, so that our system of government will be justified by its works.

For many years the American people have been watching, and from time to time as individuals taking part in the great struggle for a fair division of the newly produced wealth of the world between the inventors and organizers who inaugurated new enterprises, the capitalists great and small who risked their money and frequently lost it, the laborers whose toil produced more than ever before, and the consumers who purchased the product which cost less capital and less labor than ever before. When labor has used its weapon of the strike to secure from the employer better wages, shorter hours, better conditions of working and of living, the general public sympathy has been with the laborer, alienated only occasionally by unreasonable demands or acts of violence. The force of the strike was applied to the pocket of the employer. Agreement to labor's demands was the price of continued profits.

There has, however, been a change in the character of these economic struggles. The massing of the population in cities, where millions are dependent from day to day for their food and water, and heat and light, and health and safety, upon the uninterrupted operation of great business enterprises for production and transportation, has brought a new point of application for the force of the strike. The effective threat of a general coal strike, or a general railroad strike, is not that if such and such demands are not complied with, the coal companies or the railroad companies will cease to make profits. It is that if such and such demands are not complied with, millions of Americans will be deprived of things necessary to their existence. The demands may be right or they may be wrong. Whether they be right or wrong, the people of the country who are dependent upon the continued operation of those industries must in some way secure compliance with the demands, in order to save their lives, unless the makers of the demands relent or are controlled.

This situation presents with startling distinctness the question whether our American popular government is to continue, or is to be changed into a class dictatorship.

The people over whom one class or section holds lawful power of life or death to compel compliance with its demands is not sovereign. It does not govern. It is subject to the control of the dominating class. The demands may be moderate to-day, but they are moderate only through the forbearance of the controlling class; and, ordinary knowledge of human nature teaches us that, with power unrestrained, the demands will become oppressive to-morrow. The question is not of form. It is one of substance. It is, "Who exercises the real power of government, the people or the class?" If it be the class which rules, while it will doubtless be for a time less brutal here in purpose than the proletariat of Lenin and Trotzky, the government will be in its essence the same. It will be a class control over the majority, established and maintained through fear of actual physical injury, fear of cold, and hunger, and darkness, and pestilence, the stopping of the machinery upon which life depends. The philosophical justification of the strike aimed at the life of the community cannot be found short of Trotzky's proposition: "Terror as the demonstration of 'the will and strength of the working class is historically justified, precisely because the proletariat was able thereby to break the political will of the Intelligentsia,'" and so forth. The real force of such a strike is represented by Trotzky's other words: "The proletariat says, 'I shall break your will, because my will is stronger than yours, and I shall force you to serve me.'"

If we are to maintain the principles of our Government of all the people by all the people, we must apply those principles now to this situation. If we are a self-governing people, we must govern and not be governed. We should not attempt to make any man work against his will. We should not attempt to take away the right to strike. It is labor's great protection. But we should by law limit the right to strike at the point where it comes in conflict with the community's higher right of self-preservation. No man and no set of men can justly claim the right to undertake the performance of a service upon which the health and life of others depend, and then to abandon the service at will. The line between such a performance and an ordinary strike should be drawn by law.

Inseparably connected with the right of control by the governing people is the duty of justice resting upon them. If the people by law prohibit organized labor from holding them up to enforce its demands, the people are bound to provide means to ascertain whether the demands are just, and for enforcing them if they are found just. That duty calls for the establishment of a competent and impartial tribunal, and for the enforcement of its decisions. The present methods are as irrational as private war among citizens who go armed with deadly weapons to compel compliance with what they deem to be their rights and privileges. It can be dealt with only as private war has been dealt with, not by acquiescence, not by prohibition alone, but by prohibition accompanied by adequate remedies in lieu of private compulsion.

The new relations of labor to the industries in which it is employed point in the same direction. Everywhere labor is acquiring rights in its employment, rights in the business, rights to share in the profits, in the regulation and in the control. These new rights carry with them new duties. There is no such thing as a right without a correlative duty resting upon the possessor of the right. All rights are relative. All rights are limited by the nature of the subject to which they apply. The countryman who removes to a great city finds his liberty limited for the safety of the community. The man who, whether as employer or as laborer, engages in the great mass enterprises upon which the life of our communities now depend will have sooner or later to recognize that his liberty is limited for the safety of the community. The right of capital to combine and organize carries the duty to submit the new power thus acquired to limitations for the safety of the community. The right of labor to combine and organize carries with it the duty to submit the new power thus acquired to limitations for the safety of the community. We are dealing with the subject now by piecemeal, partially, applying inappropriate and inadequate provisions of old war-time statutes, stretched out upon technicalities to cover times of peace. The subject should be dealt with as a whole, frankly, considerately, courageously, in the exercise of the power of this great Republic, to protect civil society, and in performance of the duty of this Republic to do justice to every class of its citizens.

Whoever approaches the task with unselfish purpose will find that it involves no denial of legal right or social justice, but the just application of the ancient rules of the Common Law, and the essential principles of civil liberty; and it is a fair prophecy that, when the voice of the American Democracy has asserted through effective action its just power of government, no one will accept the decision more loyally than the liberty-loving and patriotic men who make up the great body of organized labor in the United States.

During all the years of the war the Republican Party was loyal to its National traditions. While the strength and service of the whole people were required to carry on the war, yet in the United States alone among the nations, power and authority were retained by a strictly partisan government. The dignity and gratification of office, the exercise of authority, the disposal of vast revenues, the incense of popular applause were confined to the members of the Democratic Party. To be consulted, to be trusted, to be rewarded, was the part of the Democrats. The part of the Republicans was to stand outside the circle of authority, to give, and to serve, under the direction of their political opponents. Because they loved their country, they did give, and they did serve to the limit of their means and their strength. They put aside the natural impulses of party opposition, and distrust, and resentment, and devoted all their powers to the support of the Democratic Administration with an unselfish patriotism worthy of all honor, and full of cheerful hope for the future of America.

As we look back, we see already, do we not, that theirs was the better part? Not office, or emolument, or praise was the reward of those who only served; but a spirit purified, and a vision enlarged by the habit of unselfish service for America.

The defence of free self-government against class domination demands another service. Some will suffer, some votes will be lost, some offices will be sacrificed; but American Democracy will be saved. Shall Republicans not answer? Will they temporize? Can they refuse?

WAR MEMORIALS

SPEECH AT THE CONVENTION OF THE NATIONAL FEDERATION OF ARTS, HELD IN THE METROPOLITAN MUSEUM, NEW YORK CITY, MAY 15, 1919

I CAME here this afternoon partly to join my friends, both in the Museum and in the Federation in a welcome, and partly to express in the most informal way my concurrence in the general views which have been so much better expressed by Mr. Gray [1] in the paper which has just been read.

The idea of creating memorials of the great war, which will be useful, such as public buildings, schools, bridges, highways, parks, will always have many advocates — very sincere advocates, because our country is fortunate in having a vast number of public-spirited citizens who are earnestly engaged in civic betterment and are most desirous to have better public schools and buildings and bridges and parks.

So true is this, that the idea encounters a danger — and the danger is that earnest people, anxious for the advancement of these useful projects, will seize upon the memory of great persons, of great events, as a means to accomplish their individual desires, and that, instead of a project which is really memorial, there will be a project which is really useful under color of being memorial.

There is never a great man who dies, that there are not many people who wish to seize hold of his name for the pur-

---

[1] Morris Gray, President of the Museum of Fine Arts, Boston. Unable to be present, his paper was read by Mr. Edward Robinson, Director of the Metropolitan Museum. In the course of his paper, Mr. Gray said, "We must consider the ideals with which Americans entered into the war, the ideals of right, justice and liberty."

pose of achieving something that they have long desired to achieve. And there is always danger of falling into that error.

Now I think that in this Federation we ought to consider ourselves as charged with the advocacy, or at least the protection, of an entirely different conception. I don't know anything about art. On the ground of knowledge, I ought to resign from the Federation. I have only a series of ill-understood and half-appreciated ideas, picked up through long and priceless companionship with McKim [1] and Burnham [2] and Millet [3] and St. Gaudens [4] and many another man, who assumed a public duty and were inspired by a noble, patriotic enthusiasm. As the result of their community of spirit, their coöperation of effort, the great white city at Chicago was built up twenty-six years ago.

From that event there followed two great results for our country: One was that millions of people, coming from all over the land, — from simple and humble homes in little villages and on farms, as well as from the large cities, — gained by the mere observation of what art had done a new idea of the possibility of the enrichment of life by beauty. From that time one could perceive a gradual change in the attitude of public servants — members of Legislatures, of City Councils, of Congress. Executive and administrative officers began to show the effect of a change of spirit on the

[1] Charles Follen McKim (1847–1909) was a distinguished architect, head of the well-known firm of McKim, Mead & White, of New York City. Among his most notable achievements are the Columbia University buildings in New York, additions to the White House at Washington, and more especially, the Boston Public Library.

[2] Daniel Hudson Burnham (1846–1912), was a distinguished architect of Chicago. He drew the plans of the Chicago World's Fair, and many noted buildings in various parts of the United States.

[3] Francis D. Millet (1846–1912), American artist and war correspondent, who went down with the *Titanic* in 1912.

[4] Augustus Saint-Gaudens (1848–1907), "rightly regarded as the greatest sculptor produced by America, and his work had a most powerful influence on art in the United States." *Encyclopaedia Britannica*, 11th edition, 1911.

part of their constituents. From that time dates a renaissance in the public life of our country of those old ideals of simple beauty, which governed Jefferson at Monticello and in the University of Virginia; which governed Washington in the laying out of our National Capitol, in building the White House; which governed those great colonial artists from whom came the Old State House in Boston, and the City Hall, simple and beautiful among all the sky-scrapers of lower New York, and scores of other buildings scattered about the land.

The second result was that the men who created the miracle of the White City on the Lake, never lost the impulse of public progress, and they communicated that noble impulse to their associates and their successors. And from that impulse came this organization, made effective through the inimitable capacity of Frank Millet to win others to all that is best in art and in humanity.

Now this organization undertook a great responsibility. It was the first attempt to demonstrate among the people of the country at large the fact that art is not a luxury or a fad of the very rich. It appeals to that broad constituency that makes the opinion and determines the action of the United States. And the fundamental idea that gives life to the Federation is that, when all the material things have been accomplished, when men, women and children have all they need to eat and drink, clothes to wear, houses to cover them, schools for education — when all that has been done, there is still something more needed; and that one thing more, is the addition to the sum of human happiness of a love for beauty in art — and because in art, also in nature.

The attempt to make men better by mere precept, mere preaching, mere commands, mere statutes, mere orders from above, mere advice from superior persons, must necessarily fail, unless for the lower tastes, for the vices of display and gluttony and drunkenness and brutal, gross enjoyment, there be substituted something else. You cannot drive out the lower gratifications but by the substitution of the higher.

And the fundamental idea of this Federation is not merely love of art for itself, it is not merely the gratification of our own tastes — it is a great public purpose for the elimination of the base by the substitution of the higher and nobler qualities that go with love of beauty, of art, and of nature.

Now we come to an opportunity — an occasion. All the people of the country are deeply stirred by the spirit of service and sacrifice, — by the sacrifices, the losses of the Great War, — desirous to express themselves in some way that will carry to themselves, to their associates, to the world, to the future, their gratitude, their appreciation, their honor and reverence for those who have made the sacrifice, and for the spirit which moved them. How is that to be expressed?

I agree with Mr. Gray that this purpose is something which should stand by itself. It is greater than schools or bridges or public buildings. And I think it would be lamentable if it were to be treated as a subordinate thing, to be tacked on merely to some useful project.

What is it that the spirit of America, which took this peaceful people into the Great War that we all abhorred — should do to express itself to the far-distant future? How can we express the feeling that we have?

Well, for that, there is but one recourse — that is the function, the mission of art. That is what art is. It is the expression of the spirit which the plain man and woman are unable to find words to express. And unless the art of America can find ways to express that spirit, so that for distant ages, for generations to come long hence, there will be an inspiration derived from the spirit that led the young Americans to their death in France and Flanders, then we fail.

I think we ought to appeal to the art of America to express the spirit of America to the future! It need not be always great and expensive. In the little town, a simple memorial may — like that letter of Lincoln to the mother with five sons who died for their country — be the most beautiful and impressive expression, more so than great buildings. If we really have in our hearts the spirit that moved America in the Great War, we shall search for that expression, and we shall lay upon the artists of America the burden of finding the visible expression that will be a revelation to us of what we really feel, as well as a revelation to ages to come. Unless we do that, we fail.

Oh, it should not be that the exaltation of spirit that moved America from its materialism and its dull and sleepy prosperity, shall be lost for our country hereafter! It should not be that future generations shall be unmoved by the mighty forces which have moved us! But that spirit can be carried to them only by the performance of that highest function of art. No books can carry it. No history can convey it. It can be found and read in no newspaper files. Only the interpretation of the spirit by art can carry that incalculable blessing to the future generations of our country!

And so I think that it is the noble office of this Federation, throughout all the states to which its members will return after this meeting is over, to put into the deliberations of those who are considering how the memories of our country at its noblest and purest, shall be carried on to the future — a just conception of what their duty demands, of what their duty to their country demands.

It is no idle entertainment for us. We have the duty to see to it so far as we possibly can, that all the committees and the public officers are themselves inspired by the spirit which they are endeavoring to cause to be interpreted for the perpetuity of our institutions — the preservation and the enlargement for future generations of a conception of the liberty and the justice for which America fought and Americans have died!

NEW YORK REGIONAL PLAN

REMARKS IN BEHALF OF A PROJECT OF THE RUSSELL SAGE
FOUNDATION, IN THE ENGINEERING SOCIETY'S BUILDING,
NEW YORK CITY, MAY 10, 1922

"What would the world be without architects? A howling wilderness. Without
houses, temples, city halls, Woolworth buildings, men would be crawling animals.
And, without the sense and cheeriness of beauty, dangerous animals.

Praise to the Beaux-Arts Architects for their austere methods and their understanding of their *sacerdoce*. Praise to them because they feel interested in all kinds
of builders.

Mr. Root is one. In his variegated career he has never failed to apply the austere
principles of the Beaux-Arts people: order, logic, the importance of the line and of
the true perspective; each thing at its proper plan.

As Secretary of War, as Secretary of State, he has increased the solidity of the
foundations of the nation.

It is a privilege to have worked with him and it was my good fortune to have, for
years, this privilege.

His task is not finished. He is now, for the nation, a consulting architect, and all
men who appeal to him enjoy the feeling of a delightful intercourse with a man great
by his heart and great by his brains, the new medallist, Elihu Root." — *Extract of
remarks of His Excellency M. Jules J. Jusserand, New York, May 3, 1922, when Mr.
Root received the medal of the Société des Architects Diplomés par le Gouvernement
Français.*

I HAVE come here, not to tell you what is going to be done,
but simply to express my warm sympathy with the Plan,
and my great appreciation of the labors and the interest and
the devotion of the gentlemen who have undertaken this
work.

For fifty-seven years now I have lived on the gridiron like
St. Lawrence, on that gridiron laid down upon this island by
the commissioners of 1811, who arbitrarily laid out our rec-
tangular streets up and down and across the island without
any reference to the topography of the land; and I have seen
the city grow from less than a million to its present enormous

proportions. It is not so pleasant a place to live in as it was. With the growth of the city has come great crowding, most uncomfortable crowding. The conditions under which young men and women get to and from their work in the morning and evening are most disagreeable, hardly decent, and in the business parts of the city it is difficult to get light and air and even steerage-way through the streets. It is not only there; it is in parts of the city where the greater portion of the population live that the conditions are most distressing. I have been in the habit of saying that I do not think one can obtain a virile and dominant race where the children have paving stones between themselves and the earth.

This project is in some degree to ameliorate those conditions for the future. Not only is life in business overcrowded and hampered, but the conditions of distribution make living exceedingly expensive. New York is no place to live for any one with small means. Most extravagant incomes are necessary to enable any one to live here now as well as a person of very small means can live in one of our smaller towns.

We have not quite succeeded in building a city. Something is wrong about it. The gridiron has not worked satisfactorily. It is worth while to try to find out what the trouble is. In the first place, the difference between a very large collection of human beings in a small territory and a small collection of them, between a big city and a small town, is not so much a difference in degree as it is a difference in kind. When you pass from your small town to your big town, you get problems, difficulties, injurious conditions entirely different in kind from those that exist in the small town, and they ought to be dealt with intelligently.

A city is a growth. It is not the result of political decree or control. You may draw all the lines you please between counties and states, a city is a growth responding to forces not at all political, quite disregarding political lines. It is a growth like that of a crystal responding to forces inherent in the atoms that make it up.

And the force from which that growth comes is the force of individual enterprise, based on the desire for movement, the desire for a living, for wealth, for comfort, for society, all these desires existing in the hearts and acting on the minds of a vast number of units. That is the great force of life; that is the great force of modern civilization, and that is the thing that government cannot imitate. That is why the government could not run the railroads. That is why the government cannot run the shipping. For no Congress and no President can imitate or create a substitute for the net result of the infinite number of forces in individual human beings.

Those are the forces that build up a city. The individual human beings, in response to whose urge cities grow, never think about the conditions that are to be created by the bringing together of a great mass of other people like themselves. If we build a house, we build it in what we think is a convenient and comfortable, pleasant place to have a home. A thousand others, ten thousand, a hundred thousand, all have the same idea, but nobody thinks about the water supply; nobody thinks about the sewerage; nobody thinks what it is going to cost to deliver coal there; nobody thinks how far it is going to be from market; nobody thinks about the multitude of difficulties that are created by a great aggregation of human beings within a small territory. As a result, the growth of the city is without any intelligent thought whatever regarding the great difficulties that a city has to meet.

There is one other quite important influence added to this incessant reaching out for homes, and this following of the homes with stores, with schools, with hospitals, all without any thought about the fundamental needs of a city; and that is the real estate operator in pursuit of his honorable business. He gets hold of tracts of land here and there which he can map, and cut up into blocks and building lots, and advertise and sell. He is the man who very largely determines the growth of a city. He is not thinking about the difficulties the city will meet. He is thinking about the people he can induce to come to buy the lots and build houses on them.

Now, growth can be directed, just as trees can be trained and pruned and made to grow this way or that; if they are wanted for particular purposes they can be adapted to those purposes. This project is to get an intelligent idea of how the growth of this city in the future may be directed, with common and general judgment about the way in which it is desirable that it should grow, so that it will meet as fully as possible the difficulties that are inseparable from mass human life. I think the project is practicable. I think that the existence of plans known to everybody will give just enough direction to the movement of the multitude of separate impulses, to lead the growth along the right lines.

One of the distressing things about this town is that architects have the greatest difficulty in securing immortality through their works. An architect designs a noble building, it is erected, and in a few years somebody comes along and pulls it down to build something else. It is discovered that it was in the wrong place; it was not located with reference to any intelligent idea about how the city ought to grow and was going to grow. My heart has often ached to see buildings destroyed which I thought were going to carry down to future generations the names of friends of mine who had designed and erected them.

Now we see the difficulties from the lack of plan in the development of the city in the past hundred years. What these gentlemen are doing now is not going to make much difference to most of us, but it is going, so far as we help it, to pay our debt to the future; it is going, so far as we help it, to give to the future generations who occupy this great city some good things that they will inherit from us. It is not only the city, it is not only the state, it is this great country— for this city is an agency of the whole country. The city exists because it has a great country behind it. It does not exist for itself. It lives because it discharges a distinct function for all the people of America. To-day it is not discharging that function creditably. This project when carried out, I think, will enable it to render the service that is expected from it and in return for which incalculable wealth is poured into it, and to deserve the dignity and the honor befitting the great Republic for which it is the metropolis.

If this project is supported and developed and made public, if it strikes the imagination of the people and receives the support of the public authorities and of public opinion, we may believe that our children and our children's children will see a great metropolis in which are homes where children can see the sun and breathe the air and grow up in strength and beauty, instead of the tenement-house life that disgraces our civilization. The people living in the city give up all the beauties of nature, all the wonders of the fields and the forests and the mountain and the sea; but they may see a city where men find life worth living, among nobly planned and adequately spaced and harmoniously related streets and open spaces and architectural monuments.

Did it ever occur to you that in the City of New York we never approach anything that is beautiful and noble? We are always going by such things. There are many great and noble buildings, noble works of art, but we are always passing by them. You have to turn your head to see them. In the one city of America that had a plan — in the city for which Washington secured, in the person of L'Enfant,[1] the advantage of that sense of design in which the French are so superior — wherever you go you have before your eyes something noble and beautiful. In New York the fine things are by-products, they are side-shows.

I hope for our city in the future that the immense increment to human happiness which comes from the cultivation of taste, may be gratified and nourished by laying before the people, always, objects that are noble and beautiful, that will ennoble and beautify character, so that the people of this great city will contribute to the character of America not weakness, but strength and vigor.

[1] Pierre Charles L'Enfant, who, born in France in 1755, accompanied Lafayette to America in 1777. He rose to the rank of major in the Continental Army, and came into intimate and friendly relations with General Washington.

In conjunction with Washington and Jefferson, he drew plans for the City of Washington, which, after well-nigh a century of neglect, have not only come into favor, but the Washington of our day is being developed in conformity with them.

"Few men can afford to wait a hundred years to be remembered. It is not a change in L'Enfant that brings us here. It is we who have changed, who have just become able to appreciate his work. And our tribute to him should be to continue his work. . . .

If this city were destroyed and nothing remained but the table of this tomb on which is engraved in facsimile the plan of L'Enfant, any man of sense finding it, would say, observing that mixture of logic and beauty: this must be the work of a son of France." *Extract of Mr. Root's speech at the unveiling of a monument to Major L'Enfant at Arlington Cemetery, May 22, 1911.*

See, "Major L'Enfant and the Federal City," in a volume published in 1916 — *With Americans of Past and Present Days* — by the accomplished French Ambassador, Jules J. Jusserand.

IV

INTERNATIONAL AFFAIRS

THE LEAGUE OF NATIONS

In the autumn of 1914, President Wilson said:

"Four things will have to be settled after this war, I mean these things: First, that small nations shall have equal rights with great nations; second, that never again must it be permitted for a foot of ground to be obtained by conquest; third, that the manufacture of munitions of war must be by governments and not by private enterprise; and, fourth, that all nations must be absorbed into some great association of nations whereby all shall guarantee the integrity of each, so that any one nation violating the agreement between all of them shall bring punishment on itself automatically."

The United States entered the war against Germany on April 6, 1917. An armistice was granted to Germany, at its request, in order to conclude peace. It was signed on November 11, 1918, and the war was practically, though not technically, over. Delegates flocked to Paris from the powers at war with Germany and her allies, including countries which had broken off diplomatic relations without actually declaring war. President Wilson himself headed the American Commission and endeavored, it would seem, to carry into effect the essentials of the League, or Association, of Nations, which he had said, in the autumn of 1914, would be the outcome of the war.

The draft then known as the Constitution of the League of Nations was approved by the Peace Conference at Paris on February 14, 1919. It was reconsidered and amended in various respects under the Covenant of the League, and as adopted on April 28, 1919, it forms the opening section of the various treaties drafted by the Peace Conference at Paris and imposed upon Germany and her allies.

In the interval between the two drafts, Mr. Root had given much thought to modifications in the Constitution which would render the League, or Association, more acceptable. At the request of the Honorable Frank L. Polk, Acting Secretary during Secretary Lansing's absence with President Wilson, Mr. Root sent his amendments to the State Department on March 26, 1919, from which they were cabled to Secretary Lansing on the following day. These are the amendments annexed to Mr. Root's letter to Honorable Will H. Hays.

The Treaty with Germany, of which President Wilson was one of the negotiators, was signed by him and the other plenipotentiaries on June 28, 1919. It was laid before the Senate of the United States on November 19, 1919. On two occasions the opposition to its ratification centred around the Covenant of the League of Nations — an opposition which Mr. Root's amendments were calculated to obviate, had they been accepted *in toto*. The treaty was first rejected by the Senate on November 19, 1919, and again, as it finally appeared, on March 19, 1920.

LETTER TO THE DEPARTMENT OF STATE

998 Fifth Avenue, New York, March 26, 1919

Howard Shaw, Esq.,
    Secretary
        to Acting Secretary of State Frank L. Polk,
            State Department, Washington, D. C.

My dear Sir,

A request has come to me through Mr. S. R. Bertron and Mr. Henry L. Stimson to send to Acting Secretary Polk at White Sulphur Springs a copy of certain proposed amendments to the "Constitution of the League of Nations" which I have drafted, and to send a copy of the same to you at the State Department. The request is accompanied by the statement that you have received instructions as to the disposition to be made of the paper. I accordingly enclose the draft, and I am sending another copy to Mr. Polk at the Green Brier Hotel.

Very truly yours,

Elihu Root

CABLE FROM THE DEPARTMENT OF STATE TO THE AMERICAN COMMISSION TO NEGOTIATE PEACE, AT PARIS

Department of State, Washington, *March 27, 1919.*

Ammission, Paris.

For Secretary Lansing from Polk.

Following are proposed amendments to the Constitution of the League of Nations which have been drafted by Mr. Root:

First Amendment

Strike out Article XIII, and insert the following:

The high contracting powers agree to refer to the existing Permanent Court of Arbitration at The Hague, or to the Court of Arbitral Justice proposed at the Second Hague Conference, when established, or to some other Arbitral Tribunal, all disputes between them (including those affecting honor and vital interests) which are of a justiciable character, and which the powers concerned have failed to settle by diplomatic methods. The powers so referring to arbitration agree to accept and give effect to the award of the Tribunal.

Disputes of a justiciable character are defined as disputes as to the interpretation of a treaty, as to any question of international law, as to the existence of any fact which if established would constitute a breach of any international obligation, or as to the nature and extent of the reparation to be made for any such breach.

Any question which may arise as to whether a dispute is of a justiciable character is to be referred for decision to the Court of Arbitral Justice when constituted, or, until it is constituted, to the existing Permanent Court of Arbitration at The Hague.

SECOND AMENDMENT

Add to Article XIV the following paragraph:

The Executive Council shall call a general conference of the Powers to meet not less than two years or more than five years after the signing of this convention for the purpose of reviewing the condition of international law, and of agreeing upon and stating in authoritative form the principles and rules thereof.

Thereafter regular conferences for that purpose shall be called and held at stated times.

THIRD AMENDMENT

Immediately before the signatures of the American Delegates, insert the following reservation:

Inasmuch as in becoming a member of the League the United States of America is moved by no interest or wish to intrude upon or interfere with the political policy or internal administration of any foreign state, and by no existing or anticipated dangers in the affairs of the American continents, but accedes to the wish of the European states that it shall join its power to theirs for the preservation of general peace, the representatives of the United States of America sign this convention with the understanding that nothing therein contained shall be construed to imply a relinquishment by the United States of America of its traditional attitude towards purely American questions, or to require the submission of its policy regarding such questions (including therein the admission of immigrants) to the revision or recommendation of other powers.

FOURTH AMENDMENT

Add to Article X the following:

After the expiration of five years from the signing of this convention any party may terminate its obligation under this Article by giving one year's notice in writing to the Secretary General of the League.

FIFTH AMENDMENT

Add to Article IX the following:

Such Commission shall have full power of inspection and verification personally and by authorized agents as to all armament, equipment, munitions, and industries referred to in Article VIII.

Add to Article XXIV the following:

The Executive Council shall call a general conference of members of the League to meet not less than five or more than ten years after the signing of this convention, for the revision thereof; and at that time, or at any time thereafter upon one year's notice, any member may withdraw from the League.

PHILLIPS
Acting

CORRESPONDENCE WITH THE HONORABLE WILL H. HAYS, CHAIRMAN OF THE REPUBLICAN NATIONAL COMMITTEE

WASHINGTON, D. C., *March 24, 1919.*

HON. ELIHU ROOT,
    New York, N. Y.:

DEAR SENATOR ROOT, —

Americans are seeking earnestly for further light on the question of the so-called League of Nations.

In the same spirit in which Republicans during the recent war measured their every act by how they could contribute most to effective action, so now they are determined to meet this new phase of the war problem in that revived spirit of fervent Americanism which is the glorified result of our experience of fire and blood, moving with a full appreciation of this country's duty as a responsible factor in the world of to-day and to-morrow, and with the earnest determination to do all that can possibly be done toward the maintenance of peace without sacrificing our own supreme nationalism, the preservation of which in its integrity is the greatest safeguard for the future, not only for the citizens of this country but for all peoples everywhere.

With a seriousness commensurate with the magnitude and complexity of the problem, the people are seeking the fullest information and best judgment to enable them to reach a correct conclusion. I know that I express the feeling of great numbers of your fellow citizens when I say that they will be under real obligation to you if you will present your views upon this vital subject.

Trusting you may see your way clear to meet this obvious demand, I am, with great respect,

Sincerely yours,

WILL H. HAYS

Chairman

NEW YORK, MARCH 29, 1919,

THE HONORABLE WILL H. HAYS, Chairman, etc.

DEAR SIR, —

I have received your letter of March 24, and I give you herewith, at perhaps inordinate length, my views regarding the proposed convention for a league of nations.

I am sure that all of us earnestly desire that there shall be an effective international organization to preserve the peace of the world, and that our country shall do its full share toward the establishment and maintenance of such an organization. I do not see much real controversy about that among the American people, either between parties, or within parties, or otherwise.

There is, however, a serious question whether the particular proposed agreement which is now under discussion by the Peace Conference in Paris under the title, "Constitution of a League of Nations," will accomplish that end in its present form, and whether it cannot be made more effective and free from objection. A careful study of the paper, under the urging of intense interest in the subject, has led me to the conclusion that a large part of its provisions will be of great value; but that it has very serious faults, which may lead to the ultimate failure of the whole scheme unless they are remedied, and some faults which, unnecessarily and without any benefit whatever to the project, tend to embarrass and hinder the United States in giving its full support to the scheme.

I think there should be several very important amendments to the agreement.

This seems to be the general view. Mr. Taft, who joined the President in advocating the agreement, says it ought to be amended, almost as strongly as his former Secretary of State, Senator Knox, says the same thing. When Mr. Lodge and Mr. Lowell had their great debate in Boston, both said the agreement ought to be amended.

A discussion of the merits and faults of the scheme with a view to amendment is now the regular order of business. It was to give an opportunity for such a discussion that the paper was reported to the Paris Conference and made public by the committee that prepared it.

At the time of the report Lord Robert Cecil, who represented Great Britain in the Committee, said: "I rejoice very much that the course which has been taken this afternoon has been pursued. It seems to me a good omen for the great project in which we are engaged that before its final completion it should have been published to the world and laid before all its people for their service and for their criticism."

Signore Orlando, who represented Italy, said: "We all expect from the discussion and development of the present act a renewal of the whole world; but, as the present debate has for its object to bring the whole scheme before the public opinion of the world, I wish to bring to that debate my professional contribution."

M. Léon Bourgeois, who represented France in the Committee, said: "Lord Robert Cecil has said: 'We now present to the Conference and to the world the result of our work'; but we do not present it as something that is final, but only as the result of an honest effort, to be discussed and to be examined not only by this Conference, but the public opinion of the world."

At that very time M. Bourgeois suggested an amendment about which I shall say something presently, and he went on to say: "The observations we have made on some points will, we hope, be of some value in the further discussions, since we are at the beginning of the examination of the whole plan."

These gentlemen represented all the great Allies by whose side we have been fighting in Europe, and it is plain that they expected and wished that the scheme which they had reported should be subjected to public discussion and criticism in their own countries and in ours. It is also plain that they saw no reason why the proposed agreement should be rushed through in such haste that there would not be an opportunity for public discussion and criticism and for communicating the results to the Conference.

Under our Constitution it is the business of the Senate to take the lead in such a discussion, to compare the different opinions expressed in the several states, and to draft in proper form the amendments which the public judgment seems to call for. It is unfortunate that the Senate has not been permitted to perform that duty in this case. It seems to me that the Senate ought to have been convened for that purpose immediately after the 4th of March. In addition to the regular and extra sessions of Congress the Senate has been convened separately in special session forty-two times since it was first organized, ordinarily to confirm a few appointments or pass on unimportant treaties — never for any reason more important than exists now.

There is a special reason why the Senate should consider this proposed agreement. Ordinarily, treaties are negotiated by ambassadors, ministers, or delegates, and their work is supervised and corrected, if need be, by the President and Secretary of State at Washington, who from their different point of view frequently see things the actual negotiators overlook. In this case, since the President himself is negotiating the Treaty in Paris, there is no one in Washington to supervise the negotiation, and there is no one with authority to give the negotiators the benefit of independent official judgment, unless the Senate is to perform that function.

This situation throws upon the people of the country the duty to answer the expectations of the Conference by studying and discussing and expressing their opinions on the various provisions of the proposed agreement, and to make their expressions of opinion heard the best way they can.

The avowed object of the agreement is to prevent future wars. That is what interests us. We are not trying to get anything for ourselves from the Paris Conference. We are not asking any help from the other nations who are in the Conference, but we should like to do our part toward preventing future wars. How does the proposed scheme undertake to do that?

To answer that question, one must call to mind the conditions to which the scheme is to be applied.

All the causes of war fall in two distinct classes. One class consists of controversies about rights under the law of nations and under treaties. In a general way these are described as justiciable or judicial questions. They are similar to the questions between individuals which courts are all the time deciding. They cover by far the greater number of questions upon which controversies between nations arise.

For more than half a century the American government has been urging upon all the world the settlement of all such questions by arbitration. Presidents Grant, Arthur, Harrison, Cleveland, McKinley, Roosevelt, and Taft strongly approved the establishment of a system of arbitration in their messages to Congress. Thirty years ago our Congress adopted a resolution requesting the President to invite negotiations with every other government, "to the end that any differences or disputes arising between the two governments which cannot be adjusted by diplomatic agency may be referred to arbitration and be peaceably adjusted by such means."

President McKinley in his first inaugural declared: "The adjustment of difficulties by judicial methods rather than force of arms has been recognized as the leading feature of our foreign policy throughout our entire national history."

We have illustrated the benefits of this method of settling

disputes by the Alabama Arbitration in 1872, the Bering Sea Arbitration in 1893, the Alaska Boundary Tribunal in 1903, the North Atlantic Fisheries Arbitration in 1910.

The two great International Conferences at The Hague in 1899 and in 1907 established a permanent Court of Arbitration, and rules of procedure. They also made great progress in agreeing upon and codifying the rules of international law which this court was to administer.

There was a weakness in the system devised by the Hague Conference. It was that arbitration of these justiciable questions was not made obligatory, so that no nation could bring another before the court unless the defendant was willing to come, and there was no way to enforce a judgment.

But the public opinion of the world grew. Nations began to make obligatory treaties of arbitration with one another. Hundreds of such treaties were made. The United States made some thirty such treaties with most of the principal countries in the world, agreeing absolutely to arbitrate questions arising under international law and upon the interpretation of treaties. A strong opinion arose in favor of establishing an international court composed of judges who would devote their entire time to the business of the court. The Second Hague Conference adopted a plan for such a court; and while Mr. Knox was Secretary of State he negotiated a treaty with the other great powers for its effective establishment. It became evident that the world was ready for obligatory arbitration of justiciable questions.

After the Great War began, the American "League to Enforce Peace," at the head of which are Mr. Taft and Mr. Lowell, made it the first plank in its platform that "All justiciable questions arising between the signatory powers not settled by negotiation shall — subject to the limitation of treaties — be submitted to a judicial tribunal for hearing and judgment, etc."

A similar group in Great Britain, of which Lord Bryce was a leading spirit, made the first plank in its platform the following:

"The signatory Powers agree to refer to the existing Permanent Court of Arbitration at The Hague, or to the Court of Arbitral Justice proposed at the Second Hague Conference, if and when such Court shall be established, or to some other arbitral tribunal, all disputes between them (including those affecting honor and vital interests) which are of a justiciable character, and which the Powers concerned have failed to settle by diplomatic methods."

And both of these groups proposed to provide for enforcing the judgments of the court by economic pressure or by force.

The other class of disputes which give rise to war consists of clashes between conflicting national policies as distinguished from claims of legal right. They do not depend upon questions of law or treaty, but upon one nation or ruler undertaking to do something that another nation or ruler wishes to prevent. Such questions are a part of international politics. They are similar to the questions as to which our courts say: "This is a political question, not a judicial question, and we have no concern with it." The question whether Russia should help Serbia when Austria invaded Serbia in July, 1914, is an illustration. Our own Monroe Doctrine is another illustration. That is not an assertion of any legal right, but it is a declaration that certain acts will be regarded as dangerous to the peace and safety of the United States, and therefore unfriendly.

Such questions are continually arising in Europe and the Near East, and the way in which the European countries have been in the habit of dealing with them has been to bring about a conference of the representatives of the different nations, to discuss the subject, and find some way of reconciling the differences or of convincing the parties to the dispute that it would not be safe for them to break the peace. For example, in 1905, when the German Emperor's dramatic challenge of the policy of France as to Morocco had made war seem probable, the Algeciras Conference was brought about, largely by the influence of President Roosevelt, and that conference resulted in preventing war. In 1912, when the Balkan wars had brought Europe apparently to the verge of universal war, the ambassadors of all the great powers met in London, and the result of their conference was to avert war. So, in the last week of July, 1914, Sir Edward Grey tried to bring about another conference for the purpose of averting the great war in which we have been engaged; but Germany refused to attend the conference; and she refused because she meant to bring on the war, and knew that if she attended a conference it would become practically impossible for her to do so.

The weak point about this practice of international conferences in times of danger was that they were left solely to the initiative of the individual nations; that nobody had a right to call a conference, and nobody was bound to attend one.

The great and essential thing about the plan contained in this "Constitution for a League of Nations" is that it makes international conferences on political questions compulsory in times of danger; that it brings together such conferences upon the call of officers who represent all the powers, and makes it practically impossible for any nation to keep out of them. This effect is produced by the provisions of Article XV, relating to the Executive Council of the League, or upon demand of either party to the body of delegates. Article XV is the central and controlling article of the agreement. Putting out of consideration for the moment Article X, which relates to a mutual guaranty of territory, Articles VIII and IX, which relate to the reduction of armaments, and Article

XIX, which relates to mandatories, all the other important articles in the agreement are designed to make effective the conference of the powers resulting from the submission of a dispute upon a question of policy under Article XV.

Especially important among these ancillary articles is Article XI, which declares war or threat of war to be a matter of concern to the whole League; Article XII, which prohibits going to war without the submission of the dispute and without allowing time for its settlement, or contrary to a unanimous recommendation of the Executive Council or an award of arbitrators (if there shall have been an arbitration); and Article XVI, which provides for enforcing the provisions of Article XII by economic boycott, or, if the powers choose to do so, by military force.

I think these provisions are well devised, and should be regarded as free from any just objection, so far as they relate to the settlement of the political questions at which they are really aimed. The provisions which, taken together, accomplish this result are of the highest value. They are developed naturally from the international practice of the past. They are a great step forward. They create an institution through which the public opinion of mankind, condemning unjust aggression and unnecessary war, may receive effect, and exert its power for the preservation of peace, instead of being dissipated in fruitless protest or lamentation. The effect will be to make the sort of conference which Sir Edward Grey tried in vain to get for the purpose of averting this Great War obligatory, inevitable, automatic. I think everybody ought to be in favor of that.

I repeat that this scheme for the settlement of political questions such as brought about the present war is of very great practical value, and it would be a sad thing if this opportunity for the establishment of such a safeguard against future wars should be lost.

This plan of automatic conference, however, is accompanied by serious defects.

The scheme practically abandons all effort to promote or maintain anything like a system of international law, or a system of arbitration, or of judicial settlement, through which a nation can assert its legal rights in lieu of war. It is true that Article XIII mentions arbitration, and makes the parties agree that, whenever a dispute arises "which they recognize to be suitable for submission to arbitration," they will submit it to a court "agreed upon by the parties." That, however, is merely an agreement to arbitrate when the parties choose to arbitrate, and it is therefore no agreement at all. It puts the whole subject of arbitration back where it was twenty-five years ago. Instead of perfecting and putting teeth into the system of arbitration provided for by the Hague Conventions, it throws those Conventions upon the scrap-heap. By covering the ground of arbitration and prescribing a new test of obligation, it apparently, by virtue of the provisions of Article XXV, abrogates all the two hundred treaties of arbitration by which the nations of the world have bound themselves with each other to submit to arbitration all questions arising under international law, or upon the interpretation of treaties.

It is to be observed that neither the Executive Council nor the body of delegates to whom disputes are to be submitted under Article XV of the agreement is in any sense whatever a judicial body or an arbitral body. Its function is not to decide upon anybody's right. It is to investigate, to consider, and to make recommendations. It is bound to recommend what it deems to be expedient at the time. It is the states which act, and not the individuals. The honorable obligation of each member is a political obligation as the representative of a state. This is a method very admirable for dealing with political questions; but it is wholly unsuited to the determination of questions of right under the law of nations. It is true also that Article XIV mentions a Court of International Justice, and provides that the Executive Council shall formulate plans for such a court, and that this court shall when established be competent to determine matters which the parties recognize as suitable for submission to it. There is no agreement or direction that such a court shall be established or that any questions shall be submitted to it.

International Law is not mentioned at all, except in the preamble; no method is provided, and no purpose is expressed to insist upon obedience to law, to develop the law, to press forward agreement upon its rules and recognition of its obligations. All questions of right are relegated to the investigation and the recommendation of a political body, to be determined as matters of expediency.

I confess I cannot see the judgment of three generations of the wisest and best of American statesmen, concurred in by the wisest and the best of all our allies, thus held for naught. I believe with them that — necessary as may be the settlement of political questions — it is necessary also to insist upon rules of international conduct founded upon principles, and that the true method by which public right shall be established to control the affairs of nations is by the development of law and the enforcement of law, according to the judgments of impartial tribunals. I should have little confidence in the growth or permanence of an international organization which applied no test to the conduct of nations except the expediency of the moment.

The first change which I should make in this agreement accordingly would be to give effectiveness to the judicial settlement of international disputes upon questions of right — upon justiciable or judicial questions — by making the arbitration of such questions obligatory under the system established by the Hague Conferences, or before the proposed Court of Arbitral Justice, or, if the parties prefer in any particular case, before some specially constituted tribunal; putting the whole world upon the same footing in that respect that has been created between the United States and practically every nation now represented in Paris, by means of the special treaties which we have made with them. The term "Justiciable Questions" should be carefully defined, so as to exclude all questions of policy, and to describe the same kind of questions the Supreme Court of the United States has been deciding for more than a century.

When that is done, the reference to arbitration in Article XII will have some force and effect instead of being, as it is now, a mere idle form.

The second change which I think should be made is to provide for a general conference, followed by regular conferences at stated intervals, to discuss, agree upon, and state in authentic form the rules of international law, so that the development of law may go on, and arbitral tribunals may have continually a more perfect system of rules of right conduct to apply in their decisions.

I send you herewith drafts of two suggested amendments designed to accomplish these results.

The distinction between the treatment of questions of legal right and questions of policy which I have drawn above has an important bearing upon the attitude of the United States toward the settlement of disputes.

So far as the determination of justiciable questions arising under the law of nations or under treaties is concerned, we ought to be willing to stand on precisely the same footing with all other nations. We should be willing to submit our legal rights to judicial decision, and to abide by the decision. We have shown that we are willing to do that by the numerous treaties that we have made with the greater part of the world agreeing to do that, and we should be willing to have the same thing provided for in this general agreement.

With regard to questions of policy, however, some different considerations are apparent.

In determining the extent of our participation in the political affairs of the Old World, we ought to be satisfied that a sufficient affirmative reason exists for setting aside to that extent the long-established policy of the United States to keep the Old and the New World from becoming entangled in each other's affairs and embroiled in each other's quarrels. Just so far as such a reason exists, we ought to go, but no further.

We have to start in the consideration of such a subject with the words of Washington's farewell address: "Europe has a set of primary interests which to us have none or a very remote relation. Hence, she must be engaged in frequent controversies, the causes of which are essentially foreign to our concerns. Hence, therefore, it must be unwise in us to implicate ourselves by artificial ties in the ordinary vicissitudes of her politics, or the ordinary combinations and collisions of her friendships or enmities." And Jefferson's advice to Monroe: "Our first and fundamental maxim should be never to entangle ourselves in the broils of Europe; our second, never to suffer Europe to intermeddle with cis-Atlantic affairs."

Unquestionably, the Old and the New Worlds have come into much more intimate relations since the time of Washington and Jefferson, and they have many more interests in common. Nevertheless, the basis of the expressions I have quoted remains, in substance. The people of the United States have no direct interest in the distribution of territory in the Balkans or the control of Morocco, and the peoples of Europe have no direct interest in the questions between Chile and Peru, or between the United States and Colombia.

Based upon this fact, the Monroe Doctrine has hitherto kept the Old World and the New in two separate fireproof compartments, so that a conflagration in one did not extend to the other. There never was a time when the wisdom of the Monroe Doctrine for the preservation in peace and safety of the United States was more evident than it is now. Some facile writers of late have pronounced the Doctrine obsolete and useless, but I know of no experienced and responsible American statesman who has ever taken that view, and I cannot help feeling that such a view results from insufficient acquaintance with the subject.

There has, however, arisen in these days for the American people a powerful secondary interest in the affairs of Europe coming from the fact that war in Europe and the Near East threatens to involve the entire world, and the peaceable nations of Europe need outside help to put out the fire, and keep it from starting again. That help to preserve peace we ought to give, and that help we wish to give. In agreeing to give it, the following considerations should be observed.

We are not asking, and do not need, any help from the nations of the Old World for the preservation of peace in America, nor is any American nation asking for such help. The difficulties, the disturbing conditions, the dangers that threaten, are all in the affairs of Europe and the Near East. The real reason for creating a league of nations is to deal with those difficulties and dangers — not with American affairs. It is, therefore, wholly unnecessary for the purpose of the League that purely American affairs should be included within the scope of the agreement.

When we enter into the League of Nations, we do so not with any desire to interfere in the concerns of foreign nations, but because the peaceable nations of Europe ask us to put our power behind theirs to preserve peace in their part of the world. It is not reasonable, therefore, that such participation as we agree to in the activities of the League should be made the basis of an inference that we are trying to interfere in the Old World, and therefore should abandon our objection to having the Old World interfere in America.

With reference to the most important American questions, Europe as a whole on one side and the United States on the other occupy positions which, however friendly, are nevertheless in opposition. It must be remembered that the League of Nations contemplates the membership, not only of our present allies, but ultimately of all the nations of Europe. Now, the Monroe Doctrine was declared against those nations of Europe. It was a warning to them not to trespass on American territory, and, admitting exceptions and speaking only in the most general way, the nations of Europe are on one side of that question, and the United States is on the other. To submit the policy of Monroe to a council composed chiefly of European powers is to surrender it.

I will add — without taking up space to discuss it — that I cannot escape the conclusion that to ratify this agreement as it now stands would itself be a surrender of the Monroe Doctrine, and that the agreement as it now stands gives to the United States no effective substitute for the protection which the maintenance of that Doctrine affords.

The same thing is true of immigration. The nations of Europe in general are nations from which emigrants go. The United States is a nation to which immigrants come. Apart from Great Britain, which would be bound to look after the similar interests of Canada and Australia, Europe and America are bound to look at questions of emigration and immigration from different points of view, and under the influence of different interests — friendly indeed, but opposing.

It hardly seems reasonable that under these circumstances the United States should be penalized for complying with the request of its friends in Europe to join them in the preservation of peace primarily for their benefit, and not for ours, by giving up our right to self-protection, when that is wholly unnecessary to accomplish the object of the agreement. I think, therefore, that these purely American questions ought to be excepted from the jurisdiction of the Executive Council and body of delegates, and I have prepared and annexed hereto a third amendment in the form of a reservation, this being the method which was followed without any objection, to accomplish the same purpose, at the close of both the Hague Conferences.

The fourth point upon which I think there should be an amendment is Article X, which contains the undertaking "To respect and preserve as against external aggression the territorial integrity and existing political independence of all members of the League."

Looking at this article as a part of a perpetual league for the preservation of peace, my first impression was that the whole article ought to be stricken out. If perpetual, it would be an attempt to preserve for all time unchanged the distribution of power and territory made in accordance with the views and exigencies of the Allies in this present juncture of affairs. It would necessarily be futile. It would be what was attempted by the Peace of Westphalia at the close of the Thirty Years' War, at the Congress of Vienna at the close of the Napoleonic wars, by the Congress of Berlin in 1878. It would not only be futile: it would be mischievous. Change and growth are the law of life, and no generation can impose its will in regard to the growth of nations and the distribution of power upon succeeding generations.

I think, however, that this article must be considered not merely with reference to the future, but with reference to the present situation in Europe. Indeed, this whole agreement ought to be considered in that double aspect. The belligerent power of Germany, Austria, Bulgaria, and Turkey has been destroyed; but that will not lead to future peace without a reconstruction of Eastern Europe and Western Asia. The vast territories of the Hohenzollerns, the Hapsburgs, and the Romanoffs have lost the rulers who formerly kept the population in order, and are filled with turbulent masses without stable government, unaccustomed to self-control, and fighting among themselves like children of the dragon's teeth. There can be no settled peace until these masses are reduced to order. Since the Bolsheviki have been allowed to consolidate the control which they established with German aid in Russia, the situation is that Great Britain, France, Italy and Belgium, with a population of less than 130,000,000, are confronted with the disorganized but vigorous and warlike population of Germany, German Austria, Hungary, Bulgaria, Turkey and Russia, amounting approximately to 280,-000,000, fast returning to barbarism and the lawless violence of barbarous races. Order must be restored. The allied nations in their Council must determine the lines of reconstruction. Their determinations must be enforced. They may make mistakes. Doubtless, they will; but there must be decision, and decision must be enforced. Under these conditions, the United States cannot quit. It must go on to the performance of its duty, and the immediate aspect of Article X is an agreement to do that. I think, therefore, that Article X should be amended so that it shall hold a limited time, and thereafter any member may withdraw from it. I annex an amendment to that effect.

The fifth amendment which I think is needed is one suggested by M. Bourgeois in his speech at the Conference, which I have quoted above. It is to the provisions regarding the limitation of armaments. The success of those provisions is vital. If they are not effective, the whole effort to secure future peace goes for nothing. The plan of this League is contained in Articles VIII and IX. They provide that there shall be a reduction of national armaments to the lowest point consistent with national safety; that the Executive Council shall formulate plans for a general agreement as to the amount of these reductions; and that when an agreement has been made by the powers, the parties will not conceal from each other, but will give full and frank information regarding their industries capable of being adapted to warlike purposes, the scale of their armaments, and their military and naval programmes. Article IX provides for a permanent commission to advise the League on the execution of these provisions. This full information is essential. Otherwise, one nation will suspect another of secret preparation, and will prepare to protect itself in the same way, so that the whole scheme of limitation will be destroyed. There would be some justification for this, because there are some nations of whom it would be idle to expect the truth on such a subject: their public officers would regard it as a duty to conceal and mislead. The only way to prevent that sort of thing is by giving the Permanent Commission power of inspection and verification. Every country should assent to this, just as every trustee and treasurer is willing to have an independent audit of his accounts. I annex such an amendment.

Enough has been said already to indicate that this Constitution of a League of Peace cannot be regarded as a final and conclusive instrument. It necessarily leaves much to be determined hereafter. We do not know yet what nations are to be the members of the League, what nations are to be represented in the Council, what the limitations of armaments, what the regulations for the manufacture of munitions, or what the parties understand to be the scope of the provision for freedom of transit and equitable treatment for commerce.

The provision of Article XIX (of which I fully approve), relating to mandatories to aid or take charge of administration in new states and old colonies, necessarily leaves both the selection of the mandatories and the character of their powers and duties unsettled. All these uncertainties are not matters for criticism, but of necessity, arising from the situation. Still more important is the fact that no one knows when or upon what terms the Central and Eastern powers are to be admitted to the League. The whole agreement is at present necessarily tentative. It cannot really be a league of peace in operation for a number of years to come. It is now and in the immediate future must be rather an alliance of approximately one half of the active world against or for the control of the other half. Under these circumstances it would be most unwise to attempt to give to this agreement finality, and make the specific obligations of its members irrevocable. There should be provision for its revision in a calmer atmosphere, and when the world is less subject to exciting and disturbing causes. In the meantime the agreement should not be deemed irrevocable. The last amendment which I annex is directed to that end.

If the amendments which I have suggested are made, I think it will be the clear duty of the United States to enter into the agreement.

In that case it would be the duty of Congress to establish by law the offices of representatives of the United States in the body of Delegates and the Executive Council, just as the offices of ambassadors and ministers are already provided for by law; and the new offices would be filled by appointment of the President with the advice and consent of the Senate under Article II, Section 2, of the Constitution of the United States.

Very truly yours,

ELIHU ROOT.

REVISED DRAFT OF THE PROPOSED COVENANT

WASHINGTON, D.C., JUNE 21, 1919

THE HONORABLE HENRY CABOT LODGE,

MY DEAR SENATOR:

YOU were good enough to ask that, after studying the whole of the proposed treaty with Germany and the amendments already made to the league of nations part of it, I should write you my opinion as to the amendments and as to the action which would be wise in view of existing international conditions.

I should be glad to see the peace terms and the League of Nations Covenant separated, as proposed in the resolution offered by Senator Knox, so that the latter could be considered by the people of the country without coercion from the necessities of speedy peace.

To avoid repetition, I enclose a copy of a letter which I wrote to Mr. Will H. Hays, March 29, 1919, proposing amendments to the League of Nations Covenant, and giving the reasons for them.[1] Amendments similar in substance were proposed at about the same time by many Americans familiar with public affairs, both in and out of the Senate. The amendments subsequently made in the Covenant by the Paris Conference, while to some extent dealing with the subjects of the amendments so proposed, are very inadequate and unsatisfactory.

Nothing has been done to provide for the reëstablishment and strengthening of a system of arbitration or judicial decision upon questions of legal right. Nothing has been done toward providing for the revision or development of international law. In these respects principles maintained by the United States without variation for half a century are still ignored, and we are left with a programme which rests the hope of the world for future peace in a government of men,

---

[1] For the text of the proposed amendments, see pp. 245-247.

and not of laws, following the dictates of expediency, and not of right. Nothing has been done to limit the vast and incalculable obligation which Article 10 of the Covenant undertakes to impose upon each member of the League to preserve against external aggression the territorial integrity and political independence of all members of the League all over the world.

The clause authorizing withdrawal from the League upon two years' notice leaves a doubt whether a mere charge that we had not performed some international obligation would not put it in the power of the Council to take jurisdiction of the charge as a disputed question and keep us in the League indefinitely against our will.

The clause which has been inserted regarding the Monroe Doctrine is erroneous in its description of the doctrine and ambiguous in meaning. Other purely American questions, as, for example, questions relating to immigration, are protected only by a clause apparently empowering the Council to determine whether such questions are solely within the domestic jurisdiction of the United States. I do not think that in these respects the United States is sufficiently protected against most injurious results which are wholly unnecessary for the establishment and maintenance of this league of nations.

On the other hand, it still remains that there is in the Covenant a great deal of very high value which the world ought not to lose. The arrangement to make conferences of the powers automatic when there is danger of war; provisions for joint action as of course, by representatives of the nations concerned in matters affecting common interests; the agreement for delay in case of serious disputes, with opportunity to bring the public opinion of the world to bear on the disputants, and to induce cool and deliberate judgment; the recognition of racial and popular rights to the freedom of local self-government; and the plan, indispensable in some form, for setting up governments in the vast regions deprived by the war of the autocratic rule which had maintained order — all those ought not be lost if that can possibly be avoided. The condition of Europe requires prompt action. Industry has not revived there. Its revival requires raw materials. To obtain these credit is necessary, and for this there must be security for the fruits of enterprise, and for this there must be peace. Satan is finding evil work for idle hands to do in Europe — evil work that affects the whole world, including the United States.

Under these circumstances, what ought to be done?

I am clear that, if the Covenant has to be considered with the peace terms included, the Senate ought to include in its resolution of consent to the ratification an expression of such reservations and understandings as will cure, so far as possible, the defects which I have pointed out. You will probably be unable to do anything now about the system of arbitration and the development of international law. You can, however, put into the resolution of consent a reservation refusing to agree to Article 10, and I think you should do so; you can clarify the meaning of the withdrawal article, and you can also include in your resolution the substance of the third amendment which I proposed in my letter to Mr. Hays, of March 29, relating to purely American questions, and I think you should do so. These clauses of the resolution shape themselves in my own mind as follows:

The Senate of the United States advises and consents to the ratification of the said treaty with the following reservations and understandings to be made a part of the instrument of ratification, viz.:

(1) In advising and consenting to the ratification of the said treaty, the Senate reserves and excludes from its consent the tenth article of the Covenant for the League of Nations, as to which the Senate refuses its consent.

(2) The Senate consents to the ratification of the said treaty reserving Article 10 aforesaid, with the understanding that whenever two years' notice of withdrawal from the League of Nations shall have been given, as provided in Article 1, no claim, charge, or finding that international obligations or obligations under the Covenant have not been fulfilled will be deemed to render the two years' notice ineffectual or to keep the power giving the notice in the League after the expiration of the time specified in the notice.

(3) Inasmuch as in agreeing to become a member of the League of Nations the United States of America is moved by no interest or wish to intrude upon or interfere with the political policy or international administration of any foreign State, and by any existing or anticipated dangers in the affairs of the American continents, but accedes to the wish of the European States that it shall join its powers to theirs for the preservation of general peace, the Senate consents to the ratification of the said treaty, excepting Article 10 aforesaid, with the understanding that nothing therein contained shall be construed to imply a relinquishment by the United States of America of its traditional attitude toward purely American questions, or to require the submission of its policy regarding questions which it deems to be purely American questions, to the decision or recommendation of other powers.

This reservation and these expressions of understanding are in accordance with long-established precedent in the making of treaties. When included in the instrument of ratification, they will not require a reopening of negotiation, but if none of the other signatories expressly objects to the ratification with such limitations, the treaty stands as limited as between the United States and the other powers.

If any doubt were entertained as to the effect of such action, the doubt could be readily dispelled by calling upon the four other principal powers represented in the Council to state whether they do in fact object to the entrance of the United States into the League with the understandings and reservations stated in the resolution.

As to these limiting clauses, I wish to say something further. As to Article 10:

First. It is not an essential or even an appropriate part of the provisions for a league of nations to preserve peace. It is an independent and indefinite alliance, which may involve the parties to it in war against powers which have in every respect complied with the provisions of the league of peace. It was not included in General Smuts's plan, the provisions of which have been reproduced almost textually in the League Covenant. It stands upon its own footing as an independent alliance for the preservation of the *status quo.*

Second. If we agree to this article, it is extremely probable that we shall be unable to keep our agreement. Making war nowadays depends upon the genuine sympathy of the people of the country at the time when the war has to be carried on. The people of the United States certainly will not be willing ten years or twenty years hence to send their young men to distant parts of the world to fight for causes in which they may not believe or in which they have little or no interest. If that is the attitude of the people when we are hereafter called upon to wage war under Article 10, no general, indefinite agreement made years before will make them disposed to fight; and we shall be in about the worst possible position, of having made an agreement and not keeping it.

Our people ought not to be forced into such a position, and we ought not to make any agreement that is liable to force them into such a position.

The recent controversies over the disposition of Kiaochow and of Fiume illustrate very well the way in which territorial arrangements are likely to be made in councils of the great powers controlled by expediency. I would not vote to bind our country to go into a war in years to come in defense of those arrangements.

If it is necessary for the security of western Europe that we should agree to go to the support, say, of France if attacked, let us agree to do that particular thing plainly, so that every man and woman in the country will understand the honorable obligation we are assuming. I am in favor of that. But let us not wrap up such a purpose in a vague universal obligation, under the impression that it really does not mean anything likely to happen.

Third. It is reported that Switzerland is much disturbed over the invitation to join the League of Nations and wishes to preserve her neutrality, because her people are partly French, partly German, and partly Italian, and she wishes to keep out of all quarrels which may involve those nationalities. In this country the census of 1910 showed that 35 per cent (more than one-third) of our people were of foreign birth or the children of foreign parents. We can call upon these people to stand by America in all American quarrels, but how can we control their sympathies and their action if America interferes in foreign quarrels and takes sides in those quarrels against the countries to which they are attached by tradition and sentiment? How can we prevent dissension and hatred among our own inhabitants of foreign origin when this country interferes on foreign grounds between the races from which they spring? How can we prevent bitterness and disloyalty toward our own Government on the part of those against whose friends in their old homes we have intervened for no cause of our own? Article 10 confronts us with consequences very similar to those which Washington had in mind when he advised us to keep out of the quarrels of Europe and to keep the quarrels of Europe out of America. It is by following this wise policy that the United States has attained a position of unity and of disinterestedness which enables her to promote peace mightily, because she is not a party to the quarrels that threaten to disturb peace. She is free from suspicion; she is not the object of hatred or distrust; her friendship is valued; and her word is potent. We can be of infinitely more value to the peace of the world by keeping out of all the petty and selfish quarrels that arise than we can by binding ourselves to take part in them. Just so far as it is necessary to modify this settled historic American policy in order to put into effect a practical plan for a league of nations to preserve peace, we ought to go, and we ought not to go one step further. The step proposed by Article 10 is not necessary for such a plan and we ought not to take it.

As to the statement of understanding about American questions contained in the foregoing paragraph No. 3, the most ardent advocates for accepting the League Covenant exactly as it stands insist that the provisions already inserted about the Monroe Doctrine and other purely American questions mean just what this proposed resolution says. If that be true, then nobody can object to the resolution which puts the meaning beyond question. It is important, not only for the interest of America but for the peace of the world, that such provisions should be free from doubt and occasion for dispute. If, on the other hand, their view is wrong and the provisions already inserted may be construed not to mean what the resolution says, then the resolution certainly ought to be included in the consent to the ratification.

There is one other thing to be mentioned — that is, the recital of the proposed resolution (No. 3) disclaiming any intention by the United States to intrude upon or interfere with the political policy or internal administration of any foreign State. I think that to be of real importance, because I perceive evidence of an impression in Europe that the part

taken by the representatives of the United States at Paris in
the local questions and controversies of Europe indicates an
abandonment by the United States of her traditional policy
and a wish on her part to dictate to European States and
control European affairs, thus assuming responsibility for
those affairs. That impression should be dissipated. It is
not well founded. I am sure that the people of the United
States have no such intention or wish. Such interposition in
the affairs of Europe as our representatives have been engaged in was properly but a temporary incident to the fact
that we had engaged in the war, and had therefore to discuss
the terms of peace; and we should make it clear that we
neither assume responsibility for nor intend interference in
the affairs of Europe beyond that necessary participation
under the organization of the league of peace, which we enter
upon by the request of the European nations themselves.

To return to the subject of arbitration and the development of international law, I certainly should not advise regarding the League Covenant in its present form as the final
word upon an organization for the preservation of the peace
of the world. I think that when the Senate consents to the
ratification of the treaty with some such reservations as I
have indicated, it ought also to adopt a separate resolution,
not a part of the action upon the treaty, but practically at
the same time, formally requesting the President without
any avoidable delay to open negotiations with the other
powers for the reëstablishment and strengthening of a system
of arbitration for the disposition of international disputes
upon questions of right, and for periodical meetings of representatives of all the powers for the revision and development
of international law.

I think that hereafter, when the life of Europe has become
settled, when credit and industry are reëstablished there and
governments are stable and secure, and we know what reduc-

tion of armaments the powers are going to consent to, the United States should insist upon a revision of the League Covenant. I am sure that the changed circumstances will then permit material improvement.

Faithfully yours,

ELIHU ROOT.

SPEECH AT A MEETING UNDER THE DIRECTION OF THE NATIONAL REPUBLICAN CLUB, IN THE PRESIDENTIAL ELECTION OF 1920

NEW YORK CITY, OCTOBER 19, 1920

The League of Nations figured largely in the Presidential election of 1920, especially in the closing weeks of the campaign, and Mr. Root expressed in the following speech his view of the official attitude of the Republican Party.

IT is my purpose to speak this evening of the League of Nations. The subject is too extensive for anything like a full or systematic presentation in such a speech, and it is a subject that ought to be kept free from the over-emphasis which sometimes makes campaign oratory interesting. There are some observations, however, which may be useful.

I think a large majority of the American people earnestly wish for an organization among civilized nations, through which the nations shall coöperate to prevent future wars, and that the United States shall do her full share in that organization. I certainly desire this very strongly, and I shall assume that you have the same feeling.

The pending contest for the Presidency presents the question: How will our votes on one side or the other affect the attainment of that desire? Shall we promote the peace of the world by electing Mr. Cox or by electing Mr. Harding?

As a basis for considering this question, let me restate the situation. After the Armistice which ended the Great War, a conference of all the states which had been at war with the Central Powers was called in Paris, for the purpose of agreeing upon the terms of peace to be offered to Germany and her allies. The terms were agreed upon, were communicated to the Germans, and, after some slight modifications, produced by their protests, were included in a treaty signed by the Allied and Associated powers on one side and Germany on the other, on the 28th of June, 1919. In this treaty was included a series of provisions called "A Covenant of the League of Nations." These provisions did not form any part of a contract between the Allied and Associated powers and Germany, but formed a contract of the Allied and Associated powers with each other, none of the Central powers being made members of the proposed League, although provision was made for the adherence of neutral powers which had not been engaged in the war.

The general scheme of the proposed League was that there was to be a Council, meeting from time to time, composed of representatives of the five principal Allied and Associated powers and of four other members of the League. When a controversy arose between members of the League and was not submitted to arbitration, it was to be submitted to the Council, which was to investigate and make a report containing a statement of the facts and its recommendations. All parties agreed not to go to war until three months after the award of arbitrators, or the report of the Council, which was to be made within six months after the submission of the dispute. If the report was unanimous, except as to the disputing nations, the parties agreed not to go to war at all with any other party complying with the recommendations of the report. A country violating these stipulations against making war pending the consideration of the case, or upon a party which complied with a unanimous recommendation of the Council, was to be deemed to have committed an act of war against all members of the League. Such a country was to be subject to an economic boycott and deprived of all financial, commercial, or personal intercourse with the members of the

League. The Council was to recommend to the several governments concerned what effective military, naval, or air force the members should severally contribute to the armed forces to be used to protect the covenants of the League.

There were also provisions for an Assembly, to be composed of a representative of every member of the League, and any dispute might be transferred by a party from the Council to the Assembly for consideration, report, and recommendation, with the same effect as if the dispute had been left with the Council. There were many other incidental provisions, but these which I have mentioned, in Articles XV and XVI of the Covenant, contain the gist of the whole scheme.

It will be perceived that this plan relied upon the effect of four things taken together to prevent war.

First, Upon delay to afford time for investigation, and for passions to cool and sober judgment to prevail.

Second, Upon having the facts ascertained and determined and made public to all the world, so that the misunderstandings and deceptions under which the people of a country are so often led to consent to war may be obviated.

Third, Upon having a fairly representative body not a party to the dispute express publicly a responsible and matured opinion as to how the controversy ought to be settled, and thus bring to bear upon the action of the parties the well-informed opinion of the civilized world.

Fourth, If any party to the agreement were to violate it by making war without the stipulated delays necessary for arbitration or investigation and report, or were to make war in violation of the unanimous opinion of the other nations, then, upon the practical outlawry of that party from the advantages of trade, commerce, and customary intercourse with the members of the Society of Nations, with all the consequences flowing from such an outlawry.

There were other more or less incidental provisions. One

provided that there should be a future agreement as to disarmament — a matter which manifestly could not have been determined upon at that time. Another provided for a future report by the Council of a plan for a Court of International Justice. Under that an effort is now being made to cure the marked weakness of the Covenant on the side of international law and judicial or arbitral decisions on questions of legal right. Another provided for an international labor organization. Another provided for the administration of government in backward states by mandatories until the inhabitants should be ready to maintain orderly government themselves.

There was also a provision standing by itself quite outside of the general scheme of the League for the preservation of peace, and forming no part of that scheme, but creating independently of it a hard and fast alliance between the members of the League to preserve in perpetuity the territorial and political *status quo* as it was determined upon by the Conference at Paris and included in the Treaty signed in June, 1919. It was in the following words —

ARTICLE X. The members of the League undertake to respect and preserve as against external aggression the territorial integrity and existing political independence of all members of the League. In case of any such aggression or in case of any threat or danger of such aggression, the Council shall advise upon the means by which this obligation shall be fulfilled.

It will be perceived that this obligation had nothing to do with any delay or investigation or report or recommendation, or with the public opinion of the world at the time of the future controversy. It was an independent obligation upon each member of the League to enforce for all future time the decisions of the Conference of 1919, which was then parcelling out the vast regions of Eastern Europe among various peoples, and it was without regard to whether those decisions should prove to have been right or wrong.

When this treaty came before the Senate for its advice and

consent to ratification, serious objections were raised both in and out of the Senate. Because of the peculiar way in which the treaty was negotiated, it would have been strange if there had not been objections. Ordinarily, treaties are negotiated by ambassadors, or ministers, or specially appointed plenipotentiaries, and their work is supervised at home by the Secretary of State and the President who, looking on from outside the conference chamber, have the opportunity of independent judgment and mature reflection free from the prepossessions and pressure of the actual negotiation. This is of the greatest importance in any complicated negotiation. This treaty, however, was negotiated by the President himself, and the first responsible independent judgment of a nature to correct the mistakes to which every negotiator is subject came when the treaty reached the Senate.

The principal objections may be roughly classified as follows:

1. Objections to the general defensive alliance with all members of the League established by Article X.

2. Objections to submitting to the Council of the League questions of purely American policy, such as the Monroe Doctrine, or questions of immigration, upon which the European countries, approaching the subject from an entirely different point of view and with opposing or different interests, would almost necessarily differ from the American policy.

3. That the scheme practically thrust aside the whole system of development of international law and of arbitral decision which had been the settled policy of the United States for many generations, and depended for the treatment of questions of right as well as questions of policy upon the Council, which would be composed, not of judges, but of diplomatic representatives of the powers.

4. That the scheme created a super-government which would destroy the independence of the United States.

5. That the working of the plan under the Covenant was not so arranged as to articulate with the constitutional government of the United States; that under it the President alone could practically carry on the entire foreign affairs of the United States by agents of his own selection, to the practical exclusion of the popular branch of our government.

While these objections were being developed, there was a strong popular pressure for action. The fact that the Covenant was included in the Treaty of Peace with Germany, which was not a party to the Covenant, made it apparently impossible to have peace without accepting the Covenant. Europe was in a desperate condition, and it was the common understanding that she could not restore her industry and peaceful life without the aid of America through America's accepting the Covenant and becoming a member of the League. Accordingly, to avoid the delay of renegotiating the treaty in order to meet its objections, the Senate adopted the policy of meeting the objections by a series of reservations, and the majority of the Senate voted to consent to ratification of the treaty with these reservations. It was well understood then, and is well understood now, that the other parties to the treaty would have been content to accept those reservations; and, if Mr. Wilson had been willing, the treaty would have been ratified and America would have been a member of the League. Mr. Wilson, however, was not willing. He insisted upon the treaty absolutely unchanged, and a sufficient number of Democratic Senators to defeat the treaty as modified followed him by voting against ratification.

That is practically where we stand to-day. Mr. Cox declares that he will insist upon the treaty just as Mr. Wilson negotiated it, and upon that understanding Mr. Wilson is supporting Mr. Cox for the Presidency. The Democratic platform says substantially the same thing.

On the other hand, Mr. Harding, who voted for the ratification of the treaty with the Senate reservations, declares that he would do it again under the same circumstances.

The Republican platform says:

The Republican Party stands for agreement among the nations to preserve the peace of the world. We believe that such an international association must be based upon international justice, and must provide methods which shall maintain the rule of public right by the development of law and the decision of impartial courts, and which shall secure instant and general international conference, whenever peace shall be threatened by political action, so that the nations pledged to do and insist upon what is just and fair may exercise their influence and power for the prevention of war.

Mr. Harding said in his speech of August 28:

There are distinctly two types of international relationship. One is an offensive and defensive alliance of great powers. . . . The other type is a society of free nations, or an association of free nations, or a league of free nations, animated by considerations of right and justice, instead of might and self-interest, and not merely proclaimed an agency in pursuit of peace, but so organized and so participated in as to make the actual attainment of peace a reasonable possibility. Such an association I favor with all my heart, and I would make no fine distinction as to whom credit is due. One need not care what it is called. Let it be an association, a society, or a league, or what not. Our concern is solely with the substance, not the form thereof. . . . I would take and combine all that is good and excise all that is bad from both organizations [the Court and the League]. This statement is broad enough to include the suggestion that if the League, which has heretofore riveted our considerations and apprehensions, has been so entwined and interwoven into the peace of Europe that its good must be preserved in order to stabilize the peace of that continent, then it can be amended or revised so that we may still have a remnant of the world's aspirations in 1918 builded into the world's highest conception of helpful coöperation in the ultimate realization.

Mr. Harding has reaffirmed these statements again and again, and they must be taken as representing the policy of his administration if he be elected.

It is plain, therefore, that the issue is not between a league of nations and no league of nations. The question is whether the agreement creating the League shall be accepted absolutely unchanged, or shall be modified to meet the American objections. If Mr. Cox should be elected, he would be bound to continue the old struggle to force the Senate to accept the League Covenant without change, which has kept us out of the League for more than a year. If Mr. Harding is elected, he will be bound to say to the foreign governments who are already in the League: "Here are certain objections to certain provisions of the League Covenant which stand in the way of America's entering the League. I would be glad to have the provisions of the agreement changed so as to obviate these objections." Then would follow an ordinary common-sense negotiation as to the best way to obviate the objections. Regarding this process I have to say

1. I think the American objections can be met and obviated without interfering with the scheme of the League or impairing its usefulness.

2. Without pretending to any special knowledge, I think there are clear indications that the other nations concerned are willing to make such changes as are necessary to meet the American objections.

3. I think the objections ought to be met and obviated. The Covenant contains some provisions which are unnecessary, unwise, and injurious, and they ought to be changed.

4. There is nothing unusual or distressing about negotiating the necessary changes. If the other parties are willing — as they seem to be — it will be a simple matter. Several European nations have already given notice of half a dozen changes in the Covenant which they propose to urge at a meeting of the Assembly of the League next month. The only reason why the changes necessary to meet American objections have not already been considered is that Mr. Wilson simply would not negotiate for them.

It is a heart-breaking thing for the negotiator of a treaty

to find that something he has committed himself to and insisted upon must be changed. He has naturally become an earnest partisan of his own ideas. Very likely he has committed himself by arguments and statements made in one way or another during the negotiations, so that he himself cannot very well change. He is naturally intolerant of those who do not agree with him. It is almost impossible for him to avoid thinking of them as insects or brutes, as ignorant or malicious.

Yet, the correction of negotiators' mistakes by independent reviewing authority is a necessity established by universal international experience.

This is one of the difficulties incident to the direct negotiation of a treaty by a president. Being the negotiator, he cannot review his own work impartially, and it is very difficult for him to avoid considering changes proposed by others as something personal to himself.

Fortunately, Mr. Harding will labor under no such disadvantage.

If the objections to provisions in the League Covenant were frivolous and without any substantial basis, one might question the sincerity of the objectors. No such view, however, can be maintained for a moment. The principal objection urged against the provisions of the Covenant is the objection to Article X. It is this article which Mr. Wilson declares to be the heart of the League, and for that reason it is the chief subject of controversy. It is this article above all others that Mr. Cox will be bound to insist upon if he be elected, and it is this article above all others which Mr. Harding will be bound to reject if he be elected.

Let us examine it. It is an undertaking, not by the League, but by the members of the League, not merely to respect, but to preserve as against external aggression, the territorial integrity and existing political independence of all members of

the League. That is what the United States will undertake
to do if it ratifies the League Covenant with this provision
unchanged. Unquestionably, that is an agreement to go to
war in case external aggression against any member of the
League be of such a character that war is necessary to repel
it — such for instance as the invasion of Poland by the Russians, and, apparently, the invasion of Ukrainia by the Poles.
The agreement is a guaranty of territory and independence,
to be supported by war if necessary.

President Wilson's own utterances leave no doubt upon
that. When the Senate Committee on Foreign Relations met
the President to discuss the treaty, Senator Knox asked:
"What would be the obligation of the United States in case
of external aggression against some power . . . and it is perfectly obvious and accepted that it cannot be repelled except
by force of arms?" And the President replied that Article X
would impose "an absolutely compelling moral obligation
upon the United States." The President added that a moral
obligation is "superior to a legal obligation, and has a greater
binding force." The proceedings of this meeting were recorded by a stenographer, and the record shows these statements.

In a plenary session of the Peace Conference May 31, 1919,
to consider the treaty with Austria which incorporated the
League Covenant, the representatives of Roumania and
Serbia objected to having their sovereignty limited in the
treaty by provisions regarding their treatment of racial and
religious minorities within their territory; and Mr. Wilson in
an able and impressive speech urged that they ought to be
satisfied with these limitations, because their territory and
independence were guaranteed by the military force of the
great powers. There were two stenographic records of that
proceeding. One was the official record in French, a translation of which has been widely published in books and peri-

odicals, and was printed in the *Congressional Record* nearly a year ago, apparently without any question as to its authenticity. The other was a somewhat different version, produced during the present month by an American stenographer, who took down what was said, and given out at the White House in answer to a speech by Senator Spencer, quoting the translation of the official version.

There has been much discussion upon the differences between the two reports. Whatever the differences may be, there is no difference whatever between them in respect of the proposition which I am now making: that the President urged these small powers to accept limitations upon their sovereignty because they were guaranteed by the armed force of the great powers.

According to the official version, the President said:

One of the essential conditions is the most equitable distribution possible of territories, in accordance with the affinities and desires of the populations. Once this is done, the Allied and Associated Powers will guarantee the maintenance of them as nearly as possible, (under) just conditions which we shall have reached. It is they who shall undertake the engagement and burden thereof. Inevitably, the main responsibility will rest upon them, since it is they who, by the force of things, have made the most considerable effort during the war. It must not be forgotten that it is their force which is the final guaranty of the peace of the world. Under these conditions, is it unjust, that in the language, not of dictators, but of councillors and friends, they now say: "We cannot guarantee frontiers if we do not believe that these frontiers satisfy certain principles of right and that they will not leave causes of trouble and conflict remaining in the world."

The same reasoning applies to the minorities. It is with the same idea in mind that the status of the minorities has been mentioned.

If you wish that the principal Allied and Associated Powers guarantee the very existence of the states, is it unjust that they should have satisfaction on the conditions which they deem indispensable to avoid future causes of war? ... If the world is again perturbed, if the conditions that we consider as fundamental are again put into question, the guaranty which is given to you means that the United States will send their armies and their fleet from one side of the ocean to the other.

Under the version given out at the White House, the President said:

And back of that lies this fundamentally important fact that, when the decisions are made, the Allied and Associated Powers guarantee to maintain them. It is perfectly evident upon a moment's reflection that the chief burden of their maintaining will fall upon the greater powers. The chief burden of the war fell upon the greater powers; and, if it had not been for their military action, we should not be here to settle these questions, and therefore we must not close our eyes to the fact that in the last analysis the military and naval strength of the Great Powers will be the final guaranty of the peace of the world. . . . How can a power like the United States for example (for I can speak for no other), after signing this treaty, if it contains elements which they do not believe will be permanent, go three thousand miles away across the sea and report to its people that it has made a settlement of the peace of the world? It cannot do so, and yet there underlies all of these transactions the expectation on the part, for example, of Roumania and of Czechoslovakia and of Serbia that, if any covenants of this settlement are not observed, the United States will send her armies and her navies to see that they are observed. In those circumstances is it unreasonable that the United States should insist upon being satisfied that the settlements are correct?

Upon both of these reports it is perfectly plain that the consideration upon which Roumania and Serbia were urged to consent to a limitation of their sovereignty was a guaranty of that sovereignty by the United States with the justified understanding that the guaranty (if need be) would be made good by sending armies and fleets across the sea. That guaranty was contained in Article X, and that is what Article X means.

I do not question Mr. Wilson's belief that the dispositions of the treaty for which he was contending on the 31st of May, 1919, were just and fair. I do not question his belief that all the other multitude of dispositions of those treaties which undertook to make over Eastern Europe were fair, or were expedient, or were the best that could be done under the circumstances; but, without disrespect, I do question Mr. Wilson's infallibility. I do question the complete control of abstract justice in the processes by which the four men who dictated those treaties reached their conclusions. I have an impression that there was the accommodation of conflicting interests, the giving of something here to get something there, the yielding of some things in order to avoid losing others, the shading of justice by expediency which has characterized such conferences since history began. At the best they were not inerrant. It would have been impossible not to overlook some things, and to make some mistakes. I have a strong impression that some of their conclusions were mistakes.

And I think it most objectionable that the American people shall enter into a solemn and positive agreement to guarantee and maintain by force of arms for all time the dispositions of territory and sovereignty which these four men made in the year 1919. That is a part of what Article X undertakes to do.

About the worst thing in the relations between nations is to make a treaty and break it. To maintain the faith of treaties is a prime necessity for the peace of the world. To manufacture treaties that are to be but scraps of paper is fatal to the moral standards through which alone peace can be preserved.

We are told: "There is nothing in the Covenant which in the least interferes with or impairs the right of Congress to declare war or not declare war, according to its own independent judgment, as our Constitution provides."

But, if we have entered into the guaranty of Article X, and circumstances arise which require war to make good the guaranty as described by the President in his speech of May 31, 1919, then refusal of Congress to pass the necessary resolution would be a breach of the Covenant, and the only independent judgment of Congress would be whether our Government should keep the treaty or break it.

What is the probability of the United States making good such a guaranty?

Making war nowadays depends upon the genuine sympathy of the people of the country at the time when they are called upon to fight. It must be a cause the people are interested in, believe in, are willing to fight for, and make sacrifices for at the time. No agreement made by any government years before will carry the American people into a war in which they are not interested, or which they do not at the time deem just. There was a time when governments controlled peoples, and could make war at will; but, in these days no government of a free democracy can deliver its people upon the field of battle except by the people's will at that time.

It is a practical certainty that, if the American Government enters into the obligations of Article X, so positive in its terms, so broad in its scope, so unlimited in its duration, the time will presently come (as it has already come swiftly to Western Europe) when the United States will be called upon to make good its guaranty by force, and when the people of the United States will be unwilling to make the sacrifice of life and treasure to carry on war in a distant land for a cause of which they know little, and for which they care less. The presence of such a stipulation in the League Covenant is an element of structural weakness in the scheme, for a covenant violated in any material part ceases to be enforceable.

In all efforts to secure united action among nations in this world of widely differing character and opinion and standards of conduct and interests, it is a matter of vital importance, not merely to secure agreements which correspond to abstract standards of right, but to limit agreements so that they will not violate too suddenly and sharply existing standards of conduct, with the result that they are not observed, and the whole agreement falls.

When the Peace Conference met in Paris there were two quite separate and distinct duties before it.

One of these duties was to determine and impose upon the Central Powers the terms of peace. The other duty was to propose to the world an organization for the preservation of future peace.

The first duty was the final stage of the war itself. It was the imposition of the will of the conquering nations upon the conquered nations. It involved taking away great territories from the vanquished nations, and distributing them to the Greeks, and Serbs, and Roumanians, and Czechoslovaks, and Poles, and Italians, and French, and Danes. It was the exercise of power, through military force, accomplished through the long years of struggle and sacrifice of the Great War. It was a necessary part of this process that the nations to which lands were distributed should be put in peaceable possession and established in possession. The United States was a party to the process because she was a party to the war, and the process was a part of the war. We can all see now how truly the Senate said long ago that that process should have been the first matter of urgent speed, and should have been completed while the armies of the Allies were in being, and the immediate exercise of power was possible.

The second duty of the Conference, to propose an organization for the preservation of future peace, was entirely different in its character. All neutral nations were equally concerned in that. It involved the proposal of an organization, not for the purpose of making war or of imposing the results of war, but which presupposed a world already at peace, and which was to be adapted to preserve the peace already existing. It was not an organization for the exercise of physical force, but by the universal agreement of the civilized world it was to be an organization to make effectual the exercise and dominance of moral force in the conduct of nations. The world was tired of alliances to prevent war by force. We had learned through centuries of experience that such alliances do not prevent war, but merely vary the combination of the warring elements, and we had learned that no good intentions (however sincere) in the making of the alliance could avert that inevitable result. The elements of the problem had been exhaustively studied, and were well understood by good and thoughtful people in all civilized countries. They realized that the world cannot be made good, moral, peaceable, by compulsion; that the mere opposition of force to force involves no progress toward better things; that the only line of progress is through the growth of the moral qualities that make for peace; and that an organization must be created which shall afford alternatives to war in the opportunity to secure justice by peaceable means, which shall educate moral forces through the exercise of moral forces, which shall promote respect for law, a sentiment for justice, a knowledge of truth, a desire for conciliation. Everybody knew that this would be a slow process, as all processes of advancing civilization have been slow; but it was well understood that real progress toward peace and justice could be made only through such a process, and we all believed that the terrible lessons of the Great War would have greatly accelerated the process throughout the world.

This was the conception of the scheme for a League of Nations before Article X was injected into the instrument. The scheme was imperfect. In some respects it undertook too much, and in others too little. It needs revision, and it will have revision; but, with the exception of Article X, it follows the lines of development in morals which I have undertaken to describe.

I have said that Article X was no part of the main scheme of the League of Nations. I go further, and assert that Article X is inconsistent with the purpose and spirit of the

League. Article X is an attempt to carry over and continue for all time, as a part of the organization to preserve peace, the exercise of power by the conquered nations in closing the war. It is an alliance to enforce perpetually through the operations of the League the decisions of Mr. Wilson and his associates in the year 1919. It is a throw-back to the old discredited alliances of the past. It speaks a language of power, and not the spirit of progress. It is an attempt to do what the Holy Alliance sought one hundred years ago (with just as noble expressions of purpose) — to impose by force the judgment of the rulers of the present generation upon all future generations. This is injected into a plan for the development of moral force, which must grow if it is to live, and must keep pace with the continually changing conditions and ideals of successive generations. If the League is to live, it must provide for justice in each generation according to the conceptions of the time. Not only is the thing to be done inconsistent with the spirit and purpose of the League, but the method of doing the thing is inconsistent with the independence and liberty of free nations through which alone the League can live. What free nations need for their independence is not a guaranty of favor by the more powerful. It is a guaranty of justice under law, supported by civilized public opinion. Nearly five years ago Mr. Wilson proposed to the Latin-American countries the same agreement with the United States which is contained in Article X. They rejected it, because they feared — or some of them feared — that the guaranty by the more powerful nation meant an attempt to control on the part of that nation. They feared the guaranties which we have seen in Haiti and San Domingo. That same assumption of superiority and right to control may be plainly seen in Mr. Wilson's address of May 31, 1919, to the Roumanian and Serbian delegates. Partnership between the great and the small is a dangerous enterprise. Human nature too often is unable to resist the temptations of power. The exercise of such superiority of power by the strong over the weak, as Mr. Wilson described to the Roumanians and Serbs, is inconsistent with that independent and equal condition of the nations upon which alone can a true league for progress toward peace be based.

The conception which would make the alliance of Article X the heart of a league to promote the peace of the world is a negation of the opinion held by the wisest, most experienced, and most devoted men who have labored in all civilized countries for generations to advance the cause of peace. It is a negation of the opinions held without exception by the rulers and statesmen who have led the policies of the United States for generations. It is a mistaken conception, and it ought to be repudiated by the American people, not merely for their own interest, but in the interest of the peace of the world.

THE SECOND HAGUE PEACE CONFERENCE

INSTRUCTIONS TO THE AMERICAN DELEGATES TO THE CONFERENCE OF 1907 [1]

At the weekly reception, on August 12 (24), 1898, Count Mouravieff, Russian Minister for Foreign Affairs, handed to the diplomatic representatives a circular note, proposing a peace conference and inviting their governments to send representatives to consider "The maintenance of general peace and a possible reaction of the excessive armaments which weigh down upon all nations." The city of The Hague was chosen as the place of meeting, and the Conference itself, composed of the representatives of twenty-six nations, met in that city on the 18th of May, 1899, and adjourned July 29, with several conventions to its credit, especially the Convention for the Pacific Settlement of International Disputes.

The United States was represented in that Conference. In addition to the United States and Mexico, whose delegates attended, Brazil was invited, but sent no representatives. The other Latin-American states were without diplomatic agents at St. Petersburg, and were not included in the invitation.

Mr. Root was unwilling that the Second Conference should be held without their presence, and, with the moral support of Mexico, he secured an invitation to all of them. — Indeed, he did more: he secured the postponement of the Second Hague Conference until 1907, in order that it should not meet, as was contemplated, in the summer of 1906, when the Americas would be represented at the Third Pan-American Conference to be held, as it actually was, that year, at Rio de Janeiro. All of the American states were represented at the Second Hague Conference, with the exception of Honduras, whose delegates arrived in the closing days of the session, too late to take part in the proceedings, and Costa Rica, which appointed none. The Second Hague Peace Conference consisted of the representatives of forty-four nations.

Mr. Root's instructions to the American delegation speak for themselves. It is, however, permissible to state that a no less competent judge than the late Louis Renault considered them *la sagesse elle-même*.

Department of State,
Washington, May 31, 1907

To MESSRS. JOSEPH H. CHOATE, HORACE PORTER, URIAH M. ROSE, DAVID JAYNE HILL, GEORGE B. DAVIS, CHARLES S. SPERRY, and WILLIAM I. BUCHANAN.

GENTLEMEN, —

You have been appointed delegates plenipotentiary to represent the United States at a Second Peace Conference which is to meet at The Hague on the 15th of June, 1907.

[1] Foreign Relations of the United States, 1907, pt. 2, pp. 1128–1139.

The need of such a Conference was suggested to the Powers signatory to the acts of the Hague Conference of 1899 by President Roosevelt, in a circular note by my predecessor, Mr. Hay, dated October 21, 1904, and the project met with a general expression of assent and sympathy from the Powers; but its realization was postponed because of the then existing war between Japan and Russia. The conclusion of the peace which ended that war presenting a favorable moment for further developing and systematizing the work of the First Conference, the initiative was appropriately transferred to His Imperial Majesty the Emperor of Russia as initiator of the First Conference. The Russian Government proposed that the programme of the contemplated meeting should include the following topics:

1. Improvements to be made in the provisions of the Convention relative to the peaceful settlement of international disputes, as regards the court of arbitration and the international commissions of inquiry.

2. Additions to be made to the provisions of the Convention of 1899 relative to the laws and customs of war on land — among others, those concerning the opening of hostilities, the rights of neutrals on land, etc. Declarations of 1899. One of these having expired, question of its being revived.

3. Framing of a convention relative to the laws and customs of maritime warfare, concerning, —

The special operations of maritime warfare, such as the bombardment of ports, cities, and villages by a naval force; the laying of torpedoes, etc.

The transformation of merchant vessels into war-ships.

The private property of belligerents at sea.

The length of time to be granted to merchant ships for their departure from ports of neutrals or of the enemy after the opening of hostilities.

The rights and duties of neutrals at sea; among others, the questions of contraband, the rules applicable to belligerent vessels in neutral ports; destruction, in cases of *vis major*, of neutral merchant vessels captured as prizes.

In the said convention to be drafted, there would be introduced the provisions relative to war on land that would also be applicable to maritime warfare.

4. Additions to be made to the Convention of 1899 for the adaptation to maritime warfare of the principles of the Geneva Convention of 1864.

We are advised by the Ambassador of Russia, in a note dated March 22 (April 4), 1907, that all of the Powers have declared their adhesion to this tentative programme. The following remarks, however, have been made in respect thereof.

The Government of the United States has reserved to itself the liberty of submitting to the Conference two additional questions: viz., the reduction or limitation of armaments and the attainment of an agreement to observe some limitations upon the use of force for the collection of ordinary public debts arising out of contracts.

The Spanish Government has expressed a desire to discuss the limitation of armaments.

The British Government has given notice that it attaches great importance to having the question of expenditures for armament discussed at the Conference, and has reserved to itself the right of raising it.

The Governments of Bolivia, Denmark, Greece, and the Netherlands have reserved to themselves, in a general way, the right to submit to the consideration of the Conference subjects not specially enumerated in the programme.

Several governments have reserved the right to take no part in any discussion which may appear unlikely to produce any useful result.

The Russian note proposing the programme declared that the deliberations of the contemplated meetings should not deal with the political relations of the different states, or the condition of things established by treaties; and that neither the solution of the questions brought up for discussion, nor the order of their discussion, nor the form to be given to the decisions reached, should be determined in advance of the Conference. We understand this view to have been accepted.

In regard to the two questions which were not included in the proposed programme, but which the United States has

reserved the right to present to the Conference, we understand that notice of the reservation has been communicated
to all the Powers by note similar to that from the Russian
Ambassador dated March 22 (April 4), 1907; so that each
Power has had full opportunity to instruct its delegates in
respect thereof. The United States understands that, as to
the topics included in the programme, the acceptance of the
programme involves a determination that such topics shall
be considered by the Conference, subject to the reserved
rights of particular Powers to refrain from discussion of any
topic as to which it deems that discussion will not be useful;
but that as to the two topics which we have reserved the
right to present, there has been no determination one way or
the other, the question whether they shall be considered by
the Conference remaining for the determination of the Conference itself in case they shall be presented.

It is not expedient that you should be limited by too rigid
instructions upon the various questions which are to be discussed, for such a course, if pursued generally with all the
delegates, would make the discussion useless and the Conference a mere formality. You will, however, keep in mind
the following observations regarding the general policy of the
United States upon these questions:

1. In the discussions upon every question, it is important
to remember that the object of the Conference is agreement,
and not compulsion. If such conferences are to be made occasions for trying to force nations into positions which they
consider against their interests, the Powers can not be expected to send representatives to them. It is important also
that the agreements reached shall be genuine and not reluc-
tant. Otherwise they will inevitably fail to receive approval
when submitted for the ratification of the Powers represented. Comparison of views and frank and considerate
explanation and discussion may frequently resolve doubts,

obviate difficulties, and lead to real agreement upon matters which at the outset have appeared insurmountable. It is not wise, however, to carry this process to the point of irritation. After reasonable discussion, if no agreement is reached, it is better to lay the subject aside, or refer it to some future conference, in the hope that intermediate consideration may dispose of the objections. Upon some questions where an agreement by only a part of the Powers represented would in itself be useful, such an agreement may be made, but it should always be with the most unreserved recognition that the other Powers withhold their concurrence with equal propriety and right.

The immediate results of such a conference must always be limited to a small part of the field which the more sanguine have hoped to see covered; but each successive conference will make the positions reached in the preceding Conference its point of departure, and will bring to the consideration of further advances toward international agreement opinions affected by the acceptance and application of the previous agreements. Each conference will inevitably make further progress and, by successive steps, results may be accomplished which have formerly appeared impossible.

You should keep always in mind the promotion of this continuous process through which the progressive development of international justice and peace may be carried on; and you should regard the work of the Second Conference, not merely with reference to the definite results to be reached in that Conference, but also with reference to the foundations which may be laid for further results in future conferences. It may well be that among the most valuable services rendered to civilization by this Second Conference will be found the progress made in matters upon which the delegates reach no definite agreement.

With this view you will favor the adoption of a resolution

by the Conference providing for the holding of further conferences within fixed periods, and arranging the machinery by which such conferences may be called and the terms of the programme may be arranged, without awaiting any new and specific initiative on the part of the Powers or any one of them.

Encouragement for such a course is to be found in the successful working of a similar arrangement for international conferences of the American republics. The second American Conference, held in Mexico in 1901–1902, adopted a resolution providing that a third conference should meet within five years, and committed the time and place and the programme and necessary details to the Department of State and representatives of the American states in Washington. Under this authority the Third Conference was called and held in Rio de Janeiro in the summer of 1906 and accomplished results of substantial value. That Conference adopted the following resolution:

> The governing board of the International Bureau of American Republics (composed of the same official representatives in Washington) is authorized to designate the place at which the Fourth International Conference shall meet, which meeting shall be within the next five years; to provide for the drafting of the programme and regulations and to take into consideration all other necessary details; and to set another date in case the meeting of the said Conference cannot take place within the prescribed limit of time.

There is no apparent reason to doubt that a similar arrangement for successive general international conferences of all the civilized Powers would prove as practicable and as useful as in the case of the twenty-one American states.

2. The policy of the United States to avoid entangling alliances and to refrain from any interference or participation in the political affairs of Europe must be kept in mind, and may impose upon you some degree of reserve in respect of some of the questions which are discussed by the Conference.

In the First Conference the American delegates accompanied their note upon the report of the committee regarding the limitation of armaments by the following declaration:

That the United States, in so doing, does not express any opinion as to the course to be taken by the States of Europe. This declaration is not meant to indicate mere indifference to a difficult problem because it does not affect the United States immediately, but expresses a determination to refrain from enunciating opinions upon matters into which, as concerning Europe alone, the United States has no claim to enter. The words drawn up by M. Bourgeois, and adopted by the first commission, received also the cordial interest and sympathy with which the United States, while carefully abstaining from anything that might resemble interference, regards all movements that are thought to tend to the welfare of Europe.

Before signing the arbitration convention of the First Conference, the delegates of the United States put upon record the following declaration:

Nothing contained in this Convention shall be so construed as to require the United States of America to depart from its traditional policy of not intruding upon, interfering with, or entangling itself in the political questions or policy or internal administration of any foreign State; nor shall anything contained in the said Convention be construed to imply a relinquishment by the United States of America of its traditional attitude toward purely American questions.

These declarations have received the approval of this Government, and they should be regarded by you as illustrating the caution which you are to exercise in preventing our participation in matters of general and world-wide concern from drawing us into the political affairs of Europe.

3. The attitude of the United States as to consideration of the subject of limiting armaments was stated in a letter from the Secretary of State to the Russian ambassador dated June 7, 1906. That letter, after expressing assent to the enumeration of topics in the Russian programme, proceeded to say:

The Government of the United States is, however, so deeply in sympathy with the noble and humanitarian views which moved His Imperial

Majesty to the calling of the First Peace Conference that it would greatly regret to see those views excluded from the consideration of the Second Conference. [Quoting from the call for the First Conference.]

The truth and value of the sentiments thus expressed are surely independent of the special conditions and obstacles to their realization by which they may be confronted at any particular time. It is true that the First Conference at The Hague did not find it practicable to give them effect, but long-continued and patient effort has always been found necessary to bring mankind into conformity with great ideals. It would be a misfortune if that effort, so happily and magnanimously inaugurated by His Imperial Majesty, were to be abandoned.

This Government is not unmindful of the fact that the people of the United States dwell in comparative security, partly by reason of their isolation and partly because they have never become involved in the numerous questions to which many centuries of close neighborhood have given rise in Europe. They are, therefore, free from the apprehensions of attack which are to so great an extent the cause of great armaments, and it would ill become them to be insistent or forward in a matter so much more vital to the nations of Europe than to them. Nevertheless, it sometimes happens that the very absence of a special interest in a subject enables a nation to make suggestions and urge considerations which a more deeply interested nation might hesitate to present. The Government of the United States, therefore, feels it to be its duty to reserve for itself the liberty to propose to the Second Peace Conference, as one of the subjects of consideration, the reduction or limitation of armaments, in the hope that, if nothing further can be accomplished, some slight advance may be made toward the realization of the lofty conception which actuated the Emperor of Russia in calling the First Conference.

The First Conference adopted the following resolutions:

The Conference is of opinion that the restriction of military charges which are at present a heavy burden on the world, is extremely desirable for the increase of the material and moral welfare of mankind.

The Conference expresses the wish that the Governments, taking into consideration the proposals made at the Conference, may examine the possibility of an agreement as to the limitation of armed forces by land and sea and of war budgets.

Under these circumstances this Government has been and still is of the opinion that this subject should be regarded as unfinished business, and that the Second Conference should ascertain and give full consideration to the results of such examination as the governments may have given to the possibility of an agreement pursuant to the wish expressed by the First Conference. We think that there should be a sincere effort to learn whether, by conference and discussion, some practicable formula may not be worked out which would have the effect of limiting or retarding the increase of armaments.

There is, however, reason to believe not only that there has been the examination by the respective governments for which the First Conference expressed a wish, but that the discussion of its results has been forestalled by a process of direct communication between a majority of the governments having the greatest immediate interest in the subject. These communications have been going on actively among the different governments for nearly a year, and as a result, at least four of the European Powers have announced their unwillingness to continue the discussion in the Conference. We regret that the discussion should have taken place in this way rather than at the Conference, for we are satisfied that a discussion at the Conference would have afforded a greater probability of progress toward the desired result. The fact, however, cannot be ignored.

If any European Power proposes consideration of the subject, you will vote in favor of consideration and do everything you properly can to promote it. If, on the other hand, no European Power proposes consideration of the subject, and no new and affirmative evidence is presented to satisfy you that a useful purpose would be subserved by your making such a proposal, you may assume that the limitations above stated by way of guidance to your action preclude you from asking the Conference to consider the subject.

4. The other subject which the United States specifically reserved the right to propose for consideration is the attainment of an agreement to observe some limitation upon the use

of force for the collection of ordinary public debts arising out of contract.

It has long been the established policy of the United States not to use its army and navy for the collection of ordinary contract debts due to its citizens by other governments. This Government has not considered the use of force for such a purpose consistent with that respect for the independent sovereignty of other members of the family of nations which is the most important principle of international law and the chief protection of weak nations against the oppression of the strong. It seems to us that the practice is injurious in its general effect upon the relation of nations and upon the welfare of weak and disordered states, whose development ought to be encouraged in the interests of civilization; that it offers frequent temptation to bullying and oppression and to unnecessary and unjustifiable warfare. It is doubtless true that the non-payment of such debts may be accompanied by such circumstances of fraud and wrong-doing or violation of treaties as to justify the use of force; but we should be glad to see an international consideration of this subject which would discriminate between such cases and the simple non-performance of a contract with a private person, and a resolution in favor of reliance upon peaceful means in cases of the latter class.

The Third International Conference of the American States, held at Rio de Janeiro in August, 1906, resolved:

> To recommend to the governments therein that they consider the point of inviting the Second Peace Conference at The Hague to examine the question of the compulsory collection of public debts, and, in general, means tending to diminish between nations conflicts having a peculiarly pecuniary origin.

You will ask for the consideration of this subject by the Conference. It is not probable that in the first instance all the nations represented at the Conference will be willing to go as far in the establishment of limitations upon the use of force in the collection of this class of debts as the United States would like to have them go, and there may be serious objection to the consideration of the subject as a separate and independent topic. If you find such objections insurmountable, you will urge the adoption of provisions under the head of arbitration looking to the establishment of such limitations. The adoption of some such provisions as the following may be suggested, and, if no better solution seems practicable, should be urged:

The use of force for the collection of a contract debt alleged to be due by the Government of any country to a citizen of any other country is not permissible until after —

(*a*) The justice and amount of the debt shall have been determined by arbitration, if demanded by the alleged debtor.

(*b*) The time and manner of payment, and the security, if any, to be given pending payment, shall have been fixed by arbitration, if demanded by the alleged debtor.

5. In the general field of arbitration two lines of advance are clearly indicated. The first is to provide for obligatory arbitration as broad in scope as now appears to be practicable; and the second is to increase the effectiveness of the system so that nations may more readily have recourse to it voluntarily.

You are familiar with the numerous expressions in favor of the settlement of international disputes by arbitration on the part both of the Congress and of the Executive of the United States.

So many separate treaties of arbitration have been made between individual countries that there is little cause to doubt that the time is now ripe for a decided advance in this direction. This condition, which brings the subject of a general treaty for obligatory arbitration into the field of practical discussion, is undoubtedly largely due to the fact that the

Powers generally in the First Hague Conference committed themselves to the principle of the pacific settlement of international questions in the admirable convention for voluntary arbitration then adopted.

The Rio Conference of last summer provided for the arbitration of all pecuniary claims among the American States. This convention has been ratified by the President, with the advice and consent of the Senate.

In December, 1904, and January, 1905, my predecessor, Mr. Hay, concluded separate arbitration treaties between the United States and Great Britain, France, Germany, Spain, Portugal, Italy, Switzerland, Austria-Hungary, Sweden and Norway, and Mexico. On the 11th of February, 1905, the Senate advised and consented to the ratification of these treaties, with an amendment which has had the effect of preventing the exchange of ratifications. The amendment, however, did not relate to the scope or character of the arbitration to which the President had agreed and the Senate consented. You will be justified, therefore, in assuming that a general treaty of arbitration in the terms, or substantially in the terms, of the series of treaties which I have mentioned will meet the approval of the Government of the United States. The first article of each of these treaties was as follows:

Differences which may arise of a legal nature, or relating to the interpretation of treaties existing between the two contracting parties, and which it may not have been possible to settle by diplomacy, shall be referred to the permanent court of arbitration established at The Hague by the Convention of the 29th July, 1899, provided, nevertheless, that they do not affect the vital interests, the independence, or the honor of the two contracting States, and do not concern the interests of third parties.

To this extent you may go in agreeing to a general treaty of arbitration, and to secure such a treaty you should use your best and most earnest efforts.

Such a general treaty of arbitration necessarily leaves to be determined in each particular case what the questions at issue between the two governments are, and whether those questions come within the scope of the treaty or within the exceptions, and what shall be the scope of the powers of the arbitrators. The Senate amendment which prevented the ratification of each of these treaties applied only to another article of the treaty, which provided for special agreements in regard to these matters and involved only the question who should act for the United States in making such special arrangements.

To avoid having the same question arise regarding any general treaty of arbitration which you may sign at The Hague, your signature should be accompanied by an explanation substantially as follows: "In signing the general arbitration treaty the delegates of the United States desire to have it understood that the special agreements provided for in article — of said treaty will be subject to submission to the Senate of the United States."

The method in which arbitration can be made more effective, so that nations may be more ready to have recourse to it voluntarily, and to enter into treaties by which they bind themselves to submit to it, is indicated by observation of the weakness of the system now apparent. There can be no doubt that the principal objection to arbitration rests, not upon the unwillingness of nations to submit their controversies to impartial arbitration, but upon an apprehension that the arbitrations to which they submit may not be impartial. It has been a very general practice for arbitrators to act, not as judges deciding questions of fact and law upon the record before them under a sense of judicial responsibility, but as negotiators effecting settlements of the questions brought before them in accordance with the traditions and usages and subject to all the considerations and influences which affect diplomatic agents. The two methods are radically different, proceed upon different standards of honorable obligation, and frequently lead to widely differing results. It very frequently happens that a nation which would be very willing to submit its differences to an impartial judicial determination is unwilling to subject them to this kind of diplomatic process. If there could be a tribunal which would pass upon questions between nations with the same impartial and impersonal judgment that the Supreme Court of the United States gives to questions arising between citizens of the different states, or between foreign citizens and citizens of the United States, there can be no doubt that nations would be much more ready to submit their controversies to its decision than they are now to take the chances of arbitration. It should be your effort to bring about in the Second Conference a development of the Hague Tribunal into a permanent tribunal, composed of judges who are judicial officers and nothing else, who are paid adequate salaries, who have no other occupation, and who will devote their entire time to the trial and decision of international causes by judicial methods and under a sense of judicial responsibility. These judges should be so selected from the different countries that the different systems of law and procedure and the principal languages shall be fairly represented. The court should be made of such dignity, consideration, and rank that the best and ablest jurists will accept appointment to it, and that the whole world will have absolute confidence in its judgments.

The arbitration convention signed at the First Hague Conference contained no authority for the adherence of non-signatory Powers, but provided:

The conditions on which the Powers who were not represented at the International Peace Conference can adhere to the present Convention shall form the subject of a separate agreement among the contracting Powers.

This left all the Central and South American states outside of the treaty. The United States has from time to time endeavored to secure an opportunity for them to adhere; and it has now been arranged that this shall be accomplished as a necessary preliminary to their taking part in the Second Conference. The method arranged is that on the day before the opening of the Conference a protocol shall be signed by the representatives of all the Powers signatory to the treaty substantially as follows:

The representatives at the Second Peace Conference of the States signatories of the convention of 1899 relative to the peaceful settlement of international disputes, duly authorized to that effect, have agreed that in case the States that were not represented at the First Peace Conference, but have been convoked to the present Conference, should notify the Government of the Netherlands of their adhesion to the above-mentioned convention, they shall be forthwith considered as having acceded thereto.

It is understood that substantially all the Central and South American states have notified the Government of the Netherlands of their adherence to the Convention, and upon the signing of this protocol their notices will immediately take effect and they will become parties competent to take part in the discussions of the Second Conference looking toward the amendment and extension of the arbitration convention. You will sign the protocol in behalf of the United States pursuant to the full powers already given you.

6. You will maintain the traditional policy of the United States regarding the immunity of private property of belligerents at sea.

On the 28th of April, 1904, the Congress of the United States adopted the following resolution:

Resolved by the Senate and House of Representatives of the United States of America in Congress assembled, That it is the sense of the Congress of the United States that it is desirable, in the interests of uniformity of action by the maritime States of the world in time of war, that the President endeavor to bring about an understanding among the principal maritime

Powers, with a view of incorporating into the permanent law of civilized nations, the principle of the exemption of all private property at sea, not contraband of war, from capture or destruction by belligerents. *Approved* April 28, 1904.

This resolution is an expression of the view taken by the United States during its entire history. Such a provision was incorporated in the treaty of 1775 with Prussia, signed by Benjamin Franklin, Thomas Jefferson, and John Adams, and it was proposed by the United States as an amendment to be added to the privateering clause of the Declaration of Paris in 1856. The refusal of the other Powers to accompany prohibition of privateering by such a provision caused the Government of the United States to refuse its adherence to the Declaration.

The Congressional resolution was in response to the recommendation of President Roosevelt's message to Congress in December, 1903, quoting and enforcing a previous message by President McKinley in December, 1898, which said: "The United States Government has for many years advocated this humane and beneficent principle, and is now in a position to recommend it to other Powers without the imputation of selfish motives."

Whatever may be the apparent specific interest of this or any other country at the moment, the principle declared is of such permanent and universal importance that no balancing of the chances of probable loss or gain in the immediate future on the part of any nation should be permitted to outweigh the considerations of common benefit to civilization which call for the adoption of such an agreement.

In the First Peace Conference the subject of the immunity of private property at sea was not included in the programme. Consideration of it was urged by the delegates of the United States and was supported by an able presentation on the part of Mr. Andrew D. White. The representatives of several of the great Powers declared, however, that in the absence of instructions from their governments they could not vote upon the subject; and, under the circumstances, we must consider that gratifying progress was made when there was included in the Final Act of the Conference a resolution expressing the wish "that the proposal which contemplates the declaration of the inviolability of private property in naval warfare may be referred to a subsequent Conference for consideration."

The subject has accordingly been included in the present programme and the way is open for its consideration.

It will be appropriate for you to advocate the proposition formulated and presented by the American delegates to the First Conference, as follows:

The private property of all citizens or subjects of the signatory Powers, with the exception of contraband of war, shall be exempt from capture or seizure on the high seas, or elsewhere, by the armed vessels or by the military forces of any of the said signatory Powers. But nothing herein contained shall extend exemption from seizure to vessels and their cargoes which may attempt to enter a port blockaded by the naval forces of any of the said Powers.

7. Since the code of rules for the government of military operations on land was adopted by the First Peace Conference, there have been occasions for its application under very severe conditions, notably in the South African war and the war between Japan and Russia. Doubtless the Powers involved in those conflicts have had occasion to observe many particulars in which useful additions or improvements might be made. You will consider their suggestions with a view to reducing, as far as is practicable, the evils of war, and protecting the rights of neutrals.

As to the framing of a convention relative to the customs of maritime warfare, you are referred to the Naval War Code promulgated in General Orders 551 of the Navy Department, of June 27, 1900, which has met with general commendation by naval authorities throughout the civilized world, and which, in general, expresses the view of the United States, subject to a few specific amendments suggested in the volume of international law discussions of the Naval War College of the year 1903, pages 91 to 97. The order putting this code into force was revoked by the Navy Department in 1904, not because of any change of views as to the rules which it contained, but because many of those rules, being imposed upon the forces of the United States by the order, would have put our naval forces at a disadvantage as against the forces of other Powers, upon whom the rules were not binding. The whole discussion of these rules contained in the volume to which I have referred is commended to your careful study.

You will urge upon the Peace Conference the formulation of international rules for war at sea, and will offer the Naval War Code of 1900, with the suggested changes and such further changes as may be made necessary by other agreements reached at the Conference, as a tentative formulation of the rules which should be considered.

8. The clause of the programme relating to the rights and duties of neutrals is of very great importance and in itself would furnish matter for useful discussion sufficient to occupy the time and justify the labors of the Conference.

The various subjects which the Conference may be called upon to consider are likely to bring out proposals which should be considered in their relation to each other, as standing in the following order of substantial importance:

(1) Provisions tending to prevent disagreements between nations; (2) Provisions tending to dispose of disagreements without war; (3) Provisions tending to preserve the rights and interests of neutrals; (4) Provisions tending to mitigate the evils of war to belligerents.

The relative importance of these classes of provisions

should always be kept in mind. No rules should be adopted for the purpose of mitigating the evils of war to belligerents which will tend strongly to destroy the rights of neutrals, and no rules should be adopted regarding the rights of neutrals which will tend strongly to bring about war. It is of the highest importance that not only the rights but the duties of neutrals shall be most clearly and distinctly defined and understood, not only because the evils which belligerent nations bring upon themselves ought not to be allowed to spread to their peaceful neighbors and inflict unnecessary injury upon the rest of mankind, but because misunderstandings regarding the rights and duties of neutrals constantly tend to involve them in controversy with one or the other belligerent.

For both of these reasons, special consideration should be given to an agreement upon what shall be deemed to constitute contraband of war. There has been a recent tendency to extend widely the list of articles to be treated as contraband; and it is probable that if the belligerents themselves are to determine at the beginning of a war what shall be contraband, this tendency will continue until the list of contraband is made to include a large proportion of all the articles which are the subject of commerce, upon the ground that they will be useful to the enemy. When this result is reached, especially if the doctrine of continuous voyages is applied at the same time, the doctrine that free ships make free goods and the doctrine that blockades in order to be binding must be effective, as well as any rule giving immunity to the property of belligerents at sea, will be deprived of a large part of their effect, and we shall find ourselves going backward instead of forward in the effort to prevent every war from becoming universally disastrous. The exception of contraband of war in the Declaration of Paris will be so expanded as to very largely destroy the effect of the Declaration. On the other hand, resistance to this tendency toward the expansion of the list of contraband ought not to be left to the neutrals affected by it at the very moment when war exists, because that is the process by which neutrals become themselves involved in war. You should do all in your power to bring about an agreement upon what is to constitute contraband; and it is very desirable that the list should be limited as narrowly as possible.

With these instructions there will be furnished to you copies of the diplomatic correspondence relating to the Conference; the instructions to the delegates to the First Conference, which are in all respects reaffirmed, and their report; the international-law discussions of the Naval War College of 1903; the report of the American delegates to the Conference of the American Republics at Rio de Janeiro in 1906; and the report of the American delegates to the Geneva Conference of 1906 for the revision of the Red Cross Convention of 1864.

Following the precedent established by the commission to the First Conference, all your reports and communications to this Government will be made to the Department for proper consideration and eventual preservation in the archives. The record of your commission will be kept by your secretary, Mr. Chandler Hale. Should you be in doubt at any time regarding the meaning or effect of these instructions, or should you consider at any time that there is occasion for special instructions, you will communicate freely with the Department of State by telegraph. It is the President's earnest wish that you may contribute materially to the effective work of the Conference and that its deliberations may result in making international justice more certain and international peace more secure.

I am, gentlemen, your obedient servant,

ELIHU ROOT

LATIN–AMERICAN COÖPERATION

LETTER OF INSTRUCTIONS TO ROBERT BACON
JULY 20, 1913

By letter of December 14, 1910, Andrew Carnegie created a fund of ten million dollars, to be administered by trustees of his own choice, "to hasten the abolition of international war, the foulest blot upon our civilization."

At the meeting of the Trustees of that date, Mr. Root was elected President and Chairman of the Board of Trustees of the Carnegie Endowment for International Peace, which positions he still holds in 1924.

For the purposes stated in the following letter of instructions, Mr. Robert Bacon was asked to undertake a mission to South America. He did so, and was extraordinarily successful in his endeavors. His report, entitled "For Better Relations with our Latin-American Neighbors," is not merely an account of his mission, but lays down the principles which it is believed should guide the Government of the United States in its relations with the American republics.

WASHINGTON, D. C., JULY 20, 1913

HON. ROBERT BACON,

SIR:

I beg to confirm your appointment, by formal action of the Carnegie Endowment for International Peace, as the representative of the Endowment to visit South America at such time as you shall determine upon during the present year. The object of this mission, which you have already gratified us by promising to undertake, is to secure the interest and sympathy of the leaders of opinion in South America in the various enterprises for the advancement of international peace which the Endowment is seeking to promote, and by means of personal intercourse and explanation to bring about practical coöperation in that work in South America. You are already aware, and will readily make plain to our friends in South America, that Mr. Carnegie has placed in the hands of trustees the sum of ten million dollars, the income of which is to be devoted by them to the promotion of international peace. The Trustees, upon consideration of the way in which they should seek the end for which the trust was established, formulated the following statement of specific objects to which the income of the trust should be devoted.

(a) To promote a thorough and scientific investigation and study of the causes of war and of the practical methods to prevent and avoid it.

(b) To aid in the development of international law, and a general agreement on the rules thereof, and the acceptance of the same among nations.

(c) To diffuse information, and to educate public opinion regarding the causes, nature, and effects of war, and means for its prevention and avoidance.

(d) To establish a better understanding of international rights and duties and a more perfect sense of international justice among the inhabitants of civilized countries.

(e) To cultivate friendly feelings between the inhabitants of different countries and to increase the knowledge and understanding of each other by the several nations.

(f) To promote a general acceptance of peaceable methods in the settlement of international disputes.

(g) To maintain, promote, and assist such establishments, organizations, associations, and agencies as shall be deemed necessary or useful in the accomplishment of the purposes of the corporation, or any of them.

To accomplish these objects the work of the trust has been organized in three divisions: (1) the Division of Intercourse and Education, of which Dr. Nicholas Murray Butler, President of Columbia University, is Acting Director; (2) the Division of Economics and History, of which Dr. John Bates Clark is Director; (3) the Division of International Law, of which the Secretary of the Endowment, Dr. James Brown Scott, is Director. The various objects above enumerated have been appropriately assigned to these three divisions. The methods and details of activity on the part of each of the divisions you will find indicated in a series of monographs, which will be handed to you herewith. From these you will perceive two things: First, that it is the purpose of the Trustees, not that the trust organization shall become a missionary seeking to preach the gospel of peace or directly to express its own ideas to the world, but rather to promote and advance in each country and in all countries the organization and activity of national forces in favor of peace. It is not so much to add a new peace organization to those already existing in the world as it is to be a means of giving renewed vigor to all the activities which really tend in a practical way toward preventing war and making peace more secure. Second, that in aid of the work of each of these three divisions an extensive and effective organization has been perfected in Europe as well as in America, including a great number of the most eminent and highly respected statesmen, publicists, and leaders of modern thought.

The respect and friendship which the Trustees of the Endowment entertain for the peoples of Latin America and for many distinguished Latin Americans with whom many of the Trustees have most agreeable relations of personal friendship, lead us to desire that the work of the Endowment may have the same active and useful coöperation in South America that it has already secured in Europe. For this purpose we should be glad to have you make to the gentlemen whom you meet in the South American capitals a full and thorough explanation of the history and purposes and methods of the Endowment.

You will observe that one of the means by which the Division of Intercourse and Education proposes to advance International good understanding is a series of international visits of representative men. Accordingly, under the auspices of the Division, directly or indirectly, Baron d'Estournelles de Constant of France, the Baroness von Suttner of Austria, and Professor Nitobe of Japan have already visited the United States, and President Eliot of Harvard University has visited India, China, and Japan, and Dr. Hamilton Wright Mabie is now in Japan. Your visit to South America comes in this

category, but it has a more definite and specific purpose than
any of the other visits which I have enumerated or which are
contemplated under the head that I have mentioned; for it is
not merely to strengthen good understanding by personal
intercourse between a representative North American and
representative South Americans, but it is also to introduce to
representative South Americans personally the work and
purposes and ideals of the Endowment, and to invite our
friends in South America to cordial and sympathetic union
with us in promoting the great work of the trust.

It is not expedient or desirable in advance of your visit to
be too specific regarding the scope and method of coöperation
which may be possible with our South American friends, but
you will readily observe in the monographs handed to you a
number of ways in which such coöperation may be accomplished with but little delay. For example: (a) The formation
of national societies of international law, to be affiliated with
the American Institute of International Law. (b) The presentation to the different governments of the opportunity to
participate in the proposed Academy of International Law at
The Hague by providing for the sending on the part of each
government of a representative student to that academy, if
organized. You will notice that the organization of such an
academy to bring together students from the whole world
under the leaders of thought in international law each summer depends very largely upon the question whether the governments of the world feel the need of such an institution
sufficiently to give it their formal support by sending a representative student. (c) The appointment of national committees for the consideration of contributions to the programme
of the next Hague Conference and making arrangements for
the intercommunication of such committees among all the
American countries. (d) The establishment of national societies for international conciliation, to be affiliated with the

parent Association for International Conciliation at Paris. (e) To arrange for systematic furnishing of data for the work of the Division of Economics and History, in accordance with the programme laid down at Berne by the congress of economists in the summer of 1911. You will observe that Dr. Kinley, who was appointed a member of the Committee of Research with special reference to South America, will follow you in a visit to South America within a short period, and will suggest specifically the things that can be done in aid of the researches of this division. Your office in this respect should be to prepare the way for Dr. Kinley's reception and coöperation with him.

The Trustees of the Endowment are fully aware that progress in the work which they have undertaken must necessarily be slow and that its most substantial results must be far in the future. We are dealing with aptitudes and impulses firmly established in human nature through the development of thousands of years; and the utmost that any one generation can hope to do is to promote the gradual change of standards of conduct. All estimates of such a work and its results must be, not in terms of individual human life, but in terms of the long life of nations. Inconspicuous as are the immediate results, however, there can be no nobler object of human effort than to exercise an influence upon the tendencies of the race, so that it shall move, however slowly, in the direction of civilization and humanity and away from senseless brutality. It is to participate with us in this noble, though inconspicuous, work that we ask you to invite our friends in South America, with the most unreserved and sincere assurances of our high consideration and warm regard.

Very faithfully yours,

(Signed) ELIHU ROOT

President.

THE CARNEGIE ENDOWMENT FOR
INTERNATIONAL PEACE

REMARKS BEFORE THE BOARD OF TRUSTEES
WASHINGTON, APRIL 21, 1922

DISTRESSING as have been the conditions regarding
peace throughout the world in the last few years, I
think that, on the whole, the opportunities arranged for the
working force of this Endowment have rather tended to confirm the wisdom of the program which we had laid out.

The original idea of a peace society was of an organization
for the purpose of persuading people at large in favor of
peace, through peace meetings, peace publications, peace
writings.

I need not say to the older trustees here that quite early in
our experience we came to the conclusion that, if we were to
use profitably the funds that were put in our hands, it would
be necessary for us to pass off the field of mere persuasion
and writing and speaking (since this tended to the repetition
of platitudes and saying to people already convinced the
things which they had heard hundreds of times); to get to
the bottom of the real facts, and, in addition, to carry to the
minds of the people more of an understanding of what international relations are — what the basis of them is, what their
rights and the limitation of their rights are, what their duties
and obligations are, and what the methods are by which
those rights can properly be maintained and those duties
actually performed.

Now, that is the kind of thing that we have been at work
upon; and I think that all the Divisions have been doing most

useful work during the last year. The things that Dr. Butler has mentioned about the expenditures of money in France, Belgium, and Serbia were essential. We have reached a point where we have been talking and writing for years to people who have come finally under the stress of dire misfortune. We have to do something to make them understand that it was not mere talk; that there was real friendship and real sympathy, a real desire to render a service of comradeship in their misfortunes. And while this is not a charitable institution and so has no right to spend money merely to relieve distress, the $550,000 spent as an earnest of our sincerity and our friendship is worth a great deal.

In regard to the economic history of the war, if you will look at the histories which followed the Napoleonic wars, — to take the most striking example, — you will see that the impression left of the records which became public was that they were records of military organization, military problems, diplomatic controversies, diplomatic successes and diplomatic failures. It was all governmental and military; the people underneath, who were ground down, had no records at all. The object of this work in which Dr. Shotwell is engaged is first to preserve, and second to bring about the first stage of translating, the records of the people who suffered, the people who really paid the costs, and the people who had always been neglected in history. It was evident that, to give them a chance, a fund was required, together with strenuous and extensive efforts. Somebody had to do it, and there was nobody to do it but ourselves. I feel confident that future generations will find, in the material that is being got up now by competent editorial boards all over the civilized world under Dr. Shotwell's general direction, the basis for a new and more persuasive discussion of the subjects of war and peace and for more and correct information as to what it is safe and wise for nations to do.

As to the work of the Division of International Law, that is a business of instruction, a business of education, a business, not of making all members of a democracy international lawyers, but of putting everywhere possible the material by means of which the leaders of opinion in all communities may know what are the real rights and duties of their country, so that it may be possible for the people who do not study and are not competent to understand, to get a source of intelligent and dispassionate information. And that process has been going on steadily.

We had one very important illustration of the advantage of it during the past year. I really do not know how the Far Eastern work of the late Conference upon the Limitation of Armament could have been done without MacMurray's book which had been published just a few months before by the Endowment. If we had not had those two big volumes, published by the Endowment, upon our tables for access at any moment, it would have been exceedingly difficult, if not impossible, to arrange the nine nations represented in the Conference upon a basis of agreement for the treatment of Chinese questions, so as to facilitate the heroic efforts of the Chinese people to develop an effective and stable self-government. We were continually referring to them: the members could turn to such a page and find such a treaty and such an agreement, and have the real facts readily accessible. If the tentative arrangement toward helping the Chinese in their struggle works out as I think it will, the publication of those books at the time when they were published will be worth to the world all the money that has been spent on the Division of International Law from the beginning. There were a dozen other books to which we continually referred. The assistance of the Division of International Law of this Endowment in that Conference very well illustrates the way in which help can be given. When I used to

come in here, I was as likely as not to find some Frenchman
or Japanese or Dutchman, or members of the other delegations, either consulting with Dr. Scott or in the library.
There was a feeling that this was a kind of neutral ground,
that this was a place where they could get sympathy and
help. It was unlike going to the American Government.
They could come here as they could not go to the State Department. And many a rough place was smoothed out and
many an excitement was cooled down in that way.

The work of the Endowment has gradually changed from
the production of public excitement in favor of peace to the
application of public feeling in favor of peace.

THE PERMANENT COURT OF INTER-NATIONAL JUSTICE

REMARKS AS MEMBER OF THE ADVISORY COMMITTEE OF JURISTS AT THE HAGUE, PREFACED BY LETTERS FROM MR. FRANK L. POLK, SECRETARY OF STATE *ad interim*, AND SIR ERIC DRUMMOND, SECRETARY-GENERAL OF THE LEAGUE OF NATIONS, JUNE 17 TO JULY 24, 1920

The movement for the judicial organization of the world has assumed concrete if not definite form and shape within the lives of people now living.

The institutions which are now established at The Hague, if not the conception, are in a very real sense the gift of the English-speaking peoples.

The American Delegation to the First Peace Conference meeting at The Hague in 1899, was instructed by Secretary of State Hay to propose a Court of Justice, which, with the support of the British Delegation and under the leadership of its First Delegate, Sir Julian Pauncefote, assumed the form of the present Permanent Court of Arbitration at The Hague.

The American Delegation to the Second Conference meeting at The Hague in the summer of 1907, was instructed by Secretary of State Root to propose a Permanent Court of International Justice somewhat similar to the Supreme Court of the United States. The project was introduced by the American Delegation, and after weeks of debate the idea was approved, incorporated in a draft convention of some thirty articles dealing with the organization, jurisdiction and procedure of a Permanent Court, but the formal institution of the Court of Arbitral Justice — for such it was then called — was to be deferred until the nations had reached an agreement through diplomatic channels upon the method of appointing the judges and thus constituting the court. Unfamiliarity with the subject, with the consequent lack of experience, and, above all the lack of time prevented an agreement upon a method of appointing the judges which would have been generally satisfactory to the forty-four Powers in conference.

After the adjournment, steps were taken to institute the Court, and it was well on its way to establishment when the great war diverted the thoughts of the world from peace and its judicial maintenance.

With the defeat of Germany and the signing of the Armistice on November 11, 1918, the way was open to peace, and in the Covenant of the League of Nations, although a provision in its behalf was lacking in the earlier drafts, an article provided for the establishment of a Permanent Court of International Justice.

An Advisory Committee of Jurists (ten in number) took up the project where it had been left in 1907, and the smaller conference of 1920 succeeded where the larger one of 1907 had failed.

The Advisory Committee met at The Hague in the summer of 1920. Its first session was held on June 16th, at which Baron Descamps, of Belgium, was elected President, and Dr. Loder, of Holland, Vice-President. At a later session (July 5th), M. de Lapradelle, of France, was chosen *rapporteur*. It closed with the signature of the proposed draft on July 24, 1920.

The draft of the Advisory Committee was a court idea in as strict a sense of the word as is the Supreme Court of these United States, in which nation could sue nation within a limited but generous jurisdiction, and in the absence of a nation duly invited, judgment could be rendered.

As the draft emerged from the Council and from the Assembly of the League of Nations on December 14, 1920, it was to all intents and purposes the draft convention for the establishment of a Court of Arbitral Justice, with a method of appointing the judges proposed by Mr. Root and unanimously adopted by the Council and Assembly. The judges were elected at a meeting of the Assembly in September 1921, and the Court itself was formally installed in the Peace Palace at The Hague in the course of 1922.[1]

The following letters state the call and the proposed membership of the Advisory Committee, and Mr. Root's addresses following the letters show the process through which an acceptable method of appointing the judges and thus constituting the Court, was devised.

DEPARTMENT OF STATE
WASHINGTON, *March 9, 1920.*

MY DEAR MR. ROOT, —

I have the pleasure to transmit herewith, at the request of the Secretary General of the League of Nations communicated through the American Ambassador at

---

[1] The Judges met for organization in the Peace Palace of The Hague on January 30, 1922, and the Court formally opened its sessions in the Peace Palace on February 15, 1922. Its original membership was as follows:

President, Mr. B. C. J. Loder (Netherlands)
Vice-President, Mr. Charles André Weiss (France)
Judges, Mr. Rafael Altamira (Spain)
　　　　Mr. Dionisio Anzilotti (Italy)
　　　　Mr. Ruy Barbosa (Brazil)
　　　　Mr. Antonio S. de Bustamante (Cuba)
　　　　Viscount Finlay (Great Britain)
　　　　Mr. Max Huber (Switzerland)
　　　　Mr. John Bassett Moore (United States of America)
　　　　Mr. Didrik Galtrup Gjedde Nyholm (Denmark)
　　　　Mr. Yorosu Oda (Japan)
Deputy Judges, Mr. Frederik Valdemar Nikolai Beichmann (Norway)
　　　　Mr. Michel Jovanovitch (Serb-Croat-Slovene State)
　　　　Mr. Demetre Negulesco (Roumania)
　　　　Mr. Wang Chung Hui (China)

Paris, a letter inviting you to serve on an International Committee composed of eminent jurists to prepare plans for a Permanent Court of International Justice.

I am with high regard,

Very faithfully yours,

FRANK L. POLK

[Secretary of State *ad interim*]

Enclosure:

As stated above.

The Honorable Elihu Root, New York City.

SUNDERLAND HOUSE,

CURZON STREET, LONDON, W. 1.

16th February, 1920.

SIR, —

I am instructed by the Council of the League of Nations to inform you that it has been decided to invite certain distinguished international lawyers to form themselves into a Committee, to be convened at an early date, to prepare plans for the establishment of the Permanent Court of International Justice and to ask you to be a member thereof.

The Article of the Covenant of the League of Nations under which the Committee is to be established is as follows: —

Article XIV

The Council shall formulate and submit to the Members of the League for adoption plans for the establishment of a Permanent Court of International Justice. The Court shall be competent to hear and determine any dispute of an international character which the parties thereto submit to it. The Court may also give an advisory opinion upon any dispute or question referred to it by the Council or by the Assembly.

The duties which fall to the Court will cover a wide sphere, and will be of the very highest importance.

The Council in no way underrates the sacrifice which it asks you to make in devoting a period of what will no doubt be arduous labour to helping to plan and create it; nor does it fail to realize that the work which it is asking you to interrupt is itself of very great importance. But the Court is a most essential part of the Organization of the League of Nations. If it is established on sound and statesmanlike principles, it can contribute perhaps more than any other single institution to maintain the peace of the world and the supremacy of right amongst the nations. It must be established as soon as possible after the coming into effect of the Covenant; and it is hoped that this Committee may find it possible to present its report to the Council of the League in sufficient time for that body to be able to submit it to an early meeting of the Assembly.

It is understood that the question of a Permanent Court of International Justice has been carefully examined by certain of the countries named in the Annex to the Covenant, some of which have already forwarded plans for the constitution of the Court to the Secretary-General. It is therefore suggested that the Committee should consider these plans, and should also invite the other countries named in the Annex to forward any proposals they may have prepared.

You are no doubt aware that both the Austrian and the German Governments have made certain proposals for the composition of the Court and that the Allied and Associated Governments have promised that these proposals would be submitted for detailed consideration to the Council of the League of Nations when it prepares a plan for the establishment of a Permanent Court in accordance with Article XIV of the Covenant.

The Council suggest therefore that the Committee, of which you are invited to be a member, should not overlook these assurances in preparing plans for the establishment of the Permanent Court of International Justice.

Invitations to join the Committee are also being sent to the following gentlemen:—

Mr. AKIDZUKI, Former Ambassador of His Majesty the Emperor of Japan.

M. RAFAEL ALTAMIRA, Senator, Professor of the Faculty of Law of the University of Madrid.

M. CLOVIS BEVILAQUA, Professor of the Faculty of Law of Pernambuco and Legal Adviser to the Minister of Foreign Affairs of Brazil.

BARON DESCAMPS, Minister of State for Belgium.

SEÑOR DRAGO, Former Minister for Foreign Affairs of the Argentine Republic.

PROFESSOR FADDA, Professor of Law at the University of Naples.

M. FROMAGEOT, Legal Adviser to the Ministry for Foreign Affairs at Paris.

Mr. GRAM, Former Member of the Supreme Court of Norway.

Dr. LODER, Member of the Court of Cassation of the Netherlands.

LORD PHILLIMORE, Member of the Privy Council of His Majesty the King of England.

Mr. VESNITCH, Envoy Extraordinary and Minister Plenipotentiary of his Majesty the King of the Serbs, Croats and Slovenes at Paris.

I have the Honour to be, Sir,
Your obedient Servant,
ERIC DRUMMOND,
Secretary-General

EXTRACTS FROM DEBATE IN COMMITTEE, JUNE 17, 1920

MR. ROOT: I have offered this resolution [1] in entire harmony with the view expressed by the President of the

---

[1] RESOLVED: That the Committee adopts as the basis for consideration of the subject referred to it the Acts and Resolutions of the Second Peace Conference at The Hague in the year 1907.

That the provisions of the several plans for an International Court of Justice already elaborated by Representative Jurists of

Sweden,	Switzerland,
Norway,	Germany,
Denmark,	Austria,
Holland,	

be laid before the Committee and considered as the subjects to which they respectively relate are taken up for consideration.

Committee as to the consideration of the large questions (important questions) which underlie the whole subject referred to the Committee.

The resolution was drawn up for the accomplishment of several objects:

(1) To give notice to all the world that this committee will consider the great subject referred to it, not as an opportunity for the expression merely of our individual opinions, but under a sense of duty to build upon the basis of the past development of the subject to which so many members of the committee have already contributed so well. I should be glad to have the world know that we begin here again the course of a development of the law of nations, the principle of justice in international affairs. There is throughout the world much respect and reverence for the self-sacrifice and devoted work done at The Hague in the conferences of 1899 and 1907. I think the committee should make clear the relations which it means to bear to all that work and all that was accomplished then, and I am sure that the clear understanding that the committee is beginning its labors in this spirit will be very grateful to the people of all the civilized countries of the world. I know that it will be so among the people of my own country.

(2) We have received from the Secretariat of the League of Nations, in printed form, plans for a Court of International Justice having very high authority. The jurists of Norway, Sweden, Denmark, Holland, and Switzerland have met and discussed this very subject, and they have formulated their conclusions and have formally communicated them to the Secretariat of the League of Nations, and these conclusions have been transmitted to us. Also, Germany and Austria have sent expressions of their views. In some way we should indicate to all these nations the sentiment of profound respect that we have for the work that they have done. We should

treat their recommendations or suggestions with due respect and not pass them *sub silentio*. This resolution was designed to carry to the minds of our friends in these countries the knowledge that we recognize the work that they have done with great respect and with the purpose of due consideration.

Another idea is involved in the resolution. It is that there may be something invidious if we try to select among these plans one rather than another for a basis of discussion. There can be nothing of that kind if we take the conclusion of all countries reached at the second Hague Conference. And we here come from but a few countries. We cannot come from more than ten if there are only ten of us. But let us see that the people of other countries from which no citizen sits here understand that we are going to consider in our work not only the feelings of the people of the countries from which we come, but the feelings and the opinions of the people of all countries. Let us lay down in some such declaration as this a broad foundation of unanimous international consideration of international subjects. I hoped that this resolution would carry to the people of all countries the idea that we were going to start by considering as the basis of our discussion the conclusions that they had taken at the second Hague Conference.

The working out of this resolution would be precisely as the president has suggested — that we take up the provision and form of Court adopted at The Hague as the basis for discussion. For example, if we determine to take up first the subject of the jurisdiction, the competence of the court, the provision of The Hague resolution would be the basis of discussion and the provision of the Five Powers plan would be read as relevant to that. Whatever there may be in the Austrian or the German plan, relevant to that, should also be read, and then we could proceed to our discussion. The

object, the effect of the resolution will not be so much to affect the order of our work as it will be to declare the principal point from which we propose to start.[1]

JUNE 18, 1920

MR. ROOT: We have now come face to face with the difficulty which prevented the adoption of the plan for a permanent court by the second Hague Conference of 1907.

That difficulty was the unwillingness of the large states to permit the members of the court to be named by the majority, which would always be composed of the representatives of the smaller states, and, on the other hand, the unwillingness of the smaller states to permit to the larger ones a preponderance of power and authority, which was deemed to be inconsistent with the theory of equal rights of sovereign states.

One view has been stated by a part of our colleagues, and the other by another part, and those two views are opposed. A statement of them does not solve them — it does not solve the question. The simple adoption of one view by itself would apparently send the plan of the court to the Council of the League of Nations with the most difficult question unsolved.

It seems to me that both views are, in a broad sense, right. We must accept and sincerely support the equal rights of every sovereign state — that is the foundation of the law of nations. On the other hand, we must realize that an aggre-

[1] The resolution as adopted by the Committee reads as follows:

"The Committee begins its deliberations by rendering in the first instance homage to the labors of the Peace Conferences of The Hague, which have already prepared with exceptional authority the solution of the problem of the organization of a court of international justice.

"Ready to consider in addition the projects emanating from governments, from conferences initiated by governments, of scientific international associations, and of jurists of every nationality, whose labors have preceded its own, it will take note of all sources of information which are at its disposition in order to justify the confidence of the Society of Nations."

gation of fifty millions or one hundred millions of people will have more active interest — more important affairs — dependent upon the action of the court than an aggregation of one million or one hundred thousand; so that the equality of sovereign states in law does not agree with the inequality of practical interests, which depend not upon the grouping of individuals in states but upon their production, their trade, their commerce, their activity — the two do not fully agree and each has some right to its view.

For example, we may say that, in the cases of arbitration which have been brought before the present arbitration Court at The Hague, only few countries have been concerned, and doubtless there are many countries whose mode of life and whose international affairs are such that they will seldom, if ever, have recourse to any court. Now our problem, it seems to me, is to reconcile these two views, which approach one another from very different points — the one coming from the constituted and indisputable point of legal equality of states, and the other from the practical standpoint of a deep and extensive practical interest in the subject. Can we not find some mode of constituting this court which will be consistent with both, and which will preserve the true interests of both? That, it seems to me, is the most serious problem which is committed to us.

Similar situations frequently arise in life. A number of citizens of any free country have to determine some question regarding which they have an equal right because they are equal politically, with equal voice in the affairs of their country. At the same time, some of them have a much greater interest in the matter which is to be disposed of than the others. It is not at all uncommon that, in the exercise of the free right of equal citizenship, such dispositions of practical matters are made as to recognize their greater practical interest.

Can we not accomplish that task? Allow me to refer to an example which naturally arises in the mind of an American. When the present Constitution of the United States was formed there was precisely the same kind of question raised in the Federal Convention of 1787.[1] We were all independent sovereign states — some large, some small. The large states were unwilling to permit the majority of the smaller ones the control which would come from equal representation, and, on the other hand, the smaller states were unwilling to allow to the larger ones the preponderance of power which would arise from the recognition of their greater population and wealth. That *impasse* was disposed of by the creation of two chambers, one in which the states are represented equally, and another in which the population is represented, without reference to the sovereign states in which the people reside. Now I mention that, not for the purpose of proposing that disposition here, but for the purpose of illustrating the way in which such a question has been disposed of, and disposed of so that for one hundred and thirty years it has worked practically and satisfactorily. That disposition has been followed by many nations. In Central and South America similar questions have been solved in a similar way: and in every country where there is a bicameral legislative body you will find that there is a reconciliation, by means of the two chambers, of certain conflicting ideas. Now that is the method of development of political freedom. That is the method of the development of civilization — finding practical methods of reconciling, for useful activity, conflicting political theories; and that is our task.

I must confess that, after much groping, much searching, among many proposals, I have not yet found any which was entirely satisfactory to me; but I have found so many which

---

[1] It is of more than passing interest to note that a copy of Madison's *Debates in the Federal Convention* lay on the table before each member of the Advisory Committee of Jurists at the time of Mr. Root's address.

came very near, that I am certain we shall reach it by discussion, by comparison of views, by the enlightenment which comes from hearing the expression of opinion from different points of view. I am confident from what has been done that we shall reach a practical solution, although I cannot get to it now completely — there is some objection to every suggestion.

I think there is another thing, however, that may now be said. We are a committee invited by the Council of the League of Nations to prepare a plan, which is to be formulated and submitted by the Council to the members of the League for adoption; it is to be a plan for the establishment of the permanent court of international justice. Now, let me say in passing that I believe that the court we create should be a court to coexist with, and bear due and appropriate relations to, the existing permanent Court of Arbitration at The Hague — not to be substituted for it, but to form part of the same system of international judicature. I propose not to discuss, but to suggest for consideration, this question: How far should our plans articulate with the existing organization of the League of Nations, the formation of the Council, the formation of the Assembly? Should we form a plan having close relation to that political organization, or should we form a plan which ignores that organization? It does not follow from the fact that the organization of the League of Nations is political, excepting Articles 13 and 14, relating to the court, that there can be no intimate relations between that political authority and the formation of the court. It may be that we can find there the solution of our question. At Paris, the Peace Conference secured a *modus* — which did not satisfy, entirely, both views — in the constitution of one chamber, the Assembly, in which every power great and small is equal to every other, and another, the Council, in which there is a preponderance of the great powers.

Now, is it possible that the Council and the Assembly will accept and put into force the plan of the court if the plan ignores their existence? How are courts constituted originally? However perfect may be the distinction between judicial and political powers, the personnel of the judiciary must necessarily have its origin in the political power. In my own country, the justices of the Supreme Court and all the Federal Courts are appointed by the President. The judges of the Court of Cassation in France owe their appointment to political authority. Our colleague, Lord Phillimore, whose judgment upon a judicial question would be without fear or favor as to any political authority, nevertheless derives his appointment from political power. Under every plan suggested, the judges come from a political authority.

I beg to suggest, for the consideration of my colleagues, whether possibly the election of judges by the concurrent vote of the Assembly and the Council might not point out, for our purpose, the same solution of this difficult question which already has been accomplished on the political side. That would have several advantages. The effect of the necessity of concurrent action by two bodies is that neither one can do anything which is oppressive in respect of the interests specially represented by the other. That is so in the making of all laws, and it is so when appointments are to be made by legislative bodies. The effect of the practical working would be that in the Assembly, where the smaller powers are in majority, they would protect the interests of the smaller states, and that in the Council, the larger powers, having a preponderance, would protect such practical interests of their greater trade and their greater production and their greater interests as would be submitted to the court. The practical effect would be that the selection would be made at the time of the meeting of the Assembly — that would be necessary; and one could discuss and consider individual names at that time.

Now the practical method of reconciling differences between two bodies is a committee of conference — a small committee of conference. In that committee all considerations of good faith, all justifiable doubt or apprehension of injury to interests, would be considered without the difficulty that comes from publicity. This selection of judges is an intensely practical thing, and care must be taken not to have it undertaken in such a way as to drive off and practically exclude all the best men. The best men in all countries will be unwilling to permit their names to be put before all the world in the contest for something which perhaps they would have to make great sacrifice to accept. The best men, the men we want, are the men whom you have to urge to come in; these men will not be candidates. On the other hand, if you elect a man who seems to be the best, you must have some way of finding out whether he will serve. For example, the Council selected as a member of this committee a very old and valued friend of mine in the Argentine, M. Drago — a most admirable selection. M. Drago could not come: he was so situated that he could not come from the Argentine to give this summer for the consideration of this subject. How many times, if you are going to elect a judge, will you not find that situation. Of the members of this committee, a majority are not the ones originally named.[1] Even

---

[1] Mr. Akidzuki declined the appointment and was replaced by Mr. Mineichiro Adatci, Japanese Minister to Belgium.

The Brazilian Government being unable to spare Mr. Bevilaqua, he was represented by Mr. Raoul Fernandez until late in the session, when he formally replaced Mr. Bevilaqua.

Dr. Drago was obliged to decline the appointment on account of ill health. His death on June 9, 1921, alone prevented him from being elected a Judge of the Permanent Court of International Justice.

The name of Professor Fadda was withdrawn, and Mr. Arturo Ricci-Busatti, Jurisconsult of the Italian Ministry for Foreign Affairs was appointed in his stead.

M. Fromageot was unable to leave the Foreign Office to accept the appoint-

for this service, to get the committee, a process had to be worked out for finding out who could leave his home and his occupation to come and render the service. This committee was constituted by an authority absolute. When Sir Eric Drummond wrote to a jurist inviting him to render this service, we all knew that the Council, for which Sir Eric spoke, had absolute authority to make the person receiving the letter a member of the committee. You cannot get that by the ordinary process of election. In an ordinary method of election the candidate will not say that he will serve before he knows whether it will be offered to him, and the election therefore has to take place before the electors know that the candidate will serve; and the practical method of dealing with that is some such method as this conference committee between the two bodies.

I do not state this view as a conclusion, but as a method which has occurred to my mind as being perhaps nearer to the accomplishing of our object than anything else that has been suggested, the object being, in any arrangement we make, that both the divergent interests shall have a negative power to prevent injustice and an affirmative power to propose action and in dealing with the practical questions. If

ment, and was ultimately replaced by M. Albert de Lapradelle, Professor of International Law at the University of Paris. M. André Weiss, likewise Professor of International Law at the University of Paris, had previously declined the appointment to replace M. Fromageot. He was elected an original Judge of the Permanent Court of International Justice in 1921, and upon its installation, in the following year, was chosen its Vice-President.

Mr. Gram being unable to attend because of his health, Mr. Francis Hagerup, formerly Prime Minister of Norway and a member of the Second Hague Peace Conference, and Minister to Sweden, was appointed in his place.

Mr. Milenko R. Vesnitch felt obliged to accept the Premiership of his country, and was thus unable to attend, as he otherwise would have been glad to do.

It is thus seen that of the twelve Jurists originally invited, only five accepted and attended the sessions of the Committee; and of the ten members actually present — for neither Dr. Drago nor Mr. Vesnitch was replaced — two were chosen original Judges of the Court: Mr. Altamira, of Spain, and Dr. Loder of Holland, who, in addition, was its first President.

these two powers exist, it should be worked out in some such practical way as that in which free self-government is carried on in every country where it exists. That is all that occurs to me now except that I, on this question, shall preserve an open mind for the most respectful consideration of the suggestions of my colleagues on the committee.

JUNE 21, 1920

MR. ROOT: When I was called upon to speak at the last session, I was about to make some observations upon the general subject of the theory which underlies our whole procedure in the formation of the court, and to follow such observations very briefly by some other reference to the practical necessities imposed upon us by our assignment to duty here.

There are two fundamental principles laid down by the members of the committee, with which I think we all agree, and by which I think we are ready to have any suggestions that we make decided. One is the proposition that the end of this court which we are about to recommend is justice. Unless the court succeeds in doing justice, it is worthless. We shall have failed in our efforts. The other proposition is the equality of sovereign states; to that we all agree; that we are bound to maintain, for it is the very basis, the *substratum*, which underlies the law of nations: without that there is no law, and we return to the days of barbarism and unrestrained brute force.

In applying the first principle, we are seeking justice. The task is one of the adaptation of means to an end: it is that we may recommend that the proposed court be so constituted that it will, with the greatest certainty possible to human nature, do justice — a practical adaptation of human means to secure a divine end.

In applying the other principle, that of the equality of sovereign states, it is necessary to consider the nature of the transaction on which we enter and to see whether the principle covers the transaction. The principle is limited definitely. The equality of states does not mean that they are equal in numbers, in extent of territory, in wealth, in power: it means that they are equal in the sovereign right to control their own actions and in freedom from accountability to others. It relates to the rights of each state over its own territory, its own subjects or citizens. Every state is exercising that right in agreeing or refusing to agree to any arrangements we propose. Monaco, Luxembourg, Haiti, San Domingo, have the same inalienable right to consent or refuse to consent as Great Britain or France. That is the exercise of equality. In brief, it is equality in the exercise of the rights of sovereignty.

When, however, we come to the creation of a court, we pass beyond the exercise of the rights of sovereignty. In constituting a court which is to render judgments limiting the rights of nations, we shall not be merely exercising the powers of sovereignty. What sovereign right has France to limit the sovereignty of Italy, of Great Britain? What sovereign right has Italy to name a judge to say if the power of France should be limited? From whence does this power come? From the sovereignty of Italy? It comes from consent. It has its origin in consent; not in the theory of sovereignty, not in the law of nations. It is purely conventional. The right of Italy to name a judge who can give decisions limiting the sovereign rights of France comes not from the sovereignty of Italy but from the consent of France.

As the function to be observed is a function not resting in sovereignty, but resting in consent, then, in determining whether the consent should be given mutually, and upon what terms, we must consider not merely the theory of national equality, but the conditions and circumstances of the agreement which we are proposing to make. You have passed off the field of exclusive application of the theory of equality of nations. You have passed on to a different field, in which to determine what course should be followed; you must consider everything as relevant that is reasonable. You cannot say you wish to consider alone the doctrine of equality; you cannot say you must exclude from consideration all those circumstances from which one nation derives the greater interest in a subject matter than another. All relevant facts must be considered.

Take, for example, the Universal Postal Union. The nations which made that agreement for the Universal Postal Union were equal undeniably; but is that equality treated as the sole test of the stipulations included in the agreement? No! There are, I think, seven classes, the nations being classified according to the benefits which they derive from their business, and also according to their resources for bearing the expense. Great Britain, Japan, Italy, France, the United States, Germany, Austria-Hungary, pay many times as much as the smaller states.

That is an illustration of the way in which practical common sense deals with the basis of agreement for a special object between equals; and that has been carried into the basis of the League of Nations, the nations being obliged to bear the expense in the proportions of the Universal Postal Union.

The moment you depart from the basis of unanimous agreement — which in diplomatic conferences connotes the uncontrolled equality of states — and submit anything to the determination of a majority, you have left the field of sovereignty and subjected yourself to the application of other considerations than those of the equality of states.

What kind of agreement will it be reasonable for all our countries, in the exercise of their equal sovereign rights, to enter upon? It is to attain justice. But to agree merely to attain justice is to accomplish nothing. For all civilized nations are already agreed to do justice to each other.

What we are to seek is a practical means of so limiting the weaknesses, the passions, of so enlightening the ignorance and awakening the understanding of men engaged in the affairs of nations, that there will be the highest possible probability of justice being done.

The object is to secure an institution which, by the application of just principles, will curb exercise of power; and it is because that is an essential object to be attained that we find throughout the history of the effort to create such a court a clear division of the smaller nations on one side and the larger on the other. The division which occurred in 1907, and which is here before us to-day, is the best proof that among the fundamental necessities of the case is the curbing of power. Whose power is to be curbed? Not the power of Haiti, San Domingo, and their like, but the power of Great Britain; of France; of the United States. We are not called upon by the general voice of the civilized world to make an effort toward the establishing of a court to curb the power of Norway; of Holland. The great powers, with their immense armies and navies, in the presence of which the smaller nations of the world feel that their lives are in danger unless justice prevails, and a practical method of securing justice be agreed on, are to be curbed. This court will be a court to curb the power of these great nations on the one hand, and to give protection to smaller nations on the other.

It follows that the nations are not similarly situated in respect of this project. The surrender of power to limitations imposed by a court is a surrender made chiefly by the great powers. Small powers surrender practically nothing, but they get protection, which the great powers do not.

I repeat that the great powers and the smaller powers who have been opposed since 1907 are not similarly situated in respect of this question. One is the group that is giving, another the group that is receiving, and you cannot solve a question of that description, which affects different states in a different manner, in which the states have different kinds of interests, by the application of the theory of the equality of states. You must deal with it as a question to be considered upon the basis of the realities that are to be affected; and it is not reasonable to suppose that these great states will consent to have their power limited, to surrender their sovereignty to a tribunal the constitution of which is to be entirely within the control of the smaller states. The simple constitution of the court by a majority of equal states would place them in the hands of the smaller states, who give little and get much, and always they would have the power to override the larger states, which give much and get little.

It is not wise always to think of states as if they were not composed of individual human beings. There is a particular distinction which divides the people of nearly every country. Every mind will revert readily to the differences between the military party and the peaceful party in a country in its relations with the other states. During the recent war, at times there was a tendency toward peace, when the peaceful people of Germany wished to end the war, and then a movement the other way, and the military party secured the ascendancy again. In every country there are these parties, and they are always in conflict. What we must do is to present a reasonable proposal to ensure that the principles of peace and of justice may take the control in each country.

The principle of the equality of states has, in recent years, met another principle. The growth of democracy in the world has been accompanied and produced by the growth of the conception of individual personal independence.

Our recommendations with respect to the court will have to be submitted, not to the foreign offices; they will have to be submitted to those great democracies of hundreds of millions of people, knowing but little about international affairs, ill-informed, not accustomed to consider or to discuss or to act upon them. And they control the foreign offices. The government must reach decisions which commend themselves to the great popular mind in our modern democratic governments. With these hundreds of millions of plain people the theory of equal sovereignty is accepted, but it is a weak motive as compared with the idea that a man counts as much in his own country as in another. No theory of sovereignty or equality is going to get out of this man's head in France, in England, in the United States, that he is just as good and just as much entitled to his voice in the world as the man in another country. And you propose to each member of this multitudinous sovereignty, that his country shall surrender its sovereign rights of control to a tribunal made up in such a way that a man across the border weighs as much as one thousand men on his side. See what result you get. The tendencies of intercourse, and these efforts that are drawing countries nearer together, are leveling the differences and favoring individual manhood and the rights of a universal majority as against the extension of the application of equal sovereignty. The people of the United States number more than a hundred million, and if you ask the one hundred million to consent to the sovereign rights of their country being limited in a court in which the one half-million in Honduras can outvote them, all the foreign offices in Christendom can never succeed in getting this recognized.

After all, there is that element of individual right and interest involved in all these international troubles; the greater part of the troubles are troubles where a country is championing the cause of its nationals.

Remember that the question that is to be put to the public in these great countries is not a question of consent to the application of sovereignty: it is a question of creating power by consent, a power which is not founded in sovereignty, but a new power with a right to control the action of the several states.

Now, I would not for a moment be thought to be pessimistic or critical in my judgment of the probable conduct of any country, which, under whatever agreement we make, finds itself engaged in the construction of a court; but I have to look facts in the face. There are backward nations, many quite shut up within themselves, some of them centuries behind in political development. Those very nations which are the most backward are the nations which have the least interest in the court.

But, according to the simple method of constituting a court following the principle of equality, all those backward nations would have the vote.

Some nations which are included within the theory of equality are countries in which the principle of exterritoriality is still applied, and they will have a vote; and the proposal is that, because equality has been accorded to them, and the security of international law under the equality of nations, those countries in which the principles of jurisprudence are so far different from those which obtain in the greater part of the civilized world, that it has been necessary to maintain exterritorial tribunals, are to have an equal voice in constituting this court. What I have said relates only to the weight and value of opinion in these backward nations; but there is another thing to be said: the nations will not come to the constitution of this court with minds that are *tabulæ rasæ*.

The experiences of life, the life of nations, show that there will be combinations. I say, not that there *may* be, but that there *will* be. Human nature has not changed radically. The men who ought to be in this court are the men who ought to be sought by somebody competent to offer to them the appointment. We shall have to seek them and urge them to consent to exile themselves from their homes, to abandon their careers, to commit their future for an appointment in this court; and the men who ought not to be there are the men who will intrigue to get there, the self-seeking men, the men who cannot rise to the highest places in their own courts and seek places in this court; and they will seek support, while the best spirits will quietly go on with the performance of their own duties. That is certain.

Who can go back and say that this is not so? And what will be the response? People are asked to create a court, and to give their consent to create a power, which may be exercised in the way that I have described, to control them. It is not so that governments perform their duty and maintain their people's rights.

If they are to consent away that power, they must see that the power they consent away will be guarded, and for these reasons which I have stated very crudely. I consider that we must adjust the differences of opinion in some practical way, or that we shall have no court.

JUNE 22, 1920

MR. ROOT: Reflecting upon the suggestion of M. de Lapradelle and his reference to me, some of his suggestions seem to meet the requirements of the situation. I have made a memorandum in which I have sought to follow the idea M. de Lapradelle has expressed, and to incorporate the most valuable propositions in the plan submitted to the meeting by you, Mr. President.

1. Election by Assembly and Council.
2. Qualifications of candidates to be judicial eminence and character.

3. List of persons deemed to be qualified to be furnished before the meeting of the Assembly, by the members of the permanent Court of Arbitration at The Hague. The members appointed by each nation to propose not less than two nor more than four names, one half to be from nations other than that by which the proposals are made.

4. Votes on the list thus formed to be as provided by Lord Phillimore.

5. So far as vacancies may remain unfilled by election from this list, other names may be proposed by the Assembly and Council to be considered and voted upon in like manner.

6. In all elections all electors to be under honorable obligation to regard the qualifications, and to seek adequate representation in the Court for the different systems of jurisprudence existing among civilized peoples.

I assume two fundamental propositions:

That the permanent Court of Arbitration at The Hague which now exists should remain, not be superseded; and that the new Court should form a part of the judicial system of which the old Court is a part.

There are four different functions to be allotted to these two different judicial institutions:

1. To determine questions of strict law and questions arising from contracts;

2. To determine questions depending upon the principles of justice applicable in the absence of rules of strict law or contract provisions;

3. To determine facts which are unknown or are disputed;

4. Conciliation.

These four points are to be provided for in this system of which the old Court is part, and the new Court will be part.

We must first consider that this new Court must be provided for as a part of the system of which the League of Nations is part. We cannot accept the invitation of the

Council, and recommend a plan for a court which is not going to form a part of that system.

I think that the participation of members of the permanent Court of Arbitration is very desirable, because we have in that list men who are recognized in each country as being specially familiar with the subject with which the court is to be familiar, and with the personnel in other countries which are interested.

Such a provision appropriates the initiative of the Norwegian Parliament in the work of the Nobel Committee. If I am wrong, Mr. Hagerup will correct me. In the selection of the persons to whom the Peace prize is to be given and the scientific prize, the award is made upon lists furnished by previous recipients, of the award, and several classes of men specially selected who are called upon each year to propose names. Here we have a special class of persons who are called upon to propose names. Looking into the working of the government of each country in domestic questions, it would make a great difference if the government of this country or that, proposed names through a purely political officer, who had only the idea of domestic politics in his mind, and who had to accomplish some object of domestic politics. Every court is subject to that, and it is very desirable that we should make such dispositions that the persons in each country who make this suggestion shall be persons who are not what is called "playing politics," but persons who have the international mind; and that is what I take it we wish to accomplish by the selections proposed by the heads of universities.

I think that the participation of the members of the permanent Court of Arbitration rather comes at the beginning, than at the end, as suggested by M. de Lapradelle. If it comes at the end, it would be as arbitrators, to determine a difference between the Council and the Assembly.

It is only the final decision which is important. The pressure of necessity will be more valuable than the power of decision by someone else. The legislation of the world practically is accomplished in the same way; differences between two opinions are recognized under the pressure of necessity; there must be a law on such and such subject, and the advocates of the opinions which differ are compelled to reconcile their differences, because there must be a law. Here there must be justice; and if the electors do not agree, they are condemned for incapacity. If the members of the court have the opportunity to propose this list, the origin of it will be a guaranty of qualification, and if the electors cannot agree upon one named, the opportunity to propose names outside the list will guarantee that someone be found.

I think that the last proposal, that in all elections the electors are under an honorable obligation to regard the qualifications stated and to seek adequate representation on the court for the different systems of jurisprudence — I think this is a view in which we all agree, and it seems to me that that includes valuable ideas that have been proposed by a member of the Committee.

I claim no patent or copyright on it; I admit that it is stolen property.

June 25, 1920

Mr. Root: A fundamental rule, which is the necessary corollary of the principle of sovereignty, is that no sovereign state may be sued without its consent. It is common among all enlightened states to give consent to suits against the government by individuals; but in the different states there are different methods and different limitations. Great Britain differs widely in that respect from the United States, and both differ from France, and so on. I think it would be very difficult for us to draft a system which would be satisfactory to all the states; a system containing the limitations and methods of procedure, so that we should not be introducing a further compulsory system. We should be calling upon different states to abandon their own ideas about the conditions under which they should be sued; and, of course, the less we do of that, the better — the less we hurt the sensitiveness of sovereignty, the better.

Another consideration is that the present system affords a much better method of reaching justice for individuals than to leave the individual himself to carry on his suit. The practical working of that protection which governments feel bound to give to their citizens is that a particular citizen, feeling himself aggrieved by something which has been done or refused in another country, goes to his own government, which presents a claim if it considers that he has a just right; the question is made the subject of diplomatic adjustment; and in ninety-nine cases out of a hundred the question is settled. Now, that is a process which, in all civilized countries, is recognized as desirable, and which ought to be promoted, — the settlement of claims; the adjustment of differences, — and if you are going to leave an individual to the prosecution of claims against a country, you have not that procedure because you cannot compel countries to carry on diplomatic correspondence with an individual. I doubt if any advantage would be given to individuals by forming a court to hear their complaints against foreign countries which the government of their own country did not consider just. If I have a complaint against Holland, and my own government does not think it just, I ought to be content. I think that in that view there is one word in the description of the court that we are to recommend which is very adequately descriptive, and that is the word "International." It is to be an international court; and questions which it is to try and determine are to be, indeed, questions that affect the rights of individuals, but questions that are made international by adoption on the part of the nation of the individual who seeks the decision.

In looking over the list of arbitrations which have been brought before the present Court, I find that the majority relate to the rights of individuals. It is only occasionally that one finds a national right as distinct from an individual right. For example: Spain, France, Great Britain all are conducting claims of their citizens against Portugal. Now I am quite certain that those individuals could not maintain a procedure in any international court. They would not have the means — the force — the power — the momentum — to carry the procedure; but it is because their countries deem that their cause is just that they are enabled to go into court — that there is a cause for decision. . . .

It is so desirable, so important to justice, that an individual may have recourse against a foreign country in which he may happen to suffer, that the practical common sense of mankind has created a jurisdiction and a practice under which every claim of that kind that is just is represented by the government of the country of which the claimant is a citizen. It is a matter of duty: it would be regarded as shameful for a government to refuse to prosecute a just claim. So I think those organizations accomplish their own result and I think, too, that there ought to be no cause which a man's own government does not think just.

June 26, 1920

Mr. Root: I think that the object of our association is not simply to prevent war between ourselves, but to prevent war in the whole world, to prevent that contagious disease being established anywhere.

It would be a very backward country, closed to the true principles of international justice, which forbade access to its court to aliens. I am in favor of conferring upon the Court the competence to hear all international questions, and I think that such a solution would be in conformity with the terms of the covenant.

Lord Phillimore will remember an old English saying — "leg over leg the dog went to Dover" — which means progress step by step; and I think we are now faced by the question whether we can achieve another step. At the second Hague Conference, in 1907, the world reached the point of agreeing on the principle of obligatory arbitration. After the first Hague Conference hundreds of treaties were made by which states agreed with each other upon making arbitration obligatory within certain definite limits.

These treaties stated in substance the same criterion of jurisdiction for obligatory arbitration that is stated in Article 13 of the Covenant, with certain reserves — for honor, independence, and vital interests. I myself took part in between twenty and thirty treaties, — Mr. Scott says twenty-six, — for instance, the treaty between the United States and Japan which referred questions of treaties and rules of international law to arbitration. There were similar treaties, one with Holland, one with Belgium, with Norway, with Italy, and France, and Great Britain. The model for these treaties was a treaty between France and Great Britain. The contracting parties in this treaty freely accepted compulsory arbitration with certain reserves.

I think those reserves were dictated by considerations of prudence and caution rather than by any clear conception of their necessity. There could be no question arising under the terms of a treaty which could need such reserves, because no country makes a treaty which would compromise its independence, its vital interests, or its honor. Nor were such reserves needed for the application of the rules of international law, because, if there is anything in the world that is beyond question, it is that the basis of international law is the recognition of the independence of all sovereign states.

The formula which is in Article 13 was not conceived in the inner consciousness of the gentlemen in Paris. It was a statement that had resulted from long discussion and conference among the international jurists of many countries.

I am inclined to think that making general the effect of all these individual treaties for obligatory arbitration — making the effect general by conferring jurisdiction upon the Court without any further treaty — is not a very long step in advance, but it is a step in advance which we probably ought to take. I should not say so if it were not for the great number of treaties by which all countries have expressed their willingness to submit such questions — so as to oblige them to submit such questions — to arbitration. I think there is a special reason why we should try to agree upon such a step: it is because of the relations which must exist between the Court that we are about to recommend and the political organization of the Society of Nations. The provision of the Covenant is: —

Article 12

The Members of the League agree that, if there should arise between them any dispute likely to lead to a rupture, they will submit the matter either to arbitration or to inquiry by the Council, and they agree in no case to resort to war until three months after the award by the arbitrators or the report by the Council.

In any case under this Article the award of the arbitrators shall be made within a reasonable time, and the report of the Council shall be made within six months after the submission of the dispute.

Article 13

The Members of the League agree that, whenever any dispute shall arise between them which they recognize to be suitable for submission to arbitration and which cannot be satisfactorily settled by diplomacy, they will submit the whole subject-matter to arbitration.

Disputes as to the interpretation of a treaty, as to any question of international law, as to the existence of any fact which if established would constitute a breach of any international obligation, or as to the extent and nature of the reparation to be made for any such breach, are declared to be among those which are generally suitable for submission to arbitration.

For the consideration of any such dispute the court of arbitration to which the case is referred shall be the Court agreed on by the parties to the dispute or stipulated in any convention existing between them.

The Members of the League agree that they will carry out in full good faith any award that may be rendered, and that they will not resort to war against a Member of the League which complies therewith. In the event of any failure to carry out such an award, the Council shall propose what steps should be taken to give effect thereto.

Now, that imposes upon all members the obligation to submit either to arbitration or to the Council — that is obligatory. It leaves the party which considers its case weak in law the choice — the option — to refuse arbitration and go to the Council. How does the Council act? Not under the honorable obligation to decide justly questions of right. The members of the Council do not vote upon any question submitted to them. The states which they represent vote. The honorable obligation of a member of the Council is not to decide upon the rights of the party: his honorable obligation is to decide in accordance with the interests of his country. The principle is not that of right, but of expediency. It is adapted to the settlement of questions of policy; it is ill-adapted to the determination of questions of right.

Now, it would be an unfortunate thing if we were to establish the principle that, whenever a nation is charged with wrong-doing by another nation, the nation charged shall have the choice as to whether there shall be a decision upon the rights of the nation that is claiming them, or a decision as to the expediency of permitting it to go on with the injustice.

I believe, and I am confident of the agreement of all my colleagues here, that the hope of the world must rest upon the establishment of the rule of public right. I believe that can be accomplished only by the establishment of institutions adapted, first to the application, and next to the advance and extension, of the principles of right. Along that line there is a possibility of growth. Under the decisions of the Council there is no growth. A question is decided upon the expediency of the moment; the next question begins where the first began, and the next begins just where the first and second began. It is the expediency of the moment which must always direct the decisions of the Council. But when a system of law is applied by impartial courts, each new case begins where the other ended, and there is progress, and in time the system of international law will grow to universal assent and appreciation, and the world will become accustomed to obey the law. I think it is very desirable that we should make the attempt to secure the assent of the nations to a provision that this alternative obligation of the states to send the difference either to arbitration or to the Council, shall — within the narrow limits of contract and of positive law — be fixed so that upon a question of right of contract or of law the application shall be executed by going to the Court, while upon all other questions the alternative shall remain — to go to the Court, either the new or the old, or to the Council.

I think we should endeavor to take this further step of marking the distinction, — which is not considered or expressed in the provisions regarding the Council, — the further step of marking the distinction between questions of right and questions of policy, and, within these narrow limits, of calling upon the nations of the earth to agree that the questions of right based on contract or positive law shall go to a court which shall decide judicially; and I think we can accompany that provision by a strong recommendation to the Council and the Assembly, that with the least possible delay the process which began with the first, continued with the second, and was about to be further continued in the third Hague Conference, shall be recommenced; a recommendation that with the least practicable delay another general conference be called for the purpose of reconsidering the principles of international law, of considering and declaring what is left of them since the war, — of the rules formerly accepted which have been weakened, — so that the world may know what its law is, and for the purpose of extending agreement upon the rules of law.[1]

If that could be done, and the rule could be adopted that such a conference shall take place at stated intervals, then our Court, having jurisdiction over questions of positive law as distinguished from vague considerations of justice, will, year after year and generation after generation, be exercising continually enlarging jurisdiction, each new agreement upon the rules of law adding to the jurisdiction of the Court, and we shall have begun an institution which for centuries to come will become of constantly increasing value. You will find in the decisions of such a court, charged with the maintenance of law, a check upon the undue exercise of power — political power, unregulated by law, with no law that it is bound to respect, a power which makes it especially important that the law shall be developed and respected and made the object to which the thoughts of man shall turn for a guide for their conduct.

So, Mr. President, I like the provisions of Article 21 of the Five-Power Plan, that is, the plan of Norway, Sweden, Holland, Denmark, and Switzerland, declaring that the Court is competent to judge between members of the Society of Nations.

Article 21

The Court is competent to judge between Members of the League of Nations without their previous consent, on all matters relating to the following:

(a) The interpretation of a treaty.

(b) Any question of international law.

---

[1] A resolution to this effect was presented by Mr. Root and adopted by the Committee. As voted, it is contained in the text of this volume, p. 439.

(c) The existence of any fact, which if established would constitute a breach of any international obligation. (Compare Covenant Art. 13.)

(d) The extent and nature of the reparation to be made for breach of any international obligation.

(e) The interpretation of a judgment given by the Court.

Mr. Hagerup asked me a question. I consider that the 21st Article of the Five-Power Plan does take the definition of the 13th Article of the League Covenant. I think we should follow strictly that definition. I think it would be unwise to go further than that.

I think that the real question is not what our powers are, but what the power of the Council and the Assembly may be, if they have the power to make the jurisdiction obligatory within the limitations of the expression of the pact. I should think that would be a question of the authority vested by each state in its representative in the Assembly. There is a question: it might be that we should recommend that provision, and at the same time say that, if in the opinion of the Council and the Assembly they have not the authority under the Treaty to make such a provision without the further consent of the nations, they should submit it, asking for such consent.

I have a single observation. I consider it inevitable that there should be a revision of the pact; there is a general assent to that proposition, and I should hope that, if we agree upon such a recommendation as this, it will become a part of the revision.

JUNE 29, 1920

MR. ROOT: I am inclined to agree with everything that has been said. I think that perhaps we need not scrutinize too closely the terms used in the Covenant of the League of Nations. I think that Articles 12, 13, and 14 were designed rather to indicate a general purpose than to clothe that purpose in precise scientific terms.

The scheme in the mind of the framers of the pact is fragmentary, incomplete, rather suggestive than definite.

Now, if we were clothed with power to act, if what we should do were the making of a treaty, if we were to make a covenant, perhaps it would be necessary for us to scrutinize every word used there.

But we are not. We are to recommend to the Council a plan for a permanent Court of Justice. It seems to me that we should make recommendations which will be in harmony with what we believe to be the general purpose of the framers of the pact. I think that all our colleagues who have spoken here have been seeking that result, more or less specific. Now, if we find that the attainment of the general purpose is not within the terms of the pact, but that it will require a further convention, and that purpose agrees with our judgment of what the Court should be, then I think we should recommend that they do whatever is necessary to accomplish the purpose.

It may be that we might make a recommendation in the alternative, instead of undertaking ourselves to construe the words used; we might perhaps say that we recommend this, and if in the opinion of the Assembly and the Council, a further convention is necessary, we recommend that such convention should be brought about. Otherwise, we shall fail to supplement the vaguely expressed purpose by precisely the things which a commission of trained jurists are supposed to be competent to explain.

Now, as to the general purpose. I think that the gentlemen who framed these clauses of the pact had, in a general way, in their mind the existing state of arbitration. I do not think that they had scrutinized textually the provisions of 1899 and 1907, but I think that they had the existing (as we say, Lord Phillimore) state of the art in general in their minds.

Now, when we examine, the Conference of 1907 had done three things:

1. They had enlarged and perfected the provisions of 1899 for the Permanent Court of Arbitration at The Hague.

2. They had made a declaration, a *vœu*, in which they say: "La conférence est unanime à reconnaître le principe d'arbitrage obligatoire," etc.

3. They had adopted a project of a convention "relative to the establishment of a Court of Arbitral Justice." And "with a view to promoting the cause of arbitration" (Art. 1 of the project). And they had continued with a complete project for that court, which failed to become effective only because of the inability to agree upon the selection of the judges.

They had provided in that project for a court composed of judges appointed, or elected, for a period of twelve years, making it a permanent Court of Justice in the sense that we have agreed to make this a permanent Court of Justice.

I understand that in the original form, when it was first reported, this permanent Court was called "High Court of International Justice." But it was deemed appropriate to change that name and make it "Court of Arbitral Justice."

I think it is quite clear that the framers of Articles 12, 13, and 14 were dealing with a general situation which rested then in their minds, for instance, as it was left by the Conference of 1907, and supplemented by a great number, some hundreds, of treaties of obligatory arbitration.

When they provided for arbitration, and then charged the Council with preparing a project for a "Permanent Court of International Justice," they had the same view of the relations between the arbitration and the new Court which was the basis of the project and the declaration of 1907.

Now, if that incomplete sketch of the purpose does not in

itself contain terms sufficient to bind the nations united in the Society, I think we should, as a part of our recommendation, point out how these provisions should be supplemented, in order to accomplish their great purpose.

There is another feature of this which I will not dwell upon now, because it would divert our minds from the precise subject we are discussing: that is, the submission in a unilateral form, as distinct from a bilateral agreement to submit a dispute. I mean that, instead of requiring the parties to agree upon the question to be determined, the party seeking a decision against the other should state its case itself, in its own way: and the other party should state its case, its countercase, itself, and in its own way: and let the Court decide, instead of requiring the parties to agree beforehand upon the question which is to be decided. But that is a different thing from this; it is involved in the same, but it is different.

To return to the primary question we have been discussing.

I do not know what conclusion I should reach if I were to sit down to study carefully the view expressed by Lord Phillimore as to certain meanings of the terms of the pact. I might agree and I might not. But this is of little importance, since I agree with the conclusions. I do not know whether I would agree with Mr. Loder in his view; but, being naturally indolent, I wish to avoid having to determine in my own mind this question, so long as I agree with Mr. Loder in his conclusions. So I say, let us not attempt to construe the words, to fix the precise limits of the authority to be found in the words of the pact, but let us ignore that part and recommend what we think ought to be done, and recommend that they do what is necessary to accomplish that.

Let me add: I am sure that we should be doing what the gentlemen who invited us to render this service wish to have done. I am sure they wish us not to be technical and narrow in our work, but to give them the benefit of our honest and careful judgment.

I have seen on the Agenda of the Assembly one number on the reconciliation of the French and English texts of the pact: this they will have before them. Let us not stick to the terms of the text, but give them suggestions which will be valuable to them in their future work: so I think that the formula which Mr. Hagerup introduced is admirably suited to be a basis of settlement. I would only add to it a clause by way of parenthesis, of footnote, of marginal note, saying that if, in their opinion, further covenant or consent is necessary to accomplish this, we recommend that this be done.

On the subject of procedure. As you justly remark, it has been considered and discussed and thrashed out many times. I think that the conclusions which are contained under what we call the Five-Power Plan are very clear and satisfactory in the main — the same plan from which Article 21 has been read. When we come to that, would it not shorten the work if we took those provisions — treated it as if it were a Committee report on the 1899-1907 Convention, and make that the basis of our consideration?

JULY 1, 1920

MR. ROOT: Mr. President, expressions of opinion by the members are that our discussion has proceeded so far that we could begin to reach conclusions. Accordingly, and following the rule that the proposers of a measure in a deliberative body are charged with the duty of perfecting it, after discussion, Lord Phillimore and myself yesterday afternoon undertook to put in order the proposal for the organization of the Court, which in a fragmentary way we had presented already; and I have the result of our labors, which I will now lay before the Committee. With the permission of the Committee, I move its adoption, and I will ask a vote upon it, paragraph by paragraph as soon as it suits the convenience of the Committee.[1]

Mr. President. In order to bring this before the Committee in such a manner that action can be taken on it, I ask the members to vote upon what has been read and I ask its adoption.

Of course, I do not wish to ask for an immediate vote — I merely wish to proceed in such a form that we should be moving toward a specific action. I do not want the vote upon this at once, before the Members of the Committee are ready to vote. — I wish the Committee to act upon it — not at once — to-day, to-morrow — but in a few days — on Monday.

ANNEX

THE ROOT–PHILLIMORE PLAN

Article 1

The Permanent Court of International Justice provided for by Article 14 of the Covenant of the League of Nations shall consist of independent judges who shall be chosen regardless of their nationality and who shall possess the qualifications required, in their own countries, for elevation to high legal office whether administrative or judicial, or shall be jurisconsults of recognised authority in international law.

Article 2

There shall be eleven judges and four supplementary judges who shall hold office for a term of nine years and who shall be elected by the Assembly and the Council of the Society of Nations. Each of these bodies shall vote separately and the votes of a majority of the members present and voting in each body shall be necessary to an election.

---

[1] The so-called "Root-Phillimore" Plan consists of two parts. The first, printed as an annex to the present address, is composed of seventeen articles. It deals with the appointment of the Judges and the constitution of the Court. The second part consists of Articles 18–32. Of this second part only an article here and there is printed, where necessary to an understanding of Mr. Root's remarks.

Article 3

If, after the first vote in each electoral body, it shall appear that any vacancies in the Court remain unfilled, a second vote shall be taken in like manner to fill such vacancies; and separate votes shall be taken in like manner until all the existing vacancies are filled.

Article 4

For the purpose of reconciling any differences which may arise between the two electoral bodies in regard to the persons to be elected, they may, at any time when they deem it suitable, appoint a Committee composed of three from each body for the purpose of conferring and recommending the conciliation of such differences. If such differences should prove ultimately irreconcilable, the appointment to the vacancies unfilled shall devolve upon the judges who have already been agreed upon.

Article 5

The supplementary judges shall be separately elected in like manner.

Article 6

A list of persons qualified and fit to exercise the judicial office shall be laid before the Assembly and the Council respectively before the time of election. Such list shall be made up in the following manner: At least three months before the time of election, the Secretary-General of the League of Nations shall apply in writing to the members of the Permanent Court of Arbitration at The Hague from each country which shall have appointed such member, requesting the members from each country, acting as a body, to propose not more than four names of persons whom they deem to be qualified and available for judges.

Article 7

All of the persons so proposed shall form the list to be laid before and considered by the Assembly and Council and the judges shall be elected from that list. In the event, however, of the Assembly and Council not agreeing, the Committee of Conference shall be at liberty to recommend to the Assembly and Council a person outside the list.

Article 8

The members of the Permanent Court of Arbitration in each country are requested to consult with the highest judicial officers, the heads of universities and learned societies, to the end that the nominations made may be of persons who are the most competent and experienced and of the highest judicial character and reputation.

Article 9

Judges or supplementary judges shall complete the hearing of cases of which they have cognizance even though the period for which they have been elected shall have expired.

Article 10

In case any judge or supplementary judge shall become incapable or unfit for the performance of a judicial office, upon the unanimous representation of this fact by the Court to the Secretary-General the place of the judge shall become vacant and notice shall be given of an election to fill the vacancy at the next meeting of the Assembly and Council.

Article 11

In all elections of judges and supplementary judges the electors shall be under honorable obligation to take into account the existence of the necessary qualifications and to seek so far as practicable to have represented in the Court the different forms of civilization and juridical systems which exist among the Members of the Society of Nations; but there shall be but one member of the Court elected from any one State.

Article 12

The Court shall elect its own President and Vice-President. It shall also appoint its Registrar or may designate the Registrar of the Permanent Court of Arbitration to be its Registrar.

Article 13

The President and Vice-President shall be elected for a term of three years and shall be eligible for reëlection.

Article 14

A judge may not exercise his judicial functions in any case in which he has, in any way whatever, taken part in the decision of a national tribunal, of a tribunal of arbitration, or of a commission of inquiry, or has figured in the suit as counsel or advocate for one of the parties. A judge cannot act as agent or advocate in any international cause during his term of office.

Article 15

Vacancies in the office of judge and supplementary judge shall be filled as in the case of original appointments, and in every case the appointment shall be for the full term of nine years.

Article 16

The parties cannot challenge a judge of the Permanent Court of International Justice. If, for a specific reason, the President of the Court considers that one of the judges ought not to sit in a particular case, he shall so inform him and thereupon it becomes the duty of the judge to abstain from sitting. A judge who believes that he ought not to sit in a particular case can take the initiative with the President with reference thereto.

In case of disagreement on this point between the President and the judge it is competent for either to appeal to the Court in plenary session for a decision of the question.

Article 17

The number of judges may be increased by the Assembly from time to time to not exceed fifteen judges and six supplementary judges in the aggregate.

JULY 1, 1920

MR. ROOT: Mr. President. Mr. Ricci-Busatti has referred to what I said as to carrying out the meaning of the framers of the pact.

I said that with reference to making a competent court and conferring upon it the competence of obligatory arbitration, to make obligatory judicial decisions, making it compulsory upon nations who agree to go before the Court and submit their rights to the Court. Now we have agreed upon that, I take it, that the new Court shall have certain jurisdiction which shall be obligatory upon all the members of the League of Nations.

Now that is a thing that it has taken a very long time to bring the independent nations of the world to do. A long time. In 1899 they were unwilling to submit themselves to a general obligation. In 1907 they were unwilling. The obligation must be definitely limited or they will be unwilling now.

The question is to preserve this great step in advance, of making the submission to the Court obligatory, by being certain that we do not make the obligatory jurisdiction too vague, too broad, too indefinite. We may, by improving the description of the competence of the Court, destroy the Court, because the nations will be unwilling to agree. For example, if for the word "rule" we substitute the word "principle," we enormously enlarge the jurisdiction of the Court, in obligatory arbitration, because we all have our ideas about the principles of International Law. Some of those ideas have met with universal acceptance, and where they have, they have become law. Some of them have not. As to some of them, there are different opinions in different countries — those have not become law; and you will find many nations willing to submit to obligatory jurisdiction in respect of those principles which have become law, who would be unwilling to submit to an obligatory jurisdiction which would enable the judges to base the judgment on their opinion of the principles.

We should run into the same difficulties which the Prize Court Treaty encountered. That treaty provided that, if there was a treaty, that treaty should govern. If there were no treaty stipulations and no law, the Court should apply the general principles of justice and equity.

That treaty failed because there were countries which were unwilling to agree to submit their rights to the decision of the Court without knowing what were the principles of justice and equity that the Court would apply.

The Conference of London was called and held for the purpose of discussing and agreeing upon those principles. Yet, after that even, there being some rules that were not agreed upon, the treaty failed. Now we shall meet the same fate with our treaty, unless we observe the warning given to us by the past.

Nations differ as to what are the principles of equity and justice, that is to say, the principles of international law which are based upon equity and justice. Nations differ, and they will not submit themselves unless to a Court applying the principles which have ripened into rules of law.

They will submit to the obligation of those rules, the laws that all have agreed upon. Now this text, whether we improve it or not, has been agreed upon; that is its great advantage. These forms of expression have been agreed upon by all the countries collected in Paris which were able to agree upon them, and the immense force of that agreement toward bringing an assent to the plan we propose is an advantage that must not be disregarded. I grant that M. de Lapradelle could improve this form of expression very much, but all the prestige of M. de Lapradelle's name and reputation cannot carry sufficient weight to counterbalance that which already exists in the Covenant.

My mind returns to the proposition I made a few moments ago on another subject, that if we expect the provisions for obligatory arbitration to be accepted by all these states, we must make the limits of that obligatory jurisdiction very definite, very limited, very narrow, comparatively narrow.

The framers of the pact were not able to agree upon any jurisdictions, except those which related to the interpretation of treaties and to the questions of international law.

I think we should not attempt anything more than that. I think it would be very unwise. If we could get all the states to agree to subject themselves to the obligatory jurisdiction of the Court upon questions of treaties, or upon questions of law, we should have made a great step in advance.

Now, it seems to me, we must not go too far. For us to undertake to lay down the rules which are to govern the judges is, in the first place, going beyond our functions; that is to make law; that is not our function; ours is to organize the Court. The judges will know how to determine what law is — international law; they do not want *us* to tell them how. Why should we undertake to impose our opinion as to how they should perform their duty?

But if we undertake to do so, I find upon a brief examination of this paper no occasion to dispute Clause 1 or 2, submitted by the President.

The first rules to be applied by the judge for the solution of international differences are the conventional international laws.

The second to apply: "International custom, being practice between nations accepted by them as law."

I do not know — none of us can tell — whether others will agree to that; it satisfies mé, but we are going to submit a plan which more than fifty states must accept. None of us can tell whether, by undertaking to establish the rules that the Court is to apply, we shall not prevent the other states from joining.

When we come to the third rule, however, I find myself quite at a loss. The third rule to apply according to this draft is: "the rules of international law as recognized by the juridical conscience of civilized nations." What does it mean? Does it mean something which has been recognized by the juridical conscience of civilized peoples, and yet has not become a rule of international law?

Who can tell what the conscience, the juridical conscience, has recognized?

The same may be said of the fourth part: "international jurisprudence as a means for the application and development of law." What are the limits, the tests of the jurisprudence, the international jurisprudence, as an organ of application and development of the law?

These two numbers — 3 and 4 — would be additional to the conventional and customary international laws adopted by the states as rules, and would constitute an enlargement of the jurisdiction of the Court, destroying all limits to jurisdiction.

A nation having perhaps, or not having, a member of its own nation on the Court, may find that under the heading of international justice recognized by the juridical conscience of the peoples, or under the heading of international jurisprudence, the principles, the rules for which it has been contending during all its diplomatic history are overruled. That is not law; that is not the application of rules; that is conferring power upon the Court, upon their own will and judgment, to say what the rules should be and to become the rulers of nations.

If we lay down these rules for the control of the Court, we

are saying to all the nations of the world: "You surrender your rights to say what justice should be." Can we oblige a nation to contribute to constitute a court, and bind itself to submit its rights to that court, without its consent; a court that can apply not merely the law, but what it deems to be international jurisprudence, to be the conscience of civilized peoples, in addition to what the civilized peoples have accepted as law.

Let us keep within the law in this first great step by which we hope to overcome the doubts that have always held the people back. Let us first get the civilized world to agree to accept the judgments of the Court upon questions of law, and then let us go further. You cannot get them now to agree to anything beyond that.

With regard to the question which has been put: the very eloquent expressions of the President upon the basis of judicial decision meet with my entire approval.

The precise question here, however, I think, is not the general question of the basis of judicial action but the question how far the world is now ready to go in committing itself to obligatory arbitration; and it appears to me, in surveying the present condition of opinion and feeling in the world, that the nations are not now ready to go to the full length of committing themselves to obligatory arbitration throughout the field which the President has so justly described.

I think that the world is ready now to commit itself to obligatory arbitration before a court which has jurisdiction to interpret contracts, and to apply those rules of justice and equity which have been agreed upon by the whole world and therefore have entered into the body of international law.

I think the world is ready to commit itself to submit beforehand to the jurisdiction of the Court to the extent of those rules which have been generally accepted, universally accepted, and therefore have become the law of nations.

I do *not* think the world is ready now to commit itself to obligatory arbitration before a court which is to apply those principles of justice, which have not been agreed upon so as to become part of the law of nations; because there are different conceptions in different countries and different races, and under different conditions, as to what all those principles of justice require, widely different conceptions.

I have no doubt that in a multitude of cases nations will be willing to submit to the full jurisdiction described by the President — in the majority of cases, I have no doubts.

But that is a different thing from agreeing beforehand to submit all cases, — binding themselves beforehand to submit all cases, — even though they may involve those questions as to what the law should be upon which the nations of the earth are still in dispute; even though they may involve the questions upon which the nations from which the judges of the Court are drawn differ radically as to what justice requires.

When it comes to such questions, I think that the true course is to go to arbitration. When it comes so far as to involve questions and rules not beforehand agreed upon, then I think that there should be arbitration, not obligatory jurisdiction.

I base my view — the view that the world will not now make a general agreement beforehand, to submit to the jurisdiction of the Court which is at liberty to apply its ideas of justice and equity beyond the limits where those ideas have been agreed upon so as to become international law — I base my view upon two practical experiences.

Some years ago treaties were signed between the United States and Great Britain, and the United States and France, providing for the submission of all justiciable questions to arbitration. I was then a member of the Senate, and advocated the ratification of those treaties. I had for many weeks to meet the arguments against entering into such agreement based upon the fact that the term "justiciable questions" was not definite and was too vague, and permitted the Court to decide whatever the Court thought fit, without being limited by rules of law, and would make it possible to apply any conceptions of justice, however much they might differ from the conceptions entertained in the United States. That view prevailed so strongly that the treaties were amended by the Senate to such a degree that the President considered it useless to ratify them, and they failed.

You will perceive that in this case I was occupying the very position which our President has stated to-day: only he has stated it with greater cogency and ability than I was able to do.

But I was met with that difficulty of lack of definitions which would keep the Court within any limits, which would draw the line at the accepted, and generally accepted, law of nations; and I became convinced that it would be impossible to secure the adherence of my own country to a treaty of obligatory arbitration which should go beyond that line. I hope that we may reach that point. I believe that if we can establish this Court in its application of the law of nations, it will so justify itself in the eyes of the world as to remove doubts and allay alarm and banish suspicions; but I think it must grow; I think it will be impossible to begin it except within narrow limits, and let it justify itself. The only hope of securing assent to a treaty that I can see, is by drawing the line between those justiciable questions that are within the law of nations generally agreed upon, and those questions which are without that law.

The other experience was that to which I have already referred in regard to the Prize Court Convention, which Great Britain has refused to ratify, notwithstanding the benefits of the Conference of London, because she was unwilling beforehand to submit herself to obligatory jurisdiction of a court at liberty to apply, not merely the law of nations agreed upon, but the principles of justice and equity. She said: "We want to know the principles of justice and equity which will be applied"; and because these could not be known the Court was a failure.

Now there are these two cases, and I think that we ought not to ignore them. It is far more important that we make a beginning, that we have a court, however narrow its jurisdiction, than it is that we have one with more jurisdiction, which fails.

In the first place, of course, the jurisdiction of the Court in all cases of consent would include everything that Baron Descamps has said. It would include all justiciable questions. I think that would include not only questions which are submitted to the Court under general or special treaties of arbitration, but it would include the vast majority, great preponderance of cases which come before the Court under its involuntary jurisdiction: that is to say, if there be a case where one country is brought in by another under the general agreement which we are talking about, establishing the existence of the involuntary arbitral power, and there is involved in the case only a disputed question of justice, but no question upon which there are international differences as to what the rules are — in all such cases the parties would agree that the Court should have full scope to apply any rule of known law.

There still remains the exceptional case in which the judgment must turn upon some rule or principle, or asserted principle, of justice, some disputed principle, some question upon which your court and mine, your country and mine have been in dispute, some principle upon which, perhaps, for generations the foreign offices of the different countries have been unable to agree.

Now it is those exceptional cases that governments have to consider when they are proposing to bind themselves by universal agreement. When you come to the actual application, the actual working of the Court, the exercise of justice will be general and unquestioned, except in those exceptional cases. Can you imagine a case where a great, independent, sovereign, sensitive power is taken to the Court against its will, to have judgment pronounced upon it, and the Court says: "There is no law of nations upon which you can be condemned, but we consider you are acting against the principles of justice, and therefore judgment goes against you"?

I do not think that the nations of Europe are ready to bind themselves yet to the possibility of having the law decided, not by the process through which international law is made, but by the opinions of the Court making the law.

In such cases, if a country is brought in against its will to have the law applied to it, and the Court finds that the law does not cover the case, then there will be two things: the Court can go on to say that the case is not within their jurisdiction. The other is: to make not a judgment but a recommendation.

I think we must remember that, if we say that the Court may apply "the general principles of justice, the juridical conscience of the world," although they may not in this particular case be agreed upon, then we have stricken out the limitation which we have already agreed upon; and there are then no limits whatever to jurisdiction, absolutely none, for the words "principles of justice" are not words of definition: they shift according to the longitude and latitude of the nations and constitutions to which they apply.

I have been in favor, Mr. President, of applying the principles which I have expressed to all the jurisdiction of the Court, *except its compulsory jurisdiction.* If you undertake to apply those principles to compulsory jurisdiction, you have destroyed the limits of jurisdiction: it is no longer a limited jurisdiction, it is an unlimited jurisdiction; and I am certain that we shall never in our day receive the assent, the general assent, of the world to obligatory, compulsory jurisdiction without limits.

The framers of the pact found themselves unable to go beyond the limited provisions. We have agreed upon restating, for the jurisdiction of the Court, those identical provisions, but if we now say: the Court may apply the general principles of equity and justice, we wipe out these limits.

The Court has jurisdiction to pass judgment upon questions relative to the interpretation of treaties, to questions of international law, to the existence of facts which, if stated, constitute a breach of international obligations. All those are statements of definite limited jurisdiction. We have agreed by general consent to make those the limits of the compulsory jurisdiction of the Court, the limits of jurisdiction before which one nation may compel another to come. The moment that we say that the Court may apply the general principles of equity and justice, we destroy these limits, and we make an unlimited compulsory jurisdiction.

In every country, Mr. President, there are two parties in respect of this subject of the judicial settlement of international disputes. I think it is very desirable that we should place before the world a proposition which will help the friends of judicial settlement, the friends of arbitration, to win consent from their countries and not to make it a proposition so broad as to lead to their certain defeat.

July 6, 1920

Mr. Root: I think I have said all that I ought to say on this subject, except to answer Mr. Altamira's question, and as to that there is something I have to say. For the subject is one which I included in my instructions as Secretary of State to the Delegates of the United States at the Second Peace Conference.

I will, with Mr. Altamira's permission, however, defer explaining the view which I took then and will take now, until the time comes when some amendment may be proposed to the text, and I will not delay the vote upon the main principle at present.

When the question is raised, as we shall find it will be, by a proposal for specific amendments, then I shall be glad to explain my view.[1]

Lord Phillimore suggests that I should be better understood if I stated what position I took in 1907.

It should be your effort to bring about in the Second Conference a development of The Hague Tribunal into a permanent tribunal composed of judges who are judicial officers and nothing else, and who are paid adequate salaries, who have no other occupation and who will devote their entire time to the trial and decision of international causes by judicial methods and under a sense of judicial responsibility. These judges should be so selected from the different countries that the different systems of law and procedure and the principal languages shall be fairly represented. The Court should be made of such dignity, consideration, and rank that the best and ablest jurists will accept appointment to it, and that the whole world will have absolute confidence in its judgments.[2]

I am of the same opinion still.

One other thing I wish to say, and that is, that one of the chief advantages of the plan which has been called after Lord Phillimore and myself seems to me to be, that it solves the question of unfairness by giving to the small nations a veto upon anything unfair on the part of the large nations, and giving to the large nations a veto upon anything unfair on the part of the small nations.

And it does that by availing ourselves of the existing organization, and does not found the Court upon a postulate of national discord and intrigue.

[1] For Mr. Root's further statement on this phase of the question, see pp. 380–382.
[2] For the entire text of the instructions, see p. 292.

Anything which says that the large nations shall have this and that and the small nations shall have this or that, is introducing into the origin of the Court the very principle which we wish to exclude.

The judge will be compelled to say, "I have been selected by such and such a nation"; and another judge will say, "I was selected by such and such a nation."

Under this system no judge will have been selected by any nation — they will all be elected by the votes of the members of these two existing bodies, and there will be no objection to the Court doing what I believe it should do: establish itself in the confidence of mankind.

Two bodies voting separately. It is the way Parliaments — legislatures — are accustomed to vote.

Upon the day of election the Assembly will meet and will consider the list of candidates and vote. On the same day the Council will meet, and consider the list of candidates, and vote. They will compare lists. It is not necessary for us to arrange the details of procedure. . . .

The only thing I feel strongly about is this: that we should not undertake to make too particular directions.

Every working organization, every court, makes its rules in the court for the performance of its plain duty in accordance with its convenience and its judgment as to the best way of obtaining the result.

Every minute direction that we give is likely to be the cause of objection. Little things often cause stronger objections than great ones, and this is the plan that we recommended and you have adopted, and every unnecessary provision we put in is an added danger to the plan.

So, when we have provided that the Assembly and the Council shall vote separately and, in the words of Mr. Loder, "shall vote independently one of the other," it is unnecessary for us to go on and tell them just how they shall perform their duties. They have intelligence which we should insult by instructing them how they should do it. There is not a parliament in the world which would not know how to perform a duty of this kind: and they would resent being told how to perform that duty. . . .

JULY 7, 1920

MR. ROOT: I agree with what Mr. Hagerup has said, both as to the difficulties of getting a meeting at The Hague, and as to the desirability of accomplishing just what Mr. Loder proposes; in some ways it is a question of adjustment. I think with both of them that it is desirable that suggestions shall not be confined to one's own country, and if you will bear with me I will give you an additional reason which seems to me to cover both of these conclusions.

I think that Mr. Hagerup is right about coming to The Hague — the members of the Court would not come to The Hague for the purpose of preparing a list of candidates: the object is not adequate, the thing to be accomplished is not adequate, and it is a great undertaking to have a meeting at The Hague of all the nations. The Managers of the League of Nations are already beginning to be troubled with the expenses of the organization, the staff and entertainment, and the whole thing; it is a great undertaking and a difficult thing to do; and merely to come and consult about the proposal of names for election is not adequate to bring people together. They would not come from Japan, they would not come from America, and the result would be that the meeting would fail, or that it would be composed of other representatives, from other nations, — ad hoc, — and the Court would be discredited, because for the permanent Court of Arbitration at The Hague I think it would be the worst possible thing, to be asked to do a thing it could not perform.

But what is it that we wish to attain? Not a common judgment but the best informed judgment about men from all parts of the world, and we want to get that best informed judgment from the approximate locality in which the men live and have done their work. That is not strictly confined to nations; it is rather a matter of the general system and the grouping of nations.

It is going to be very difficult to get the best men for this Court, because you have got to find men who are fit for it and who can and will serve.

Now these two things are things about which information, the most valuable information, will come not necessarily from a particular nation but from a group of nations.

Take, for instance, the case of Messrs. Bustamante[1] and Zeballos,[2] who have been mentioned. There are men in that great area which, in the new world, follows the laws and customs of Spain, many men, competent and known to all the people of Central and South America. The members of the Permanent Court in that part of the world are accustomed to the same system of law, with intimate relations between their countries; they will know who the men are who are fit to serve and they will ascertain who the men are who will serve: you cannot collect that information by coming to The Hague. We have got to find out in the United States what men we should be proud to send to act upon the Court. Somebody has got to find out in Great Britain who is fit to go and who is willing to go; that information has got to come from the neighborhood, and I think there should be consultations between the United States and Canada, for instance, between South America and Spain, between the countries in Northern

[1] Antonio Sanchez de Bustamante (1865–0000), distinguished lawyer of Cuba. Elected one of the original members of the Permanent Court of International Justice.

[2] Estanislao Severo Zeballos (1854–1923), a distinguished publicist of the Argentine Republic, former Secretary of State, member of the Institute of International Law and President of the International Law Association.

and Western Europe, where the men of prominence all know each other so well — between the men in Western and Eastern Europe. I think these Conferences are going to be the source of the really valuable information, upon which the selection would be made. Accordingly, I think that it is very valuable that the members should not be confined to naming people from their own countries.

But there is a little practical difficulty about adopting the form suggested by Mr. Loder, — that one country cannot propose more than one of its own citizens, — and I think the safer form would be to require that half of them should be from other nations: that obviates the difficulty a little — I should put it, not more than four, and to require that half should be from other countries.

In answer to the question whether there will be enough candidates: —

I should think there would be no difficulty. The President suggested the difficulty the other day that there would be too many. I think it will right itself. I observe the limit of four is the same as that of the Permanent Court, and there are 130 members on the Permanent Court now. It is no burden to make selections from a list of this size. You have only to check those names which you find notable, and then to consider the names checked.

On the other hand, I think that every country should make proposals. It is their duty, and if it should appear that a sufficient list was not forthcoming, it would be the duty of the Secretary General to inform the members that they were not doing their duty, and that would bring proposals.

One advantage about putting it in that way would be that you might get so great a consensus of opinion from the members of the Permanent Court upon certain men that it would determine their election, and the Assembly and the Council would not feel justified in going against that opinion.

I have had for many years experience in this same kind of thing. Of course, we have a very large country in the United States; but there, all the judges of the Federal Court are appointed by the President. I have for many years, with different Presidents, successive Presidents, been in the habit of having the President say to me,"I have to appoint such a judge to such a position, who ought to come from your part of the country: who is there whom I can appoint?" Now the process followed always was this. I would go home to New York and I would go to the judges of the Federal Court and say: "Whom do you know; who is there who will take this place?" I would ask the leaders of the bar; and sometimes — often — one would be named. I would go to him. He would say, "No, I cannot serve." Another would say, "I cannot serve"; and so on, until finally I would find one who was fit and willing to serve. That process has to go on *there*, where the men are whom you are trying to get into the Court, and nowhere else; it is a practical experiment that has to go on.

I am certain that, when this Court has established itself, the process will be: not all peoples trying to get judges into it, but the Court, through the Secretary General, applying to the people in different parts of the world: "Cannot you get us a good man for this vacancy?" "Cannot you find a good man for us?" That is going to be the question put — "Find a good man for us who is willing to serve."

The discussion has proceeded on two different questions.

First, the question of the number to be formed by the members of the Permanent Court.

Upon that I am indifferent. I am sure there will be sufficient lists; I am sure that the object of securing good lists will be attained if it is put into the hands of the members of the Permanent Court.

But there is a form of provision in the Five-Power Plan which seems to me to be very good. It differs from that proposed by Lord Phillimore and myself and differs from Mr. Loder's suggestion, but it is a different road to the same result.

"Each member [of the League of Nations] may nominate a number of candidates equal to the number of vacancies," etc.

I now come to the other question, the proposition of M. de Lapradelle.

To abandon the proposal of names by the members of the Permanent Court, and to require that the Governments of the states propose the names: that is the essence of M. de Lapradelle's proposal.

Now, when Lord Phillimore and myself put into the proposal that bears our name the provision for the naming of the candidates by the members of the Permanent Court, we did so largely because of our respect and admiration for the President of the Committee.

We went as far as we thought it was possible to go, and have in part succeeded in incorporating the President's proposal. We could not put in a provision for election by the members of the Court, because we knew that it would not be accepted.

We could not put in the provision for a meeting here at The Hague, because we were certain that the members would not and could not come. What we put in the paper was the President's proposal in so far as we could go with him.

We have no — I certainly have no — pride of authorship in it. I do not look at it as a proposal I am under obligation to defend.

It is now proposed to abandon it altogether, absolutely. I think that the proposal involves a complete change in the theory of the constitution of the Court.

To that change I am not ready to agree.

It is true that the members of the Permanent Court are appointed by governments; it is true also that in the Assembly and the Council the election will be made by the representatives of governments; but I think we should propose a plan for a court which will impose upon all the governments of the world, not to consider their political relations but to consider the fitness of the men who ought to be appointed to the Court.

And I know but one way to do that: that is, not by imposing limitations upon the governments, for we cannot do that; governments will make their appointments upon their own motives and in accordance with their own powers. We can do it only by demanding the proposal of names, not of men whom governments wish, but of men who are known to be competent, impartial, judicial in their character, men of character, capable of rising above and ignoring the question of governmental politics and policy.

If we do not put in this plan some disposition which imposes this consideration upon the world, the plan will be a failure.

Governments will speak when the Assembly votes, and when the Council votes, governments will speak: but why should governments speak in making up the list of candidates?

Now, practically, it will be far better that the governments do not commit themselves as to the names to be in this list.

In the first place, you would get no expression of opinion from any government upon the men who are citizens of another country.

As I look back upon years spent as the foreign minister of my own country, I realize that I would not for a moment have thought of proposing the name of someone from Holland, without asking whether it would be agreeable to the

Government of Holland, or of someone from France, without ascertaining whether it would be agreeable to the Government of France. No foreign minister who knows his business, who is fit for his place, will undertake to render judgment upon the qualifications of a distinguished citizen of another country and to commit his government to it. It cannot be done.

As to the naming of its own citizens, the government is to be heard when the election comes. That election will name but a small number of those who are proposed. The representative of a government will have to exercise judgment; there will be adjustments of ideas — he must have freedom. How foolish for his government to have committed itself officially beforehand; how embarrassing to have committed itself beforehand. The discharge of the functions of the government in this way requires that the official proposal of names should be so made that the government is not committed until it comes to the election.

And for this reason it is of the greatest value that the proposal of names should come from these gentlemen, from the judges and scientific men of repute who are members of the Permanent Court, who speak not for their governments, who do not commit their governments — who speak from their own knowledge. So that every government can come to the election without having been committed beforehand.

I think that the provisional naming of these candidates by the governments will be wholly impracticable as a working scheme, and that it will be necessary to find someone who can make up the list so that the government will not have been committed by it but will have a free hand.

For this reason we should make up the list from persons proposed by the members of the Permanent Court.

I think that, if we were to charge the governments to name their list of candidates, and then the governments elect from them, we should have gone a long way back toward the character of the Council; we should have made this Court but little different from the Council, which deals with politics; we should have a body created upon political considerations, a body representative of governments of particular countries, instead of a body selected upon the ground of fitness to administer justice, which is superior to all divisions.

JULY 8, 1920

"In the event, however, of the Assembly and Council not agreeing, the Committee of Conference shall be at liberty to recommend to the Assembly and Council a person outside the list." [Extract from Article 7.]

MR. ROOT: That provision was designed to accomplish two things — one to obviate the difficulty . . . of seeming to try to rob governments of a part they should have. If it should happen that the government was dissatisfied with the names proposed by its own members, it then would have the opportunity of making its voice heard at the election. This is necessary for the reason that the plan must be accepted by governments. . . .

The other idea was this. Our object was to secure a working scheme which will produce judges; and while we want to guard against abuse, still we must not prevent it from being a working scheme.

Now, all human experience shows that from time to time, when there are two persons or bodies having equal authority and each has a similar position, each opposed to the other, it becomes impossible to unite them — to get them to agree on a proposal, without conciliation.

And, moreover, to give an opportunity for that kind of conciliation, the widest latitude in seeking this third person must be allowed. I think this is something in the nature of things.

It may well be that there are objections to the person

voted for by the Council, and that they can find some third man satisfactory to everybody — I would give full scope in order to accomplish that. In other words, there may be such a point-blank opposition that the only solution will be finding a dark horse.

I think the practical sense of the question requires that we give them the full opportunity to find that animal.

By requiring the lists to be made up from recommendations by members of the Permanent Court of Arbitration — jurists accredited by their own countries from all over the world — we shall have established a standard of competence, a standard of conduct, and it would be quite impossible that the dark horses should not be persons conforming to that standard.

When the situation comes of a deadlock between the Council and the Assembly, and next between the members of the Committee, it will not be on this full list — it will be on some particular situation — there may be only two or three names which answer to the requirement. . . .

Let me answer the remarks made to me by Mr. Loder and Mr. Altamira. When the situation comes it will be an exception. . . . [1]

There may be only two or three names which answer to the requirements. The representatives of men who cover that great ground occupied by the law and procedure of Spain should have places that must be filled; the places naturally assignable to the countries following the common law of England must be filled. The place which would, of course, be assigned to the customs and jurisprudence of Japan must be filled. It is particularly a question of selecting someone who has the knowledge and sympathy necessary for an understanding of the causes coming up from some part of the world:

[1] For Mr. Root's previous remarks on the question, see p. 370.

it may be from Scandinavia; it may be from Eastern Europe; and you will not then have a great list: there will be just a few names, and among those you may have no selection from one side or the other.

Now there ought to be the fullest opportunity to get out of that situation, and it may well be that the purpose of getting different men of such understanding and character and eminence that everyone will agree to them may be accomplished; but should they be unwilling to be named, you might have to get someone who would be willing to serve for the purpose of breaking that deadlock.

I find two different forms of expression — one used by me in the instructions to the delegates of the United States to The Hague Conference, and one used by Lord Phillimore and myself in Article 11 of this project. Both were designed to accomplish the same object: it is an object which can be accomplished, not by definition but by description, and the cause in my mind was the practical discovery of the extreme difficulty which I had, and which others around me had, in understanding the procedure and the forms of expression, the manner of thought of persons who have lived under a different system of jurisprudence, a different phase or form of expression of civilization.

For many years it was my duty to review and pass judgment upon proceedings which had gone on under Spanish law.

I found that it was extremely difficult for me to understand what they were doing, and I had to apply myself assiduously to the study of their proceedings, the names and words they used, the things they were doing in the Spanish courts.

I found that the countries following the lead of Spain had a most admirable system, most admirably adapted to the habits and the customs of life that they followed but wholly unadapted to my own country; and that the method of procedure, the forms of action in my own country would be wholly unadapted to the customs and habits of the Spanish-American people. All over the world the same thing exists. The jurisprudence of each country is the growth of its customs and habits, the ways of doing business of the people of the country; in every country the procedure is the growth of the life of the country. Now what we want here is a court which will understand the sympathies, the thought, the opinions, the prejudices, the forms of expression, the ways of acting of all the people of the world — of the civilized world.

It is not a means of securing a judge for one country or another, but it is a means of securing an understanding court, a court that will understand the case brought before it, sought in those instructions which I gave to the delegates to the Conference of 1907.

Now there may be many different forms of words employed to secure that, — perhaps one as well as another, — because it is not capable of definition. In different countries, the culture varies slightly or greatly, and it is difficult to draw the line; but in general I think it is wise to have something that will indicate that we want to have a court so distributed that among the judges on the bench there will be an understanding, a sympathetic understanding of all cases that may be brought before them.

July 9, 1920

Mr. Root: Is not really the most important experience, judicial experience? The judicial habit of mind, the judicial open-mindedness. If you are going to specify the kind of experience, it seems to me that that ought not to be omitted. The experience on the bench of Mr. Loder's Court, the experience on the bench of Lord Phillimore's Court, would be a most admirable qualification for the position on this new Court. It is not merely to have an international arbitrator, it is having the judicial habit of open-mindedness.

I have here the clause covering this subject, drafted by one whom we all recognize as a master — Mr. Louis Renault; and after much discussion adopted by the Second Hague Conference.

July 13, 1920

Mr. Root: I have long thought that it was desirable that an agreement should be made among all civilized nations for the treatment of acts of violation of those principles of humanity and justice and morality, which are universally recognized — the treatment of such acts very much as the slave-trade is treated.

Accordingly my feelings, my sentiments are in accord with the motive of the proposition made by our President and so eloquently seconded by M. de Lapradelle.

I should be glad if we might in some way express or indicate that we are not deaf and blind to the subject; in some way show that we feel that there is a grave question to be determined; that we do not ignore it, even if we may not express a definite view about it. I find in my own mind, in attempting to work the subject out, some very serious difficulties which probably exist also in the minds of our colleagues.

In the first place, as has already been well said, there must be a law to be applied by any court that is created. At present the Law of Nations operates only upon nations. If an individual does an act which violates some rule of the Law of Nations, he is subject to punishment only so far as that law is a part of the municipal law of his own country, or of the country within whose jurisdiction, the country in which he does the act. It is because an act violating the Law of Nations is against the peace and dignity of that particular country that he is punished in it.

Now, so long as that is true, no one else can punish the act without an infringement upon the sovereignty of the country within whose jurisdiction the act is done, and it becomes a question of the maintenance of individual sovereignty and the modification of individual sovereignty. How far, to what extent, in what cases, will an individual sovereign state admit the right of other sovereignties to punish its citizens for acts done within its jurisdiction? that is the fundamental question which must be determined — a very grave and serious and also a difficult question, which cannot be decided unless upon long consideration.

It is liable to involve a divided allegiance. For example: I am an officer in the Army of the United States; I am ordered by my superior to do a certain act, and I do it. Someone is of the opinion that that act was a violation of the Law of Nations, and the political authority of my own country, to which I owed allegiance, is overruled by other sovereigns. It is plain that upon a matter of that description there must be accurate definition, careful limitation, in order to obviate such a result as that.

It would be impossible for the nations, for certain states, to admit that their own citizens might be punished upon the initiative of the Assembly or the Council of the Society of Nations for what the Assembly thought, or the Council or any court might judge, to be crimes against international public order, because that general authority would mean indeed creating a super-government; it would be creating a central authority which would have control over all theretofore independent sovereign states, and would be able to seize upon the individual and punish him irrespective of the views of his own country; the exercise of such a power must be most carefully limited.

I am inclined to think that there is a special field of justice which is quite different from what we are now discussing, and that is the application of laws of war — to acts in war — men caught red-handed in pillage and murder should be punished summarily: it is necessary as a part of the law, and it is quite different from the thing we are discussing now — the exercise of a peaceful jurisdiction in time of peace for crimes committed. I am inclined to think that it will be necessary that there be a definition of certain acts which shall be either avowed or disavowed by the states. If avowed by the state, then the state must be responsible; if disavowed, then the person caught doing the act must be treated as in the case of the slave-trade, which is disavowed under whatever flag it is carried on.

I think you have got to create special classes of violators of declared law who have been disavowed by their own countries and ought to be made subject to punishment. If there is a law of such a nature and a corresponding jurisdiction is established, it would gradually expand; that is the natural course; that is about the only way in which the varied opinions and prejudices of the multitude of people in this world can be brought together — step by step — to begin with a simple institution which has the seeds of growth and then let it justify itself.

II. In such a case it would be necessary to provide for the obligation of all the states to surrender the person charged, because one could not give to a court of any one state the authority to go into the territory of another state, sovereign state, and take the person from them; that would be an act of war.

I should rather have the moving party to be any sovereign state — that is to say, such jurisdiction as it is found possible to create should be put in movement by a state, coming into court and declaring that such and such an act had been done by such and such a person whose action had been disavowed by his own country.

Now, what would be the nature of the proceeding — what would be the authority? A super-government — that must not be, for that could not continue to exist: there is no Roman empire; — what would it be?

I suppose that the authority which calls upon a state to surrender the accused, which judges him and absolves or convicts the accused of the crime of murder, must be the sovereignty of some other country.

And the question to be determined initially is then: Are the several states of the world willing to modify their sovereign authority; and if they are, how far, to what extent and in what manner are they willing to modify?

When that has been ascertained, you can make a court and the course for us to follow is to make an expression of opinion, or rather that we should suggest, recommend, that this subject be committed to the Conference proposed in the paper which the President has already read, be committed to a Conference for consideration and recommendation, because of all the countries everyone would have to be consulted and we cannot settle it.

JULY 24, 1920

MR. ROOT: May I make a suggestion? I think clearly that, under the terms of the invitation to us, we are under obligation to place in the hands of the Secretariat of the League of Nations the result of our deliberations.

In the second place, I think we should request the Secretary to advise the Council that any further information or explanation, which the Council may desire, will be furnished by the Reporter, if he is willing to undertake it. No, we should say the President or the Reporter of the Committee. It would naturally be the reporter, however, as he would have all the information, explanation, etc.

Thirdly, I think that it should be distinctly understood and go into the *procès-verbal* of to-day, that the Committee will not advocate or argue our conclusions to any extent whatever. We have been asked to advise, and we have advised, and we rest. It would be undignified to urge the adoption of our advice.

ADDRESS BEFORE THE ASSOCIATION OF THE BAR OF THE CITY OF NEW YORK, OCTOBER 21, 1920

It is a pleasure to take part in this series of discussions because I think it is a very valuable and praiseworthy project on the part of the Association, and I am glad to be able to contribute what I can by talking for a few minutes about the subject scheduled for this evening. It is a very proper subject to discuss here, because this Association has had something to do with it. When the constitution for the League of Nations was proposed and published by the conferees at Paris, with a request for suggestions, the Special Committee of this Association upon International Law held a meeting for the purpose of considering what they ought to do in that field.

The result of that meeting was that there was a unanimous resolution passed, without reference to party, race, creed, or previous condition of servitude, by the Committee, recommending and urging that there be included in the agreement or League of Nations, the following:

The High Contracting Powers agree to refer to the existing Permanent Court of Arbitration at The Hague, or to the Court of Arbitral Justice proposed at the Second Hague Conference, then established, or to some other arbitral tribunals, all disputes between them, including those affecting honor and vital interests, which are of a justiciable character, and which the powers concerned have failed to settle by diplomatic methods. The powers so referring to arbitration agree to accept and give effect to the award of the Tribunal.

Disputes of a justiciable character are defined as disputes as to the interpretation of a treaty, as to any question of international law, as to the existence of any fact which, if established, would constitute a breach of any international obligation, or as to the nature and extent of the reparation to be made for any such breach. Any question which may arise as to whether a dispute is of a justiciable character, is to be referred for decision to the Court of Arbitral Justice when constituted, or, until it is constituted, to the existing Permanent Court of Arbitration at The Hague.

That resolution was communicated to the Secretary of State of the United States, and was cabled by him to Paris. After the communication to the gentlemen at Paris, an amendment was made to the League agreement. I will say nothing because I know nothing on the question whether this was *propter hoc* or simply *post hoc*. The substance of the amendment was to include in the Covenant for the League the definition as to justiciable questions given in the resolution of the Committee of this Association upon International Law. That resolution, as I understand, was subsequently approved by the Association in plenary session. The article of the League Covenant originally read as follows:

The members of the League agree that whenever any dispute shall arise between them which they recognize to be suitable for submission to arbitration and which cannot be satisfactorily settled by diplomacy, they will submit the whole subject matter to arbitration.

That is the way it stood before, and being simply an agreement to arbitrate questions recognized as being suitable for arbitration, did not amount to very much. But the amendment inserts the following words:

Disputes as to the interpretation of a treaty, or as to any question of international law, as to the existence of any fact which, if established, would constitute a breach of any international obligation, or as to the extent and nature of the reparation to be made for any such breach, are declared to be among those which are generally suitable for submission to arbitration.

Then it goes on:

For the consideration of any such dispute the Court of Arbitration to which the case is referred shall be the Court agreed upon by the parties to the dispute or stipulated in any convention existing between them.

The members of the League agree that they will carry out in full good faith any award that may be rendered, and that they will not resort to war against a member of the League which complies therewith. In the event of any failure to carry out such award, the Council shall propose what steps should be taken to give effect thereto.

You will see that that carries into the article in a general way the definition of justiciable questions included in your resolution. That is a long step forward, because what are known as the Taft Treaties of Arbitration, treaties negotiated while Mr. Taft was President, between the United States and France and between the United States and Great Britain, failed because they provided for referring to arbitration all justiciable questions and the term "justiciable" was deemed so general and vague, so without any precedent upon which to draw the line as to what was justiciable and what was not, that it was considered that an agreement to refer to arbitration all justiciable questions would involve or might involve all sorts of questions, whether of policy or of right. This definition obviates the chief objection which led to the failure of the Taft Arbitration Treaties.

In the League Covenant it is also stated in Article XIV that —

The Council shall formulate and submit to the members of the League for adoption plans for the establishment of a Permanent Court of International Justice. The Court shall be competent to hear and determine any dispute of an international character which the parties thereto submit to it. The Court may also give an advisory opinion upon any dispute or question referred to it by the Council or by the Assembly.

Sometime in the early spring I received an invitation from the Council of the League of Nations, identical with an invitation which was sent to some dozen gentlemen residing in different countries, inviting us to become members of a committee, or, as they call it on the other side, a commission, to devise and recommend a plan for the Permanent Court of International Justice, which the League Covenant required the Council to formulate and to submit to the members of the League for adoption. The invitation was to prepare and recommend to the Council of the League a plan by which they might comply with this provision of Article XIV, which required them to formulate and submit a plan for a Permanent Court of International Justice.

For many years, people concerned with international affairs have realized that one difficulty about arbitration is that arbitrators too often are apt to treat the cases brought before them as a matter for settlement, for adjustment. They have come to consider, apparently, that their function is to do with the case what seems to them to be the wisest and most expedient thing for all parties and all interests concerned. They tend to act under a sense of diplomatic obligation rather than under a sense of judicial obligation. The great difficulty about arbitration has really been, not that nations were unwilling to submit questions of law, questions of right, the kind of questions that our courts pass upon as between individuals in municipal law, to impartial judgment, but that they had not much confidence in getting impartial judgment, because they found that the arbitrators, when they got together, went into negotiation as diplomats, and no one could tell what would come out of it. The party having a strong case, no matter how strong, being no matter how absolutely right upon the question of legal right, might find itself defeated because it seemed to the arbitrators on the whole that it perhaps would be better that it should not have its legal rights, but that the case should be settled as conveniently as possible.

Now, this proposed Permanent Court of International Justice was designed to differ from the ordinary arbitral tribunal in that respect. It was designed to be a court in which judges would sit and decide according to law, and let the consequences take care of themselves. And that was the problem presented to this Committee which met at The Hague in the second week of June last.

The Committee was composed of members from ten different countries. Lord Phillimore from England, M. de Lapradelle from France, Baron Descamps from Belgium, Judge Loder from Holland, Mr. Hagerup from Norway, Mr. Altamira from Spain, Mr. Adatci from Japan, Mr. Ricci Busatti from Italy, Mr. Raoul Fernandez from Brazil, and myself. Nobody represented any government. We were called there as experts purely, and on just as purely expert work as if a lot of engineers had been called together to propose a plan for a bridge.

At the outset, one might suppose that it was quite a simple thing to get up a plan for a court; but there were some very serious difficulties involved.

A plan had been prepared at the urgent instance of the American delegates to the Second Hague Conference in 1907 — a plan for a permanent court of international justice. The name that was given to it then was the Court of Arbitral Justice, and that was the name that found its way into our Bar Association resolution — referring to the "Court of Arbitral Justice" proposed at the Second Hague Conference. A general scheme of a court was devised in 1907 and reported to the Second Hague Conference — and was adopted. But, it did not take the form of an operative convention or treaty, because it was found impossible to agree upon the constitution of the court. That is, it was found impossible to agree upon the way in which the judges should be selected. There was a certain jealousy or suspicion or prejudice or perhaps just apprehension, on the part of the small countries toward the big countries, which made the small countries unwilling to allow the big countries to have a voice in the naming of the judges, proportionate to their size, proportionate to the influence they thought they ought to have. On the other hand, the big countries were not willing to allow the great numerical preponderance of small countries to override them and to make up the court by overwhelming them with their votes. Great Britain and France and Germany and Russia would not consent that Luxembourg and Switzerland and Haiti and San Domingo should outvote them. There was no question about that in their minds. So that the great countries would not consent to a vote in which each country was to have a voice — an equal voice — in the selection of the judges, and the small countries would not consent to a vote in which the big countries had any greater voice than each of them had. There the thing stopped, and the Court failed in 1907 upon that.

It was a serious difficulty, and many efforts had been made in the meantime between 1907 and the coming on of the war to try to get over that — but without success.

Now, in making up the plan of the Court, this Committee, sitting at The Hague, adopted a plan for dealing with this subject, which was taken very largely from the experience of the government of the United States. It was pointed out that in 1787, when the Constitution of the United States was framed, just such a question presented itself to the Convention. There were the big states, and they were not willing to be overborne by the numerical superiority of the small states; and there were the small states, not willing to yield their equal rights and give the big states any greater voice in the government of the country than they had. And that was settled by making the two legislative bodies and giving all the states — great and small — an equal voice in the Senate, and giving the population its voice according to numbers in the House of Representatives, so that Nevada has just as much voice in the Senate as New York, while New York has forty-three times the voice in the House that Nevada has. Now, there was a practical adjustment of just the same kind of a difficulty, and after months of discussion, the Committee came to a realization of the fact that, after all, this was a mere adjustment of means to an end. It was not a question of sovereignty. Many of them came to the meeting firmly resolved never, never to surrender the sovereignty of their small countries — not to yield one jot or tittle. But, they finally came to the conclusion that after all this was a court in which the sovereignty of everybody was liable to be limited by judicial decision; and that no one had a right to have that done, but it must be done solely by consent. So it was not a question of the exercise of sovereignty; but, it was a question of consent — to be given by sovereignty; and the right of sovereignty was satisfied if everybody had the same right to consent or refuse to consent.

Following that line, it was perceived that under the organization of the League of Nations — there were two bodies organized on exactly the same principle as the Senate and the House of Representatives of the United States — the Council, in which the big states were predominant, and the Assembly, in which the small states were predominant; and accordingly the question of electing the judges was settled by providing that they should be elected just exactly as laws are passed by our Congress, requiring in the election of a judge the concurrent, separate votes of both of those bodies, just as the passing of a law in the government of the United States requires separate and concurrent votes of both the bodies of the national legislature. Then the difficulty that they might not agree was met by importing bodily into the system our American Committee of Conference, in which so many thousands of laws have been thrashed out and settled upon when it seemed impossible that the Senate and the House could agree; and provision was made that if, after a certain number of votes, there was no agreement, a committee of conference was to be appointed, and that they were to have full scope to find somebody whom they could recommend to both houses for election. And on that basis, that old

bugaboo of 1907 was dissipated, and that is the way in which
the Court is now proposed to be organized. You will perceive
that that is essentially fair because it enables each party in
the community of nations to exercise a veto against unfairness by the other. The Assembly can always prevent the
Council from being unfair. That is, the small nations in the
Assembly can always prevent the big nations from being unfair. And the big nations, small in number, in the Council
can always prevent the small nations, in great number in the
Assembly, from being unfair. They can each force fair treatment of the subject and effect a satisfactory solution.

Then, there was another question which was very serious,
and that was the question of jurisdiction. The plan of 1907
provided for no obligatory jurisdiction. It merely provided
that this Court was to have jurisdiction over all questions —
international questions — submitted to it. But, here was a
provision in the Covenant of the League, that all questions,
disagreements, disputes, which were not submitted to arbitration, were to be sent to the Council or brought before the
Council. Now, the Council was not a body of judges. It was
a body of diplomats. The obligation of a member of the
Council is not to do justice as a judge, but to protect the interests of his country for which he casts his vote; and the
natural effect of giving the option either to arbitrate or to
go to the Council would be that the nations which felt their
case to be weak in the matter of law or justice would always
refuse to arbitrate and instead go to the Council, where it
could be negotiated. Accordingly we came to the conclusion
that we ought to have obligatory arbitration upon questions
of strict legal right, and we put that into the plan, in the
exact words of the resolution of this Association and of the
amended Article XIII of the Covenant which embodied those
words. We provided that the Court should have jurisdiction
of all questions that were submitted by both parties — inter-

national questions — and should have jurisdiction over all questions of international law, interpretation of treaties, or the direct effects of the obligation over which the dispute arose.

There was one other subject which was quite important, and that was the question whether countries in litigation were to be represented in the Court. That was a difficult subject, because the first answer, if you were to ask any national or municipal lawyer, would be — no. Yet, upon very full consideration, we all came to the contrary conclusion, and I have no doubt that it was quite proper. Of course, there are representatives of many countries in the Court. Every member of the Court comes from a different country, and we had a provision that no more than one shall come from one country; but few small countries can be included in the Court, and so we provided that a country not included should have a right to have a judge from among its own people put into the Court for the purposes of that case. And the reasons for it are these: The greatest obstacle to doing justice as between nations is a failure of nations to understand each other. I don't believe anybody can appreciate that without actual experience. Many years ago I was called upon to argue in the Supreme Court of the United States a case relating to the effect of a French judgment in this country. I see Mr. Coudert in front of me smiling because he remembers the case. There had been a suit brought by the administrator of the old firm of Alexandre, the maker of kid gloves, against A. T. Stewart & Company over some contract for gloves. The suit was brought in Paris, and judgment was obtained there, for I don't remember how many millions of francs, and suit on that judgment was brought here in the Circuit Court of the United States. Judge Wallace held the judgment to be conclusive, and he at that time said that it would be merely impudent for us to assert that the French system of doing justice was not just as good a system for doing justice as our own. I studied the subject very carefully, and I came to the conclusion that Judge Wallace was right — with a qualification, and the qualification was this: The French system was adapted to doing justice between people who had French ideas and did their business in the French manner, and an American would have very little chance under it. On the other hand, the American system is adapted to doing justice as between people who have American ideas, and who do their business in an American way, and a Frenchman would have very little chance under it.

Well, you find that difficulty everywhere in international affairs, and in no other class of people in the world can you find it more inveterate than among lawyers. We passed hours and hours and days in that committee in discussing subjects where the only difference was not in our discussion or in what we were saying, but in a different set of ideas in the backs of our heads; and it requires experience to understand that there is such a difference of ideas. Lord Phillimore and myself, the two representatives of the common-law-system countries, found ourselves up against a granite wall very often; and I suppose that the continental lawyers found themselves in the same attitude as to Lord Phillimore and myself. It required long and patient effort to find out what we were talking about. Now, we agreed that in order that justice should be done in the international Court, there ought to be some one man at least in the Court who understood the habits, the customs, and the reactions of the nation that is a party to any proceeding, and the result was that we provided for such a court — for the present — of eleven judges and four alternates or supplemental judges, to be elected by the separate and concurrent votes of these two bodies. They are to be judges sworn as judges under the honorable obligation of the judicial office, doing no other business, and they are to sit there and decide international cases according to law.

There were also a great number of ancillary provisions about the Court. The judges are to be paid regular salaries. They are to reside during the sessions of the Court at the seat of the Court. The seat of the Court is to be The Hague. There are provisions for special tribunals upon the request of the parties during vacation. There is a provision for a Chief Judge. Upon application of the parties, the Chief Judge is to designate three judges to take up a case which may be urgent during vacation time. The Court will always be ready to do business. At the same time we provided for the continuance of the old Permanent Court of Arbitration at The Hague for the purpose of dealing with questions which involve subjects not altogether justiciable but appropriate for arbitration, so that that old tribunal, which has some of the characteristics of John the Baptist, is not to be destroyed.

I should have mentioned the fact that the election of these judges is to be from a list which is made up by the members of the old Permanent Court of Arbitration at The Hague. The members of that old court from each country are to send to the Secretary General at The Hague two names for each vacancy when this new Court is to be put into operation. My friend, Mr. Straus, whom I see smiling before me, and Judge Gray and Mr. John Bassett Moore and myself will have to get together and propose the names of two men whom we think fit to be judges and who, we have ascertained in some way satisfactory to ourselves, will probably be willing to serve as judges, and send them on to the Secretary. All the countries are to do that. And from the list thus made out, these two bodies, the Council and the Assembly, are to make their selections so that you will get the sort of personnel for the Court as far removed as practicable from the ordinary influences of politics for what there is in it.

Of course, the action of the Committee, which was unanimous, does not decide anything. The Committee simply reports to the Council of the League of Nations, by which it was constituted, and the Council now has this plan before it. I do not know what they are going to do with it. In some form or other it will be laid before the Assembly of the League of Nations, which is to meet next month in Geneva. I do not know what they will do with it. It may be that there will be so much opposition to the obligatory feature of arbitration, that they will strike it out. I do not know. I hope not. But, whatever they do with it, that step is taken. Another step forward has been taken, and it is there by the unanimous agreement of fairly competent representatives of ten different nations situated in different parts of the world, widely differing in their interests and characteristics and size and wealth — by the unanimous agreement of a fairly representative body of men familiar with the subject — a plan for the formation of a court to deal with international questions upon grounds of public right, just as the Supreme Court of the United States, and the Court of King's Bench of Great Britain, and the Court of Cassation of France, deal with questions of municipal right.

I say that a unanimous agreement has been formulated for a plan of such a court. Now, this is a step in advance in the processes of civilization. All the processes of civilization are slow. All advances shock somebody, and an attempt to go too fast, too far at once, almost always ends in failure. "Leg over leg the dog went to Dover." I have often thought in observing the progress of improvement of the law in Washington that every good bill had to have a period of gestation. I remember a bill which did great signal service had been knocking at the door of Congress from year to year for thirteen years. It started with nobody for it, and finally someone opened the door and said, "Why don't you come in?"

And that is more so in international affairs. Every step forward has to come in contact with the ingrained habits, preconceptions, involuntary reactions of vast multitudes of people, and they have got to be treated just as a nervous horse is treated. If you go at him too fast, you get into trouble. Now, it is very much so about this judicial business. You have got to go step by step. It is five, nearly six years now since the Constitutional Convention of this state adopted a provision for the reorganization and condensation of state government and what is known as the budget system. A great majority of the Convention had agreed upon it, but it was overwhelmingly defeated at the polls. Yet more than twenty states have adopted it since, and the Governor's Commission, appointed by the Governor who at that convention opposed it, has now recommended the same thing. Substantially all the important advances upon the Constitution of 1846 that were made by the Convention of 1867 in this state were adopted afterward, although their plan was rejected at the time.

Now, this idea of arbitration, this idea of affording a substitute for war by the processes of justice, was laughed at in 1899. It was adopted by the 1899 Conference only because they had to do something to save the Tsar's face. The Tsar had called the Conference of 1899 for the purpose of agreeing upon disarmament, and Germany and some other countries were unwilling to have the subject discussed; but the Conference was called and they had to do something, and so they considered that they would give the children something to play with, and they got up this arbitration proposal. All the wise people said, "Oh, don't bother about it." Very likely, if our government had not sent the Pious Fund case there for arbitration between the United States and Mexico, and if it had not been for the backing of the Government of the United States proceeding upon the universal sentiment of the people of the United States in favor of giving this substitute for war a chance by the attainment of justice through judicial procedure, the Court would not have amounted to anything. But it did; and it was enlarged and improved upon, and it was the adoption of that plan in 1899 which made possible the improvement of the plan by the Conference of 1907. The former Conference provided the basis for the 1907 plan for a Permanent Court of Arbitration, and this in turn was what made it possible for this Committee to agree upon the concrete plan for a court; and whether this plan be adopted as the Committee agreed upon it, or not, it is a step in the direction upon which hereafter the great progress of civilization toward justice in place of war will go on.

That is all, I think, I have to say on this Court. It is a pleasure to talk to lawyers about it. Perhaps I should speak on one more little thing about the Court, and that is — procedure. There is not much procedure provided for. I did not think it was advisable to propose to the Committee the adoption of the New York Code. There is really very little procedure, but a few little things which we thought were necessary were put into the plan of the Court. Where you have a great many countries, all with different procedures, it is necessary to be quite general in your rules, and one result of this is, I am sure, that you will get along much better in dispensing justice.

I want to add that I had very great pleasure later in the summer, in September, of going back to The Hague after finishing the work of the Committee, and presiding in an arbitral tribunal and rendering the first judgment of the Permanent Court of Arbitration at The Hague in the Peace Palace — practically inaugurating that building; and I wish I could tell Mr. Carnegie about it. It was a controversy in which England and France and Spain and Portugal were concerned over the liability of Portugal in the seizure of properties in possession of the religious orders in Portugal at the time of the Revolution in 1910. The arbitration was agreed upon in 1913 before the war, and M. Lardy, the old Swiss Minister at Paris, and M. Lohman, the Dutch jurist, and myself were made the arbitrators. The war suspended the proceedings, but they were revived after the war, and in September, the case was brought to an end by the judgment; so there is actual demonstration that the old Permanent Court of Arbitration at The Hague still lives.

ANNUAL ADDRESS AS PRESIDENT OF THE AMERICAN SOCIETY OF INTERNATIONAL LAW
WASHINGTON, APRIL 26, 1923

On February 24, 1923, President Harding transmitted with his approval a recommendation dated February 17, 1923, of Secretary of State Hughes, that the United States should, with certain reservations, join the Permanent Court of International Justice established at The Hague. These reservations were:

I. That such adhesion shall not be taken to involve any legal relation on the part of the United States to the League of Nations or the assumption of any obligations by the United States under the Covenant of the League of Nations constituting Part I of the Treaty of Versailles.

II. That the United States shall be permitted to participate through representatives designated for the purpose and upon an equality with the other states members respectively of the Council and Assembly of the League of Nations in any and all proceedings of either the Council or the Assembly for the election of judges or deputy judges of the Permanent Court of International Justice or for the filling of vacancies.

III. That the United States will pay a fair share of the expenses of the Court, as determined and appropriated from time to time by the Congress of the United States.

IV. That the statute for the Permanent Court of International Justice adjoined to the protocol shall not be amended without the consent of the United States.

In support of Secretary Hughes's recommendation, Mr. Root delivered the following address.

The Permanent Court of International Justice, which is now in operation at The Hague, was established by a protocol signed on the 16th of December, 1920, and ratified by substantially all the civilized nations, great and small, with the exception of the United States, Germany, Russia and Mexico. The court is composed of eleven judges, and four deputy judges, to act in case of illness or absence. They are all required to be "independent judges, elected regardless of their nationality, from among persons of high moral character, who possess the qualifications required in their respective countries for appointment to the highest judicial offices, or, who are jurisconsults of recognized competence in international law," and it is required that they shall represent the main forms of civilization and the principal legal systems of the world. They are elected for terms of nine years and are eligible to re-election. They receive fixed salaries and are prohibited from exercising any political or administrative function while in office. The court elects its own president and appoints its own clerk, and makes its own rules. A session of the court is required to be held every year and, unless otherwise provided by the rules of the court, the session begins on the 15th of June and continues until the calendar of cases is cleared. A quorum of nine judges is required for hearing and decision, except in certain special cases in which summary procedure is provided for. Before entering upon the discharge of his duties, each judge is required to make a solemn declaration in open court that he will exercise his powers impartially and conscientiously.

The court is open to all states and only to states. The general jurisdiction of the court is of three classes: First, all cases which the parties submit to it; second, all cases provided for in treaties and conventions; third, as to all states which shall have signed a special clause contained in the protocol accepting compulsory jurisdiction, all cases whatever between such states concerning (a) interpretation of a treaty; (b) any question of international law; (c) the existence of any fact which, if established, would constitute a breach of an international obligation; (d) the nature or extent of reparation to be made for the breach of an international obligation; (e) the interpretation of a judgment rendered by the court. The court has certain special jurisdiction over disputes in labor cases.

The court is required to apply (1) international conventions, whether general or particular, establishing rules expressly recognized by the contesting states; (2) international custom as evidence of a general practice accepted as law; (3) the general principles of law recognized by civilized nations; (4) judicial decisions (without giving them binding force) and the teaching of the most highly qualified publicists of the various nations as subsidiary means for the determination of rules of law.

This court does not supersede but is in addition to the old so-called Permanent Court of Arbitration at The Hague, from which it differs widely.

The old court of arbitration was not, properly speaking, a court. It was merely a panel of persons available to act as judges, made up by appointments of not exceeding four persons by each of the states taking part, and a clerk's office to carry on the administrative business made necessary whenever an arbitral tribunal was selected from this panel.

Experience has shown that this plan of constituting the court specially for the purpose of each particular controversy was not a very good way for getting legal rights decided, because as a general rule arbitrators selected by one side or the other in a particular controversy, tend to represent that side of the controversy with the result that there is negotiation and compromise rather than judicial decision. Doubtless some controversies which involve fact and feeling rather than fact and law can most usefully be settled in that way, and for that reason the old so-called court of arbitration has been left and the new court, which is a real court, has been established, composed of permanent judges whose selection has no relation whatever to any particular controversy, whose number is so great as to make their body superior to any special local influence, who are conspicuous and distinguished figures in the international world, who are members of a great institution, the high reputation of which they must be solicitous to preserve, and who must necessarily year by year acquire increased competency for the discharge of their judicial duties.

This is substantially the same kind of change which was made by the United States in 1787 when they abandoned the plan provided in the 9th article of the old Articles of Confederation for the appointment of a special commission to hear and determine each controversy between states, and vested in one Supreme Court the judicial power to determine controversies between two or more states, under the third article of our present Constitution.

The proposal that the United States shall adhere to the protocol of December 16, 1920, which established the Permanent Court of International Justice, is quite distinct from the question whether the United States should become a member of the League of Nations so much discussed during the years 1919 and 1920. The two different projects approach the great problem of preserving peace from different angles and by different methods. They differ radically in their nature and in their effects.

The organization of national representatives in an Assembly and Council provided for by the League of Nations Covenant was in substance provision for a special form of diplomatic procedure, adapted like all diplomatic procedure to deal with questions of national policy. The Assembly and Council are not composed of natural persons. They are composed of states represented by natural persons. It is not M. Bourgeois or Lord Balfour, who speaks and votes in the

Council. It is the Republic of France and the British Empire speaking and voting through M. Bourgeois and Lord Balfour. It is not Señor Augustine Edwards or Lord Robert Cecil who speaks and votes in the Assembly of the League. It is Chile and South Africa speaking and voting through them. The honorable obligation of each individual, taking part in the proceedings of the Council and Assembly, is the obligation of a diplomatic agent towards his own country. There is none of that special personal obligation which constrains the conscience of a judge upon his oath and his self-respect to decide any controversy in accordance with law and the facts, without subordination to political power.

All diplomatic procedure has the purpose of avoiding or preventing conflict. The methods are varied according to the requirements of the particular situation. An ambassador may call upon a foreign minister and discuss a question with him. Foreign Offices may carry on extended correspondence, arguing the same matter of difference. The good offices or the mediation of a friendly power may come in to bring the parties together. Identic circular notes may be sent out to secure an expression of agreement on the part of several powers. Conferences may be called of a few powers specially interested in some particular controversy, such as the Conference of Ambassadors in London by which Sir Edward Grey maintained peace after the Balkan wars; such as the Naval Conference in London in 1908 and the Conference for the Limitation of Armaments in Washington in 1921. More general conferences may be called to deal with many subjects of common interest, such as The Hague Conferences, the Red Cross Conferences. The meetings of the Assembly and Council of the League of Nations are diplomatic conferences held at stated times and places. All the conclusions reached are reached by diplomatic agreement just as truly as if those conclusions resulted from diplomatic correspondence or from conversation in a Foreign Office, or from a conference *ad hoc* like the Arms Conference.

To these stated conferences is furnished a Secretariat rather more elaborately equipped to carry into effect conclusions that may be agreed upon than the ordinary secretariat which every international conference has to have.

The Court of International Justice, on the other hand, completely excludes the essential characteristics of the League organization and procedure.

No diplomatic agreement is sought or attained. No member of court represents, or is at liberty to represent any state whatever.

Their duty is not to deal with policies or agreements, but to decide questions of fact and law in cases brought before them. Each judge's obligation is not to represent his country, or any country, not to execute the orders of any foreign office, not to reflect the policy of any government, but upon his own conscience to hear and decide upon the evidence and the law in accordance with his own personal judgment.

The court is absolutely independent and is subject to no control by the League of Nations or by any other political authority.

It is plain that there is a line of cleavage between this court on the one hand, and the political organization of the League on the other, which is the same as the line drawn by the Supreme Court of the United States between its own functions in dealing with judicial questions and the functions of the legislative and executive branches of our government in dealing with political questions. This is not arbitrary but exists in the nature of things because it is plain that states acting in the League organization could not really decide judicial questions, while a court organized for the decision of such questions could not decide questions of governmental policy without abandoning its function of a court and assuming the entirely different function of a political agent.

There is sometimes a failure to appreciate the different offices of these two distinct methods of international procedure.

The diplomatic method is the necessary method of dealing with immediate exigencies and dangerous crises in affairs. Under such circumstances there is no other way to prevent disaster. Argument and persuasion and explanation, the removal of misapprehensions, the suggestion of obstacles and advantages, conciliation, concession, stipulations for the future, and the still more serious considerations to which diplomacy may finally resort, all these are employed to deal with immediate and acute situations. The slow processes of judicial procedure are not adapted to deal with such exigencies.

It should be observed, however, that these diplomatic processes have been going on from the beginning of history and especially for the last three centuries since the Thirty Years' War and each diplomatic effort begins just where similar efforts began centuries ago. Maps change, trade changes, dominant powers change, means of attack and defense and of benefit and injury change; but the nature of man does not change and the appeal of the expediency of the moment to human passions and desires is always the same. The achievements of diplomacy dealing with successive international crises are reprieves of civilization, not steps in the progress of civilization.

On the other hand consider the entirely different office of an international court. The least of the benefits which such an institution can furnish is in its decision of particular cases. That is frequently of high importance because however unimportant in itself, the question decided may appear to be, such questions are frequently the origins of general ill-feeling. They frequently halt the whole progress of diplomatic effort towards a good understanding. One of the curious human features of international affairs is that two peoples will accept without irritation an impartial decision upon a question between their two countries when, if the Foreign Minister of either country had agreed to the same thing voluntarily, he would have been hung in effigy.

You will recall that in 1898 a Joint High Commission was created by Great Britain and the United States for the purpose of disposing of a great number of pending controversies between the United States and Canada. The Lord Chancellor of England, Lord Herschell, came over to head the British Section, and Vice-President Fairbanks headed the American Section. They met alternately in Ottawa and Washington. They appointed committees. They discussed the numerous questions at issue and they separated without being able to settle anything whatever because neither party could yield upon the Alaskan boundary question. The Alaskan boundary question was determined by the decision of the tribunal which sat in London in 1903 and thereupon progress towards settlement of controversies began all along the line and before the Great War came in 1914, every question had been settled, so that no controversies remained on the diplomatic calendar to hinder alliance between all the English speaking peoples. It frequently happens in this way that a judicial question upon which neither side can yield without a sense of humiliation is like a key log of a jam, the removal of which sets free the whole mass to follow its natural course down the stream. In such a case it may be of vast importance to both countries to have a question decided while it may be quite unimportant which way it is decided.

More important is the part that the existence of adequate machinery for judicial settlement plays as a necessary feature of any process towards the outlawry of war. No one can expect a world free from controversy. Disputes will constantly arise so long as human nature remains the same.

They must be settled in some way. If not settled peaceably, then from time to time when they are important and exciting, they will lead to force. That cannot be prevented by mere negatives. The only practical recourse is by furnishing some adequate means of peaceable settlement; and throughout the entire field of disputes arising upon claims of right, human experience has devised no means of peaceable settlement so effectual as the opportunity to secure the judgment of a competent and upright court of justice.

More important also is the value of an international court as an agency in the development of international law, for there lies the path of progress. It is only by advance in the establishment of law that the peace loving peoples of the world can move forward towards the permanent establishment of the rule of public right in lieu of impulse and selfishness and brutal force.

Consider the underlying conditions which make it difficult to maintain peace. Chief among these are the essential differences of temperament and character and traditions and preconceived ideas and inherited modes of thought and feeling and action and differing conceptions of what is just and right and permissible in conduct. Out of these arise inevitable misunderstandings and opposing views of national rights and national duties. In this field interested motives find fertile soil for the cultivation of prejudice and passion and the determination of patriotism on both sides to insist on one country's supposed rights at all hazards, while one side or the other is surely mistaken. This process goes on among civilized peoples, the vast majority of whom on both sides are sincerely in favor of peace. The one force which civilization possesses capable of checking this process towards conflict is this public opinion in favor of peace. How can that opinion be made effective? Why has it not been more effective in the past? The plain answer is that public opinion when called upon to address itself to the living questions of the moment is uninformed. It is ill-informed. It is frequently misinformed. It is differently informed in different countries and if required to argue out in the heat of controversy, from first principles, the right and wrong of national action, or proposed action, it becomes confused and ineffective; it has no adequate force of crystallization. The plain remedy is to secure general agreement upon rules of right conduct between nations upon which the public of all civilized countries may base their judgment so that universal opinion may be clear and potent. The rules must conform to the common conceptions of morality but they must not be mere moral truths. They must translate moral truths into terms of action. They must be definite and certain to be effective tests of conduct. Their formulation and acceptance must inevitably be a long, slow process, but all advances in civilization have been by long, slow processes. It has been by such a process that the law of nations in its present extent has been built up. For centuries governments have been gradually discussing with each other the ways in which nations ought to act under such and such conditions and rescuing from the great mass of temperamental differences certain matters of international relation upon which all nations could agree, and formulating rules which all nations could accept; and thus very gradually the field of difference has been narrowing and the field of agreement has been enlarging. These rules constitute the law of nations.

We sometimes hear the remark that the Great War has destroyed international law. The future would be dark indeed if that were so. But it is not so. It is true that many of the rules of international law, designed to regulate the conduct of war, were grossly violated. Upon this two observations suggest themselves. One is that the whole field of international law to regulate the relations of nations in peace is unaffected. The other is that you cannot destroy a law by breaking it. The whole community of individuals or of nations can destroy a law by acquiescing in the breaking of it, but no lawbreaker can destroy the law he breaks. There has certainly been no acquiescence in the wholesale violation by Germany, of the law relating to war. On the contrary it was the testing of Germany's conduct by these rules of international law which led the civilized world outside of the Central Powers to condemn Germany and was the chief element in forming the clear and definite public opinion which ranged against her the forces that led to her final defeat, and the essential basis of the reparations by the infliction of which Germany is being punished now, is the German violation of law in beginning and carrying on the war by land and sea. The public opinion of the civilized world found in the clear rules of the law which it had established a certain basis for its judgment and it has reasserted and re-enthroned the law which was apparently overwhelmed for the moment.

Democracies cannot live without law. Autocrats can issue commands but democracies must govern themselves by public opinion and there can be no effective public opinion without established rules of conduct. A world of democracies must be governed by public opinion in support of law or it will be a world of anarchy.

In this modern world of rapid change, the development of international law by the old processes of diplomatic correspondence has not kept pace with the changing conditions calling for the application of the law. Within our lifetimes two new methods of expediting the process have been devised. The first is the holding of conferences for the purpose of discussing and agreeing upon additional and more effective rules — a process which ought to be resumed without any avoidable delay. The other is the establishment of this permanent court to pass upon questions of international law in dispute between nations and which, according to all human experience with courts of justice, will inevitably develop the law as it decides cases under the law.

Dangerous as analogies are, when I hear expressions of little esteem for the slow processes of international law because they do not prevent excited peoples from the use of force, I cannot help thinking of the relation between curative and preventive medicine. When a patient is laid low by an acute disease, it does not help him for the physician to talk about sanitary science. Medicine and surgery must deal with that case as best they can at the moment. Nevertheless if future cases of disease are to be prevented, if the community is to be more healthful, if the death rate is to be lower, if there is to be less tuberculosis, less yellow fever, less typhoid, rules of sanitary conduct of life must be established and understood and followed and enforced by public opinion. The place to begin is in the beginning before disease has taken possession and become acute.

The question now presented is whether the United States shall take part with the other civilized nations in supporting the International Court of Justice, which the United States has so long urged those same nations to join her in creating.

Manifestly the presumption is in favor of the United States supporting the court. Both self-respect and self-interest require that the United States should stand by its own policy. We cannot decently urge the creation of such a court as this upon the rest of the world through a long series of years and then repudiate the court when they consent to it, unless we offer some adequate reason. Is there any such reason?

Several suggestions have been made:

(1) It is said that the court originated in the League of Nations and should therefore be avoided.

The Court did not originate in the League of Nations. It

originated in the proposal of the United States to the First Hague Conference of 1899. Upon the urgency of the United States in The Hague Conference of 1907, the project was worked out and agreed upon in its essential features, except the method of selecting the judges and that conference adopted a resolution in these words:

The Conference recommends to the signatory powers the adoption of the annexed draft convention for the creation of a court of arbitral justice and the bringing it into force as soon as an agreement has been reached respecting the selection of the judges and the constitution of the court.

The difficulty which prevented a complete agreement upon the court in 1907 was very simple but very stubborn. The community of nations which was represented in the Second Hague Conference consisted of a small number of large and powerful states and a large number of small and physically weak states. Upon any question to be determined by a vote of states, the small states would have complete control. Yet the large states had greater population, greater interests to be affected by the court and as compared with the majority of the small states greater experience and familiarity with the kind of questions the court would have to pass upon. The small states were jealous of their equal sovereign rights and would not concede superior rights of sovereignty to any other state, however great and powerful, and so they insisted upon each sovereign state having one equal vote in the selection of judges to make up the court. On the other hand, the great states were wholly unwilling to submit themselves to the control of the small states. That was the difficulty upon which the court project stuck fast in the Conference of 1907 and the solution of which was referred to the governments of the nations by the Conference. During most of the time between the Conference of 1907 and the Great War the government of the United States was engaged in trying to work out with the other principal powers some solution of this question. Several plans were proposed and draft treaties were made and passed around from foreign office to foreign office, without reaching any satisfactory conclusion up to the time of the War. During all this time America was urging the court upon the other powers under the administration of Mr. Taft, as it had done under the administrations of Mr. Roosevelt and of Mr. McKinley.

At the close of the war when the League of Nations came to be made, no power either to act as a court, or to create a court was vested in the League, but the duty of finding a way of solving this old unsettled question which already rested upon the foreign offices of the different powers, was imposed upon the Council of the League by the 14th article of the Covenant, which provided:

The Council shall formulate and submit to the members of the League for adoption, plans for the establishment of a Permanent Court of International Justice.

The Council was charged to submit a plan to the several states just as the projects of The Hague Conventions were submitted to the several states and became effective only through the several treaty ratifications.

For the purpose of performing this duty of devising a plan to be submitted, the Council invited ten gentlemen from different parts of the world, supposed to be specially familiar with the subject, to meet as a commission to discuss and recommend a plan. In this commission there was one member from each of the following countries: France, Great Britain, Italy, Japan, Belgium, Brazil, Holland, Norway, Spain and the United States. Nobody represented any country. They were all there purely as experts, as if physicians were called together to consult about a case, or engineers to consult about a bridge.

This commission found and recommended what seemed to them to be a reasonable solution of the critical question. The solution was that as there were already in existence two organized bodies, one of which (viz., the Assembly of the League of Nations) was dominated by the smaller powers, and the other of which (viz., the Council of the League of Nations) was dominated by the larger powers, the judges of the court should be elected by the separate concurrent votes of these two bodies — a majority vote in each being necessary to an election, and that this election should be from an eligible list of persons nominated by the members of the old Permanent Court of Arbitration at The Hague, from each country represented in that organization. In this way, each class of nations — the small class of large nations and the larger class of small nations, would have power to prevent unjust or unreasonable conduct by the other class.

This plan, with the details of which I will not detain you, was approved and was submitted to all the states who were members of the League of Nations and was accepted by those states by signing and ratifying the protocol of December 16, 1920. After the ratification of the protocol by the greater part of the civilized nations, an election was held and the plan worked admirably and resulted in the selection of a court of the highest quality both of character and ability, which has organized and entered upon the discharge of its duties and has already disposed of a number of important and difficult questions.

It should be observed that the protocol or treaty constituting this court makes it a world court and not a League court; and especially it should be noted (1) that all states, including the United States, are made competent suitors before the court; (2) that the citizens of all states, including the United States, are made eligible for election to be judges of the court, as the election and membership of a distinguished American indicates; (3) that all states which were members of the old Permanent Court of Arbitration at The Hague, including the

United States, are entitled to make nominations which shall form a part of the eligible list from which judges are to be elected. In the summer of 1921 the American group of members of the old Hague Court of Arbitration were formally invited, pursuant to the protocol of December, 1920, to make nominations for judges. The American group did not deem it advisable to act officially upon that invitation at that time without some authoritative expression of the policy of the United States regarding the court. The members of the American group, however, other than Mr. Moore, did not hesitate to express their unanimous personal opinion that the wisest possible choice among the citizens of the United States for membership in the Court would be Mr. Moore himself. (4) That in electing a judge, the members of the Assembly and of the Council of the League of Nations are not exercising any power vested in them by the League or by the Covenant. They are executing a special power vested in them by the treaty which creates the court and which authorizes them to act as special electoral bodies under the authority of the treaty. (5) That the protocol contains an express invitation to states not members of the League, including the United States, to become parties to the treaty by adherence.

Only two things appear to remain to complete the full participation of the United States. One is that the United States shall undertake to pay its reasonable portion of the very moderate cost of maintaining the court. The other is that the United States shall have the right to be represented in the election of judges on the same footing as other powers. The President has proposed in a message to the Senate that by adherence to the protocol, the United States shall agree to contribute to the expenses upon condition that it is accorded the right to share in the election.

(2) It is said that by adhering to the protocol, the United States would in some way become entangled in the League of Nations to which it does not wish to belong.

This apprehension can result only from a lack of clear understanding of what is proposed. The protocol recognizes two distinct classes of states, one, the states that are members of the League of Nations and the other, states that are not members of the League of Nations. It is proposed that we adhere to the protocol expressly as a state which is not a member of the League of Nations. The only obligation we assume is to pay a sum of money towards the support of the court, the amount to be determined by our own Congress. The only right we acquire is to have a voice in the selection of judges. We may or we may not choose to litigate before the court. If we do choose to litigate, we establish no relations to anyone except the perfectly definite and well understood relations of a litigant in any court.

(3) It is said that by reason of the fact that not only the British Empire but the self-governing dominions of that Empire have votes in the Assembly of the League of Nations, Great Britain would have six votes to our one upon the election of judges.

Whatever cogency that argument may have had as bearing upon the question whether the United States should enter the League of Nations, in which the Assembly had important functions to discharge, it has no practical bearing upon the present question for the reason that the vote in the Assembly in the election of judges is a matter of no practical concern to the United States and it is a matter of no practical advantage to the British Empire.

By the express terms of the protocol of December 16, 1920, no power can have more than one of its nationals in the court. The selection of that one national from each of the five great powers is secured by their votes in the Council, sitting as an electoral body under the authority of the protocol. One of these will be the British Empire. Another will be the United States, each having one vote and only one vote. The difficult task of the Assembly is to distribute the remaining six judges and four deputy judges, ten in all, among between forty and fifty smaller or weaker powers. The very essence of the arrangement for a separate vote by the Assembly is that in that distribution there shall be no domination by the great powers, but the smaller powers shall have an opportunity to arrange the distribution among themselves. The United States has no business to interfere with it and ought not to wish to interfere. She could neither gain nor lose a member of the court by interfering. The British Empire could neither gain nor lose a member of the court by interfering. The self-governing dominions of the British Empire cannot gain a member of the court by their votes because their citizens are all nationals of the British Empire and there can be but one national of that Empire in the court. The objection is purely theoretical and formal, affecting no real interest of the United States, not worthy of consideration in view of the tremendous issues which depend upon securing universal support of the civilized world for this great world court of justice any more than the special relations which exist, or have existed, between the United States and Liberia, Haiti, Santo Domingo, Cuba, Nicaragua and Panama are entitled to consideration. The only real interest we have in the votes of the Assembly is our interest in common with all good and decent people in the world that the best possible judges shall be elected and if Esthonia, Latvia, Lithuania, Albania, Poland, the Balkan States, the West Indies and Central America are willing that these highly civilized self-governing nations, confederated with the United Kingdom in the British Empire should take part with them in making the selections in which the great powers have no concern, we ought to be content, just as France, and Italy and Japan are content, and to be gratified because we all know that it will make for the selection of a better court.

(4) It is said that the jurisdiction of the court ought to be compulsory. To that I personally agree. The commission which formulated and reported the plan for the court, recommended that jurisdiction should be compulsory; but some nations were unwilling to go to that extent.

No one can say with reasonable confidence that the United States would not have been one of those unwilling nations if the question had been put to it. The uniform attitude of the Senate upon a long series of arbitration treaties has been an attitude of refusal to give to any tribunal whatever compulsory jurisdiction affecting the interests of the United States upon any class of questions. At all events, some nations were unwilling to consent to compulsory jurisdiction. Was the project to be abandoned for that reason? That is not the way to make progress towards the adoption of any idea in this world of widely differing opinions and prejudices. The way to make progress is to secure agreement just as far as possible, get it recorded, get it acted upon so far as it permits action, commit the whole world to it as irrevocably as possible, and then upon the next occasion start on the basis of that agreement and try for a further step, and when that has been accomplished, try for a still further step. Patience and persistency and faith are the conditions of success in getting ideas adopted in a world composed of states in all stages of social and political development. If you exercise these qualities and your idea is right, you will win through. If you insist upon all or nothing at the outset, you fail. One should always remember that the only international agreement that is worth anything is a real agreement; that opinion and feeling cannot be changed by force; that such a change is an internal process which naturally requires time.

The protocol of December 16, 1920 secures the court upon the character and constitution of which the nations were ready to agree. It secures the jurisdiction of the court so far as the nations are ready to agree, and in two ways it opens the door for enlarging the jurisdiction of the court by making it compulsory just as soon as the nations become ready to agree. First, it confers jurisdiction not merely upon matters specially submitted, but in the case of general treaties for judicial settlement so that if any two nations are willing to have all juridical questions as between them judicially settled as of course, they can make a treaty to that effect and thereupon the court would have compulsory jurisdiction as between these two nations. Second, the door is kept open by the inclusion in the protocol of a provision under which nations who are willing to give the court compulsory jurisdiction may assent to such jurisdiction and thereby create it. Some twenty, mostly of the smaller powers, have signed that optional clause so that as between them the court has compulsory jurisdiction. If the United States wishes the court now to have compulsory jurisdiction, the natural course would be for the Senate to advise the President in response to his message that the Senate is ready to approve the signing not merely of the protocol, but of the optional clause in the protocol which affords compulsory jurisdiction.

I wish to express my warm agreement with what Senator Borah has recently said about outlawry of war.[1] To that end I sincerely hope that the approval of the United States may be given to this international court which represents the highest point yet reached by agreement of the nations in af-

[1] On February 13, 1923, Senator Borah introduced a resolution, one portion of which relates to the subject mentioned by Mr. Root. It is as follows:

Resolved, That it is the view of the Senate of the United States that war between nations should be outlawed as an institution or means for the settlement of international controversies by making it a public crime under the law of nations and that every nation should be encouraged by solemn agreement or treaty to bind itself to indict and punish its own international war breeders or instigators and war profiteers under powers similar to those conferred upon our Congress under Article I, section 8, of our Federal Constitution which clothes the Congress with the power "to define and punish offenses against the law of nations."

fording the same substitute for war by judicial decision of international cases that has been so effective in doing away with private war among individuals.

I hope also that following upon that approval, the influence of the United States will be employed to bring about a new conference of all the nations entitled to take part in the making of international law, to formulate and agree upon the amendments and additions, which should now be made, to reconcile divergent views and to extend the law to subjects not now adequately regulated, but as to which the interests of international justice require that rules of law shall be declared and accepted.

I look forward with confidence to the time when the rules so formulated and accepted as universal law, will declare all wars of aggression to be criminal violations of the law of nations. I look forward to the time when the refusal of any nation proposing war, to submit to an impartial court the decision of the question whether facts exist to justify it in war upon defensive grounds, will be deemed a confession of guilt; and I look forward to the time when the universal opinion of civilization, having such a clear and certain basis for the formation of judgment, will visit upon the aggressor its swift and heavy condemnation against which no nation may prevail.

War cannot be outlawed by proclamation, or by resolution, or by mere agreement, or by mere force. War can be outlawed only by arraying the moral force of the civilized world in support of definite rules of conduct which exclude war, and by giving to that moral force institutions through which that force may be applied to specific cases of attempted violation. One of those necessary institutions is a court by whose judgment the great multitude who desire the peace of justice may know what is just.

The question presented by the President's message is really only a question of moral support. The amount of contribution towards the support of the court to be determined by our own Congress, would be negligible. We undertake to do nothing, and to give nobody authority or power to do anything to us. The question is merely whether we shall give our moral approval to the establishment of the same kind of court which our government has been urging for a generation. It is less than three years since both political parties in the United States practically agreed upon the American attitude, expressed by one of those parties, in its platform, in these words:

> . . . stands for agreement among the nations to preserve the peace of the world. We believe that such an international association must be based upon international justice and must provide methods which shall maintain the rule of public right by the development of law and the decision of impartial courts.

Since that time the only proposal of any practical step towards giving effect to the belief expressed in the words which I have just quoted, is the proposal contained in this message of the President. No one has proposed any alternative method to give effect to that belief.

Can it be that the people of the United States do not care whether or not anything is done to make it possible to outlaw war?

THE CONDITIONS AND POSSIBILITIES REMAINING FOR INTERNATIONAL LAW AFTER THE WAR

ANNUAL ADDRESS AS PRESIDENT OF THE AMERICAN SOCIETY OF INTERNATIONAL LAW, WASHINGTON, APRIL 27, 1921

THE American Society of International Law may appropriately renew its discussions of the subject to which it is devoted, by a review of the effects of the World War both as to the law itself and as to the international relations under which the law is to be applied.

It is obvious that we cannot go on assuming that the laws and customs of war on land and at sea, the rules which regulate the rights and duties of neutral powers and persons in case of war, retain the authority which we supposed them to possess in the month of July, 1914. These rules imposed their obligation upon all parties to the great conflict, and, when violated by one party, they could not reasonably be deemed to restrain the other belligerents. So, the world went on for several years without much reference to them; and the question now is: How far do they exist?

In many ways the conditions which gave rise to those rules have been materially changed. The new modes of conducting war, under which practically entire peoples are mobilized either for combat or supply, have apparently destroyed the distinction between enemy forces and non-combatant citizens, so that the differences which underlie the law of contraband disappear. The whole people would seem to be an enemy force, and all goods destined for their use would appear to be contraband. The historic declaration of Paris that "the neutral flag covers enemy goods with the exception of contraband of war," and that "neutral goods with the exception of contraband of war are not liable to capture under the enemy's flag," would seem to have been swallowed by the exception, and the doctrine that "free ships make free goods" and that "blockades in order to be binding must be effective" appear to have become idle phrases. The submarine, the Zeppelin, and the airplane, wireless telegraphy, the newly achieved destructive power of high explosives and of poisonous gases, have created conditions affecting both belligerents and neutrals not contemplated when the old rules were established, and in many respects the old rules are not adapted to deal with the new conditions.

More important still is a fact which threatens the foundation of all international law. The doctrine of *Kriegsraison* has not been destroyed. It was asserted by Bethmann-Hollweg at the beginning of the war, when he sought to justify the plain and acknowledged violation of international law in the invasion of Belgium upon the ground of military necessity. The doctrine practically is that, if a belligerent deems it necessary for the success of its military operations to violate a rule of international law, the violation is permissible. As the belligerent is to be the sole judge of the necessity, the doctrine really is that a belligerent may violate the law or repudiate it or ignore it whenever that is deemed to be for its military advantage. The alleged necessity in the case of the German invasion of Belgium was simply that Belgium was deemed to be the most advantageous avenue through which to attack France. Of course, if that doctrine is to be maintained, there is no more international law, for the doctrine cannot be confined to the laws specifically relating to war on land and sea. With a nation at liberty to declare war, there are few rules of peaceful intercourse, the violation of which may not be alleged to have some possible bearing upon a military advantage; and a law which may rightfully be set aside by those whom it is intended to restrain is no law at all.

The doctrine has not been abandoned. It was formally and authoritatively declared by the German Government and acted upon throughout the war. We can find no ground to justify the conclusion that a plainly unrepentant Germany does not still maintain the soundness of the doctrine as a part of its historic justification, nor has there been any renunciation by the allies of Germany. We must, therefore, face the fact that the law which during the course of three centuries had become apparently firmly established upon the universal acceptance and consent of all the members of the community of civilized nations is shaken to its foundation by the repudiation of its moral obligation on the part of the four Central powers, — Germany, Austria-Hungary, Turkey, and Bulgaria, — which at the outbreak of the war had over 144,000,-000 inhabitants.

Few more futile public performances can be found in the history of international intercourse than the long diplomatic discussions which accompanied the earlier years of the war between neutral nations and Germany, about the rules of international law and their application to the conduct of Germany's military and naval proceedings, while Germany had already publicly declared that she would not deem herself bound by any rules that she found to be disadvantageous to herself. The same will be true in the future if the same condition exists. It will be impossible to maintain the restraint upon national conduct afforded by the rules of international law so long as so great a part of the civilized world asserts the right to disregard those rules whenever it sees fit. Either the doctrine of *Kriegsraison* must be abandoned definitely and finally, or there is an end of international law, and in its place will be left a world without law, in which alliances of some nations to the extent of their power enforce their ideas of suitable conduct upon other nations.

Another threatening obstacle to international law exists in the rapid development of Internationalism. This is presented by the avowed purposes of the Third Internationale, aiming at the destruction of national governments and the universal empire of the proletariat; by the fact that the brutal and cruel despotism of Lenin and his associated group has been able to maintain its ascendancy over the vast territory and population of Russia, calling itself a dictatorship of the proletariat but making itself a dictatorship over the proletariat as well as all other classes, and ruling in the name of a world-revolution for the accomplishment of the purposes of the Third Internationale. It is presented also by the universal propaganda carried on with almost religious fervor in all countries and seriously affecting the leadership of labor in many countries. That propaganda, exceedingly subtle and ingenious throughout the world, has toppled over the wits of parlor Socialists from their insecure foundations of education superior to their intelligence, and is making them the unconscious agents of promoting political principles which they would abhor if they understood them, and of aiding sinister projects for profit in which they personally have no part. The organization of the civilized world in nations is confronted since the war with a vigorous and to some degree prevailing assertion that a much better organization would be that of government by class, existing in all nations and superior to all.

International law, of course, is based upon the existence of nations. There is no common ground upon which one can discuss the obligations of international law with the Third Internationale; and just so far as the ideas of Lenin and Trotsky influence the people of a civilized country, just so

far the government of that country is weakened in the performance of its international obligations.

The existence of nations is not an accident of locality or of
language or of race. It is one phase of the struggle of mankind for liberty. The independence of nations is an assertion
of the rights of different groups of men having in the main
different customs, traditions, habits of thought and action,
ideas of propriety and of right, to have local self-government.
This is true whatever the form of government; whether it be
a monarchy or an aristocracy permitted by the people of the
country, or a republic in which rulers are elected by the
people, the distinction is the same between government in
accordance with the people's own conceptions of right and
propriety, and government by an alien force having different
and incongruous conceptions. There are few more injurious
influences in international affairs than the inability of the
people of one country to understand or to realize the differences between themselves and the people of other countries
in fundamental and often unexpressed preconceptions. These
differences affect the understanding in the different countries
of every act done and every word used. They are not matters
of reason, to be solved intellectually like a problem of Euclid.
They are the results of long ages of tradition, modes and
habits of thought, inherited assumptions regarding the conduct of life. One race of men take off their shoes and keep on
their hats, another race take off their hats and keep on their
shoes under similar conditions, to express similar sentiments
of respect. To the people of one country polyandry is the
natural social organization; to the people of another, polyg-
amy; and to the people of others monogamy is natural and
appropriate. The people of some countries consider that
justice is best attained by applying a system of excluding
evidence according to rigid rules of relevancy and competency, while the people of other equally civilized countries

consider that the same result may be best attained by admitting in evidence anything that anybody chooses to say on
the subject. None of these differences is the result of the
working out of problems by pure reason. They come from
the fact that peoples of different countries and of different
races do not think alike and cannot think alike, because their
intellectual processes are the resultants of different traditional
conceptions combined with the apparent logical premises of
each problem.

The most grinding possible tyranny is to be found in the
intimate control of a people by other races or rulers who do
not understand the people whom they rule. The vice of
tyranny is so widespread, the tendency to tyrannize over
others is so universal, especially among those who think
themselves better than others, that only the highest intelligence creates exceptions to the rule of oppression in alien
control. The declaration of the independence of nations,
large and small, is an assertion of the right to be free from the
oppression of alien control. Internationalism would fasten
that oppression upon the world without recourse.

The fundamental ideas of international law are, first, that
each nation has a right to live according to its own conceptions of life; second, that each national right is subject to the
equal identical right of every other nation. International law
is the application of these principles through accepted rules
of national action adapted to govern the conduct of nations
toward each other in the contacts of modern civilization. Internationalism, by destroying the authority and responsibility of nations and the law which is designed to control
their conduct toward each other, would destroy the most
necessary bulwark of human liberty, the chief protection of
the weak against the physical force of the strong, and substitute the universal control which the nature of men will make
an inevitable tyranny.

The long, slow process of civilization, with its peaceful attrition between individuals and between local and tribal groups, tends toward the steady enlargement of nations through the reconciliation of ideas and the adoption of common standards, making it easy for different groups to live together under the same government. Every great country shows the results of this process. Burgundy, Provence, and Brittany, Wessex, Sussex, and Northumbria, Wales, England, and Scotland, Piedmont and Naples have come to live peaceably together under governments in which each has a voice and in which each is understood. But that process cannot be forced any more than the growth of a tree can be forced. It can be promoted as the growth of a tree can be promoted. The parliament of man may come just as the parliaments of Britain and France and Italy have come, but it must be by growth and not by force or by the false pretence of agreement where there is no real agreement, or by international majorities overbearing minority nations through majority votes.

The great force of Russia, which aims to impose internationalism upon the world, therefore, halts the development of international law, the very foundations of which the existing government of Russia now repudiates. As the basis of international law is universal acceptance, either Russia must be excluded from the category of civilized nations or the law must wait upon the downfall of the present régime in Russia. In the meantime, every act which tends to support that régime, whether for sentiment or for trade, is a hindrance to the restoration of law and the rule of international justice.

Under these circumstances, how are we to take up the task of promoting the development of the Law of Nations? The task cannot be abandoned. The process which owes its impulse toward systematic development to Grotius and the horrors of the Thirty Years' War cannot be abandoned.

Never before was the need so great. The multitudes of citizens who now control the national governments of modern democracies and direct international policies cannot safely follow the passion of the moment or the idiosyncrasy of the individual public officer in their international affairs, without accepted principles and rules of action, without declared standards of conduct, without definition of rights, without prescription of duties too clear to be ignored. Otherwise the world reverts to chaos and savagery.

To determine how this Society and its members may be effective in efforts to promote the development and authority of international law, some further examination of the existing international situation will be useful. The armistice of November 11, 1918, left for the successful Allied powers two quite distinct and in some respects incongruous tasks. The first task was to decide upon the terms of peace and to require compliance with those terms. That was a matter of power, of force. It was the imposition of the will of the conquerors upon the conquered. Only the belligerent nations were concerned in it. It was a part of the war. Disarmament, reparation, disposition of conquered colonies, transfers of territory, were to be dictated as alternatives to further military punishment by the successful armies and navies. It was to be affected by the principles of reward for assistance in winning the war, of penalty for offences against civilization in beginning and carrying on the war, and by treaties between the belligerents.

The second task in necessary sequence was to give effect to the universal desire of the civilized world by bringing all civilized nations into agreement for the future preservation of peace. That was a matter, not of force, but of reason, humanity, universal instinct of self-preservation. It must be voluntary, not compulsory. It was the concern of all neutral nations equally with all belligerent nations. It presupposed a world at peace, in which peace, already attained, was to be preserved. It was to follow, not to be a part of, the compulsions of conquest.

The Versailles Conference undertook to include both of these separate, distinct, and incongruous processes in the same treaty. They framed a League of Nations for the future, they invited all neutrals to join, and at the same time and in the same instrument they undertook to impose penalties to which they required the defeated belligerents to submit. The defeated belligerents were not admitted to the League and had nothing to say about it, while the neutral members of the League naturally had no right or authority respecting the terms of peace imposed by the treaty. The two processes were tied together, however, by provisions making the League of Nations the agent of the conquerors to see to the execution of the terms imposed upon the other defeated nations. Thus certain powers were vested in the League, including neutrals, regarding the administration of occupied territory, plebiscites, scrutiny of government under mandates. These functions plainly were to be in exercise of derivative not original authority of the League, which became a mere agent of the belligerents for those purposes. Spain, Holland, Norway, for example, and any organization which represents them, can have no authority regarding a plebiscite in Silesia or the government of Danzig, except within the limits of a specific agency created by the nations which had a right won by conquest or created by treaty between such nations and Germany.

Another peculiarity of the treaty was that, although it contemplated the participation of all the belligerents, it was expressly made separable, by the provision that it should take effect when ratified by any three of the principal powers. Accordingly, when the other principal powers ratified the treaty and the United States refused to do so, the terms of peace became binding between Germany and the ratifying powers, although not between Germany and the United States. And the League of Nations, no longer a mere project, came into being and still exists, uniting for specified purposes substantially all the civilized countries except the United States, Germany, Russia, Austria-Hungary, and Turkey.

The natural tendency of these arrangements and the discussion and controversy which they engendered was toward great delay and confusion. The imposition of terms of peace was a matter calling for prompt decision and compliance while the conquering armies were in being and able to compel compliance. Under the distractions and discussions incident to the formation of a league for future peace, this vital process of closing the war dragged along until the Western armies had mainly disappeared; and many of the issues of the war have passed into a new and prolonged stage of discussion.

In the meantime, the Supreme Council of the belligerents, in which the United States continued entitled to a place which she ceased to fill, has held the centre of the international stage, trying to bring about the state of peace which the League of Nations was formed to preserve; and at the same time the League has been struggling with its special agency under the treaty, without ever having been put by its principals in the position of recognized authority; and the organization for future peace has remained incomplete in the face of continual actual war involving a majority of the people of Europe and the Near East.

In considering our course as students, lawyers, American citizens, united by common interest in the Law of Nations, I think we must assume that the conditions which I have described are temporary; that before very long the immediate issues of the war will be settled for the time being and peace will be restored; that republican Germany and her associates will abandon the arrogant assertion of the *Kriegsraison;* that the brutal and cruel despotism which now oppresses the people of Russia will meet the fate which awaits the violation of economic laws and, failing to be rescued by those friends who are coming to its assistance in this and other countries, will fall, and the people of Russia will come to their own.

When these results have been reached, there will remain the hindrances of differing forms and methods favored by the nations within and the nations without the existing League. But the idea that by agreeing at this time to a formula the nations can forever after be united in preventing war by making war seems practically to have been abandoned; and the remaining differences are not of substance and ought not to prevent the general desire of the civilized world from giving permanent form to institutions to prevent further war. In the long run, from the standpoint of the international lawyer, it does not much matter whether the substance of such institutions is reached by amending an existing agreement or by making a new agreement.

The necessary things are that there shall be institutions adapted to make effective the general civilized public opinion in favor of peace, and that these institutions shall be developed naturally from the customs, the habits of thought and action, and the standards of conduct in which civilized nations agree, and that they shall be of such a nature that the habit of recourse to them will have an educational effect and be a means of growth in justice and humanity.

The Covenant of the League, under which so many nations are now included, commits its members fully to these fundamentals, and, while it undertakes to go further and do too much, the evident tendency of its members is to reduce this excess by interpretation and amendment and bring it down to the character of real representation of the common customs and common opinions of civilized peoples in favor of peace.

On the other hand, the United States is certain to be ready to join in some form, in seeking the same result by these same essential methods. That will follow necessarily from the traditional policy of our country and the responsible declarations of our government in both the legislative and the executive branches.

Considering this field of preventive provisions as separate and distinct from the temporary exigencies of compulsory war settlements, if we examine both the League agreement and the declared policy of the United States for information as to common purposes, we shall find several different kinds of united action upon which there is practically agreement in principle, with difference only in degree or as to specific means.

We may pass over, as least important, although extremely useful, provisions for international coöperation in administrative services to facilitate trade and intercourse, or to apply regulations by common consent in matters of common interest. The International Postal Union, the control of wireless telegraphy, the ice-patrol of the North Atlantic for the safety of the ships of all nations, are examples of this kind of coöperation. The labor provisions of the Treaty of Versailles come under the same head, although they were put into the treaty without the discussion and consideration necessary to ascertain whether they ought to be adopted or whether they met a general demand or were adapted to world-conditions. Much of the time of the League organization has been devoted to matters of this character, which are really local, affecting particular groups of countries, and which would be arranged, naturally, and probably better, between the countries concerned, without burdening or involving the countries not concerned.

Most important for dealing with immediate danger to international peace is a system of international conferences upon questions of international policy. This is a natural growth from experience. The Algeciras Conference is a type. The Conference in London, which limited the effect of the Balkan wars, is another. It is a general belief that if Sir Edward Grey had secured the conference he sought in July, 1914, the war would have been averted. Whether it be by dispelling misunderstandings, allaying fears, soothing irritation, or by the repressive effect of general adverse opinion, a formal general conference of the principal nations ordinarily leads to a situation in which it is extremely difficult for any nation to begin war.

The weakness of the practice hitherto has been in the fact that no one had a right to insist upon a conference; no one was under obligation to attend a conference. The step in advance, plainly indicated as the natural development of this most useful practice into a systematic institution, is to establish an administrative agency whose duty it shall be to call such a conference in time of threatened danger, on suitable request, and to place all nations under obligation to attend the conference when called. Upon the substance of this there is no disagreement. The Council of the League does this and something more, and the difference is over the something more. The Council of the League is a perpetual, permanent conference, as distinguished from conferences *ad hoc*, to be called automatically whenever grave cause arises. No one seems to question that in one way or another there should be obligatory conferences.

Such conferences, however, deal with policy in particular exigencies, and they proceed upon motives of expediency. They are not steps in the development of the rule of right among nations. In that direction also, however, we find elements of general agreement.

The Covenant of the League of Nations in its preamble states one of its objects to be " in order to promote international coöperation and to achieve international peace and security . . . by the firm establishment of the understandings of international law as the actual rule of conduct among governments"; and in the 14th article it provides: "The Council shall formulate and submit to the members of the League for adoption plans for the establishment of a permanent court of international justice."

The American Congress in a statute enacted August 29, 1916, expressed the American view in the most solemn form. The statute says:

It is hereby declared to be the policy of the United States to adjust and settle its international disputes through mediation or arbitration, to the end that war may be honorably avoided. . . . In view of the premises, the President is authorized and requested to invite, at an appropriate time, not later than the close of the war in Europe, all the great Governments of the world to send representatives to a conference which shall be charged with the duty of formulating a plan for a court of arbitration or other tribunal, to which disputed questions between nations shall be referred for adjudication and peaceful settlement.

The latest message of the President of the United States to Congress on the 12th of the present month, said:

The American aspiration, indeed the world aspiration, was an association of nations based upon the application of justice and right, binding us in conference and coöperation for the prevention of war and pointing the way to a higher civilization and international fraternity in which all the world might share. . . . In the national referendum to which I have adverted, we pledged our efforts toward such an association, and the pledge will be faithfully kept.

The pledge to which the President plainly referred in the paragraph just quoted was contained in the Republican Platform, in these words:

The Republican Party stands for agreement among the nations to preserve the peace of the world. We believe that such an international association must be based upon international justice, and must provide methods which shall maintain the rule of public right by the development of law and the decision of impartial courts, and which shall secure instant and general international conference whenever peace shall be threatened by political action, so that the nations pledged to do and insist upon what is just and fair may exercise their influence and power for the prevention of war.

While this pledge was in the platform of one party, it was not, in fact, the subject of party controversy, and the enormous majority of over seven million votes given to the candidate standing by that platform justifies the assertion that these words state the true attitude of the American people, as that attitude is now certified in the passage which I have quoted from the President's message to Congress.

It is apparent that the attitude of the League and the attitude of America toward this subject do not differ in substance, however much they may differ as to the specific modes of effectuating the common purpose.

The duty imposed upon the Council of the League, "to formulate and submit plans for the establishment of a permanent court of international justice," has been performed, and a convention establishing such a court has been adopted by the League and has already been ratified by many of its members. It provides for a permanent court of judges elected for fixed periods, paid fixed salaries, engaging in no other occupation, and bound to proceed under an oath which imposes upon them judicial obligation as distinguished from a sense of diplomatic obligation. To this court all nations may repair for the adjudication of their differences.

So much for the nations in the League. It is also true that this court is in substance, in everything essential to its character and function, the same court which under Mr. Roosevelt's administration was urged by the United States upon the Second Conference at The Hague in 1907, and which, at the instance of the United States, was provided for in subsequent treaties between the United States and the principal European Powers, negotiated under Mr. Knox as Secretary of State in Mr. Taft's administration, but not finally consummated when the war intervened.

Here plainly there is agreement in substance, and the difficulties are formal.

The technical commission which in the summer of 1920 drafted the plan for a permanent court that has been adopted by the League, accompanied the plan by a unanimous recommendation as follows:

The Advisory Committee of Jurists, assembled at The Hague to draft a plan for a Permanent Court of International Justice,

Convinced that the security of states and the well-being of peoples urgently require the extension of the empire of law and the development of all international agencies for the administration of justice,

Recommends:

I. That a new conference of the nations in continuation of the first two conferences at The Hague be held as soon as practicable for the following purposes:

1. To restate the established rules of international law, especially, and in the first instance, in the fields affected by the events of the recent war.

2. To formulate and agree upon the amendments and additions, if any, to the rules of international law shown to be necessary or useful by the events of the war and the changes in the conditions of international life and intercourse which have followed the war.

3. To endeavor to reconcile divergent views and secure general agreement upon the rules which have been in dispute heretofore.

4. To consider the subjects not now adequately regulated by international law, but as to which the interests of international justice require that rules of law shall be declared and accepted.

II. That the Institute of International Law, the American Institute of International Law, the Union Juridique Internationale, the International Law Association, and the Iberian Institute of Comparative Law be invited to prepare, with such conference or collaboration *inter sese* as they may deem useful, projects for the work of the conference, to be submitted beforehand to the several Governments and laid before the conference for its consideration and such action as it may find suitable.

III. That the conference be named Conference for the Advancement of International Law.

IV. That this conference be followed by further successive conferences at stated intervals, to continue the work left unfinished.

Plainly, these recommendations cannot receive effect, now, or until the present emergencies of an unsettled war have been disposed of. But when the time comes, they will point the way to the performance of the object of the League "for the firm establishment of the understandings of international law," and the identical purpose of the people of the United States, so often declared by their representatives.

It is to be observed that these two — the establishment of a permanent court and the restoration of the authority of international law — are correlative parts of the same world-policy, upon the substance of which the civilized nations are in agreement.

There can be no real court without law to control its judges, and there can be no effective law without institutions for its application to concrete cases. This is the traditional policy of the United States — to establish and extend the law declaring the rules of right conduct accepted by the common judgment of civilization, and to substitute in international controversies upon conflicting claims of right impartial judgment under the law in the place of war.

The existing situation presents difficulties and embarrassments in arriving at a common understanding regarding the precise modes in which this general world-policy shall receive effect; but I, for one, am not willing to assume that the patience and good sense of the diplomacy of the world, including our own country, will be unequal to the task of so disposing of the formal difficulties as to achieve the great object upon which all are agreed.

It is further to be observed that conference upon matters of policy, either permanent or occasional, on the one hand, and the establishment of law and judicial disposal of questions of right, on the other hand, are not alternative and opposing methods. They are mutually supplemental parts of one and the same scheme to prevent war. Both are methods of bringing the public opinion of the world to bear upon the settlement of controversies. Neither covers the field without the other. Never before has there been such evidence of the power of public opinion as has been afforded by the vast propaganda through which the contending nations in the great war have tried their cases at the bar of public judgment of the world, and have sought to commend their conduct to the peoples of other nations.

The idea that any formula can be devised, under the working of which the world can be made peaceable by compulsion, is manifestly in course of abandonment. The public opinion of mankind is so mighty a force, that it is competent to control the conduct of nations as the public opinion of the community controls the conduct of individuals. But it must be an intelligent, informed and disciplined opinion. The exit of autocracies leaves the direction of foreign relations under the ultimate control of multitudinous, ill-informed, and untrained democracies. In place of dynastic ambitions, the danger of war is now to be found in popular misunderstandings and resentments.

How are these vast democracies to be justly informed as to the rights and wrongs of controversies, and the fairness of policies? It seldom happens that the great multitude of citizens can argue out from first principles the complicated and difficult questions of right and wrong involved in international relations. It seldom happens that the subject is not obscured by misinformation and misleading suggestion, and by appeals to passion rather than to judgment. The only mode of meeting this great and vital need, dictated by reason and approved by experience, is the establishment of institutions through which, when strife is not flagrant, the deliberate and unbiased opinion of mankind may declare and agree upon the rules of conduct which we call law, by which in times of excitement judgment may be guided, and by which the peoples may be informed of the limits of their rights and the demands of their duties; and by the establishment of institutions through which disputed facts may be determined and false appearance and misinformation may be stripped away and the truth be made known to the good and peaceful peoples of the world by the judgment of impartial and respected tribunals. In such institutions rests the possibility of growth and development for civilization. Through them may be established by usage the habit of respecting law. They may create standards of conduct under which the thoughts of peoples in controversy will turn habitually to the demonstration of the justice of their position by proof and reason, rather than by threats of violence, so that the time will come when a nation will know that it is discredited by the refusal to maintain the justness of its cause by the procedure of justice.

This is the work of international law, applied by an international court. The process will be slow, but all advance of civilization is slow. Not what ultimate object we can attain in our short lives, but what tendencies toward higher standards of conduct in the world we can aid during our generation, is the test that determines our duty of service. The conditions which will hinder and delay effective action for the reestablishment of law are many and serious, but we must prepare. When the time for action comes, it must find the results of study, discussion, and matured thought ready, as material for authoritative judgment by the nations, and, meanwhile, the voice of the least of us may be of some avail, urging that force be repressed and expediency be guided by the public opinion of the world, made effective by declared and accepted rules of public right applied by competent and impartial international tribunals.

THE PROHIBITION OF SUBMARINES AND POISONOUS GASES

SPEECH AT THE FIFTH PLENARY SESSION OF THE CONFERENCE ON THE LIMITATION OF ARMAMENT, WASHINGTON, FEBRUARY 1, 1922

On August 11, 1921, Secretary of State Hughes conveyed a formal invitation to the Governments of the British Empire, France, Italy, and Japan to take part in a Conference on the Limitation of Armament, to be held at Washington. The invitation, while calling attention to the effect of armament upon productive labor, and the enormous disbursements on rival armaments, stated that the time was opportune "to approach this subject directly and in conference," and that it might be found advisable "to formulate proposals by which, in the interest of humanity, the use of new agencies of warfare may be suitably controlled."

These five Powers were invited because they had the greatest armament, and therefore suffered most by its maintenance and increase.

Recognizing that the Pacific, notwithstanding its name, was a storm-center, the Conference was broadened to include the Pacific and Far Eastern questions, and China, the Netherlands, and Portugal, because of their interests in those regions, were invited to take part in that phase of the Conference. Belgium was invited upon its own request.

There were therefore two Conferences — one for the limitation of armament, composed of the representatives of five Powers; the other, for Pacific and Far Eastern questions, composed of the representatives of nine Powers.

The American delegates to the Conference were Secretary Hughes, Senator Henry Cabot Lodge, Senator Oscar S. Underwood, and Mr. Root.

Called for the 11th of November, the Conference was opened the following day. It adjourned February 6, 1922. The official languages were French and English. In accordance with diplomatic precedent, Secretary Hughes was chairman of the Conference.

An agreement for the limitation of naval armament was reached between the British Empire, France, Italy, Japan, and the United States, and a series of important agreements concerning the Pacific was adopted. This agreement and the convention prohibiting the use of noxious gases were signed February 6, 1922.

The proposals prohibiting the unrestricted use of submarines and the employment of poisonous gases were made by Mr. Root.

THE CHAIRMAN (speaking in English). The Committee on Limitation of Armament has adopted Resolutions with regard to the conduct of submarines in war, and with regard to the use of poison gas. These Resolutions have been embodied in a Treaty which is now to be presented to the Conference. I shall ask Mr. Root to present that Treaty.

Mr. Root (speaking in English). Mr. Chairman and gentlemen:

This Treaty supplements the Treaty which limits armaments by imposing certain limitations upon the use of armaments.

It is brief and I will read it.

"The United States of America, the British Empire, France, Italy, and Japan, hereinafter referred to as the Signatory Powers, desiring to make more effective the rules adopted by civilized nations for the protection of the lives of neutrals and noncombatants at sea in time of war, and to prevent the use in war of noxious gases and chemicals, have determined to conclude a Treaty to this effect, and have appointed as their Plenipotentiaries:

.   .   .   .   .   .

"Who, having communicated their Full Powers, found in good and due form, have agreed as follows:

Article 1

"The Signatory Powers declare that among the rules adopted by civilized nations for the protection of the lives of neutrals and noncombatants at sea in time of war, the following are to be deemed an established part of international law:

"(1) A merchant vessel must be ordered to submit to visit and search to determine its character before it can be seized.

"A merchant vessel must not be attacked unless it refuse to submit to visit and search after warning, or to proceed as directed after seizure.

"A merchant vessel must not be destroyed unless the crew and passengers have been first placed in safety.

"(2) Belligerent submarines are not under any circumstances exempt from the universal rules above stated; and if a submarine cannot capture a merchant vessel in conformity with these rules the existing law of nations requires it to desist from attack and from seizure and to permit the merchant vessel to proceed unmolested.

Article 2

"The Signatory Powers invite all other civilized Powers to express their assent to the foregoing statement of established law so that there may be a clear public understanding throughout the world of the standards of conduct by which the public opinion of the world is to pass judgment upon future belligerents.

Article 3

"The Signatory Powers, desiring to insure the enforcement of the humane rules of existing law declared by them with respect to attacks upon and the seizure and destruction of merchant ships, further declare that any person in the service of any Power who shall violate any of those rules, whether or not such person is under orders of a governmental superior, shall be deemed to have violated the laws of war and shall be liable to trial and punishment as if for an act of piracy, and may be brought to trial before the civil or military authorities of any Power within the jurisdiction of which he may be found.

Article 4

"The Signatory Powers recognize the practical impossibility of using submarines as commerce destroyers without violating, as they were violated in the recent war of 1914–18, the requirements universally accepted by civilized nations, for the protection of the lives of neutrals and noncombatants, and to the end that the prohibition of the use of submarines as commerce destroyers shall be universally accepted as a part of the law of nations they now accept that prohibition as henceforth binding as between themselves and they invite all other nations to adhere thereto.

Article 5

"The use in war of asphyxiating, poisonous, or other gases, and all analogous liquids, materials, or devices, having been justly condemned by the general opinion of the civilized world and a prohibition of such use having been declared in Treaties to which a majority of the civilized Powers are parties,

"The Signatory Powers, to the end that this prohibition shall be universally accepted as a part of international law binding alike the conscience and practice of nations, declare their assent to such prohibition, agree to be bound thereby as between themselves and invite all other civilized nations to adhere thereto.

Article 6

"The present Treaty shall be ratified as soon as possible in accordance with the constitutional methods of the Signatory Powers and shall take effect on the deposit of all the ratifications, which shall take place at Washington.

"The Government of the United States will transmit to all the Signatory Powers a certified copy of the procès-verbal of the deposit of ratification.

"The present Treaty, of which the French and English texts are both authentic, shall remain deposited in the Archives of the Government of the United States, and duly certified copies thereof will be transmitted by that Government to each of the Signatory Powers.

Article 7

"The Government of the United States will further transmit to each of the Non-Signatory Powers a duly certified copy of the present Treaty and invite its adherence thereto.

"Any Non-Signatory Power may adhere to the present Treaty by communicating an Instrument of Adherence to the

Government of the United States, which will thereupon transmit to each of the Signatory and Adhering Powers a certified copy of each Instrument of Adherence.

"In faith whereof, the above named Plenipotentiaries have signed the present Treaty.

"Done at the City of Washington, the —— day of February, one thousand nine hundred and twenty-two."

You will observe that this treaty does not undertake to codify international law in respect of visit, search, or seizure of merchant vessels. What it does undertake to do is to state the most important and effective provisions of the law of nations in regard to the treatment of merchant vessels by belligerent warships, and to declare that submarines are, under no circumstances, exempt from these humane rules for the protection of the life of innocent noncombatants.

It undertakes further to stigmatize violation of these rules, and the doing to death of women and children and noncombatants, by the wanton destruction of merchant vessels upon which they are passengers, as a violation of the laws of war, which, as between these five great powers and all other civilized nations who give their adherence, shall be henceforth punished as an act of piracy.

It undertakes further to prevent temptation to the violation of these rules by the use of submarines for the capture of merchant vessels, and to prohibit that use altogether. It undertakes further to denounce the use of poisonous gases and chemicals in war, as they were used to the horror of all civilization in the war of 1914–1918.

Cynics have said that in the stress of war these rules will be violated. Cynics are always near-sighted, and usually the decisive facts lie beyond the range of their vision.

We may grant that rules limiting the use of implements of warfare, made between diplomatists will be violated in the stress of conflict. We may grant that the most solemn obligation assumed by governments, in respect of the use of implements of war will be violated in the stress of conflict. But beyond diplomatists and beyond governments there rests the public opinion of the civilized world; and the public opinion of the world can punish; it can bring its sanction to the support of a prohibition with as terrible consequences as any criminal statute of Congress or of Parliament.

We may grant that, in matters which are complicated and difficult, where the facts are disputed and the argument is sophistic, public opinion may be confused and ineffective; yet when a rule of action, clear and simple, is based upon the fundamental ideas of humanity and right conduct, and the public opinion of the world has reached a decisive judgment upon it, that rule will be enforced by the greatest power known to human history, the power that is the hope of the world.

That power was the object of all the vast propaganda of the late war; that power was the means of determining the conflict in the late war; and that power, the clear opinion of the civilized world, stigmatizing as a violation of the fundamental rules of humanity and right, a specific course of conduct, will visit a nation that violates its conclusion with a punishment that means national ruin.

This treaty is an attempt to crystallize, in simple and unmistakable terms, the opinion of civilization that already exists. This treaty is an appeal to that clear opinion of the civilized world, in order that henceforth no nation shall dare to do what was done when the women and children of the *Lusitania* went to their death by wanton murder upon the high seas.

INTERNATIONAL LAW AT THE WASHINGTON CONFERENCE ON THE LIMITATION OF ARMAMENT

ANNUAL ADDRESS AS PRESIDENT OF THE AMERICAN SOCIETY OF INTERNATIONAL LAW, WASHINGTON, APRIL 27, 1922

THE business of the recent Washington Conference on Limitation of Armament was to reach agreements which would bind the parties by contractual obligation, as distinguished from the obligations imposed by law. The agreements reached, whether expressed in treaties or in formal declarations, are not complicated and are easily understood. In two fields, however, the subjects treated were so far affected by rules of international law that to understand the full meaning and purpose of the provisions agreed upon, and the reasons why they received their present form, it seems desirable to consider the law in the light of which the agreements are to be read.

One of these fields is covered by the treaties and resolutions relating to China and the formal declarations relating to Siberia. The other field is covered by the treaty and resolutions regarding submarines and other new agencies of warfare.

In the first instance, let me state the general nature of the Conference work as a whole.

The Conference was called to deal with the limitation of armament. The special occasion for it was the apparent race of competition in the building of battleships and battle-cruisers on the part of Japan and the United States, a race in which Great Britain was about to enter under the impera-

tive necessity of maintaining her ocean-borne food supply
and protecting her Far Eastern colonies and dominions. The
original parties proposed were the five great naval Powers,
actual or potential — Great Britain, France, Italy, Japan,
and the United States.

The condition of affairs in the continent of Europe made it
plain very early that it would be impossible at that time and
in that way to deal effectively with the subject of land armament, so that the work of the Conference was confined to its
primary purpose of stopping the race of naval construction
and limiting naval armament. At the outset of the Conference the United States made a very drastic proposal not only
to stop competition, but to destroy about forty per cent of
the existing strength of capital ships of the principal naval
Powers, in such a way as to leave the relative proportions of
naval strength unchanged, and that proposal was ultimately
accepted and embodied in the principal treaty resulting from
the Conference.

Such proposals, however, do not carry themselves. Competition in armament results from national states of mind,
distrust, apprehension of attack, a widespread belief that war
is imminent, so that the peoples of the respective countries
think in terms of war, prepare for war and reach a condition
of thought and feeling in which it is natural for war to come.
That state of mind must be disposed of if competition is to be
really stopped. The nations concerned must cease to think in
terms of war and must come to think in terms of peace. The
object of having a conference is to effect such a change by
friendly negotiation, explanation, doing away with misunderstanding, creating conviction of friendly intention and
good faith, with the aid on appropriate occasions of friendly
advice of third parties.

The success of such a process in the Washington Conference was registered in what is called the Four Power Treaty

between Great Britain, France, Japan, and the United States.
I doubt if any formal treaty ever accomplished so much by
doing so little. It provided that we should all respect rights,
which we were bound to do already, and that if controversy
arose about the Pacific islands (it was quite immaterial what
islands), the parties should get together and talk it over,
which was the very thing they were then doing in Washington. The consent of the Senate was not necessary to such an
agreement. It merely arranged for following an ordinary
form of diplomatic intercourse. The President had done the
same thing at Algeciras and at The Hague and at the Conference of London without asking the consent of the Senate,
and the Senate had ratified the conclusions reached at those
conferences. It was important, however, that the Senate
should give its approval in this case because the instrument
was a formal certificate to all the people of Japan and all the
people of the United States and all the civilized Powers, that
the parties to the treaty had abandoned their mutual distrust and had ceased to think about war with each other and
had resumed relations of genuine friendship. That certificate
and the truth that it represents, incidentally made possible
the abandonment of the Anglo-Japanese Alliance and made
possible the treaty for the limitation of naval armament and
dispelled one war cloud upon the horizon of a troubled world.

The Four Power Treaty was not enough, however, standing
by itself, to make the new condition stable without some
treatment of the causes of irritation which had arisen and
which might be apprehended upon the continent of Asia.
For the discussion of this subject, four other Powers having
interests in the Far East — Belgium, China, The Netherlands, and Portugal — also took part.

These causes of irritation were incident to the contacts of
western civilization with the peculiar and widely different
civilization of China. The character of the Chinese people

commands admiration, respect and sympathy. It was a product of the life of a self-contained agricultural community occupying a vast territory and content with the conditions of peace and industry within their own limits. It was little adapted, however, to resist the thrust of western enterprise ranging the world for trade and the development of wealth.

The report to the President by the American Delegation in the Conference described this aspect of Chinese civilization in these words:

The people of China are the inheritors of the oldest extant civilization of the world; but it is a civilization which has followed a course of development different from that of the West. It has almost wholly ignored the material, the mechanical, the scientific, and industrial mastery of natural resources, which has so characterized our Western civilization in its later growth, and has led among us to the creation of an intricate industrial system. The spirit of Chinese civilization has, moreover, been pacific, and lacking in the consciousness of nationality as we understand that term. In its political aspects, the ideal of that civilization was to follow the principle of self-government by the family or guild to an extreme. The throne had imposed upon the people virtually no authority and exercised virtually no functions save to preserve order and to collect taxes for the maintenance of the throne as a symbol of national or racial unity.

. . . .

China, with its age-long devotion to a political ideal which scarcely involved the concept of a state, and which had afforded its people no experience of coördinated action for political ends, was slower to adapt itself to conditions arising out of what it regarded as the intrusion of the West. Even after it had ceased actually to oppose this intrusion, it still sought to hold itself aloof and to carry on a passive resistance to the new influences which were at work. Against powerful, well-knit governments of the European type, strongly nationalistic, and in some instances availing themselves of military force, China could oppose only the will of a weak and loose-knit government, lacking even the support of a national self-consciousness on the part of its people. Against the organized industrial and commercial enterprises of the West, China had no similar organization to oppose, and no means of exploiting on any adequate scale the coveted latent wealth of the country.

We should recall the fact that international law was originally a system of rules dictated by reason and convenience and accepted by the Christian nations of Europe for the regulation of their relations with each other, and that these nations, and these alone, constituted the community of nations created by the assumption of such obligations toward each other; that this community or family of nations was first enlarged to include Christian states which had grown up outside of Europe, consisting chiefly of the American states which had their origin in European colonization; that it was not until the Treaty of Paris of 1856 that any non-Christian state was admitted to the international family by the agreement of the great European Powers admitting Turkey "to participate in the advantages of public law and of the European concert." The criterion of inclusion or exclusion was not at any time in reality religious. It rested upon the question whether a given state had the kind of civilization necessary to enable its government and its people in every respect to understand and comply with the rules of international law as those rules had been developed in the family of Christian nations. It is plain that inability in this respect might result either from a low degree of civilization or from a different kind of civilization with different modes of thought and conceptions of right conduct.

Accordingly Japan, for about forty years after she was open to intercourse with the western peoples, was not admitted to the family of nations, but the amazing facility with which she acquired an understanding of western ideas and adapted herself to the methods of what we, in the West, consider progress, led to her admission to full companionship under the law about twenty-five years ago, and she then became bound to obey and entitled to assert the rules of international law, to control her intercourse with other members of the family.

It is difficult to determine just how far China, Persia, Siam and some other states, having a civilization quite different from that of Europe and America, have been admitted to the family of the nations who are entitled to the benefits and subject to the obligations of international law. Certainly China was not admitted to that circle during the early years when the conditions were created out of which the present difficulties have arisen. She was not then in a condition to comply with and probably her people were in many respects wholly unable to understand the rules of international law. The reciprocal obligation which those rules involved could not exist and China, being unable to comply with the obligations of that law on her own part, had no right to insist upon the obligation against others. Her right was the moral right to be treated fairly and decently and her obligation was a moral obligation to treat others in the same way. It is also clear that a continuance of the same inability to perform international obligations has down to the present time prevented the full admission of China to the circle of states governed by international law, notwithstanding her inclusion in international conferences and regular diplomatic intercourse.

The customary method for regulating intercourse between the peoples who are subject to international law and the peoples who are not subject to that law has long been to provide conventionally for such regulations as are absolutely necessary. The most striking of these arrangements is the establishment of extraterritorial jurisdiction under which the citizens of the outside Power are withdrawn from the jurisdiction of local tribunals and are entitled to have their rights tried by officials of their own country, primarily by the consuls of their own country. This was the case in Turkey and it continued under the capitulations until the war of 1914. That kind of jurisdiction was provided for by our treaty of 1854 with Japan and generally in the treaties between Japan and the other civilized Powers, and it continued until the year 1894. It was provided for by our treaty of 1844 with China and still continues. We have created for the exercise of that jurisdiction in place of the consuls, the American court in China, a great and excellent court, which performs its duties most creditably. Similar treaties were made with China by the other western Powers.

As a natural corollary to this assent to the right of the foreign nation to protect its own nationals by the action of its own officers, there is a general recognition of the special applicability to the country in which the extraterritorial jurisdiction is exercised of the rule under which outside countries may land troops in disturbed regions for the protection of their own nationals. That rule cannot be stated better than it was by Mr. Hill, in a letter by him as the Assistant Secretary of State, September 11, 1900. He says:

> Although in this reply it was convenient to limit the memorandum to the occasion of landing at a treaty port, it was not designed to forego the right, which this government has always held and which on occasion it has exercised in China and in other countries, to land forces and adopt all necessary measures to protect the life and property of our citizens whenever menaced by lawless acts which the general or local authority is unwilling or impotent to prevent.

The most striking illustration of the application of this rule to China was in the Pekin expedition for the rescue of the legations from the Boxers in the year 1900.

A third subject which has been customarily regulated by treaty in such countries has been trade. Ordinarily there has been first a refusal to permit trade, finally overcome by the pressure of the outside nations and yielded with an agreement limiting the places where trade could be carried on, and expressly stipulating what customs duties should be imposed. We made such a treaty with China in 1844 and there are outstanding some fifteen or sixteen such treaties. That with Great Britain was made eighty years ago, in 1842.

A similar trade agreement involving stipulated tariff rates was included in our treaty of 1854 with Japan.

The door having thus been opened in China, it was inevitable that individual enterprise should press on to secure opportunities for profitable development of the great wealth of that vast country. As there was no law in China to regulate such development, it naturally took the form of pressure for special concessions, and naturally the governments of the seekers for concessions backed up their citizens. After the war of 1895 between China and Japan had revealed the national weakness and governmental incapacity of China, the activity in seeking profitable concessions increased greatly, and there was much favoritism and corruption, much betrayal of the true interests of China on the part of her own officials, and much jealousy and ill-feeling between the competitors for concessions and between their respective governments. It seemed as if China was in a fair way to be torn to pieces and divided between the contending Powers. In 1899 Mr. Hay undertook to put a stop to this process by his famous declaration of the "open door" policy, supplemented in 1900 by a declaration in favor of the preservation of China's territorial and administrative integrity. To these he secured the assent of all the great Powers and they did doubtless retard the process. With the lapse of years, however, the rather informal assents of the Powers to these declarations came to be treated more and more as polite assurances rather than as binding obligations, and the danger in both its aspects, danger to China and danger to peace between the outside Powers, again became threatening. It was that double danger with which the Conference had to deal before the Four Power Treaty could be regarded as permanent and the naval treaty could be concluded.

In the meantime the Chinese revolution of 1911 had overthrown the Manchurian dynasty and great numbers of the

Chinese people, under the leadership of the younger generation, many of whom had been educated in the western countries and in Japan, had been making heroic efforts to establish
a competent and stable government. They were still in the
stress of turmoil and conflict. The country was divided into
separate groups of provinces under the control of local military chieftains, maintaining their own separate armies and
frequently engaged in conflict with each other. The Pekin
government had but little power and was quite unable to enforce its authority or make good its agreements throughout
the greater part of the country.

Under the conventional arrangements with China there
had developed a vast extent of beneficial trade and industry
upon which multitudes of people in and out of China were
dependent. It was evident that to attempt then to wipe out
all the arrangements which I have described and put China
immediately upon the footing of a full member of the society
of nations unhampered in her trade, her administration and
her maintenance of order, except by the rules of international
law, would be futile and disastrous for there was no government in China competent to maintain trade, to administer
justice to foreigners, or to protect foreign life and property.
It was evident too that China must work out her own salva-
tion, that no exercise of foreign power could accomplish the
result. Four hundred and thirty million people are too great
a mass to be reformed from the outside. If China is to possess her own territory with independence and control of her
own destinies, she must learn to govern herself and to assert
and maintain her own rights as a nation.

Accordingly, the members of the Conference addressed
themselves to the task of helping China so far as it was possible in her struggle to achieve self-government. They based
their action upon a formal and unanimous agreement:

(1) To respect the sovereignty, the independence, and the territorial and administrative integrity of China;

(2) To provide the fullest and most unembarrassed opportunity to China to develop and maintain for herself an effective and stable government;

(3) To use their influence for the purpose of effectually establishing and maintaining the principle of equal opportunity for the commerce and industry of all nations throughout the territory of China;

(4) To refrain from taking advantage of conditions in China in order to seek special rights or privileges which would abridge the rights of subjects or citizens of friendly states, and from countenancing action inimical to the security of such states.

The first of these propositions stated the great objective of an independent China under international law. The second pointed out the way for the full attainment of that objective. The third reaffirmed the principle of the open door, and the fourth contained a self-denying ordinance to keep within bounds the competition of the assenting states.

Having adopted these rules of conduct, the Conference proceeded in a painstaking way to apply them to a succession of concrete cases. Anyone examining the treaties and resolutions will find that they uniformly sought a double object: first, to relieve the limitations and inconveniences flowing from the old conventional relations as far as was then practicable under the existing governmental conditions in China, and second, to afford to all sections and parties of the Chinese people a helpful incentive to unite in the establishment of an effective and stable government by making specific provisions under which such a government, competent to perform its national duties, will be the means of bringing China into the full possession of the rights and liberties assured by international law to the members of the family of nations, just as Japan has been brought into that family.

Personally I am a believer in the coming of that event. It will be a long difficult process, for it requires the new education of more than four hundred million people, but I look to

the future of that industrious, kindly, peaceable people, with
their inveterate respect for individual and family rights, not
as a yellow peril, but as a great reinforcement to the power of
ordered liberty upon the domination of which the future of
our civilization depends.

The Conference treaty relating to submarines, which is in
the way of being described as the Declaration of Washington,
was also an incident to the naval armament negotiation.

After an understanding had been reached about the respective proportions of capital ships of the five Powers, a difference developed as to the construction of submarines. Great
Britain, which had suffered more than any other Power from
the unrestricted destruction of commerce by submarines during the World War, proposed that all submarine construction be prohibited, basing the proposal upon the assertion
that the only really important function of the submarine was
as a commerce destroyer. This proposal was opposed by
Powers regarding the submarine as a useful and comparatively inexpensive instrument for coast defense against naval
attack. Everyone in the Conference condemned the use of
the submarine for the destruction of commerce as it was used
by the Germans during the war, and everyone in the Conference assented to the propriety of using submarines for
naval defense. The question was whether one view should
lead to prohibition or the other should lead to permission.
The submarine treaty was an attempt, coming strictly within
the province of a conference for the limitation of armament,
to reconcile the practical results of these two divergent views
by permitting the construction of submarines and preventing
their abuse in a way which it is hoped may prove effective.

The way in which the treaty sought to make such a prohibition effective was — First, by declaring as clearly and
definitely as possible the most important rules of existing
law for the protection of innocent life and property at sea,

through limiting the rights of warships in their treatment of vessels of commerce; Second, by an unequivocal declaration that belligerent submarines are not under any circumstances exempt from these universal rules and that if a submarine cannot capture a merchant vessel in conformity with these rules, the existing law of nations requires it to desist from attack and to permit the merchant vessel to proceed unmolested; Third, by denouncing a breach of any of these rules as a violation of the laws of war and declaring the offender liable to trial and punishment as if for an act of piracy before the civil or military authorities of any Power within the jurisdiction of which he may be found.

It will be perceived that up to this point the treaty does not undertake to make or provide for making new universal or general international law. It does four things:

It furnishes the high authority of the five great naval Powers of the world as to what the existing law is, at the same time inviting all other Powers to add to that authority by their assent.

It binds all of these five great Powers themselves to obey this law.

It establishes jurisdiction for the trial and punishment of all future violations of this law.

It classifies violations of this law with piracy.

Recall the controversy waged in Germany in the year 1916 over the question whether Germany should engage in unrestricted submarine warfare against commerce. There were two parties on opposite sides of the question and the issue for a long time appeared doubtful. The argument which apparently won the day was that such warfare was not prohibited because the rules of international law regarding visit and search and seizure were made when there were no submarines and that as submarines could not work effectually under those rules, the rules were not to be deemed applicable to them, so that unrestricted submarine warfare against commerce was no violation of international law. The general judgment of the civilized world was that the rules for the protection of innocent lives were wholly independent of the description of vessels which might undertake to regulate commerce and that no belligerent could avoid such rules by constructing ships which could not conveniently obey them. It seems highly probable that if that general judgment had been formally registered and declared before 1916, as it has been in this treaty, the decision about unlimited submarine warfare against commerce would have been the other way in Germany and the terrible destruction caused by that warfare would have been avoided.

Recall also the situation which existed after the Armistice when people were crying "Hang the Kaiser" and when the Allied countries were confronted with the fact that they could not punish the atrocious crimes committed by German officers on land and sea during the course of the war, under any jurisdiction existing at the time the offenses were committed; that is to say, they could not punish lawless violence except by lawless violence.

What I have called the third step in this treaty, the jurisdictional provision for punishment, falls in the same class of national action by international agreement as the punishment of piracy, the prevention of slave trade and the exercise of the authority vested in Congress by the Constitution of the United States (Article 1, Section 8) — "To define and punish piracies and felonies committed on the high seas and offenses against the law of Nations." The offense to be punished is against the law of nations. The sovereign authority which proposes to punish is national. The right to exercise that authority depends upon jurisdiction of the person. The place of the offense is immaterial because international law is a part of the law of the country asserting jurisdiction and is not confined to the limits of that country's own territory but extends over all the seas. The liability for these violations of international law cannot be excused by pleading the order of a superior. This is quite in accordance with the view taken by the Supreme Court of the United States that no official order of a superior officer can be superior to the law or can relieve the master of a vessel from liability for violating the law.

Perhaps this provision agreed upon by so great authority in the world may be the beginning of a system under which in general those rules of international law which express the moral sense of mankind may receive a new sanction through responsibility to law and liability to punishment of the agents through whom the rules may be violated.

It will be observed that the statement in this treaty of the rules relating to visit and search and seizure does not undertake to state all the rules of international law upon that subject. It was not intended to state all such rules. It was not intended to be a codification of international law relating to visit and search and seizure. The purpose was to state only the most important rules for the protection of innocent life so briefly and simply that every intelligent person could understand them, and to refrain from confusing the unscientific mind by the introduction of the less important details. This was required by the main consideration upon which the treaty relies for its effectiveness. The treaty is not merely a declaration of existing law. It is not merely an agreement between governments resulting from diplomatic negotiation. It is all these, but above all, it is an appeal to the public opinion of mankind to establish and maintain a fundamental rule of morals applied to international conduct in the form of a rule of international law.

We are all familiar with the assertion that international law is not really law because it has no sanction. That is only a half-truth and therefore misleading. The real sanction of international law comes from the punishing power of public opinion, a power which has been growing with great rapidity in recent years and bids fair to grow still more rapidly with the increased public participation in the conduct of foreign affairs and the constantly increasing interdependence of nations. The ordinary mode of its exercise is in control of the operations of government. The most absolutely simple exercise of it is illustrated by the effectiveness of the Chinese boycott which avails itself of no governmental action whatever. This tremendous and increasing power is not very effective as yet in support of mere governmental agreements as such, and it is not very effective in matters which are complicated and confused, which rest upon conflicting evidence and argument; but where a rule of international law is simple, easily understood and applies the moral sense of decent people the world over to human conduct, public opinion is competent to enforce that rule with tremendous effect. The advantage of having the moral sense about a particular course of conduct crystallized into a rule of law, is that it takes the subject out of the field of controversy and leaves opinion free from uncertainty. I have no doubt that the provision of this treaty which serves to put such acts as the sinking of the *Lusitania* in the same class as piracy correctly registers and formally declares the deliberate opinion of the civilized world outside of Germany and of many people in Germany, and that this formal solemn declaration of the criminal quality of the act will very greatly decrease the probability of its repetition by any nation hereafter because it will present the practical certainty of universal public condemnation which no nation can afford to incur.

This treaty takes one further step, and that is to simplify still further the whole subject by proposing a new rule of absolute prohibition against the use of submarines as commerce destroyers, and all five of the great Powers uniting in the treaty voluntarily subject themselves to the operation of that rule and at the same time ask other Powers to join them in that new rule by adhering to the treaty. This, of course, is the first step in making a new rule of international law. It follows closely the method adopted by the Powers joining in the Declaration of Paris in 1856 and in the Alabama Treaty of Washington in 1871. In that treaty of 1871, after stating the three rules regarding the duty of neutrals, to which Great Britain and the United States bound themselves, they proceed to provide for requesting the adherence of other Powers. The effect of this adoption of these three rules regarding the rights and duties of neutrals, although by only two Powers, is apparent in the subsequent conventions which have been building up international law since 1871. I think a similar effect may be anticipated from the declaration of this new rule regarding submarines by the five Powers of the Washington Conference of 1921.

Similar considerations apply to the provision of the treaty under consideration prohibiting the use of poisonous gases. That prohibition, which puts the use of poisonous gases and chemicals in the same class with the poisoning of wells, carries on in more definite and universal form a declaration contained in Article 171 of the Treaty of Versailles. That declaration was in these words:

The use of asphyxiating, poisonous, or other gases and all analogous liquids, materials, or devices being prohibited, their manufacture and importation are strictly forbidden in Germany.

This was one of the articles which was adopted by the United States in its subsequent treaties with Germany and with Austria and with Hungary, with the result that some thirty-five Powers had united in declaring that such a prohibition existed, although the article itself went no further than to impose the prohibition specifically upon Germany. The

present treaty goes a step farther and gives definite form to
the general prohibition and invites all civilized Powers to
adhere.

It will be seen from what I have said that while the Washington Conference had no concern with the making of international law, it did naturally and effectively, as incidental to
giving effect to its policy of limiting armament, take quite
important steps in the direction of developing and strengthening international law.

It took one further step by resolution providing for the
appointment of a commission to consider and report upon the
condition and requirements of international law affecting
the other new agencies of warfare which have produced so
startling an effect upon military and naval conflicts.

The time has not yet come when international affairs are
sufficiently settled to make immediately practicable a general
conference to consider, clarify, extend, and strengthen the
law of nations, but it is already high time for those who believe in a world controlled by law, to begin their preparation
for such a conference, and the Washington Conference on
Limitation of Armament, as a by-product of its own special
work, has contributed materially toward that preparation.

DEMOCRACY AND FOREIGN AFFAIRS

SPEECH AT THE BANQUET CONCLUDING THE DISCUSSIONS OF THE
INSTITUTE OF POLITICS AT WILLIAMSTOWN, MASSACHUSETTS

AUGUST 26, 1921

On July 29, 1921, the Institute of Politics opened its doors for the first time at
Williamstown, Massachusetts, under the auspices of Williams College. Its purpose
was to furnish instruction not in politics technically so-called, but in the international aspect of politics, or, in other words, the politics of foreign affairs.

Foreigners recognized as specialists in different phases of the world's work were
invited to deliver lectures. Americans of repute in their various fields met informally
around the table men and women registered for the Institute and attending its
courses.

At the end of the first session of the Institute, Mr. Root delivered the following
address.

MR. PRESIDENT, LADIES AND GENTLEMEN: I am told
that the approach of so many eminent men from various
corners of the globe, where conflicting opinions and interests
seem to portend serious conflicts, frightened Dame Nature
in the Berkshires so that she shook herself into a tremendous
storm, and uprooted your great and noble elms and tore their
mighty branches from their sides, and filled the inhabitants
of Williamstown with consternation. They have come! and
lo, the brilliant sunshine and the clear streams and the
verdant fields and forests and blue mountains rest in peace
and happiness. May it be an augury for the presently approaching future of the world.

I wish, sir, in behalf of a great body of Americans who have
not had the privilege of meeting with you, to give their
thanks to you, Mr. Garfield, for your vision and effectiveness
in conducting this Institute; to your devoted assistants, your
trustees and your faculty, who have put the resources of

this noble old institution at the service of the Institute; to the generous donor who has made it possible; and especially to the distinguished gentlemen who have taken the trouble to cross the broad Atlantic, to brave the horrors of a savage land, in order to contribute their part toward the success and effectiveness of this most extraordinary and successful meeting.

Its value cannot well be overestimated. The character of the discussion, both in your Round Tables and in your lectures, has been practical, has dealt with the actual conditions of mankind, with the concrete; and it has all been a most delightful contrast to those wildernesses of words which have ordinarily been employed in the discussion of international affairs in America in former years. Your eminence in your own countries, as well as your personal abilities, have struck the imagination of the American press, and the substance of your words has been carried to the remotest part of this great country, published in a thousand journals, commented upon in thousands of editorials. You have done that most difficult thing — you have gained a hearing upon a topic which has never until very recent years elicited the slightest interest from the people of the United States. The effect of this in itself will be very great, and as an example it will be greater still. As an earnest of the future, it is a most valuable gift that you have brought to us. Never before in the history of the world has there been so much occasion for an effort of this description. The war has left many changes, but one of the greatest is the change in the possession of power in the government of the world. The old autocracies, by their methods of conducting international affairs, practically compelled all the world to conduct their affairs in similar ways. But autocracy has passed off the stage, and now enters Democracy to rule the world.

Not only are democracies conducting the governments of

the world, not only do democracies hold in their hands the power of government, but the effect of the war has been to set free the millions of people who constitute these new governing bodies from their old habit of respect for authority in matters of opinion, to emancipate them from their old habits and customs and ways of thought and feeling and living. They demand the right of decision. They follow close upon the heels of their representatives and dictate what they shall do. Open diplomacy they demand, that we may decide. And who shall deny them? Who, subject to certain limitations imposed by common sense, wants to deny them? If the people are to rule, as they are to rule, they should know; and all the agents of government should be not only willing but insistent that the real rulers shall know.

Now the problem that all those who seek to promote a world in which peace and prosperity and noble character and opportunity for progress rest upon security and justice, have to solve, is changed completely. The old autocracies understood international affairs thoroughly, but the old autocracies were utterly selfish. The newly governing democracies are generous. They mean what is right; they are honest; they wish for peace; they abhor war, but they are most imperfectly informed. Many of them are quite oblivious to the fact that there are different backgrounds, different ways of thinking and feeling, among the peoples of other countries. It does not occur to them that a thousand years of development in another country, with another language, another literature, other customs, will have produced in the back of every man's head a set of ideas which change the value and the meaning of every word that is spoken and every act that is done.

Many of them assume that their own ideas are the ideas which ought to prevail, and which will prevail if only the world does what is right. Many of them are untrained, unin-

formed, and often misinformed. And many, many of them
are quite oblivious to the duty of acquainting themselves
with the facts of international relations and the rules that
experience has shown to be necessary in the conduct of international affairs. Many of them think that all international
affairs are simple, because they assume that these can all be
settled by adopting their idea. Many of them are quite ignorant of all the difficulties that stand in the way of reconciling the different feelings and interests and ideas of the
people of different countries.

And so in each country there is a tendency to erect an ideal
of international peace and justice and conduct evolved out
of one's own inner consciousness, like the anthropomorphic
deities of Greek mythology.

Now these plain people are our rulers, and it is they who
are to determine international questions and control the
conduct of international affairs. But there is vast disap-
pointment. They had hoped for a new and better world as
the result of the war. They find that the old passions still
sway the acts of men; that the personal, ignoble interests
control; that the clash of wits, each seeking to get the better
of the other, still goes on; and that the reaction from the
exalted virtue of great trials and tribulations is equal to the
action which it follows. And they do not know what ought
to be done, or how it ought to be done.

Now this is quite plain: If one is to sail in an airship, he
wants the builders and the crew to know their trade; and if
the democracies of the world are to control the international
affairs of civilization, they must make it their duty to learn
the business they undertake; for without that they will make
sad havoc and have to come to their lesson ultimately through
hard experience. They must learn in each country, these
plain people, the limitations upon their national rights. It
has not occurred to me that there are any material exceptions

to this rule. You will find in every country people who, in looking at the conduct of their country in its foreign relations, assume that there is only one side to every question, and that is their country's side, their own side. They must learn that they have duties as well as rights. As old Francis Lieber used to say, there can be no right without a duty. They must learn that they hold the right upon the conditions of performing the duty. They must learn that the ideal of justice is not merely justice to themselves and their wives and children, but it is justice accorded by them to others. They must learn that the ideal of liberty is not merely that they shall be free, but that they shall be willing and glad that others shall be free. They must learn to realize the rightful and unobjectionable differences between nations, and to respect the right to differ, not to treat it as cause of offense. They must learn that in international affairs, just as in family affairs and neighborhood affairs, respect for the feelings and the prejudices of others is a condition of having one's own feelings and prejudices respected. They must get rid of that feeling which exists so widely throughout the world, and which Bret Harte described, telling of a frontier village to which a stranger came, and the people looked upon him as having the moral defect of being a foreigner. They must learn to have kindly consideration and they must learn the art of mutual concession. They must become internationally minded. They must learn a broader truth, that not what a nation does for itself, but what a nation does for humanity is its title to honor and glory. They must learn that in God's good world the way to scale the heights of prosperity and happiness is not to pull down others and climb up over them, but to help all up together to united success.

This will be a long, slow process. It is not merely the difficult task of instilling knowledge into millions upon millions of minds of all degrees of capacity for receiving knowledge, but it is the slow, difficult task of moulding character, for it is a matter of character as well as a matter of knowledge. New estimates must be made of what is respectable and honorable and admirable. Human nature does not change, but human standards of conduct change. And among the plain peoples of the earth, if we are to attain to peace and justice, standards of conduct must be changed by the long, slow process which alone can accomplish this miracle. It is a matter of growth, just as the development of a tree is a matter of growth for many years. We must make the ascent from the low level of squabbling and quarreling and hatred and dislike to the level of true manhood, patient and considerate, kind and magnanimous. The curve will be so gradual that at each point the divergence from the straight line will be imperceptible.

Now how can this be done? How can this mighty change be brought about? Well, education, of course — by education. But how to educate those who are blind and cannot see, those who are deaf and cannot hear? That is the great value of what you have been doing. You probably have not been hearing any new things, you probably have not been saying any new things, but you have been putting into good intelligent form the old things which you knew long before you came here. You have tried to say a thing so that plain people could hear it, and you have been speaking to them through that great institution, the press.

The press — ah, that is the great strength of a nation! It has been doing great things on your behalf. From a thousand editorial offices every day your words have gone throughout the country, carrying on the process of education. But in the process a conflict between the old standards and the new goes on without ceasing. Misinformation goes without the corrective of adequate education, and it will lower the public standard of action. The leaders of opinion must be created, and in

that you have been doing a most useful work. Throughout
the colleges and universities of this country, and I hope of the
other countries from which you come, the printed copies of
the lectures delivered here will be widely used, and the reports of the Round Table conferences will be read by the
teachers.

Of course, you cannot in any country turn everybody into
an international lawyer or a trained diplomat. But there can
be in every community a centre of influence among the plain
people, some leader who will teach them to know the truth,
to lead the thought of his community. Every library should
have placed in it the sources of information from which the
truth about international affairs can be distributed to the
people of the community. Every high school should have a
library containing the works of those who know the truth
about international affairs, and where the pupils can study
about international affairs, and learn what they want to
know of the relations of their own nation with foreign nations;
and from these standards they will learn to be what they
want to be, powers for peace and justice.

You will perceive that this is but an extension of the
process of free government; that the same lesson has to be
learned by any race, any people who attain the blessing of
free institutions. How long and slow that process is, we all
know. We have not succeeded yet in reaching our ideal. We
have learned long ago from bitter experience that to make
men free from despotic control does not make them free from
the consequences of their ignorance. They must learn by
long and bitter experience to govern themselves. Apparent
democracy does not carry with it the assurance of honest and
efficient government. That development is acquired by slow
and hard experience. There is the rub. It is the same process as the process of attaining individual liberty under law,
which secures the recognition of the right of each person to

differ from others, while respecting the right of others to differ from him. Thus do we develop a standard for solving the questions of government. The same qualities which make a people competent for free self-government are the qualities which will make this world a world of peace and justice. There is the augury for the future. We know that men can learn the art of free self-government, and therefore they can learn the art of international peace.

The important thing is, not to be impatient, not to be discouraged because everything is not done at once as we think it ought to be. We shall all suffer, all continue to suffer, not being free from it here in this country, certainly, any more than you are free from it on the other side of the ocean. Perhaps we all have some sins to suffer for. Perhaps it is not all so unjust. But the important thing is, not to try to measure the workings of this great community of the world in the terms of our short lives. It is to observe not the conditions of the moment but the tendency of the hour — the tendency of the nations during the centuries. If ever so little they move in the right direction, then what is required is not spectacular achievement, which will make some man famous, but the steady and unresting efforts into which all of us put our lives, to be forgotten, and live only in the great result of the future.

Do not let us be discouraged. The great thing is that democracies are interested. I do not know how it is across the Atlantic, but I know here in America that in the many years that I have been observing public affairs there never has been so much interest in questions of right and wrong, what is practical and expedient and what is a people's duty, in international affairs, as to-day. I do not think this Institute would have been possible ten years ago — surely not for it to gain such a hearing. And I am enough of a believer in free self-government to be sure that, if the people will really address themselves to the subject, if they will be interested in it and apply themselves to it, they will come out all right. It is indifference that is fatal, that one does not care whether he is doing right or wrong. It is your duty to see that you are doing the right to the best of your ability, and to be clear in your own minds whether you are claiming rights which do not belong to you. There has been too much of that in the past. That is in process of being gradually done away, and done away through the first steps of the process of education. It is a new, hard lesson that the world has to learn. Mr. Choate, that fine and noble gentleman whose face was so familiar in the Berkshires, used to say: "There is nothing so painful in the world as to think." And that is the case with a great many people who do not know it. But the peoples who were competent for the war and who are competent for self-government, are going to be able to understand international questions and to deal with them.

The lessons of the war are not lost; but in the distressing circumstances which have followed it they have ceased to be felt and to be applied. The lessons of the brotherhood of man learned on the fields of France and Flanders, Italy and Poland, and the Russian frontier — the lesson of universal condemnation of ruthless and brutal greed for power; the lesson of the underlying nobility in the plain people who met there for the first time to risk and give up their lives; the beauty of service and sacrifice — these are not forgotten and they will not be. They will all remain in the consciousness of the world.

After all this petty strife and grasping have been ended, after all this selfish ambition has been forgotten, we shall recover our sense of exalted patriotism. We have all gazed from the mountain-top upon a fair land beautiful in peace and justice, and now we are wandering in the foothills, turning to the right and to the left before unexpected obstacles. But the vision is not forgotten; the impulse is not spent; the world is still seeking to regain its lost vision on the heights; the world is still seeking anxiously for the way, and it is manfully striving for that goal to which through knowledge it will slowly come.

A REQUISITE FOR THE SUCCESS OF POPULAR DIPLOMACY

ARTICLE CONTRIBUTED TO THE FIRST NUMBER OF *FOREIGN AFFAIRS*, SEPTEMBER 15, 1922[1]

THE control of foreign relations by modern democracies creates a new and pressing demand for popular education in international affairs. When the difficult art of regulating the conduct of nations toward each other, in such a way as to preserve rights and avoid offense and promote peaceful intercourse, was left to the foreign offices of the world, the public in each country could judge policies by results, and, in the various ways by which public opinion expresses itself, could reward or punish the success or failure of government. To perform that particular function it was not very important that the public should be familiar with the affairs out of which success or failure came. That condition, however, is passing away. In the democratic countries generally, the great body of citizens are refusing to wait until negotiations are over or policies are acted upon or even determined. They demand to know what is going on and to have an opportunity to express their opinions at all stages of diplomatic proceedings. This tendency is due partly to a desire to escape from certain well recognized evils in diplomacy as it has been practised. It is due in part, doubtless, to the natural disposition of democracies to revert to the conditions which existed before the invention of representative government, and thus to avoid the temporary inequalities involved in delegations of power to official representatives however selected.

[1] Reprinted with the permission of *Foreign Affairs*.

The new condition has undoubtedly been accelerated by the great war and its lessons. We have learned that war is essentially a popular business. All the people in the countries concerned are enlisted in carrying it on. It cannot be carried on without their general participation. And, whoever wins the war, all the people of all the countries involved suffer grievous consequences. There is a general conviction that there has been something wrong about the conduct of diplomacy under which peoples have so often found themselves embarked in war without intending it and without wishing for it, and there is a strong desire to stop that sort of thing. Democracies determined to control their own destinies object to being led, without their knowledge, into situations where they have no choice.

The demand for open diplomacy and contemporaneous public information, although in its application there is frequently an element of mere curiosity or news-gathering business, nevertheless rests upon the substantial basis of democratic instinct for unhampered self-government. It is incident to the awakening sense of opportunity which, among the unskilled majority, has followed the exercise of universal suffrage, the spread of elementary education, and the revelation of the power of organization. The change is therefore to be considered not as temporary but as a step in the direct line of development of democratic government, which, according to the nature of democracies, will not be retraced. The new conditions, and such developments as may grow from them, are the conditions under which diplomacy will be carried on hereafter. Of course, as in all practical human affairs, limitations and safeguards will be found necessary, but the substance will continue, and public opinion will be increasingly, not merely the ultimate judge, but an immediate and active force in negotiation.

The usefulness of this new departure is subject to one

inevitable condition. That is, that the democracy which is undertaking to direct the business of diplomacy shall learn the business. The controlling democracy must acquire a knowledge of the fundamental and essential facts and principles upon which the relations of nations depend. Without such a knowledge there can be no intelligent discussion and consideration of foreign policy and diplomatic conduct. Misrepresentation will have a clear field, and ignorance and error will make wild work with foreign relations. This is a point to which the sincere people who are holding meetings, and issuing publications in opposition to war in general, may well direct their attention if they wish to treat the cause of disease rather than the effects. Given the nature of man, war results from the spiritual condition that follows real or fancied injury or insult. It is a familiar observation that in most wars each side believes itself to be right and both pray with equal sincerity for the blessing of heaven upon their arms. Back of this there must lie a mistake. However much ambition, trade competition, or sinister personal motives of whatever kind, may have led toward the warlike situation, two great bodies of human beings, without whose consent war cannot be carried on, can never have come to two diametrically opposed genuine beliefs as to the justice of the quarrel, without one side or the other, and probably both, being mistaken about their country's rights and their country's duties. Here is the real advantage of the change from the old diplomacy to the new. Irresponsible governments may fight without being in the least degree mistaken about their rights and duties. They may be quite willing to make cannon fodder of their own people in order to get more territory or more power; but two democracies will not fight unless they believe themselves to be right. They may have been brought to their belief by misrepresentation as to facts, by a misunderstanding of rules of right conduct, or through having the blank of ignorance filled by racial or national prejudice and passion to the exclusion of inquiry and thought; but they will fight not because they mean to do wrong but because they think they are doing right. When foreign affairs were ruled by autocracies or oligarchies, the danger of war was in sinister purpose. When foreign affairs are ruled by democracies, the danger of war will be in mistaken beliefs. The world will be the gainer by the change, for, while there is no human way to prevent a king from having a bad heart, there is a human way to prevent a people from having an erroneous opinion. That way is to furnish the whole people, as a part of their ordinary education, with correct information about their relations to other peoples, about the limitations upon their own rights, about their duties to respect the rights of others, about what has happened and is happening in international affairs, and about the effects upon national life of the things that are done or refused as between nations; so that the people themselves will have the means to test misinformation and appeals to prejudice and passion based upon error.

This is a laborious and difficult undertaking. It must be begun early and continued long, with patience and persistence; but it is the very same process as that by which all the people of the great democracies have learned within their own countries to respect law and to follow wise and salutary customs in their communities, and to consider the rights of others while they assert their own rights, and to maintain orderly self-government.

It so happens that our own people in the United States have been peculiarly without that kind of education in foreign affairs. Not only have we been very busy over the development of our own country and our own institutions, but our comparatively isolated position has prevented the foreign relations of the old world from becoming matters of immediate vital interest to the American people, and they have not been interested in the subject. Naturally enough a great part of our public men have neglected to study the subject. The great body of Americans in office would study questions of transportation and tariff and internal improvements and currency because their constituents were interested in these subjects; but there was no incentive for them to study foreign affairs because their constituents were indifferent to them. The conditions are now widely different. Our people have been taught by events to realize that, with the increased intercommunication and interdependence of civilized states, all our production is a part of the world's production, and all our trade is a part of the world's trade, and a large part of the influences which make for prosperity or disaster within our own country consist of forces and movements which may arise anywhere in the world beyond our direct and immediate control. I suppose that the people of the United States have learned more about international relations within the past eight years than they had learned in the preceding eighty years. They are, however, only at the beginning of the task.

The subject is extensive and difficult, and a fair working knowledge of it, even of the most general kind, requires long and attentive study. Underlying it are the great differences in the modes of thought and feeling of different races of men. Thousands of years of differing usages, under different conditions forming different customs and special traditions, have given to each separate race its own body of preconceived ideas, its own ways of looking at life and human conduct, its own views of what is natural and proper and desirable. These prepossessions play the chief part in determining thought and action in life. Given two groups of men, each having a different inheritance of custom and tradition, and each will have a different understanding of written and spoken words, of the reasons for conduct and the meaning of conduct, and each will to a very considerable degree fail to understand the other. Neither can judge the other by itself. If the instinctive occidental reformer and the instinctive oriental fatalist are to work together, they must make biological studies of each other. Add to these differences the selfish passions which have not yet been bred out of mankind, and there inevitably follow in the contacts of international intercourse a multitude of situations which cannot be solved so long as the men of any one nation assume that the rest of the world is going to think and feel as they themselves do and to act accordingly.

The organization of independent nations, which has followed the disappearance of the Holy Roman Empire, is in the main the outgrowth of that progress in civilization which leads peoples to seek the liberty of local self-government according to their own ideas. Whatever may be the form of local governments, there can be no tyranny so galling as the intimate control of the local affairs of life by foreign rulers who are entirely indifferent to the local conceptions of how life ought to be conducted. National independence is an organized defense against that kind of tyranny. Probably the organization of nations is but a stage of development, but it is the nearest that mankind has yet come toward securing for itself a reasonable degree of liberty with a reasonable degree of order.

It is manifest that the differences of thought and feeling and selfish desire which separate nations in general, have to be dealt with in particular in the multitude of controversies which are sure to arise between them and between their respective citizens in a world of universal trade and travel and inter-communication. The process of such adjustment without war is the proper subject of diplomacy. During some centuries of that process many usages have grown up which have been found necessary or convenient for carrying on friendly intercourse, and many of these have hardened into generally accepted customs in manners or in morals which no longer require to be discussed but which every nation has a right to assume that other nations will observe. Many rules of right conduct have been accepted and universally agreed upon as law to govern the conduct of nations. In England and America, these rules of international law are authoritatively declared to be a part of the municipal law of the country enforceable by the courts. In this way the nations founded upon differences have been gradually rescuing from the field of difference and controversy, and transferring to the field of common understanding and agreement, one subject after another of practical importance in the affairs of the world. The process is in the direction of that unity of thought and feeling, the absence of which hitherto has caused the failure of all schemes and efforts for the unity of mankind. The study of international relations means not only study of some particular controversy, but study of this long history of the process of adjustment between differing ideas, and of the prejudices and passions and hitherto irreconcilable differences which have baffled adjustment and which affect the relations and probable conduct of the nations concerned. All these are in the background of every international question and are often of vital importance to its right understanding.

The process I have described has created a community of nations. That community has grown just as communities of natural persons grow. Men cannot live in neighborhood with each other without having reciprocal rights and obligations toward each other arising from their being neighbors. The practical recognition of these rights and obligations creates the community. It is not a matter of contract. It is a matter of usage arising from the necessities of self-protection.

It is not a voluntary matter. It is compelled by the situation.
The neighbors generally must govern their conduct by the
accepted standards, or the community will break up. It is
the same with nations. No nation whose citizens trade and
travel — that is to say, no nation which lives in neighborhood with other nations — need consider whether or not it
will be a member of the community of nations. It cannot
help itself. It may be a good member or a bad member, but
it is a member by reason of the simple fact of neighborhood
life and intercourse. The Bolshevik rulers of Russia are illustrating this. They have been trying to repudiate all the
obligations resulting from their country's membership in the
community of nations, and one result is that intercourse is
impossible.

This great fact of the community of nations is not involved
at all in any question about the "League of Nations" or any
other association of nations founded upon contract. The
"League of Nations" is merely a contract between the signers
of the instrument by which they agree to superadd to the
existing usages, customs, laws, rights, and obligations of the
existing community of nations, certain other rights and obligations which shall bind the signers as matter of contract.
Whether a country enters into that contract or not, its membership of the community of nations continues with all the
rights and obligations incident to that membership.

A self-respecting democracy which undertakes to control
the action of its government as a member of this community
of nations, and which wishes to respond fairly and fully not
only to the demands of its own interests but to the moral
obligations of a member of the community, is bound to try
to understand this great and complicated subject, so that it
may act not upon prejudice and error but upon knowledge
and understanding.

There is one specially important result which should follow

from such a popular understanding of foreign affairs. That is, a sense of public responsibility in speech and writing; or perhaps it would be better stated as a public sense of private responsibility for words used in discussing international affairs. More fights between natural persons come from insult than from injury. Under our common law, libel was treated as a crime, not because of the injury which it did to the person libeled, but because it tended to provoke a breach of the peace. Nations are even more sensitive to insult than individuals. One of the most useful and imperative lessons learned by all civilized governments in the practice of international intercourse, has been the necessity of politeness and restraint in expression. Without these, the peaceful settlement of controversy is impossible. This lesson should be learned by every free democracy which seeks to control foreign relations.

It cannot, however, be expected that every individual in a great democracy will naturally practise restraint. Political demagogues will seek popularity by public speeches full of insult to foreign countries, and yellow journals will seek to increase their circulation by appeals to prejudice against foreigners. Hitherto these have been passed over because the speakers and writers were regarded as irresponsible; but, if the democracy of which the speakers and publishers are a part is to control international intercourse, that irresponsibility ends, and it is the business of the democracy to see to it that practices by its members which lead directly toward war are discouraged and condemned. Offenses of this character are frequently committed in this country by political speakers and sensational newspapers; and because we are a great nation the expressions used become known in the other countries concerned, and cause resentment and bitter feeling. What especially concerns us is that these are very injurious offenses against our own country. Such public expressions by our own citizens bring discredit upon our country and injure its business and imperil its peace. They answer to the description of crime in the old indictments as an act "against the peace and dignity" of the State. They will practically cease whenever the American public really condemns and resents them so that neither public office nor newspaper advertising or circulation can be obtained by them. That will come when the American public more fully understands the business of international intercourse, and feels a sense of the obligations which it incurs by asserting the right to control the conduct of foreign relations.

THE EDUCATION OF DEMOCRACY IN FOREIGN AFFAIRS

SPEECH IN THE COMMITTEE ON FOREIGN RELATIONS AND
NATIONAL DEFENSE OF THE NATIONAL CIVIC FEDERATION,
WASHINGTON, JANUARY 17, 1923

JUDGE Parker [1] and I belong to different parties but we are in the same *bloc*.

I welcomed with a great deal of enthusiasm the proposal to form this Committee, with its special object, when Mr. Easley came to me with a letter from Judge Parker about it and I agreed cheerfully to become a member of the Committee, although I am afraid I cannot render very much service, and, as a reward for my sympathy, the Judge and Mr. Easley have asked me to make a speech.

I understand this Committee to be organized for a specific purpose: as one of the results of the conference of last November, — not as a repetition of that conference but as one of its results, — the outgrowth of the patriotic effort coming from the impulse given by a conference of that kind. Unless it does communicate power to the hearts and minds of the people taking part in it, the kind of power that results in action, such a conference amounts to nothing. One of the results of that conference is the organization of this Committee. I understand the Committee to have one general, but limited, purpose and that is to devise and put into operation means for educating the people of the United States in the fundamentals of international relations. That is something very much needed.

[1] Alton B. Parker, Democratic candidate for the presidency of the United States in 1904.

People of the United States have not bothered themselves much about international relations. From the time we swung away from the habits of thought of the old Colonial times, with the passing of the generation that had been concerned in the intimate action and reaction of mother countries and colonies, the people of the United States became absorbed in their own home affairs. They were pushing after and conquering the Continent, building up a great nation. And down to the time of the Spanish War it was not worth the while for any public officer of the United States to familiarize himself with foreign affairs, unless it was the Secretary of State. If a man wanted to be a Congressman or a Senator, and to acquire the universal approval and gratitude of his countrymen by being in Congress, he did not bother himself about foreign affairs, because his constituents did not care about them. He would study tariff questions and currency questions and immigration questions and transportation questions, because his constituents were interested in them, but he had not any time to spend over foreign affairs, because knowledge about them would not help him along at all, with the result that with all our vast machinery of education, our great system of education, continually growing, foreign affairs have been let alone.

And now we are brought into immediate and inevitable contact with them, and the whole people of the United States have taken charge of the conduct of foreign affairs, and everybody is expressing opinions about them, and a very large part of the discussion is carried on on a basis of insufficient knowledge. There are — I am keeping myself within bounds in the statement, I think, when I say there are some people in the United States who lack humility. There are some people who think they know it all when they know very little. There are many people who think they can solve all the great problems of international affairs by evolving schemes out of their own consciousness. And I have been much interested, being in the way of seeing and knowing about ever so many of these schemes, to see how uniformly they settle everything international, except the difficulties. And they are in perfect good faith, because the men who get them up don't know the difficulties exist. They not only don't understand them — they don't know they exist.

Now one of the great troubles in life is a lack of understanding by men of each other. We give but little thought to the part played in the affairs of life by habit, habits of thought and feeling and action.

There are a lot of Republicans and Democrats in this room. Why? How many of you are Republican except because you were born and brought up Republican; and how many of you are Democrats except because you were born and brought up Democrats? Of course it could not be for any other reason.

Now in every country on earth there is a set of traditions, of modes of thought and feeling and action, a set of conceptions of what is right, proper, appropriate, and decent, a set of conceptions as to what constitutes liberty, what constitutes right as between man and man, and the inheritance of those traditions and modes of thought, of feeling and judgment, in the back of every man's head constitutes more than one half of his motives of action in the present.

I have often seen discussions of questions between men of different races. It is not necessary to go so far as to a question between an Occidental and an Oriental. It is not necessary to go so far as that; but in discussions between people of the western nations of Europe, I have seen four fifths of the time taken up by discussion resulting from the fact that neither one understood what the other one had in the back of his head; and when they once had finally got to a common understanding the discussion was ended. Those differences color and affect the understanding of every word that is spoken and written.

The judgment of the purposes of others in their action, the judgment as to the probability of future action, lies back of all international affairs and of all international controversies.

Now knowledge of the history of those differences and the prejudices that spring from them, and the convictions of right and wrong in practical affairs that grow from them, is essential to a just understanding of the problems that are presented for determination by the people of America in their international relations; and the people of America as a whole know very little about them. How could they? Where are they taught? Of course there are journals — for the last sixteen or seventeen years there has been a most admirable journal of international law published, with a couple of thousand subscribers, one of the best journals anywhere in the world, full of information, but only a couple of thousand subscribers. It goes into the libraries. A man who knows how can find it. But how about the hundred million, the hundred and nine million that never heard of it? There is a journal, a quarterly review of international affairs, called "Foreign Affairs," just started this last summer. It was begun most admirably. It is adapted to give most useful information, but if they can get five or six thousand subscribers they will be making a tremendous success; and how about the other hundred and nine million? And those things go over the head. They go over the head of the man on the street. They could not even crawl down the chimney of a district schoolhouse. They are so far up.

There are many things in our monthly magazines and in our newspapers, but there is such a great mass, and the articles on foreign affairs are part of the enormous mass of material which the ordinary plain American citizen does not plow through; and the thing is to get some system by which we can get the fundamental facts about foreign affairs — the facts that it is necessary to know, in order to discuss any of the living questions of foreign relations intelligently — into the minds of the people who vote, the people who constitute the great democracy that is going to settle those questions.

I am bound to say that a great deal of the discussion that goes on about foreign affairs seems to me to proceed upon the basis of ignorance of all the premises from which one can usefully reason, regarding foreign affairs. Now this business of educating people about this new field: People are perfectly competent to learn it. Do not let us make any mistake about that. It is very much the same problem as that of learning the fundamentals of civil liberty, or self-government, very much the same, and people who are competent to do one are competent to do the other, but we have been studying the problem of self-government for three hundred years, and we have not got through yet.

We are learning; we are learning something every day about how to govern ourselves. Sometimes we do too little, and sometimes we do too much, and we do not know why it is too little, or it is too much, but we are all the time learning lessons.

Now that has come to be comparatively simple, because there are a great many people competent to teach; I mean there are a great many competent leaders of opinion, so that if a man has not thought much about such subjects, and is a little puzzled, he can strike somebody within a few rods who has thought about it and who can tell him things. We have leaders of opinion very competent to teach in matters of self-government; but we have not competent teachers in matters of foreign affairs, dealing with these strange animals that inhabit other countries. We know as little about them as I know about trading a horse or a dog or a parrot. They are strange because they differ from us. It does not follow that they are inferior to us or we are superior to them. It is because they are different, and they have the same problems toward us that we have toward them, and in order to get on in the world in which democracies control foreign affairs, democracies have got to get busy and learn the business.

It is the most difficult thing in the world to get into the human mind.

We make speeches; even this speech of mine will not go very far. I do not think more than fifty million people out of one hundred and ten million will memorize it. We write articles and print them in magazines, in pamphlets. We increase the trade in waste paper baskets immensely. Only five per cent of the power stored in coal is utilized in the steam locomotive. If we can get that — that is ever so much; but what is utilized from the output of magazine articles and newspaper articles and pamphlets and speeches? Ever so much less. If you can get, not five per cent, but one tenth of one per cent of the power that is in them utilized by getting it into the minds of the people they are intended for, you are doing very well.

Douglas Fairbanks came in to see me a few years ago over at The Hague. He had just come from London where people had given a tremendous reception to Mary Pickford — tremendous. And Fairbanks was very interesting. The lesson that he brought from that experience was that the film had opened a new means of access to the human mind. He said, "Here were tens of thousands of people, hundreds of thousands, who could not be reached by speech or by the written or by the printed word, but somehow the film had gone through the eye into their brains and disturbed them." Now there is a great deal of food for thought in that.

But our subject here is one that you cannot very well utilize for films. The question is how to get these fundamental ideas about foreign relations into the minds of the great mass of the American democracy, and I take it the first object of this Committee is to try to devise a means to do it — how to do it. And the second is, go to work and give effect, operate those means. I take it the Committee is not to advocate or oppose. It is not to constitute itself an agency for any reform or any movement of any kind. It is to do something else, and that is to find a way to enlarge the knowledge and understanding of the uncontroverted facts upon which necessarily rests all useful discussion of questions of foreign relations.

Now let us confine ourselves to that purpose. Do not let us go on trying to do anything else. You have got to train a lot of teachers to train others. It is going to be a long and difficult work. It is not something on which Judge Parker and Mr. Easley can make a final report next month, nor next year, nor the next generation. It is a long task. But somebody had to begin it. A lot of people are trying to begin it. The idea here is that the Civic Federation has united so many different elements and different points of view, that perhaps they could strike out some methods of doing this thing, of which other people had not thought. The Civic Federation was organized in order to include different points of view. That was its purpose, and it fits the spirit of that Federation to start a movement which is designed to carry truth into many minds, having many different points of view. And that is what has got to be done here.

I think that covers about what I have to say, except this: That the entrance of democracy upon the field of foreign affairs, the manifest purpose of the great body of voters in democratic countries to be themselves directly the agents who carry on the foreign affairs of their countries, involves a terrible danger as well as a great step in human progress — a great step in progress if the democracy is informed; a terrible danger if the democracy is ignorant. An ignorant democracy controlling foreign affairs leads directly to war and the destruction of civilization. An informed democracy insures peace and the progress of civilization. The question we are trying to deal with goes down to the very foundation of future civilization. If prejudice and passion and ignorant whim are to control the foreign affairs of the world, then civilization is bound to come to an end. If a democracy is going to control foreign affairs without any sense of responsibility, without any such sense of responsibility as comes from studying the subject, then peaceful relations will become impossible; discord, conflict, war, destruction, will inevitably follow. You can pick up a newspaper almost any morning and see accounts of how somebody who ought to know better is endeavoring either to gratify himself or to ingratiate himself with a prejudiced audience by abuse and insult of some foreign nation, by the use of language, which if it were employed in the intercourse between man and man within our own country, would lead to an immediate breach of the peace. Now the trouble is that the men who are guilty of that kind of language in public speech and public writing never have had brought home to them any sense of responsibility as members of a democracy to keep the peace. More fights come from insult than from injury. More wars come from international feeling because of a belief of insult and humiliation than come from any mere material thing, as a rule; not always, but as a rule. The material interests of a discussion which brings about war are seldom of the slightest consequence compared with the very first day's material expense in carrying on the war. The wars come in the main because of an excited feeling caused by apprehension of injury or by a sense of insult, and you see the members of our democracy utterly oblivious to the idea that, by taking part in foreign affairs, they become subject to any responsibility whatever. People have got to learn that. And they cannot successfully conduct or control their foreign affairs until they have learned it. When they have learned it, I think it will cease to be popular for a man to insult other nations in public, just as it has ceased to be popular for a man to insult another man in public.

Now, the first problem, I think, is, can we devise some way of getting the fundamental groundwork for judgment and discussion upon foreign affairs into the minds of the American people — a widespread system — if we can devise it. And the second thing is to go ahead and do it.

HOW TO INTEREST DEMOCRACY IN
FOREIGN AFFAIRS

REMARKS IN THE EXECUTIVE COMMITTEE OF THE COMMITTEE
OF ONE HUNDRED ON FOREIGN RELATIONS, NATIONAL CIVIC
FEDERATION, NEW YORK, MARCH 1, 1923

THE primary purpose of the Committee of One Hundred
is to get into the hands of the American people a series of
noncontroversial facts to which everyone would agree but
which nine tenths of the people of the United States do not
know — facts which form the necessary basis of all sound
reasoning upon international affairs and which will enable
them to form opinions upon controversial questions arising. . . .

With regard to the proposed Committee on Collection of
Facts and Preparation of Material, there are just three
things important and they constitute a great task.

One is to interpret the existing material to the people who
have not the time, the training, or the knowledge to interpret it for themselves. There is an enormous mass of material. Dr. James Brown Scott has worked for many years,
as the head of the Division of International Law of the Carnegie Endowment for International Peace, in having a great
mass of elementary facts set forth by approved writers, in
having the documents which are important in international
affairs translated and republished in order that they might
be placed in all the libraries of the country. Look in any
library of the United States and you will find it supplied
with that material which previously was not available. Dr.
Nicholas Murray Butler is at the head of another department

of that institution which goes by the name of the American Association for International Conciliation and which has printed in little pamphlets in octavo form, sent out by the million, all sorts of information — international agreements, speeches by important persons all over the world, et cetera.

All this material constitutes an enormous mass but the man on the street is not getting anything out of them. He can read them but they make no impression on his mind because he cannot interpret them. The thing is to get all this interpreted and put into such simple shape that the clerk in the dry goods store, the bookkeeper in the bank, the man who is working in the iron mill or the mine, the farmer and the brakeman on the railroad, can understand it. They are the people who vote. They are going to determine what is to be done in international affairs and need certain elementary data regarding national rights and, more important still, national duties and, what is also quite important for all of us, national manners. And the question now is about getting a committee that will do what the bee does with the flowers — produce honey.

Then, the next thing is to get the means by which this information, these simple lessons drawn from the facts we have at hand, can be gotten into the minds of our people — some way of cutting down the economic loss in the millions, billions, and trillions of words precipitated upon the world today, which is frightful.

Now, each head of a great organization, a number being represented here, has special means of access to a multitude of minds. That is the significance of the representation of these great organizations in the Committee of One Hundred. But it is all going to cost money.

So, there are the three things: (1) To distill useful information; (2) To convey it to the mind; and (3) To get the money to pay the expense. That is a big enough job for anybody.

I should say the first thing necessary is to enable the people to understand the meaning of the facts and to reason from the facts they see stated about the rights and duties of their own country for, after all, that is what all of the people are concerned about. That is what they have to vote upon. They have to keep the President in or put him out; to keep the congressmen and senators in or put them out, according as those officers have done or not done what they ought to do. In order to know whether they have or not, the people should have some sort of idea as to what those officers ought to do.

I think the fundamental thing at the start is to set forth the correct idea of what a nation is. The whole subject is colored by that. It is not merely a matter of individuals discussing what is wise or right or expedient. That comes in the idea of a nation and that is practical. They need information upon the difference between a nation and internationalism. You have the Third Internationale, the Bolshevik organization; then we have all these nations. What is the character of what we call a nation? My conception is that a nation is the expression of that necessity for liberty which consists of the right and opportunity for local self-government. That is the sharp line of distinction between the organization of the civilized world in nations and the proposed organization of the world by the Internationalists under which all the world will be governed as one organization — not the existing organization of nations. If they are all governed as one, there will be no local self-government. The central power will be in control. On the other hand, the organization of nations is the assertion of the right of the various communities and groups of people in this, that, and the other tract of territory to be governed in accordance with their own conception of what is right and just and fair and seemly and moral. That is not for someone else to decide. There are a multitude of ideas all over the world but the most galling tyranny is for a community to be governed by what some foreigner thinks is right. The most essential right of liberty is that the community shall be governed in accordance with its own conceptions.

That is the basis of the organization of nations and the fundamental idea upon which all these facts should be interpreted. From that you can go on to what are the necessary incidents to this national right — of local government. What we call independence is the same thing as the individual right of liberty. That carries something with it. It is the right to do certain things according to one's own will — the right to eat mutton or beef, as you choose, if you can get it; the right to send your children to the kind of school you prefer; to marry the woman you want to marry, if she is willing. But each man's liberty is limited by the precisely equivalent right of every other man.

National independence, like individual liberty, requires, as an essential, freedom from other people's domination, from other people's interference with the conduct of life. Our country, in asserting its own independence, is bound to assert the independence of other countries and not interfere with them. If they want to wear red, white, and blue hats or green or yellow hats, it is none of our business. The duty to respect independence places a limit upon what we can and ought to do with regard to the affairs of others, and what we will permit them to do regarding our affairs.

In the long course of the growth of civilization, there have developed certain ways in which nations can help one another — certain good offices, mediation, conciliation, arbitration, various forms of compulsion, justified only when the nation exercising it does so in asserting its rights; and then it has only the right to assert its own. That should be explained in such a way as to accompany it with something that will point out the practical bearings it has upon the affairs of to-day. Take, for instance, this: A lot of people wanted us to stop France from going into the Ruhr. We have no more right to do that than France would have to come over here and make us naturalize the Japanese. Many people who realized that wanted us to mediate between Germany and France. We had no right to do that unless they were willing; and an inquiry was made, apparently, to ascertain whether they were and it seemed that they were not. That ended it. That stopped us unless we were willing to violáte rights of France and Germany which we would not permit them to violate in our case.

Those are simple things which are quite lost sight of by most people when thinking on these subjects. And you can show what vital and fundamental principles are involved in this and that problem. It is a fascinating sort of thing and it ought to be worked out and put on paper, and then submitted to criticism and suggestion, and perfection. When you get that, you can put your lessons in simple, pertinent and intelligible form such as that of a leading editorial, always pointing out with your lesson in some simple way the bearing it has upon practical affairs.

INDEX

INDEX

Adams, John, quoted, 85, 86, 310.

Adatci, Mineichiro, 335 n., 395.

Admission to the Bar, matter of moral character of applicants for, 148, 149; problem of foreign applicants for, 149 ff.

Alaskan boundary, 36, 412.

Algeciras Conference, 257, 439.

Altamira, Rafael, 327, 335 n., 372, 373, 383, 395.

Alverstone, Richard Webster, Lord, 130.

American Academy of Arts and Letters, address on J. R. Lowell to, 58.

American Bar Association, address to Judicial Section of, 135 ff.; and legal education, 141 ff.; 114,

American Judicature Society, 163.

American Law Institute, address at meeting to organize, 158 ff.

American Society of International Law, addresses to; on the Permanent Court of International Justice, 391–405; on international law after the war, 427–445; on the Washington Conference on limitation of armament, 452–468.

"Americanization," 226.

Anderson, Colonel (Pittsburgh), 53, 56.

"Annapolis meeting, the," 82.

Arbitration, of international disputes, always favored by United States, 254, 305 ff., 440, 441.

Arbitration, Court of, set up by Hague conferences, 255.

Art in the United States in 1870, 105, 106.

Arthur, Chester A., President, 254.

Bacon, Robert; introduction to J. B. Scott's life of, 93–98; letter of instruction to, on his mission to South America, 315–319; 169.

Bacon, Mrs. Robert, 97.

Balfour, Arthur J., Earl, 42, 408, 409.

Balkan Wars, the, 257, 439.

Banks, and the government, 208.

Bar, the, duty of, in leading public opinion, 115, 116, and in respect to legal education, 144 ff. And see Admission to the bar, American Bar Association.

Bar Association of the City of New York, Fiftieth Anniversary of, 111 ff.

Barnes, W. H. L., 17.

Bellows, Henry W., 99.

Benson, Egbert, 78.

Bertron, S. R., 248.

Bethmann-Hollweg, Theobald T. F. A. von, 428.

Bevilaque, Clovis, 327, 335 n.

Bible, the, 39.

Billings, John S., 57.

Bismarck, Count Otto von, 100.

Bixby, Mrs., Lincoln's letter to, 68.

Blodgett, William T., 109.

Bolshevism in Russia, 223 ff.

Borah, William E., Senator, 424 and n.

Boston, strike of police in, 127, 128.

Bourgeois, Léon V. A., 252, 266, 408, 409.

Boxer uprising (1900), 38, 458.

Boyhood and Youth of Joseph Hodges Choate, 46 and n.

Bradley, Dan, 78.

Brest-Litovsk, treaties of, 170 n.

Bristol, Eli, 78.

Bryant, W. C., 99, 101.

Bryce, James, Viscount, 256.

Buchanan, William I., 295.

Bucharest, Peace of, forced upon Roumania, 170 n.

Burke, Edmund, 66, 175.

Burnham, Daniel H., 233 and n.

Bustamente, Antonio S. de, 376 and n.

Butler, Nicholas Murray, 316, 321, 498.

Cadwalader, John L., 57.

Carnegie, Andrew, address on, 49–57; his *Autobiography*, 49, 50 n.; *The Gospel of Wealth*, 50 n.; trusts, etc., founded by, 54–57; 315, 404.

Carnegie Corporation, and its trustees, 56.

Carnegie Endowment for International Peace, 55, 315–323.

Carnegie Foundation for the Advancement of Teaching, 54, 141, 142.

Carnegie Hero Fund, 55.

Cavour, Count Camillo de, 100.

Cecil, Lord Robert, 252, 409.

Central-American Court of Justice, 55.

Century Association, addresses before: on Roosevelt, 3; on J. H. Choate, 43; Seventy-fifth Anniversary of, 99 ff.

Chatham, William Pitt, Earl of, 66, 175.

Chicago, "White City," at, 233, 234.

China, threatened partition of, 37; the open door, 37, 38, 459; status of, in Washington Conference, 454 ff.; revolution in (1911), 459, 460.

Chinese civilization report on, 455.

Choate, George, 47.

Choate, George C. S., 47.

Choate, Joseph H., addresses on, 17–48; offices held by, and honors conferred on, 18, 24, 43; 57, 169, 178, 185, 295.

Choate, Joseph H., Jr., 17.

Choate, Rufus, 20, 28, 29.

Choate, William G., 47.

City-planning, 238 ff.

Civil War, J. R. Lowell and the aftermath of, 60; reaction from political effects of, 90, 91.

Clark, Erastus, 78.

Clark, John Bates, 316.

Clayton-Bulwer Treaty, abrogated, 37.

Cleveland, Grover, President, his Venezuela message, 35; introduction to McElroy's life of, 88–92; 254.

Clinton, George, 77, 82, 83, 84.

Code Napoleon, 162.

Colleges in United States, democracy of, 152, 153.

Comfort, George F., 107.

Committee of Seventy, the, 24.

Conferences, international, provided for by League of Nations Covenant, 438, 439.

Congress, sole qualification for election to, in 1918, 188; importance of electing Republicans to, during the War, 199–201.

Congress, Sixty-sixth, the, 213.

Conkling, Roscoe, 135.

Constitution of United States, Hamilton and, 83; status of, after the Civil War, 115; Anniversary of signing of, 121 ff.

Constitutional Convention of 1787, 82, 83.

Continental Congress, 81.

Cooper, J. Fenimore, 101.

Coudert, Frederic R., 399.

Cox, James M., 277, 282, 284, 285.

Criticism, effect of, on conduct of the War, 171.

Cuba, 36.

Davies, Julien, 111, 113.

Davis, George B., 295.

De Forest, Emily J., 109.

De Forest, Robert, 109.

Dean, James, 78.

Decisions of courts in United States, multiplicity of reports of, 159, 160.

Descamps, Baron, 325, 327, 365, 367, 368, 369, 370, 379, 386, 395.

Diplomacy, Popular paper on, 479–486.

Disraeli, Benjamin, 100.

Douglas, Stephen A., 72.

Drago, Señor, 327, 335 and n.

Drummond, Sir Eric, Secretary-General of the League of Nations, letters of, 326, 327; 336.

Dumas, Alexandre, 31.

Dunfermline Trust, established by Carnegie, 52, 53, 54.

Durand, Asher B., 99.

Easley, Ralph B., 489, 495.

Education in America, 39.

Edwards, Augustine, 409.

Eliot, Charles W., 57, 317.

Eliot, John, 175.

Emancipation Proclamation, the 64, 73, 74.

Emerson, R. W., 101.

English-speaking peoples, solidarity of, 61, 62, 66, 67, 131, 174 ff.

Estournelles de Constant, Baron d', 317.

Europe, American interest in affairs of, 262 ff., 275–277.

Evarts, William M., 28, 30, 32.

Evarts, Southmayd and Choate, 17.

Fairbanks, Charles W., Vice-President, 36, 412.

Fairbanks, Douglas, 494.

Federalist, the, 83.

Fernandez, Raoul, 335 n., 395.

Fiume, 273.

Foch, Ferdinand, Marshal, 42.

Foot, Moses, 78.

Foreign Affairs, education and interest of Democracy in, 489–502.

Foreign Affairs (magazine), paper on Popular Democracy in, 479–488; 492.

Four-Power Treaty, the, (Washington Conference), 454.

Franklin, Benjamin, 39, 66, 175, 310.

Frémont, John C., 25.

Fromageot, M., 327, 335 n.

Gardner, Augustus P., 200.

Garibaldi, Giuseppe, 100.

Garrick, David, 44.

George III, 133.

Germany, attitude of, in Feb., 1918, 170; armistice and treaties with Russia, 170 n., 171; domination of, means death of liberty, 179; and Russia, 179, 187; and the Ukraine, 189.

Gladstone, William E., 14, 100.

Gold, Thomas R., 78.

Goodwin, Judge, 146.

Grant, Ulysses S., President, 254.

Gray, George, 401.

Gray, Morris, 232 and n., 235.

Great Britain, J. H. Choate, Ambassador to, 18, 27, 35–39; value of his service to people of, 38, 39; J. R. Lowell, Minister to, 59; and the United States, bond between, 131, 132, 175, 176.

Grey, Sir Edward (Viscount), 257, 409, 439.

Hagerup, Francis, 335 n., 346, 355, 359, 375, 395.

Hague, The, Peace Palace at, 55.

Hague Conference, First (1899), 308, 310, 311.

Hague Conference, Second (1907), 18, 39–41; adopts plan for international court, 255; Latin-American states represented in, 295; Instructions to American Delegates to, 295–314; Russian programme for, 296, and suggestions of divers governments concerning it, 297; failure of attempt to establish international court, 395, 396, 417.

Haig, Sir Douglas (Earl), 98.

Hale, Chandler, 314.

Hale, Edward Everett, 157.

Hamilton, Alexander, address on, 76–87; Champion of the Constitution, 82 ff.; 39.

Hamilton College, statue of Hamilton presented to, 76; history of, 76 ff.; first trustees of, 78.

Hampden, John, 175.

Harding, Warren G., President, 210, 277, 283, 284, 285, 424, 425, 426, 440, 441.

Harrison, Benjamin, President, 254.

Harvard, John, 39.

Hawaii, 37.

Hawthorne, Nathaniel, 48, 101.

Hay, John, Secretary of State, arbitration treaties negotiated by, 306; 36, 37, 57, 296, 459.

Hays, Will H., letter of, to Root, 250; letter of Root to, on the League of Nations, 251–268.

Herschel, Farrar, Baron, 36, 412.

Hicks, Congressman, 207.

Higginson, Henry L., 57.

Hill, David B., Senator, 33.

Hill, David Jayne, 295, 458.

Holmes, O. W., 101.

Hopkins, Sewal, 78.

Hughes, Charles E., Secretary of State, 25, 446.

Huntington, Daniel, 99.

Ice-patrol of North Atlantic, 438.

Individual liberty, surrendered during the war, how to be recovered, 206 ff.

International law, fundamental ideas of, 432; in the Washington Conference, speech on, 452–468; sanction of, 465, 466.

International Postal Union, 438.

Internationalism, development of, 430; in Russia, 430, 431, 433.

Irving, Washington, 101.

Isthmian canal, an, 36, 37.

Jay Treaty, the, 85.

Jefferson, Thomas, President, 233, 243 n., 262, 310.

John, King, 175.

Johnston, John T., 109.

Joint High Commission, on questions between Canada and the United States, 36, 412.

Jusserand, Jules J., 13.

Justinian, 162.

Kahn, Julius, 200.

Kent, William, 161.

Kiaochow, 273.

Kinley, Dr., 319.

Kirkland, Samuel, 77, 78, 79.

Knox, Philander S., Secretary of State, 251, 255, 269, 286, 441.

Labor, organized, in United States, dictatorship of, 226 ff.

Lancashire, workmen of, and Lincoln, 67, 173, 174.

Lang, Cosmo Gordon, Archbishop of York, speech at meeting in honor of, 173 ff.

Lansing, John, 78.

Lansing, Robert, Secretary of State, and President Wilson, 221, 247.

Lapradelle, M. de, 325, 335 n., 344, 346, 364, 365, 379, 386, 395.

Lardy, M., 405.

League to Enforce Peace, the, 255.

League of Nations, organization and development of, 435 ff.; and the United States, 438 ff.; community of nations not involved in, 486.

　　Covenant of, and the United States Senate, 217 ff.; Root's proposed amendments to, 248–250, and letters concerning, to W. H. Hays, 251–268, and H. C. Lodge, 269–277; speech to National Republican Club on, 277–294.

　　Article VIII, IX, 257, 258, 266, 267, 268; X, 219, 220, 265, 266, 270, 271, 272, 273, 274, 275, 286 ff., 292, 293; XI, 258; XII, 258, 351, 355; XIII, 259, 351, 352, 355; XIV, 260, 355; XV, 257, 259; XVI, 258; XIX, 257, 258, 266, 267, 268; XXV, 259. And see Permanent Court of International Justice.

Legal education, address on standard of, 141 ff.

L'Enfant, Pierre C., 243 and n.

Lenin, Nicholas, 128, 224, 228, 430.

Library-building in Great Britain and America (Carnegie), 56.

Lieber, Francis, 141.

Limitation of armament, attitude of United States toward, in 1907, 301–303.

Limitation of armament, Washington Conference on, speech on submarines and poisonous gases, 447–451; general nature of the Conference, 452, 453.

Lincoln, Abraham, addresses on, 63–75; the Second Inaugural, 67, 68, 172; and the workmen of Lancashire, 67, 173, 174; and Hamilton, 80; quoted, 171; speech at dinner on his birthday, 202 ff.; 39, 50, 60, 148, 149, 152, 173,

186, 187. And *see* Emancipation Proclamation.

Loder, Dr., 325, 327, 335 n., 358, 374, 377, 379, 383, 385, 395.

Lodge, H. C., Senator, letter of Root to, 269–277; 252, 446.

Lohman, M., 405.

London, address presenting Saint-Gaudens's statue of Lincoln in, 63 ff.

London, Conference of (Balkan Wars), 439.

Longfellow, H. W., 101.

Louis Philippe, 100.

Lowell, A. Lawrence, 252, 255.

Lowell, James Russell, address on, 58–62; 101.

Lowell, Percival, 59.

Lusitania, sinking of, 451.

Luther, Martin, 15.

McElroy, Robert, *Grover Cleveland, the Man and the Statesman*, introduction to, 88 ff.; 182.

McKim, Charles F., 233 and n.

McKinley, William, President, 3, 254, 310, 418.

MacMurray, on the limitation of armament, 322.

Mabie, Hamilton W., 317.

Macaulay, Thomas B., Lord, 14.

Madison, James, *Debates in the Federal Convention*, 332 n.

Maistre, Joseph de, quoted, 103, 174.

Mangin, General, quoted, 125.

Marquand, Mr., 109.

Marshall, John, Chief Justice, 136.

Martin, Edward S., *Life of J. H. Choate*, 17, 46 n.

Marvel, Mr., 155.

Menken, S. Stanwood, letter to, 169–172; 178, 185.

Metropolitan Museum of Art, Fiftieth Anniversary of, 105 ff.; founders of, 107.

Military training, universal, importance of, 198, 199.

Millet, Francis D., 233 and n., 234.

Milton, John, 61.

Mitchell, S. Weir, 56.

Monroe, James, 262.

Monroe Doctrine, the, 219, 256, 263, 264, 270, 275.

Moore, John Bassett, Judge of the Permanent Court of International Justice, 401, 420.

Morgan, J. P., 109.

Morse, S. F. B., 101.

Mullet, Mr., architect, 106.

Myers, Michael, 78.

National Civic Federation, speech to committees of, 489–502.

National Federation of Arts, speech at convention of, 232 ff.

National Security League, organization of, 169; aims of, 169, 182, 189; 24.

New York City, conditions in, in 1870 112 ff.; its noble monuments, 242.

New York Constitutional Convention (1894), 33–35.

New York Convention to ratify Constitution of United States (1788), 83, 84.

New York University, 79.

Nicholas I, of Russia, 100.

Nicholas II, 128, 296, 403.

Nitole, Professor, 317.

North American Review, 51.

Orlando, Vittorio, 252.

Pan-American building, Washington, 55.

Paris, Treaty of (1783), 81.

Parker, Alton B., 489 and n.

Parkman, Francis, 101.

Pauncefote, Sir Julian (Baron), 324.

Peace Conference (1919), two duties of, entirely distinct, 291, 292.

Permanent Court of International Justice, steps leading to establishment of, 324 ff.; list of judges elected to, 325 n.; extracts from remarks in debates in the Advisory Committee, 327–390; Root-Phillimore plan for organization and procedure of, 360–362; addresses on, to Bar Association of New York, 391–405, and to American Society of International Law, 405–426.

Philippines, the, 37.

Phillimore, Walter G. F., Baron, 327, 345, 350, 356, 359, 373, 379, 384, 385, 395, 400.

Pickering, Timothy, 79.

Pickford, Mary, 494.

Pittsburgh, Institute of, 53.

Platt, Jonas, 78.

Plattsburg camps, 97.

Poisonous gases, in the Washington Conference, 467, 468.

Politicians, 74, 75.

Polk, Frank L., 247, 248, 325.

Polk, James K., President, 101.

Pomeroy, John N., 161.

Porter, Horace, 295.

Porto Rico, 36.

Private property, exemption of, from capture by belligerents, 309–311.

Proctor, Thomas R., presents statue of Hamilton to Hamilton College, 76.

Punch, quoted, 202.

Pym, John, 175.

Railroads, government control of, 207, 208.

Reading, Rufus Isaacs, Earl of, Lord Chief Justice, address at dinner in honor of, 130 ff.

Reconstruction legislation after the Civil War, 90.

Renault, Louis, 295, 386.

Republican Party, duty of, in the war, 192 ff.; speech on restoration policies of, 210 ff.

Republicanism of 1920, 69 n.

Research Institute of Washington, 54.

Rhinelander, Mr., 109.

Ricci-Busatti, Arturo, 335 n., 363, 395.

Roberts, Frederick S., Earl, 96.

Robinson, Edward, 232 n.

Roosevelt, Theodore, President, sketch of his career, 3; addresses on, 3–16; 205, 254, 257, 296, 310, 314, 418, 441.

Rose, Uriah M., 295.

Roumania, 170 n., 286, 288, 293, 294.

Russell Sage Foundation, regional plan of, 238 ff.

Russia, and Germany, 170 n., 179; Bolshevism in, 223 ff.; programme of, for 2d Hague Conference, 296.

Russian Jews in New York, attitude of, 183.

Saint-Gaudens, Augustus, his statue of Lincoln, 63 ff.; 233 and n.

Salem, Mass., J. H. Choate and, 47, 48.

Salisbury, Robert A. T. Gascoyne-Cecil, Marquis of, 36.

Saltonstall, Leverett, 17.

Sanger, Jedediah, 78.

Savonarola, Girolamo, 15.

Schuyler, Philip, 77, 79.

Scotch universities, and Carnegie, 54.

Scott, James Brown, *Robert Bacon*, introduction to, 93 ff.; 316, 323, 350, 497.

Senate of the United States, the, and President Wilson, 217 ff. And *see* League of Nations, Versailles, Treaty of.

Serbia, 286, 288, 293, 294.

Sergeant, John, 78.

Shakespeare, William, 61, 65.

Shays's Rebellion, 81.

Sherman, James S., Vice-President, 202.

Sherman, Willett, 202.

Shotwell, Dr., 321.

Slavery in the United States, and Lincoln, 63, 64, 73.

Southmayd, Mr., 30.

Spencer Selden, Senator, 287.

Spenser, Edmund, 61.

Sperry, Charles S., 295.

Steel, Bessemer process, 50, 101.

Sterling, Caroline D., wife of J. H. Choate, 17.

Steuben, Baron Friedrich von, 79.

Stimson, Henry L., 248.

Story, Judge Joseph, 161.

Sturges, Jonathan, 99.

Submarines, in the Washington Conference, 462 ff.; and poisonous gases, treaty concerning prohibition of, 447–450.

Substantive law, necessity for restatement of, 158 ff.

Supreme Court of the United States, 39.

Suttner, Baroness von, 317.

Switzerland, 274.

Taft, William H., President, 3, 251, 254, 255, 393, 418, 442.

Tariff, necessity for revision of, 215.

Taxation, necessity for revision of, 214.

Theodosius, 162.

Thomas, Charles S., Senator, 155, 156.

Thrift Stamps, 190, 191.

Treasury Department, Hamilton and, 84, 85.

Trotzky, Leon 128, 224, 228, 430.

Tuttle, Timothy, 78.

Ukraine, the, and Germany, 187.

Underwood, Oscar W., Senator, 446.

United Kingdom Trust, 56.

Universal Postal Union, 339.

United States, in 1847, 101; separate treaties of, with Germany, etc., 210; and the League of Nations, 438 ff.

Venezuela, Cleveland's message concerning, 35.

Verplanck, Gulian, 99.

Versailles, Treaty of (1919), and the Senate, 218; should be ratified with reservations, 220, 435, 436; labor provisions of, 438.

Vesnitch, Milenko R., 327, 335 n.

"Victorian Period, the," 105, 106.

Viviani, René, 42.

Wallace, Judge, 399, 400.

War-Savings Stamps, 190, 191.

Washington, George, President, and Hamilton, 80; 66, 72, 86, 175, 243 n., 262, 274.

Washington, D. C., and L'Enfant's plan, 243 and n.

Washington Conference in limitation of armament. *See* Limitation of armament.

Webster, Sir Richard. *See* Alverstone.

Weiss, André, 335 n.

Wells, Samuel, 78.

Wesley, John, 15.

West Publishing Co., 162.

Westminster Abbey, 63, 68.

Whiskey Rebellion, the, 85.

White, Andrew D., 57, 310.

Whittier, John G., 101.

Williamstown, Mass., Institute of Politics at, 469; speech on Democracy and Foreign Affairs at, 469–478.

Williston, Samuel, 161.

Wilson, Woodrow, President, his appeal for a Democratic Congress (1918), 217; his denial of the Senate's right to advise on the League Covenant, 217; and Lansing, 221; quoted, 247; and Article X of the Covenant, 286–289; 3, 169, 172, 193, 200, 206, 210, 216, 253, 281, 282, 285, 293, 294.

World War, R. Bacon's service in, 96 ff.; nature of, 176, 177; importance of moral qualities in, 180, 181; by whom won, 205, 206; questions arising from, 221, 222.

Zebalos, Estanislao S., 376 and n.